ORTHODOX CHRISTIANITY AND MODERN SCIENCE:
PAST, PRESENT AND FUTURE

SCIENCE AND ORTHODOX CHRISTIANITY

3

Orthodox Christianity and Modern Science: Past, Present and Future

Editors
KOSTAS TAMPAKIS
HARALAMBOS VENTIS

BREPOLS

This publication has been implemented within the framework of the project "Science & Orthodoxy around the World", which was made possible through the support of a grant from the Templeton World Charity Foundation, Inc. The opinions expressed in this publication are those of the author(s) and do not necessarily reflect the views of Project SOW and the Templeton World Charity Foundation, Inc.

© 2022, Brepols Publishers n. v., Turnhout, Belgium.

All rights reserved. No part of this publication may be reproduced, stored in a retrieval system, or transmitted, in any form or by any means, electronic, mechanical, photocopying, recording, or otherwise without the prior permission of the publisher.

D/2022/0095/157
ISBN 978-2-503-59668-6
eISBN 978-2-503-59669-3
DOI 10.1484/M.SOC-EB.5.125871

Printed in the EU on acid-free paper.

Table of Contents

Introduction — Orthodoxy and the Sciences, from the Past to the Future
Haralambos Ventis and Kostas Tampakis — 7

Orthodoxy Matters: Why Has a Scientific Revolution not Taken Place in the Greek East?
The Role of Orthodox Christian Traditionalism
Vasilios N. Makrides — 15

Science and Religion in Historical Perspective: Some Brief Thoughts from the Engaged Periphery
Donald A. Yerxa — 45

Ecology and Environment from an Orthodox Perspective: Current Encounters in Bulgaria
Ivaylo Nachev — 53

Science, Religion and Bioethical Issues in Greek Orthodox Journals (1998 to the present)
Sandy Sakorrafou — 63

Medicine, Suffering and Death: Palliation and the Ethics of Caring for Those we cannot Cure
Maria Bouri — 83

Teaching about Science and Religion in the Seminary
Gayle E. Woloschak — 119

Science and Theology: The Prospects for Fruitful Mutually Beneficial Cooperation
Kirill Kopeikin — 131

Humanity as the Central Theme of the Dialogue between Theology and Science
Alexei Nesteruk — 147

Theological Anthropology Today: Panayiotis Nellas's Contribution
Doru Costache — 167

The Enduring Temptation of Scientistic Reductionism as the Secular Equivalent to Ontotheology and Religious Literalism.
Haralambos VENTIS   183

Orthodox Christianity and the Archaic Experience Of Nature
Bruce FOLTZ   199

Science at the edge of Eternity
Georgios MESKOS   209

Incarnational Naturalism: A Solution to the Problem of Miracles?
Christopher C. KNIGHT   223

HARALAMBOS VENTIS AND KOSTAS TAMPAKIS

Introduction — Orthodoxy and the Sciences, from the Past to the Future

This volume is the third to emerge from the "Science & Orthodoxy Around the World" project, which is organized by the Institute of Historical Research of the National Hellenic Research Foundation and funded by the Templeton World Charity Foundation. The theme of this third SOW volume, not unlike the entire project that draws together the papers contained therein, is likely to appear suspect to skeptical readers from the outset, for all the well-meaning efforts of devout scientists to gloss over the conflict between the two partners brought into dialogue. For reasons that will be broached shortly below, science and religion are indeed strange bed-fellows, and thus not so easily reconciled as many would like to think — but neither are they sworn enemies, intrinsically opposing one another, though this latter claim must be carefully qualified.

Let us tackle their differences first: for one thing, science is intrinsically falsifiable in accordance with Karl Popper's famous criterion of falsifiability, which specifies that no theory can be considered 'scientific' unless it carries specific stipulations indicating on what grounds it can be proven wrong. Hence, science is a self-correcting probe into the unknown, focusing as it does on natural processes as opposed to miracles or supernatural events alleged by 'revealed claims.' Moreover science is a cumulative, on-going endeavor of coming to terms with every aspect of physical reality, unfazed by forbidden or unpalatable questions that may compromise heartfelt metaphysical or ideological preconceptions. Religious faiths, on the other hand, have long been upbraided since at least the dawn of Modernity and the emergence of the scientific revolution as incorrigibly dogmatic — which is to say, as unfalsifiable and rigid forays into ultimate reality (the latter comprising in itself a questionable terrain of inquiry, from a skeptical perspective). Further berated as hopelessly static and backward-oriented in character, religions are routinely dismissed as far removed in every conceivable sense from the forward-looking, open-ended scope of science. Given these ostensibly unbridgeable discrepancies between the two mindsets, how can anyone ever hope to bring them into a meaningful conversation or, even worse, make them intersect in an honest and fruitful manner?

Such sanguine efforts toward intersection, other than those of the early-Church Apologists, go back as early as the Middle Ages and the first stirrings of Natural Theology, a major branch of religious epistemology. Traditionally, Natural Theology

Haralambos Ventis • National and Kapodistrian University of Athens
Kostas Tampakis • National Hellenic Research Foundation

has striven to bring the Christian faith into dialogue with the most current intellectual systems beginning with Aristotelian philosophy, the premier scholarly edifice at that time. It combined reason with revelation, in the process devising increasingly intricate arguments aiming to offer irrefutable proof for the existence of God (the most famous of those being Anselm of Canterbury's 'ontological argument,' followed by the so-called 'cosmological' and 'teleological' ones). St. Thomas Aquinas, a towering figure of Scholasticism, borrowed copiously from Aristotle, particularly capitalizing on the latter's key notions of '*analogia entis*' and 'entelechy' respectively, with a view to infusing Christianity with a broader, extra-biblical perspective complementary to Scripture's wisdom. The former of these concepts, '*analogia entis*,' drawn from the analogical similarity presumed by Aristotle between different planes of existence, was christened to strengthen belief in the biblical view of humankind as having been made in the image of God; the human race, bestial as it may be, nevertheless shares an analogical resemblance to its Maker. 'Entelechy,' on the other hand, as the Greek polymath meant it, declared that life, far from being contingent and meaningless, is deeply teleological: it possesses an inherent purpose worth discovering, if the sub-lunar realm of *nature* (φύσις), the place of motion and growth, is to make sense to us. Concerning human beings, this grand purpose comprised the attainment of *eudaimonia*, the kind of good life that Aristotle had in mind, achieved by virtuous living and the avoidance of extremes; in the study of nature, on the other hand (although the two realms are interrelated), purpose was reflected in the celebrated four 'causes' suggested by the Greek philosopher as the combined means by which we can ascertain how the world works: these were the 'formal,' the 'efficient,' the 'material,' and the 'final' cause, the last being the most important of all. Aquinas, in his life-long effort to appropriate the best that the erudite world had to offer Christianity, reaffirmed Aristotelian teleology yet redefined life's purpose in terms of emulating not civic virtues but the Church's. As a general assessment, it could be argued that the Scholastics' bridge-making pursuits were an enticing, noble task, vibrant with intellectual alertness and a keen knowledge of heathen learning.

Unfortunately, the endeavor was innately marred with dark spots that would finally propel the developments leading to the Protestant Reformation.[1] Worst among these was the transformation of '*analogia entis*' to a hardened moral ideal sternly mandating that Christians attain divine ethical perfection as a result of their analogical similarity to God — an impossible assignment, no doubt, which was to inflict much strain and agony on the western Church's flock of that era; so much so, in fact, that many psychologically tormented believers felt compelled in their uncertainty to resort to the purchase of so-called 'indulgences,' sold by the Roman Church as certificates earning owners extra amounts of divine grace and mercy. Appalled by this odious practice, indicative of the Roman Church's institutional corruption at

---

1   For a reliable and detailed chronicle of this milestone event in European history, see Carter Lindberg, *The European Reformations* (Oxford & Cambridge, MA: Blackwell Publishers, 1996); also by Lindberg, *The Third Reformation?* (Macon, Georgia: Mercer University Press, 1983). For a shorter account, see Owen Chadwick, *The Reformation* (London: Penguin, 1972).

that time, Martin Luther and the early Reformers did not rest content with merely condemning the self-serving fraud of the Church; scratching deeper, they indicted the disastrous, in their judgment, infiltration of pagan ideas into theology, whose inroads to Christian spirituality perverted the simplicity and liberating spirit of the Gospel. To counter Scholasticism's grim hybrid, Luther and his kin contemporaries decreed a group of three *solas*: '*sola gratia*,' '*sola fide*,' and '*sola scriptura*.' The first of these sets out to directly undermine the said tantalizing principle of 'salvation by works through emulating divine perfection:' salvation, Luther argued, is not earned; it should be seen rather as a matter of grace, i.e. as a gift from God, never in terms of an achievement. In affirming the free character of salvation, Luther stood on opposite ends from the optimistic anthropology of Pelagius with its emphasis on free will and accomplishment. By rejecting redemption in terms of "merit," Luther counter proposed a rather exaggerated reading of St. Augustine and St. Paul touting humankind's debased nature and helplessness before sin. This stratagem aimed at stressing humankind's total reliance on God, by which Luther was inevitably led to a mild version of predestination that John Calvin would later harden to a problematic degree. But predestination aside, if the whole notion of salvation by works and effort is to be decisively undermined, its flawed intellectual basis must first be dented; and the Reformers' way of doing so was by introducing the remaining two 'solas': salvation comes from faith only, and (more importantly), faith is shaped by Scripture alone, never by extra-biblical sources foreign to the Gospel and easily manipulated so as to corrupt the blissful Christian vision with torturing burdens.

In due time, the coalesced Protestant principles gave rise to *Fideism*, the main counterpoint to Natural Theology. As a system of religious epistemology, Fideism relies primarily on faith, not on theory or syllogism. At the heart of it is the tenet that attempts to prove the existence of God through philosophical contrivances are neither feasible nor necessary or even desirable, for that matter (as Blaise Pascal would later reiterate in his commitment to the solid God of Abraham, Isaac, and Jacob, echoing in that manner the spirit of Jansenism, a protestant-like version of Roman Catholicism). To offer a sound witness of the Christian faith, it should suffice to present inquirers with a glimpse of the interior life of its practitioners as it is actually lived and experienced. By contrast, handing outsiders abstract 'proofs' and cerebral formulas is deemed as an exercise in futility; for intellectual ploys of this sort are in truth useless in the face of stout skepticism, not really convincing anyone in the first place, other than those who already confess faith in God. As a starting-point and to a certain degree, Fideism not only gets the work done, it also constitutes a more honest endeavor of letting outsiders know the real gist and flavor of Christianity. Nevertheless, like all human constructs, Fideism comes with a host of its own defects. Chief among these are its introverted aversion to self-examination and the ensuing unaccountability to science and Modernity. Indeed, critics such as Kai Nielsen have long bemoaned Fideism's anti-intellectualism, along with its lack of an evolving (self) critical theology. It is certainly one thing to renounce cerebral 'proofs' supposedly establishing the existence of God, as useless and patronizing; it is quite another to jettison every intellectual effort to render the faith, at least up to a point, scrutable and accountable to what is nowadays known about the cosmos and the emergence and evolution of humankind. Fideism, in particular, has been rightly blamed in this writer's view for infusing some Christian confessions with a certain amount of anti-humanism and anti-intellectualism, thanks both to its habitual introversion and (in extreme cases) the naïve insistence on Scripture's inerrancy. These are the streams which have been pouring water on the fundamentalist mill of Protestant Christianity. At least Natural Theology has never ceased to engage in rational argumentation and intellectual exchange in its perennial dedication to foster a humanist version of Christianity — a renewable edifice as much informed by revelation as by reason and the spoils of classical education (in that regard, it is worth mentioning Aquinas' astute aphorism, that he pitied people 'of one book,' even if that sole source of knowledge were Scripture itself).

It goes without saying that differences between these rival systems, Natural Theology and Fideism, are often blurred and should not be absolutized. Their complementarity is strongly evinced in the work of compatibalists such as Desiderius Erasmus, René Descartes, John Locke or more recently Karl Rahner: these are but few among several influential thinkers who have more or less argued that reason and faith are not really in conflict but counterbalance one another, even if they still prioritize either of their respective starting-points. Moreover, both methods of engaging with religion have long since grown to more sophisticated versions of their original forms; case in point, the modern school of Reformed Epistemology, a refined fideist strand which does assume the rationality of Christianity as a vital and essential feature of it, while still refraining from defending it argumentatively or by reference to external evidence.[2] Be that as it may, it should be stated that endeavors such as project 'Science and Orthodoxy all over the World' (SOW) are neither fideist nor apologetic in character or intentions; much less do they function as forums for the exchange of 'creationist' nonsense and self-righteous religious rhetoric alleging to prove the existence of God. The editors of the present volume firmly believe in the independence of science and its total freedom to pursue its queries uninhibited by dogmatic prejudices coming especially from the camp of religion. We detest even subtle, insidious forms of theocracy and uphold academic freedom, the liberty to publish unpopular, iconoclastic findings and perspectives opposing prejudices and power structures; in short, we stand in defense of anything of academic rigor that forces us to reconsider and take alternative looks on life. Accordingly, we feel that the slightest compromise to these hard-earned achievements of western intellectual culture would inevitably result in the suppression of truth and, over the long run, to nothing less than humankind's mental death.

At the same time, we believe in the value of conversation, including the conversing partnership cultivated between science and faith as is attempted herein, provided it is conducted under honest and fair terms. By the same token, we dismiss the hubris of 'scientism,' meaning the ideological presumption that quantitative approaches of the empirically testable sort are uniquely appropriate to answer life's most significant

---

2   For more, see Michael Sudduth, *The Reformed Objection to Natural Theology* (Abingdon, Oxfordshire & New York: Ashgate Publishing, 2016).

existential questions. From that angle, we view certain patronizing pronouncements from the camp of popularizers of science such as the late Carl Sagan, as hopelessly simplistic and ideologically-laden. Sagan is known for championing naturalism instead of merely advocating a healthy, much-needed dose of skepticism toward grand metaphysical claims. The difference between the two approaches is enormous and should be brought to the fore in the interests of impartiality, although the task obviously requires a more properly qualified effort than our crude allusion in this brief introductory statement would permit: an apposite response should aim to peel off the ideological layers surrounding the promotion of scientism as an ostensibly self-evident modern totem. For lack of space, let us presently say only that rather than serving the cause of truth per se, the hijacking of science by naturalistic agendas ends up upholding an undocumented materialist picture of reality that science proper cannot endorse as such. Here we are greatly aided by the counsel of William James, who addressed this very problem over a hundred years ago

> Science taken in its essence should stand only for a method and not for any special beliefs, yet as habitually taken by its votaries, science has come to be identified with a certain fixed general belief, the belief that the deeper order of nature is mechanical exclusively, and that non-mechanical categories are irrational ways of conceiving and explaining even such a thing as human life.[3]

Sagan is famous for exhorting his audience to forego the 'great metaphysical conceits' instituted by monotheistic religions in particular and to espouse in their stead the so-called 'great demotions' incurred by science — with the transition from geocentrism to heliocentrism and its consequences being foremost among those exercises in cognizance humility. To be sure, Christian theology ought to take the Copernican and Darwinian revolutions very seriously with a view to incorporating their insights into its own evolving perspective. This is a long-term project which has already begun to be implemented, albeit Orthodox theologians are unfortunately by and large still laggards in this ambit.[4] In their zealotry to pontificate, though, authors like Sagan appear to be oblivious to the conceit at the core of their own narrative, meaning their ill-informed eagerness to exhaust reality to the arbitrary limits of human conceptualization and understanding — a reductive temptation, not much unlike the religious fundamentalist's self-assured inclination to delimit the truth solely to the confines of Scripture and, where Orthodox Christianity is concerned, to tradition.

One of the main driving motives for putting this volume together is the determination to resist both kinds of temptation, particularly their indiscernible common ground, the hubristic and arbitrary alignment of what can be *known* with what actually *exists* (see Haralambos Ventis' paper). There is a religious as well as

---

3 Eugene Taylor, *William James on Consciousness Beyond the Margin* (Cambridge, MA: Harvard University Press, 2011), p. 121.
4 For a recently published analysis of the consequences and challenges posed by heliocentrism upon the maximalist Orthodox Christology and an attempt at reconciling the two, see Haralambos Ventis, 'Έχει η Ορθόδοξη χριστιανική θεολογία λόγο ύπαρξης στη μετα-κοπερνίκεια εποχή;' Δευκαλίων (*Deucalion*), 33(1–2), December 2019, pp. 132–62.

a secular version of the fallacy known as reductionism, the infamous tendency to explain away complex, naggingly inscrutable questions pertaining to ontology through subterfuges that 'cut reality down to size,' in Thomas Nagel's memorable phrase. To oppose this fallacy in either form is an excellent starting-point for attaining epistemic humility — a badly needed prerequisite for sincere and disinterested conversation. But what of the pressing question regarding the falsifiability of ontological and, by extension, of ethical religious statements? By their own admission, Christians are not relativists on either score. Science, as a project also invested in verity, may be just as adamantly foreign to relativism, as portrayed by its staunch defiance of the fluid approaches to the truth provocatively espoused by neo-pragmatists and social constructivists alike (the former being preeminently exemplified by the late Richard Rorty); at the same time, however, science is also an unwaveringly self-correcting enterprise, intrinsically open to the revision of its tentative body of knowledge, as was mentioned at the beginning of this essay. Does this in turn signify a total incompatibility between science and Christianity? In response to this challenge, a Christian may reply that while amendment is not an option as far as purely theological doctrine is concerned (i.e. with reference to Christology and the Trinity), it is quite possible and even required when it comes to cosmology and anthropology, which are now being considered afresh from a Christian perspective. It is hoped that, in the process, Orthodoxy in particular shall reactivate its long-forgotten but always valuable tool of apophaticism, an epistemological principle which broadly speaking asserts that 'no truth is ever exhausted in its verbal formulation.' If boldly utilized, apophaticism can preemptively guard against the ossification of theological statements concerning creation into dry, finalized formulas, exhaustive of the truth they purport to convey. Eschatology, too, is a precious consort here, to the extent that it raises a gap between the fullness of truth awaiting us in God's Kingdom and the limitations and partiality of historical knowledge. In essence, eschatology assumes that the Church's vessel is still adrift on its way to the eschaton's shore, and by no means already on the Kingdom's waterfront. The said gap places a tentative, provisional status on many social beliefs nowadays perceived as normal and self-evident, even from a Christian viewpoint, in line with Christ's assertion in the Gospels that 'the last shall be first and the first last,' Mt. 20:16; Mk. 10:31). In effect (and this is its foremost contribution), eschatology cancels every attempt to issue final statements on humankind and the cosmos, shielded from fallibility and potential reconsideration.

The authors of the present volume explore an assortment of issues related to science and Orthodox theology, from theoretical as well as practical perspectives. The papers are by no means exhaustive of the field. They sketch in essence a beginning, not a closure. Project SOW has run for three years now, and it is intellectually exhilarating to see the scholarship on Science and Orthodoxy bloom. Nevertheless, this final volume shows all too clearly how many additional issues could and should be examined.

The first paper by Vasilios Makrides raises a contentious issue: Why did the Scientific Revolution not take place in the Orthodox East? The author makes a bold suggestion regarding traditionalism in the Orthodox Christian tradition, and opens a venue of research which has been so far neglected. Donald Yerxa attempts to reverse the established hierarchy of Science versus Religion, in the process exporing alternatives to Science's dominance. Ivaylo Nachev moves the discussion to the very real, urgent concerns of environmentalism, focusing as he does on current relevant discussions among Orthodox Christian circles in Bulgaria. Sandy Sakorrafou tackles the growing field of bioethics and its appearance in Greek Orthodox journals, while Maria Bouri addresses the theme from the viewpoint of a practicing doctor: How are we expected to face the ethical challenges involved in caring for patients with life-limiting and incurable conditions? How do Orthodoxy and medical sciences interact, in the face of imminent death?

In the second part of the volume, Gayle Woloschak's paper moves in another direction and raises the question of why so few Orthodox seminaries, schools and departments teach the subject of science and religion. She moves on to discuss some general points to be considered in such an endeavor, and why such initiatives are more necessary than ever. Kirill Kopeikin boldly moves from the classroom to the laboratory, so to speak, suggesting that Orthodox Christianity could offer assistance in solving some of the central scientific problems of our time. Alexei Nesteruk expands he scope even further, by arguing that promotes the dialogue between Orthodox theology and science cannot be symmetric, because such a dialogue presupposes a hidden theological commitment related to the fact that both its terms have origin in human life. In fact, the self-affectivity of human life makes theology the stronger partner in the relationship. Finally, Doru Costache focuses on what a theological Anthropology could be in the present, and discusses Panayiotis Nellas's contributions to such a project.

In the last part of this volume, Haralambos Ventis discusses critically the natural human inclination towards reductionism, and discovers in it a perennial temptation scourging both scientific and religious narratives: The covert, but hubristic, assumption that reality can be domesticated by being framed in humanly recognizable coordinates. Bruce Foltz, in his contributions, traces what he calls the 'archaic conception of nature' that could be found in the works of environmental pioneers such as Leopold and Emerson, and tries to address the suspicion that a secularized world shows in such conceptions. He turns to the hesychast tradition of Orthodox Christianity to perform a critical role in legitimizing this realm of experience. Georgios Meskos discusses how modern scientists such as Julian Barbour and Lee Smolin adopt an extended physical reality to overcome issues in General Relativity and Quantum Mechanics. He further proposes, following Iain McGilchrist, that many religious experiences are the result of the structure of the physical world. Finally, in the last paper of the volume, Christopher Knight proposes what he calls 'Incarnational Naturalism' as a way to address miracles within Orthodox Theology.

The thirteen papers that comprise this volume, as these abridged descriptions indicate, range over several disciplines, periods and themes. They are certainly about the past, present and future of the relationship between the sciences and Orthodoxy, but they are also about what is still lying ahead, not in the temporal, but in the exploratory sense. As the third and final volume commissioned by Project SOW, we take the opportunity to restate to the reader our initial suggestion: This is not a academic closure of a field, but rather the tantalizing hint of the work that still lies ahead.

VASILIOS N. MAKRIDES

Orthodoxy Matters: Why Has a Scientific Revolution not Taken Place in the Greek East?

The Role of Orthodox Christian Traditionalism

▼ ABSTRACT This chapter attempts to address an old and highly debated issue, namely that of the potential connection between Christianity and the rise of modern science. More specifically, it is about the role of Western Latin Christianity, especially of Protestantism, but also of Roman Catholicism, in enabling the appearance of the so-called 'Scientific Revolution' in Western Europe, which is roughly situated between 1543 and 1687. The question that arises is what happened in Eastern and South Eastern Europe, especially with regard to scientific inquiries and the prevailing presence of Orthodox Christianity there. The article argues that a Scientific Revolution of the above sort could have never taken place in the Orthodox Christian East, which followed another path to modern times. This is due, among other things, to the strong influence of Orthodox traditionalism and its wider socio-cultural repercussions.

Introduction: Christianity and the Rise of Modern Science

This chapter attempts to address an old and highly debated issue, namely that of the potential connection between Christianity and the rise of modern science. More specifically, it is about the role of Western Latin Christianity, especially of Protestantism, but also of Roman Catholicism, in enabling the appearance of the so-called 'Scientific Revolution' in Western Europe, which is roughly situated between 1543 and 1687. We are talking here about a most radical and massive breakthrough in science and technology, which subsequently not only had a catalytic influence upon the future and the profile of Western Europe, but was also able to decisively affect the rest of the world in the long run, not least through the Western overseas expansion,

Vasilios N. Makrides • University of Erfurt

Orthodox Christianity and Modern Science: Past, Present and Future, ed. by Kostas Tampakis and Haralambos Ventis, SOC, 3 (Turnhout, 2022), pp. 15–44.
© BREPOLS ❧ PUBLISHERS   10.1484/M.SOC-EB.5.130950

colonialism and imperialism.[1] Many scholars have argued that there is something specific and unique in this West European explosive scientific development (e.g., the differences of ancient and especially mediaeval science with modern science;[2] the role of scientific societies in establishing, disseminating and popularising scientific knowledge[3]). Joseph Needham, for example, opined that science and technology in China were for most of the time historically superior to the West European ones, also regarding the application of scientific knowledge to practical human needs. Yet, this efficiency and superiority did not lead to the kind of Scientific Revolution that appeared in Western Europe. For Needham, this should be primarily attributed to the different social, intellectual and economic structures of the civilisations under consideration.[4] The same has been argued concerning other cultures, which had long, strong and important scientific heritages, such as those of India[5] and mediaeval Islam[6]. In recent years, however, there has been increased scholarly interest in the explicit or implicit influences of non-Western cultures on the rise of West European modernity including the Scientific Revolution.[7]

Be that as it may, these cases, together with many other related ones, have been amply discussed in the context of the research paradigm initiated by Max Weber, concerning the role of Western Christianity, both implicit and explicit, in the rise of West European modernity as a whole. Indeed, Weber tried to explain the 'West European unique development' (*okzidentale Sonderentwicklung*) by reference to Western Christianity, focusing primarily on ascetic Protestantism (especially Calvinism and Puritanism, but also Pietism) and considering partly the developments within Mediaeval Roman Catholicism, which had also contributed to the specific

---

1   See C. A. Lertora Mendoza Conicet, E. Nicolaïdis, and J. Vanderssmissen (eds), *The Spread of the Scientific Revolution in the European Periphery, Latin America and East Asia. Proceedings of the XX*th *International Congress of History of Science (Liège, 20–26 July 1997)*. Vol. 5 (Turnhout: Brepols, 1999); George N. Vlahakis et al. (eds), *Imperialism and Science: Social Impact and Interaction* (Santa Barbara, CA: ABC-CLIO, 2006).
2   See Reijer Hooykaas, 'The Rise of Modern Science: When and Why?', *The British Journal for the History of Science*, 20 (1987), 453–73.
3   See Martha Ornstein, *The Rôle of Scientific Societies in the Seventeenth Century*, Third Edition (Chicago: University of Chicago Press, 1938); James McClellan, *Science Reorganized: Scientific Societies in the Eighteenth Century* (New York: Columbia UP, 1985).
4   See Joseph Needham, 'Thoughts on the Social Relations of Science and Technology in China', *Centaurus*, 3 (1953), 40–48; Joseph Needham, 'Science and Society in East and West', *Centaurus*, 10 (1964), 174–97; Joseph Needham, *The Great Titration: Science and Society in East and West* (Toronto: University of Toronto Press, 1969). See also Nathan Sivin, 'Why the Scientific Revolution did not Take Place in China — Or didn't it?', in *Transformation and Tradition in the Sciences: Essays in Honour of I. Bernard Cohen*, ed. by Everett Mendelsohn (Cambridge: Cambridge UP, 1985), pp. 531–54.
5   See Virendra Singh, 'Why did the Scientific Revolution Take Place in Europe and not Elsewhere?', *Indian Journal of History of Science*, 22 (1987), 341–53.
6   See Toby E. Huff, 'The Scientific Revolution and the Arab-Muslim Background', in *History of Sciences in Islam*, edited by the al-Rabita al-Muhammadia li al-Ulama' (The Mohammadan Council of Scientists). Vol. 2 (Rabat, 2014), pp. 11–20.
7   See George Saliba, *Islamic Science and the Making of the European Renaissance* (Cambridge, MA: MIT Press, 2007); H. Floris Cohen, *How Modern Science Came into the World: Four Civilizations, One 17*th*-Century Breakthrough* (Amsterdam: Amsterdam UP, 2010).

West European rationalisation process.[8] Although due his untimely death, he left his comparative civilisational studies (including those on Orthodox Christianity) unfinished, he was able to provide a 'religious genealogy' of the otherwise more secular West European modernity and the radical transformations it brought about. Without excluding material and other factors in explaining social change, his emphasis was rather on the realm of (religious) ideas, convictions and associated interests, which may have influenced human social action accordingly.[9]

Such a perspective became quite attractive afterwards for several generations of scholars until today, who *mutatis mutandis* delved deeper into this particular area and made significant contributions. With regard to modern science, this was achieved first by sociologist Robert K. Merton in his dissertation. Influenced by Talcott Parsons, who had introduced Weber's work and ideas to American academia, Merton connected the rise of experimental science and new scientific values (e.g., intellectual autonomy and freedom, legitimation of scientific research for the glory of God) with Protestantism (especially English Puritanism, but also German Pietism).[10] As expected, such a connection generated numerous discussions and debates.[11] On the one hand, it was corroborated in many respects by further studies.[12] But it was also criticised from various perspectives,[13] more recently in the context of postcolonial studies, which have tried to unearth and re-evaluate the non-Western and non-European background of modern science.[14] Yet, the main point is that the 'Merton thesis' in general appeared to be quite plausible and was generally supported by varied evidence. To avoid misunderstandings: The emphasis put here on the role of religion was not meant to undermine a plethora of other reasons (e.g., social, political, cultural, economic, institutional) that may

---

8   See, for example, Alan C. Turley, 'Max Weber and the Sociology of Music', *Sociological Forum*, 16 (2001), 633–53; Lutz Kaelber, 'Weber's Lacuna: Medieval Religion and the Roots of Rationalization', *Journal of the History of Ideas*, 57 (1996), 465–85.
9   See Hans G. Kippenberg and Martin Riesebrodt (eds), *Max Webers "Religionssystematik"* (Tübingen: Mohr Siebeck, 2001); Gert Albert, Agathe Bienfait, Steffen Sigmund, and Claus Wendt (eds), *Das Weber-Paradigma. Studien zur Weiterentwicklung von Max Webers Forschungsprogramm* (Tübingen: Mohr Siebeck, 2003).
10 See Robert K. Merton, *Science, Technology and Society in Seventeenth Century England* [1938] (New York: Harper & Row, 1970).
11 I. Bernard Cohen et al. (eds), *Puritanism and the Rise of Modern Science: The Merton Thesis* (New Brunswick, NJ: Rutgers UP, 1990).
12 See Gerhard Lenski, *The Religious Factor: A Sociological Study of Religion's Impact on Politics, Economics, and Family Life*, Revised Edition (New York: Doubleday, 1963); Reijer Hooykaas, *Religion and the Rise of Modern Science* (Grand Rapids, MI: William B. Eerdmans, 1972); Eugene M. Klaaren, *Religious Origins of Modern Science: Belief in Creation in Seventeenth-Century Thought* (Grand Rapids, MI: William B. Eerdmans, 1977); John Brooke and Ekmeleddin İhsanoğlu (eds), *Religious Values and the Rise of Science in Europe* (Istanbul: Research Centre for Islamic History, Art and Culture, 2005).
13 See, for example, George Becker, 'The Merton Thesis: Oetinger and German Pietism, a Significant Negative Case', *Sociological Forum*, 7 (1992), 642–60.
14 See Arun Bala and Prasenjit Duara (eds), *The Bright Dark Ages: Comparative and Connective Perspectives* (Leiden: Brill, 2016).

have led — either in connection and interaction with each other or not — to the rise of modern science.[15] Thus, there are quite many theories, which take such factors (e.g., social and economic[16]) strongly into consideration. The same holds true for Weber's initial methodological approach, which was more ideational than materialist in perspective, without however ideological or political overtones. It was simply about a largely ignored and neglected factor, namely religion, that had nonetheless, even unexpectedly, contributed decisively to the rise of West European modernity as a whole. With regard to modern science, interestingly enough, some scholars have also looked at the tradition of Roman Catholicism, which was also considered to have formed a necessary (but not decisively sufficient) background for the rise of modern science;[17] consider, for instance, the role of the Roman Catholic Church especially in the Middle Ages in founding schools and universities and in disseminating knowledge (e.g., through its monastic orders and their transnational networks), which resulted in the mediaeval flourishing of learning.[18]

Quite important is also the fact that the related debates did not die out, but continue up today in various forms. More recently, the connection between Protestantism and the rise of modern science was taken up by the historian of ideas Peter Harrison, who argued that the answer to the question about the rise of modern science in Western Europe and the establishment of a dominant and influential scientific culture there is related to specific features of Western Christendom and its theological thinking.[19] He also pointed to particular theological orientations in Orthodox Christianity that

---

15 See Herbert Butterfield, *The Origins of Modern Science*, Third Edition (New York: Free Press, 1957); H. Floris Cohen, *The Scientific Revolution: A Historiographical Inquiry* (Chicago: University of Chicago Press, 1994); Steven Shapin, *The Scientific Revolution* (Chicago: University of Chicago Press, 1996); Toby Huff, *The Rise of Early Modern Science: Islam, China, and the West*, Second Edition (Cambridge: Cambridge UP, 2003); John Henry, *The Scientific Revolution*, Third Edition (New York: Palgrave MacMillan, 2008); H. Floris Cohen, *The Rise of Modern Science Explained: A Comparative History* (Cambridge: Cambridge UP, 2015); Toby Huff, *Intellectual Curiosity and the Scientific Revolution: A Global Perspective* (New York: Cambridge UP, 2011).
16 See Edgar Zilsel, *The Social Origins of Modern Science* (Dordrecht: Kluwer, 2003); Gideon Freudenthal and Peter McLaughlin (eds), *The Social and Economic Roots of the Scientific Revolution. Texts by Boris Hessen and Henryk Grossmann* (Heidelberg/New York: Springer, 2009).
17 See Alexandre Kojève, 'L'origine chrétienne de la science moderne', in *Mélanges Alexandre Koyré*. Tome 1. *L'aventure de l'esprit*, ed. by I. Bernard Cohen and René Taton (Paris: Hermann, 1964), pp. 295–306; Stanley L. Jaki, *Science and Creation: From Eternal Cycles to an Oscillating Universe* (Edinburgh: Scottish Academic Press, 1974); Stanley L. Jaki, *The Road of Science and the Ways to God* (Chicago: University of Chicago Press, 1978); Stanley L. Jaki, *Cosmos and Creator* (Edinburgh: Scottish Academic Press, 1980); Amos Funkenstein, *Theology and Scientific Imagination from the Middle Ages to the Seventeenth Century* (Princeton, NJ: Princeton UP, 1986).
18 See Lynn White, Jr., *Medieval Religion and Technology: Collected Essays* (Berkeley: University of California Press, 1978); Benjamin Nelson, *On the Roads to Modernity: Conscience, Science and Civilizations. Selected Writings*, ed. by Toby E. Huff (Totowa, NJ: Rowman & Littlefield, 1981).
19 See Peter Harrison, *The Bible, Protestantism, and the Rise of Natural Science* (Cambridge: Cambridge UP, 1998); Peter Harrison, 'Subduing the Earth: Genesis 1, Early Modern Science, and the Exploitation of Nature', *The Journal of Religion*, 79 (1999), 86–109; Peter Harrison, *The Fall of Man and the Foundations of Science* (Cambridge: Cambridge UP, 2007); Peter Harrison, *The Territories of Science and Religion* (Chicago: University of Chicago Press, 2015).

were not conducive to such results.[20] In addition, sociologist Rodney Stark argued strongly that major events in the history of the European continent including modern science could be attributed to the influence of Western Christianity.[21] Talking about Christianity here, the term should be understood in its various guises and functions; for example, as an articulated theological system of ideas, as an established political power with a pervasive societal impact, or as a comprehensive worldview.

Bearing in mind this short overview about the intrinsic connection of Western Christianity to the rise of modern science, the question that arises in this context is what happened in Eastern and South Eastern Europe, especially with regard to scientific inquiries and the prevailing presence of Orthodox Christianity there. It makes no surprise to state from the outset that a Scientific Revolution of the above sort has never taken place in the Orthodox Christian East, which has followed another path to modern times. In actual fact, modern science was gradually introduced to the East from the West, albeit with considerable delay and followed by concomitant problems and reactions. In Russia, for example, this happened at an official level due to the systematic efforts of Tsar Peter I the Great (r. 1682–1725),[22] while in the Balkans under Ottoman rule this took place at an informal level particularly from the second half of the eighteenth century onwards.[23] Most importantly, many dominant Orthodox institutions and actors in these areas reacted against the introduction of modern science to the East and openly repudiated related modern advances while remaining fixated on old and outdated scientific knowledge. The belated reactions against Copernican cosmology in the Greek Orthodox East are a case in point.[24] Seen in this way, it is safe to argue that there was certainly a common Christian background in Europe, yet its concrete articulations and the overall contours of its historical evolvement in East and West exhibited significant differences and had diverging repercussions in the long run.

Once more, this is not to claim that the Scientific Revolution was due exclusively to religious causes, since we are talking about a highly complex and multi-dimensional

---

20 See Peter Harrison, 'Science, Eastern Orthodoxy, and Protestantism', *Isis*, 107 (2016), 587–91.
21 See Rodney Stark, *For the Glory of God: How Monotheism Led to Reformations, Science, Witch-hunts, and the End of Slavery* (Princeton, NJ: Princeton UP, 2003), pp. 121–99.
22 See Valentin Boss, *Newton and Russia: The Early Influence, 1698–1796* (Cambridge, MA: Harvard UP, 1972); Michael D. Gordin, 'The Importation of Being Earnest: The Early St. Petersburg Academy of Sciences', *Isis*, 91 (2000), 1–31; Robert Collis, *The Petrine Instauration: Religion, Esotericism, and Science at the Court of Peter the Great, 1689–1725* (Leiden: Brill, 2011).
23 See Kostas Gavroglu and Dimitris Dialetis, 'Appropriating New Scientific Ideas in the Greek-Speaking Regions During the 17th and 18th Centuries', in *Die Griechen und Europa. Außen- und Innensichten im Wandel der Zeit*, ed. by Harald Heppner and Olga Katsiardi-Hering (Vienna: Böhlau 1998), pp. 69–101; Dimitris Dialetis, Kostas Gavroglu, and Manolis Patiniotis, 'The Sciences in the Greek Speaking Regions During the 17th and 18th Centuries — The Process of Appropriation and the Dynamics of Reception and Resistance', *Archimedes — New Studies in the History and Philosophy of Science and Technology*, 2 (1999), 41–72; Yiannis Karas, *Οἱ θετικές ἐπιστῆμες στόν ἑλληνικό χῶρο (15ος–19ος αἰώνας)* (Athens: Daidalos–I. Zacharopoulos, 1991).
24 See Vasilios N. Makrides, *Die religiöse Kritik am kopernikanischen Weltbild in Griechenland zwischen 1794 und 1821: Aspekte griechisch-orthodoxer Apologetik angesichts naturwissenschaftlicher Fortschritte* (Frankfurt am Main: Peter Lang, 1995).

issue that defies a mono-causal explanation. For instance, the Orthodox world lacked the centuries-long and established tradition of mediaeval university structures in Central and Western Europe, which had contributed to the creation of a vast network of local scientific cultures, as well as to a related intensive transregional communication. Further, the Balkans were from the early modern times onwards under Ottoman rule, a situation that lasted for centuries and secluded the Orthodox subjects there from an intensive and productive encounter with the radical Western modern developments including those in the scientific realm. Finally, due to historical and other reasons, Russia lagged behind for a long time and was not in a position to produce its own autonomous scientific culture — a development that took place only from the eighteenth century onwards, yet again under the formative Western influence. Here it is about the notorious multi-levelled backwardness of Eastern and South Eastern Europe in modern times, which has given rise to many debates, but also to numerous misunderstandings and concomitant stereotypes.[25] Be that as it may, it would be mistaken to deny the huge developmental gap that was separating East and West in Europe from the early modern times onwards. Such differences were noticed, for example, by an astute observer, the Corfiote traveller Nikandros Noukios (c. 1500–after 1556), who had visited various countries and cities in Central and Western Europe and had first-hand experience of the scientific and technical innovations and changes there.[26] The same scientific and technological advances in Italy had been already observed by the later Cardinal Bessarion (1403–72) even before the fall of Byzantium, who had made in the early 1440s an interesting report about them to a member of the imperial Palaiologos dynasty, the future and final Byzantine Emperor Constantine XI Palaiologos (1449–53).[27] This is not to deny the numerous contributions of Byzantine scholars to the West European cultural, scientific and technological development, who emigrated there before and after 1453.[28] We are simply talking about a general comparison between Byzantium and Western Europe, in which the overall decline of the former and the growing pre-eminence of the latter become evident at multiple levels.

---

25 See Larry Wolff, *Inventing Eastern Europe: The Map of Civilization on the Mind of the Enlightenment* (Stanford, CA: Stanford UP, 1995); Maria Todorova, *Imagining the Balkans* (New York: Oxford UP, 1997).
26 See John Anthony Cramer (ed.), *The Second Book of the Travels of Nicander Nucius of Corcyra* (London 1841; Reprinted: New York: Johnson Reprint Corporation, 1968); Jules-Albert de Foucault (ed.), *Nicandre de Corcyre. Voyages* (Paris: Les Belles Lettres, 1962); Anneliese Malina, 'Nikandros Nukios, Ἀποδημίαι. Buch I. Bericht über seine Reise durch Deutschland in den Jahren 1545–1546', in *Ὁ Ἑλληνισμός εἰς τὸ ἐξωτερικόν. Über Beziehungen des Griechentums zum Ausland in der neueren Zeit*, ed. by Johannes Irmscher and Marika Mineemi (Berlin: Akademie-Verlag, 1968), pp. 45–181.
27 See Albert Galloway Keller, 'A Byzantine Admirer of "Western" Progress: Cardinal Bessarion', *The Cambridge Historical Journal*, 11 (1953–55), 343–48; Antonis Pardos, 'Οἱ ἄξονες τῆς ἰδεολογίας τοῦ Νέου Ἑλληνισμοῦ στὴν ἄλλη Κωνσταντινούπολη. Ἡ παρακαταθήκη τοῦ Βησσαρίωνα: Λάσκαρης καὶ Μουσοῦρος ἀνάμεσα στοὺς Ἕλληνες τῆς Βενετίας', in *Ἄνθη Χαρίτων*, ed. by Nikolaos M. Panayiotakis (Venice: Elliniko Instituto Vyzantinon kai Metavyzantinon Spoudon, 1998), pp. 527–68.
28 See Jonathan Harris, *Greek Emigres in the West, 1400–1520* (Camberley, Surrey: Porphyrogenitus, 1995).

Aside from the above caveats, the role of religion in enabling or hindering certain developments (and here specifically in the scientific realm) should not be neglected, and the same holds true for our case. In this context, it is interesting to observe the weaker scientific development among the Slavs influenced by the Orthodox Christian tradition compared to that of the Slavs influenced by the Western Latin culture.[29] More specifically, there are certain characteristics of the Orthodox belief and practice system that are — in contrast to the Western Latin ones — certainly not very conducive to the development of modern science.[30] For instance, this has to do with the degree of world-affirmation and related attitudes among the Christian Churches respectively, whereas Orthodox cultures are notorious for their stronger other- and outerworldly orientations. It is thus not accidental that from such a perspective the preoccupation with the mundane, trivial and transient sciences was considered unnecessary and useless for the most important and true goals of an Orthodox Christian in life. All the more, it was even regarded as dangerous for the salvation of the soul, since it could lead to worldliness and a neglect of the spiritual priorities in life.[31] In addition, there were stronger theological legitimations of scientific inquiry in Western Europe than in the Orthodox East, especially due to a more robust natural theology.

This chapter will look more closely at another factor that has played a key role in this context. It is about the intense preoccupation of Orthodox Christians with preserving their religious tradition intact and without alterations, particularly in their need to demarcate themselves from the 'fallen Latin West'. This preoccupation, however, often led to strong traditionalist attitudes that not only uncritically glorified and venerated the past, but also turned against any change and innovation whatsoever. In addition, traditionalism led to an absolutisation of various secondary and less significant elements that had been at some time, regardless if purposely or accidentally, incorporated into the main corpus of tradition. More importantly, such an orientation exerted strong influence not only on the religious domain, which was the central one in this case, but also on the non-religious realm as well. Consequently, even necessary changes and innovations that had nothing to do with the Orthodox tradition *per se* were often repudiated as non-traditional and potentially dangerous. This traditionalist spirit and absolutisation process will be exemplified by reference to the official acceptance and endorsement of Aristotelianism by the Patriarchate of Constantinople in the seventeenth and eighteenth centuries, a fact that hindered or delayed the introduction of new scientific ideas into the Greek Orthodox world. It

---

29 See Ihor Ševčenko, 'Remarks on the Diffusion of Byzantine Scientific and Pseudo-scientific Literature Among the Orthodox Slavs', *The Slavonic and East European Review*, 59 (1981), 321–45.
30 For more details, see Vasilios N. Makrides, ''Επιστημονική Ἐπανάσταση καί Ὀρθόδοξη Ἀνατολή', in *Τό αἴτημα τῆς διεπιστημονικῆς ἔρευνας. Οἱ ἐπιστῆμες στόν ἑλληνικό χῶρο*, ed. by Yiannis Karas (Athens: Trochalia, 1997), pp. 61–91; Vasilios N. Makrides, 'Review Essay: In a Different Vein? Scientific Development in the Greek Orthodox East', *The British Journal for the History of Science*, 46 (2013), 335–40.
31 See Vasilios N. Makrides, 'Science and the Orthodox Church in 18th and Early 19th-Century Greece: Sociological Considerations', *Balkan Studies*, 29 (1988), 265–82 (pp. 271–75); Makrides, *Die religiöse Kritik*, pp. 152–71.

goes without saying that no Scientific Revolution could have ever come out of such a traditionalist milieu, one imbued with a persistent and omnipresent anti-innovative spirit.[32]

Orthodox Traditionalism and its Broader Societal Transformations

Compared to Roman Catholicism and particularly to Protestantism, Orthodox Christianity, in its various forms and local contexts, appears nowadays to be a religious system much more bound to tradition and to the Christian past, bequeathed by the early Church, the Church Fathers and the Church Councils. From an Orthodox perspective, fidelity to tradition and its intact preservation are an element of self-identification, a source of authenticity, and a cause of concomitant pride. However, the importance attached to tradition is also connected to the phenomenon of Orthodox traditionalism, which can be observed throughout history and which has repeatedly earned critical comments from various perspectives.[33] This is because the right distance between tradition-boundedness and traditionalism could not be always maintained for a number of reasons. For example, the need to keep the sole true Christian faith (Orthodoxy) intact has often led in later centuries to insulation, introversion, defensiveness and reactionary attitudes. As a consequence, this frequently led to the absolutisation of the entire corpus of tradition without any differentiations, especially due to the lack of any critical approaches to it. Tradition was then regarded indistinctly as a dense and solid whole, all parts of which were deemed as central and essential, thus without the possibility of change, adaptation or reform. It is not accidental that innovation (νεωτερισμός, καινοτομία) in religious matters was always negatively evaluated.[34] Historically speaking, the following Biblical passage was amply and diachronically quoted in various Orthodox contexts to legitimise not only traditional, but also traditionalist stances: 'Μὴ μέταιρε ὅρια αἰώνια, ἃ ἔθεντο οἱ πατέρες σου' ('Do not remove the ancient boundary markers, which your fathers have set in place') (Proverbs 22: 28). In fact, Orthodox Christians seem to be still living in many respects in the past and particularly in a pre-modern situation, as they usually try to find pertinent answers or solutions to various modern problems by reference to a normative and binding past, which is regarded as superior than the present and the future. This becomes

---

32 See Makrides, 'Science and the Orthodox Church', pp. 267–71.
33 See Hans Küng, *Theologie im Aufbruch. Eine ökumenische Grundlegung* (Munich/Zürich: Piper, 1992), pp. 67–85; Sabrina P. Ramet, 'The Way We Were — and Should Be Again? European Orthodox Churches and the "Idyllic Past"', in *Religion in an Expanding Europe*, ed. by Timothy A. Byrnes and Peter J. Katzenstein (Cambridge: Cambridge UP, 2006), pp. 148–75; Adolf von Harnack, *Das Wesen des Christentums* [1900], edited by Claus-Dieter Osthövener (Tübingen: Mohr Siebeck, 2007), pp. 124–38.
34 See Geoffrey W. H. Lampe (ed.), *A Patristic Greek Lexicon* (Oxford: Clarendon Press, 1961), pp. 693 and 907–08; Christian Hannick, 'Tradition et autorité dans la théologie byzantine', *Ostkirchliche Studien*, 59 (2010), 28–43 (pp. 39–42).

evident in the way past authorities (e.g., the Church Fathers) are usually treated in the Orthodox world.[35] Such an attitude does not mean that the Orthodox Churches and Christians abhor change or even innovative steps altogether. On the contrary, they often flirted with novel things, even if they camouflaged them under the protective veil of tradition. The whole issue relates more to the normative significance that the past holds for them, not only in terms of its tabooing, idealisation and mystification, but also concerning the resulting devaluation of the present and the future.[36]

What is highly interesting for the purpose of this chapter is the range of Orthodox traditionalism, which hardly remained limited to the religious sphere alone. In most cases and under various circumstances, it transcended it and was transformed into a broader societal traditionalism that *a priori* rejected change and innovation. It occasions no surprise then that the above Biblical passage was also used to legitimise a scientific traditionalism and deny modern scientific achievements, such as the Copernican worldview.[37] The initial, religiously motivated traditionalism, which anyway was already quite strong and influential, was extended with the passing of time to other societal sectors and could influence them accordingly. During this process, it was usually impossible to distinguish between those elements of the tradition, which could be changed, and those which could not. This development can be already observed in Byzantium in the context of the standardisation and normativisation of the Orthodox doctrine through the Ecumenical Councils (325–787/843); consider the 'Synodicon of Orthodoxy',[38] namely the decree of the 843 Synod of Constantinople that restored the veneration of icons, praised the confessors and heroes of the Orthodox faith and castigated its enemies throughout the centuries; it is proclaimed until today at the 'Feast of Orthodoxy' (also known as the 'Sunday of Orthodoxy') on the first Sunday of Great Lent in the liturgical calendar of the Orthodox Church. Additionally, the confidence about possessing the sole true Christian faith was corroborated in the context of the Byzantine 'political theology' via various eschatological interpretative schemes about the course of world history and the place of the Byzantine Empire therein.[39] The mounting tensions between the Orthodox East and the Latin West also contributed decisively to these processes, given that the Latins were accused by the Orthodox of perilous innovations in the Christian doctrine and tradition. The established Orthodox true faith had thus to be preserved at any price away from contamination and adulteration. All this fostered enhanced traditionalist and

---

35 See Pantelis Kalaitzidis, 'From the "Return to the Fathers" to the Need for a Modern Orthodox Theology', *St Vladimir's Theological Quarterly*, 54 (2010), 5–36.
36 See Vasilios N. Makrides, 'Orthodox Christianity, Change, Innovation: Contradictions in Terms?', in *Innovation in the Orthodox Christian Tradition? The Question of Change in Greek Orthodox Thought and Practice*, ed. by Trine Stauning Willert and Lina Molokotos-Liederman (Farnham: Ashgate, 2012), pp. 19–50.
37 See Makrides, *Die religiöse Kritik*, pp. 139 and 311–12.
38 See Jean Gouillard, 'Le Synodikon de l'Orthodoxie. Édition et Commentaire', *Travaux et Mémoires*, 2 (1967), 1–316.
39 See Gerhard Podskalsky, *Byzantinische Reichseschatologie: Die Periodisierung der Weltgeschichte in den vier Grossreichen (Daniel 2 und 7) und dem tausendjährigen Friedensreiche (Apok. 20). Eine motivgeschichtliche Untersuchung* (Munich: Fink, 1972).

anti-innovative attitudes among the Byzantines in the sensitive domain of religion, which became stronger and more evident after the 'Great Schism' of 1054 and during the late centuries of the empire. Generally speaking, Byzantine society had gradually become already from the period of Emperor Justinian I (527–65) more and more traditionalist. It is thus not accidental that the term 'innovation' had mostly negative connotations after the sixth century, being used to denounce heretical doctrines, rebellions or illegal actions.[40]

This Orthodox and broader societal traditionalism does not signify that Byzantium lacked any developments, changes or novel ideas and currents in various domains, ranging from religion to science. But as Kazdan and Cutler put it: *'Reforms were usually couched in terms of the restoration of the past rather than of innovation.'*[41] In other words, changes and reforms did happen, and there were many actors, both religious and secular, who asked for or tried to implement them[42] (e.g., the learned Archbishop of Thessaloniki Eustathios, Michael Psellos, Nikephoros Gregoras, Demetrios Kydones, the later Cardinal Bessarion, Georgios Gemistos-Plethon). Being deeply aware of the ongoing decline of the empire, many of them also often turned to Western Europe in order to find novel ideas and developments (including in science and technology) from which the moribund Byzantium could potentially profit.[43] This becomes more visible in late Byzantine times when the empire was facing a broader weakening and decline in many domains and needed fresh elements in order to recover and become strong again. Yet, the dominant and pervasive frame remained a strong traditionalist one that could not enable a serious break with the past and the introduction of important innovations, either moderate or radical.[44] In general, the Byzantine linkage with the past, whether Biblical or Hellenic, *'created an imaginary stability. Each phenomenon had an analogy in the past and therefore a place in the historical process or, theologically, in the economy of salvation'*.[45]

This was not only due to the socio-historical circumstances of that era, such as the pervasive anti-Latin sentiments and policies and the East-West axiological comparison, which was supposed to always prove the Byzantine superiority. It was also due to endogenous causes related to the aforementioned widespread traditionalism that created a sense of self-reliance, self-sufficiency and self-complacency. However,

---

40 See Herbert Hunger, *Byzanz, eine Gesellschaft mit zwei Gesichtern: Eine J. C. Jacobsen Gedenkvorlesung* (Copenhagen: Munksgaard, 1984), pp. 26–27.
41 Alexander Kazhdan and Anthony Cutler, 'Innovation', in *The Oxford Dictionary of Byzantium*. Vol. 2 (Oxford: Oxford UP, 1991), pp. 997–98 (p. 997).
42 See Paul Wirth, 'Tradition und Fortschritt in Byzanz', *Byzantinische Forschungen*, 12 (1987), 119–23.
43 Regarding Kydones, see Frances Kianka, 'Demetrios Kydones and Italy', *Dumbarton Oaks Papers*, 49 (1995), 99–110; Judith Ryder, *The Career and Writings of Demetrius Kydones: A Study of Fourteenth-Century Byzantine Politics, Religion and Society* (Leiden: Brill, 2010).
44 See Ihor Ševčenko, 'The Decline of Byzantium Seen Through the Eyes of its Intellectuals', *Dumbarton Oaks Papers*, 15 (1961), 169–86; Igor P. Medvedev, 'Neue philosophische Ansätze im späten Byzanz', *Jahrbuch der Österreichischen Byzantinistik*, 31/2 (1981), 529–48 (esp. pp. 530–32).
45 See Alexander P. Kazhdan, 'Innovation in Byzantium', in *Originality in Byzantine Literature, Art and Music: A Collection of Essays*, ed. by Anthony R. Littlewood (Oxford: Oxbow Books, 1995), pp. 1–14 (p. 12).

one has to also pay attention to the specific cultural coordinates of the Byzantine world, in which 'innovation' was not connected to continuing linear progress and the constant look for novelties, as in the modern context. Originality in Byzantium was more connected to the creative imitation (μίμησις) and the rather constructive (not passive) reproduction of the (ancient Greek) prototypes.[46] Modern scholarship has also tried to provide a more nuanced account of Byzantine traditionalism and the innovative potential existing in many domains,[47] not least in the scientific realm.[48] Such revisions are useful in locating divergent facets of Byzantine culture and avoiding a monolithic approach to it. Yet, the question is how much all these minor cases matter in the predominant frame of Byzantine traditionalism, its Orthodox origins, its dislike of innovations, and its long-term repercussions, which also affected the realm of science.[49] For instance, the main proponent of Hesychasm, Archbishop of Thessaloniki Gregory Palamas (1296–1359), was not *a priori* an adversary of profane knowledge, but merely objected to its inappropriate use leading to the secularisation of the high clergy.[50] Far more important is, however, the overall impact of the Hesychast movement, which displayed an outspoken contempt for mundane, profane knowledge. Although Hesychasm did not manage to put a brake on Byzantine humanism, it did curtail the eventual impulses towards more radical developments in the scientific realm.[51] No doubt, there were also humanist debates in Byzantium and even readiness, albeit at times disputed, to profit from other cultures and develop science further,[52] yet all this did not lead to a major breakthrough in science and to a true liberation from the long-established traditionalist frame of reference.

Given this overall background, it becomes understandable why the Orthodox tradition-boundedness became more intensive and influential after the fall of Byzantium and during the subsequent long Ottoman period. It was often transformed

---

46 See Alexander Kazhdan and Anthony Cutler, 'Imitation', in *The Oxford Dictionary of Byzantium*. Vol. 2 (Oxford: Oxford UP, 1991), pp. 988–89.
47 See Apostolos Spanos, '"To Every Innovation Anathema"(?). Some Preliminary Thoughts on the Study of Byzantine Innovation', in *Mysterion, Strategike og Kainotomia. Et Festskrift til ære for Jonny Holbek*, ed. by Harald Knudsen et al. (Oslo: Novus Forlag, 2010), pp. 51–59; Apostolos Spanos, 'Was Innovation Unwanted in Byzantium?', in *Byzantium Wanted: The Desire for a Lost Empire*, ed. by Ingela Nilsson and Paul Stephenson (Uppsala: Uppsala Universitet, 2014), pp. 43–56.
48 See, among others, J. V. Field and M. T. Wright, 'Gears from the Byzantines: A Portable Sundial with Calendrical Gearing', *Annals of Science*, 42 (1985), 87–138; Timothy S. Miller, *The Birth of the Hospital in the Byzantine Empire* (Baltimore: Johns Hopkins UP, 1985); Anna M. Muthesius, 'The Byzantine Silk Industry: Lopez and Beyond', *Journal of Medieval History*, 19 (1993), 1–67; Harris, *Greek Emigres*, pp. 151–88; John Haldon, '"Greek Fire" Revisited: Recent and Current Research', in *Byzantine Style, Religion and Civilization. In Honour of Sir Steven Runciman*, ed. by Elizabeth Jeffreys (Cambridge: Cambridge UP, 2006), pp. 290–325; Petros Bouras-Vallianatos, *Innovation in Byzantine Medicine: The Writings of John Zacharias Aktouarios (c. 1275–c. 1330)* (Oxford: Oxford UP, 2020).
49 See Efthymios Nicolaidis, *Science and Eastern Orthodoxy: From the Greek Fathers to the Age of Globalization* (Baltimore: Johns Hopkins UP, 2011), pp. 72–73.
50 See Nicolaidis, *Science and Eastern Orthodoxy*, pp. 98–104.
51 See Nicolaidis, *Science and Eastern Orthodoxy*, pp. 104–05.
52 See Nicolaidis, *Science and Eastern Orthodoxy*, pp. 81–92 and 106–17.

into a wider traditionalism, coupled with social conservatism and widespread anti-Westernism, aimed at stopping changes of all kinds, even those unrelated to the religious domain. This broader anti-innovationism had again a clear Orthodox background, as everything turned around the intact preservation of the sole true faith, the most valuable treasure that solely Orthodox Christians claimed to exclusively possess at that time. This becomes most evident in the first serious contacts between Jeremias II Tranos, Patriarch of Constantinople (1572–95), and Lutheran theologians from Tübingen, which took place between 1573 and 1581. Despite sincere efforts, the differences between the two sides were unbridgeable and had mostly to do with completely divergent approaches to and evaluations of the church tradition. In the end, Patriarch Jeremias reproached the Lutherans because of their constant drive for critical inquiry and innovation in church matters, which he deemed as highly dangerous. His critique was summarised in the following statement: 'Οὐκ ἵσταται ὑμῶν ἡ διάνοια' ('*Your mind does not stand still*'). The alternative was to be fully satisfied with and never question the inherited and established Christian tradition, as well as to respect past church authorities unreservedly.[53] This spirit had an immediate impact upon the general orientations of the Orthodox world at that time, which were modelled along the same traditionalist pattern of thought, and led to cultural isolationism and lack of progress. Needless to say, the differences to the then radically developing Western Europe were tremendous and immense and kept growing even bigger. It was not only the rise of the Reformation and the birth of modernity, which went hand in hand in their critical re-evaluation of the past, but also the breakthrough of the Scientific Revolution with its far-reaching consequences. Hence, this particular situation can offer some explanations as to why such a Scientific Revolution could have never taken place in the Orthodox East and why religion in the form of Orthodox traditionalism mattered a lot in this constellation.

No doubt, the Orthodox became aware, even if belatedly, of this massive Western scientific and technological progress, yet in many cases they preferred to keep a defensive attitude and articulate diverse compensation strategies in order to devalue and undermine related Western achievements. A usual one was to boast about the achievements of Greek antiquity, which Western Europe had singlehandedly usurped and utilised for its own sake, and hence to degrade the alleged Western impressive development.[54] Naturally, the argument about the dependence of modern science on the ancient Greek scientific heritage is not completely out of hand, yet normally this is not meant to underestimate the innovations and the overall breakthrough

---

53 See Dorothea Wendebourg, *Die eine Christenheit auf Erden: Aufsätze zur Kirchen- und Ökumenegeschichte* (Tübingen: Mohr Siebeck, 2000), pp. 95–115; Vasilios N. Makrides, 'Ohne Luther: Einige Überlegungen zum Fehlen eines Reformators im Orthodoxen Christentum', in *Luther zwischen den Kulturen: Zeitgenossenschaft — Weltwirkung*, ed. by Hans Medick and Peer Schmidt (Göttingen: Vandenhoeck & Ruprecht, 2004), pp. 318–36 (esp. pp. 329–34).

54 See Makrides, 'Science and the Orthodox Church', pp. 277–78; Vasilios N. Makrides, 'Greek Orthodox Compensatory Strategies Towards Anglicans and the West at the Beginning of the Eighteenth Century', in *Anglicanism and Orthodoxy 300 Years after the 'Greek College' in Oxford*, ed. by Peter M. Doll (Oxford: Peter Lang, 2006), pp. 249–87 (esp. pp. 274–76).

achieved through modern science at many levels, given that the pioneers of the Scientific Revolution gave extensive new twists to traditional ideas and practices.[55] Another compensation strategy was to consider all mundane developments of the 'fallen West' as trivial, vain and insignificant compared to the preservation of the sole true faith by the Orthodox, which was valued incomparably much more from the perspective of salvation and eternal life after death.[56] It should also be mentioned that such a reactionary Orthodox traditionalism was further strengthened by the overall conservative milieu of the Ottoman Empire, which in general could not be characterised as progressive and innovative in comparison to Western Europe, albeit for its own specific reasons.[57] This was a widespread opinion at that time, although the Greek learned cleric Eugenios Voulgaris (1716–1806) in a political essay about the then situation of the Ottoman Empire was critical of this view (δὲν εἶναι τόσον ἐχθροὶ τῆς καινοτομίας καὶ τοῦ νεωτερισμοῦ) and talked about Ottoman innovations, especially in the military realm.[58]

Orthodox Traditionalism and the Absolutisation of Corydallic Aristotelianism in the Greek East (Seventeenth–Eighteenth Centuries)

A very pertinent example to understand these processes and the broader significance of Orthodox traditionalism can be found in the absolutisation of the Aristotelian philosophy and worldview and its incorporation into the normative corpus of the Orthodox tradition in the Greek world under Ottoman rule. It was a time when the Scientific Revolution in Western Europe had already reached its peak and new scientific knowledge was widely disseminated, established and popularised. This traditionalist development did not happen randomly, but was officially approved and authorised by the Orthodox Church, mainly represented by the Patriarchate of Constantinople. The whole story can reveal quite vividly how a relative, non-religious element (in this case: Aristotelianism) received initially under specific circumstances an official church backing and was closely related to the corpus of the Orthodox tradition that had to be preserved unaltered at any price. With the passing of time, the presence of this element was further stabilised and legitimised within this corpus, so that it was also considered to form one of its integral parts that could not be changed. The circumstantial context that had initially led to the acceptance of this element fell later on into complete oblivion, whereas this element was corroborated with further arguments and canonised as being essential for the preservation of the authentic

---

55 See Stanley L. Jaki, 'The Greeks of Old and the Novelty of Science', in «Ἀρετῆς Μνήμη». Ἀφιέρωμα «εἰς μνήμην» τοῦ Κωνσταντίνου Ἰ. Βουρβέρη (Athens: Elliniki Anthropistiki Etaireia, 1983), pp. 263–77.
56 See Makrides, 'Greek Orthodox Compensatory Strategies', pp. 270–73.
57 Cf. Norman Itzkowitz, *Ottoman Empire and Islamic Tradition* (Chicago/London: University of Chicago Press, 1972), pp. 96–97.
58 See [Eugenios Voulgaris], Στοχασμοὶ εἰς τοὺς παρόντας κρισίμους Καιρούς, τοῦ Κράτους τοῦ Ὀθωμανικοῦ (St. Petersburg [?] 1771 or 1772), pp. 18–19.

Orthodox tradition. Put it otherwise, it was a process of the absolutisation of a minor and relative element, a usual development historically in Orthodox cultures because of their endemic traditionalism, which exceeds the narrow religious borders and can exert broader influence.

To begin with a reconstruction of the whole story: As is historically well known, Aristotelianism as a philosophical and cosmological system had a huge impact during the Middle Ages in Western Europe and also in the Islamic world, which was scientifically quite advanced at that time and had made significant contributions. Aristotelian philosophy was also used to corroborate the Christian dogma, especially by the Scholastics. All this contributed to the establishment of Aristotelian authority at that time, despite the fundamental incongruence of certain Aristotelian cosmological postulates (e.g., about the eternity of the world) with the Christian doctrine. In general, the overcoming of Aristotelianism in cosmology was the most serious hindrance for the advancement of modern scientific ideas, a development that happened gradually and was quite conflictual at times. In actual fact, there were many receptions of Aristotelianism in Western Europe at the time of the Renaissance and Humanism, which were still competing with each other.[59] There was first, the classical one of medieval Scholasticism, which used Aristotelian philosophy not *per se*, but basically for the sake of the dominant Roman Catholic Church and the Christian doctrine. There was also Averroism, based on Aristotle's reception by Ibn Rushd/Averroes (1126–98), which had theological underpinnings and objectives of its own. Yet, in early modern times, the growing interest for a necessary distance of scientific and philosophical knowledge from church control and purposes led to other developments. An interesting case in point was the current of Paduan Aristotelianism or Neo-Aristotelianism, articulated at the University of Padua, among others by Cesare Cremonini (1550–1631), who was also called 'Aristoteles redivivus'. Its major postulate was to free Aristotle's reception from the church and understand him in his own terms according to ancient Greek interpretations, such as that of Alexander of Aphrodisias (end of second — middle of third century CE), one of the most celebrated commentators of Aristotle. This is also the reason why Paduan Aristotelians were called 'Alexandrians' (*alessandristi*).[60] This 'secularisation' was fully in line with the overall climate of the day and the attacks against the Roman Catholic establishment, both ecclesiastical and educational.

---

59 See Charles B. Schmitt, *The Aristotelian Tradition and Renaissance Universities* (Variorum Collected Studies Series, 203) (London: Variorum Reprints, 1984); Edward Grant, 'Ways to Interpret the Terms "Aristotelianism" in Medieval and Renaissance Natural Philosophy', *History of Science*, 25 (1987), 335–58.
60 See Maria Assunta Del Torre, *Studi su Cesare Cremonini: Cosmologia e logica nel tardo aristotelismo padovano* (Rome: Antenore, 1968); Charles B. Schmitt, *Cesare Cremonini: Un aristotelico al tempo di Galilei* (Venice: Centro Tedesco di Studi Veneziani, 1980); Heinrich C. Kuhn, *Venetischer Aristotelismus im Ende der aristotelischen Welt: Aspekte der Welt und des Denkens des Cesare Cremonini (1550–1631)* (Frankfurt am Main: Peter Lang, 1996); Ezio Riondato and Antonino Poppi (eds), *Cesare Cremonini: Aspetti del pensiero e scritti*. Vol. 1 (Padua: Academia Galileiana di Scienze, Lettere ed Arti, 2000).

As far as the Orthodox East is concerned, things were in many respects different, given that there was first, a rather smooth indigenous reception of Aristotelian philosophy from the Byzantine to the post-Byzantine era without major interruptions. The continuity of the manuscript tradition of Aristotelian works attests to this.[61] After all, the Orthodox East did not have to go through the radical upheavals that characterised the passage of Western Europe from the Middle Ages to the early modern period and experienced the battle between 'the ancients and the moderns' to a lesser degree. Nevertheless, the debates between Platonists and Aristotelians during the Renaissance did find an echo in the East as well, exemplified particularly by the differences between the Platonist Georgios Gemistos-Plethon (c. 1355/60–1452) and the Aristotelian Georgios-Gennadios Scholarios (c. 1405–c. 1473), the first Patriarch of Constantinople after the fall of Byzantium.[62] Further intellectual fermentations and developments in Western Europe also kept influencing the East, including the novel early modern reception of Aristotle. This concerned the aforementioned current of Paduan Aristotelianism, which had been appropriated by the Athenian Theophilos Corydalleus (1574–1646),[63] a student of Cremonini in Padua (1609–13), emphasising the disentanglement of philosophy from theology. Corydalleus also dissociated his interpretation of Aristotle from the Plato-filtered Aristotelianism of the Byzantine era. He had also expressed various opinions not only on the relations between theology and philosophy, but also on pure church issues (such as the Eucharist and the *Transubstantiatio*[64]) that were not in congruence with the church doctrine. He further exhibited anti-theological and anti-metaphysical tendencies hinting at an autonomy of the material world. It was this situation that triggered various critiques against him for atheism or heresy by Meletios Syrigos (1585–1663) and others.[65]

---

61 See Yiannis Karas, ''Η Ἀριστοτελική παράδοση στήν περίοδο τῆς Τουρκοκρατίας (Φυσικές-Θετικές Ἐπιστῆμες)', in Πρακτικά τοῦ Παγκοσμίου Συνεδρίου "Ἀριστοτέλης" (Thessaloniki, 7–14 August 1978). Vol. 2 (Athens: Ypourgeio Politismou, 1981), pp. 414–19; Karas, Οἱ θετικές ἐπιστῆμες, 73–77; Roxane Argyropoulos and Yiannis Karas, Inventaire des manuscrits grecs d'Aristote et de ses commentateurs. Contribution à l'histoire du texte d'Aristote. Supplément (Paris: Société d'Édition «Les Belles Lettres», 1980).
62 See Nikos K. Psimmenos (ed.), Ἡ ἑλληνική φιλοσοφία ἀπό τό 1453 ὥς τό 1821. Vol. 1: Ἡ κυριαρχία τοῦ Ἀριστοτελισμοῦ. Προκορυδαλική καί κορυδαλική περίοδος (Athens: Gnosi, 1988), pp. 53–124; George Karamanolis, 'Plethon and Scholarios on Aristotle', in Byzantine Philosophy and its Ancient Sources, ed. by Katerina Ierodiakonou (Oxford: Oxford UP, 2002), pp. 253–82.
63 See, among others, Cleoboulos Tsourkas, Les débuts de l'enseignement et de la libre pensée dans les Balkans. La vie et l'oeuvre de Théophile Corydalée (1570–1646), Second Edition (Thessalonique: Institute for Balkan Studies, 1967); Christos Marazopoulos, Θεόφιλος Κορυδαλλέας. Ὁ πρωτοφιλόσοφος τοῦ ἑλληνικοῦ Νεοαριστοτελισμοῦ (Athens: Grigoris, 2008); Vasilios I. Tsiotras, ''Ο «Εἰς κοιμηθέντας» λόγος τοῦ Θεοφίλου Κορυδαλλέως καί ἡ ἀριστοτελική περί ψυχῆς θεματική του', Ὁ Ἐρανιστής, 29 (2016), 5–45.
64 See Nikolaos E. Tzirakis, Ἡ περί μετουσιώσεως (transubstantiatio) εὐχαριστιακή ἔρις. Συμβολή εἰς τήν ὀρθόδοξον περί μεταβολῆς διδασκαλίαν τοῦ ΙΖ΄ αἰῶνος (Athens 1977).
65 Cremonini was also accused of materialsm and atheism by the Jesuits and had problems with the Inquisition. See Tsourkas, Les débuts, p. 192. About Corydalleus' views on religion and philosophy, see Thomas Papadopoulos, Ἡ νεοελληνική φιλοσοφία ἀπό τόν 16° ἕως τόν 18° αἰώνα (Athens: I. Zacharopoulos, 1988), pp. 135–50.

Despite these problems, Corydalleus managed to introduce this current of Aristotelianism to the Orthodox world of the day mainly through his commentaries on Aristotle's works that circulated in large numbers in manuscript form at the various centres of Greek learning.[66] Further, this Aristotelianism and its variations became established and dominated subsequently the Greek Orthodox intellectual scene[67] (e.g., in the Danubian Principalities through Corydalleus' students, such as Ioannis Karyofyllis, *c.* 1600–after 1693[68]; in Ioannina by Georgios Sougdouris, 1645/47–1725[69]). This lasted at least until the second half of the eighteenth century when new scientific ideas started to gain momentum and became more influential. His system also came to be known under the name of 'Corydallism' (Κορυδαλλισμός), a term that at that time acquired a derogatory significance indicating the old and outdated scientific tradition that had been superseded by modern science. All this took place mostly after the death of Corydalleus himself, who is not to be blamed for the later absolutisation of the Aristotelian tradition he had introduced to the Greek Orthodox world.

More importantly, these developments took place through the intervention of the official church at various levels, which finally led to the acceptance and official legitimation of this form of Aristotelianism in the early seventeenth century. This was achieved by the controversial Patriarch of Constantinople Cyril Loukaris (1572–1638), who had also studied in Padua and had appointed Corydalleus in charge of the Patriarchal Academy of Constantinople in order to reorganise its educational programme. Given the growing tensions with the Roman Catholic expansionist policy towards Eastern and South Eastern Europe and the challenge of Uniatism, Loukaris gradually became staunchly anti-Catholic, anti-Jesuit and anti-Scholastic, also due to his first-hand experience with Catholics in these areas.[70] This is why he started making related openings to the Protestant world, which caused him a lot of disdain and critique at that time. Interestingly, the accusation of endorsing Calvinist views was raised for both Loukaris and Corydalleus.[71] Among other things, Loukaris intended to create a new educational and cultural paradigm for the Orthodox world as a way to counterbalance the growing Jesuit religious and intellectual infiltration that was

---

66 See Yiannis Karas, *Οἱ ἐπιστῆμες στήν Τουρκοκρατία. Χειρόγραφα καί ἔντυπα*. Vol. 2. *Οἱ ἐπιστῆμες τῆς Φύσης* (Athens: Estia, 1993), pp. 159–203.
67 See Psimmenos (ed.), *Ἡ ἑλληνική φιλοσοφία*, pp. 173–292.
68 See Tsourkas, *Les débuts*, pp. 211–13; Ariadna Camariano-Cioran, *Les Académies Princières de Bucarest et de Jassy et leurs Professeurs* (Thessaloniki: Institute for Balkan Studies, 1974), pp. 180–91.
69 See Kostas Petsios, *Ὁ ἐσωτερικός διαφορισμός τοῦ νεοελληνικοῦ ἀριστοτελισμοῦ κατά τόν 17ο αἰώνα: Τό συγγραφικό ἔργο καί οἱ φιλοσοφικές ἀπόψεις τοῦ Γεωργίου Σουγδουρῆ (1645/47–1725)* (Ioannina: Panepistimio Ioanninon–Dodoni/Parartima, 2007).
70 See Tomasz Kempa, 'Kyrillos Loukaris and the Confessional Problems in the Polish-Lithuanian Commonwealth at the Turn of the Seventeenth Century', *Acta Poloniae Historica*, 104 (2011), 103–28.
71 See Charalambos N. Meletiadis, 'Ἀπό τόν Θεόφιλο Κορυδαλέα στόν Ἀλέξανδρο Μαυροκορδάτο, Ἀριστοτέλους τύχες', in *Proceedings of the International Conference 'Aristotle and Christianity'* (Athens, 24–25 November 2016), ed. by the Dean's Office of the Faculty of Theology (Athens: Ethniko kai Kapodistriako Panepistimio Athinon, 2017), pp. 353–81.

taking place at that time (also in Russia[72]). To this purpose, Paduan Aristotelianism in Corydalleus' version appeared to be particularly pertinent, as it turned decisively against the Aristotelianism of the Roman Catholic establishment.

As already mentioned, Corydallic Aristotelianism was in many respects problematic for the church doctrine, thus its official endorsement by Loukaris seems to be a paradox. Nevertheless, it can be adequately explained in the context of that particular era. Basically, it was in line with Loukaris' strong anti-Catholic orientations and policies, who intended thereby to avoid the so-called '*pestifarae quaestiones*' (contaminating/corrupting questions), namely the problem of the continuous and inappropriate intermingling of philosophy/science and theology and the constant danger of theological innovations. In his view, this was basically a Western Latin problem due to the Roman Catholic policies, and luckily not an Eastern Orthodox one. Through the introduction of Corydallic Aristotelianism into the Greek school curricula, the Western dilemma could be thus avoided. In other words, Corydallic Aristotelianism offered a useful division of labour between philosophy and theology and was a quite viable alternative to the Jesuit educational influence, thus it could be claimed by the Orthodox side for specific purposes. In actual fact, Loukaris was not so much interested in creating an Orthodox humanistic education *per se*, as he clearly prioritised the unconditional and simple faith over detailed knowledge and rational syllogisms. Hence, his decision to endorse and promote Corydallic Aristotelianism was rather politically than ideologically motivated. In this way, he definitely contributed to the creation of an 'Orthodox Humanism', but his main aim was to articulate an independent intellectual frame for the Orthodox and especially clearly distinct from the analogous Jesuit one.[73]

What is important here is the fact that Loukaris' policy cannot be characterised as a traditionalist one. On the contrary, it was rather innovative, as he basically tried to renew the Greek Orthodox educational repertoire through the introduction of Corydallic Aristotelianism. This new element was due to the specific challenges that Loukaris was facing at that time and was not perceived as a permanent and an absolute one. We should not forget the problems that Aristotle's and Corydalleus' ideas presented to the Orthodox Christian tradition, which, however, some Aristotelians tried to circumvent in various ways. One such mechanism was the theory about the 'double truth', supported by Corydalleus himself, namely about one truth based on the Bible and the Christian doctrine, and about another one based on Aristotle, which were somewhat considered as mutually independent and thus unrelated. This subterfuge enabled someone to remain both a true Christian and a good

---

[72] See Nikolaos A. Chrissidis, *An Academy at the Court of the Tsars: Greek Scholars and Jesuit Education in Early Modern Russia* (DeKalb, IL: Northern Illinois UP, 2016).

[73] See Manolis Patiniotis, 'Οἱ Pestifarae Questiones τοῦ Κυρίλλου Λουκάρεως καί ἡ ἀνάδυση τοῦ κορυδαλικοῦ προγράμματος', in *Βυζάντιο–Βενετία–Νεότερος Ἑλληνισμός: Μιά περιπλάνηση στόν Κόσμο τῆς Ἑλληνικῆς Ἐπιστημονικῆς Σκέψης*, ed. by Giorgos N. Vlahakis and Efthymios Nicolaidis (Athens: Ethniko Idryma Erevnon, 2004), pp. 211–44 (esp. pp. 236–42); Manolis Patiniotis, *Στοιχεῖα Φυσικῆς Φιλοσοφίας. Ὁ Ἑλληνικός ἐπιστημονικός στοχασμός τόν 17° καί 18° αἰώνα* (Athens: Gutenberg, 2013), pp. 99–171 (esp. pp. 149–71).

Aristotelian and to avoid tantalising questions about specific Aristotelian tenets that contradicted Christian doctrine. However, this solution was heavily criticised not only by the proponents of new scientific ideas as totally mistaken,[74] but also from other Aristotelians (e.g., by Nikolaos Koursoulas, 1602–after 1652), who were in favour of the one and sole Christian truth, corroborated by Aristotelian categories (also in the traditional Thomistic sense).[75]

Hence, even if Loukaris himself was not a traditionalist in this respect, subsequent generations of Orthodox prelates and thinkers fell victim to this challenge and absolutised Corydallic Aristotelianism as a core element essential to the corpus of the Orthodox tradition and with a clear anti-Western agenda denying the modern scientific advances.[76] In their attempt to keep Orthodoxy intact from Western innovations, they were ready to extend the limits of tradition beyond the religious domain and include many contingent elements that were circumstantially accepted into or were simply associated with the wider corpus of the Orthodox tradition. Truth be told, the Orthodox were indeed under strong pressure by Western Christians at that time and their overall superiority at numerous levels and were trying to defend not only their faith, but also their own cultural and scientific traditions. Hence, their defence mechanisms led them to support the Orthodox tradition as a solid block with all its religious and non-religious features. Due to this growing traditionalism, they were unable to discern that many elements of this 'Orthodox block' (including Aristotelianism) were by no means absolute, but rather subject to change. After all, it was futile to wage a war against modern science by endorsing an outdated Aristotelian worldview, and the fact that many Orthodox kept doing this until later centuries attests to a definite loss of reality among them.

In all probability, the learned Patriarch of Jerusalem (1661–69) Nektarios (1600–76), a former student and admirer of Corydalleus,[77] personified in the best way possible the epitome of this Orthodox and scientific traditionalism. Due to his church engagement in the Holy Land, he had first-hand experience of the conflicts among the Christian Churches and confessions for the control of the holy sites there at the expense of the Greek Orthodox Patriarchate of Jerusalem. This situation rendered his anti-Western attitude even stronger. Thus, in a text of 1672 against the French Protestant Jean Claude (1619–87), he tried to refute his critical and scornful remarks about the Orthodox Church and tradition and the educational level of the Greek Orthodox world of that era. Basically, Nektarios defended the superiority of

---

74 See Linos G. Benakis, *Μεταβυζαντινή Φιλοσοφία, 17⁰⁵–19⁰⁵ αἰώνας. Ἔρευνα στίς πηγές* (Athens: Parousia, 2001), pp. 73–78.
75 See Benakis, *Μεταβυζαντινή Φιλοσοφία*, pp. 140–43; Konstantinos Petsios, *Ἡ περί φύσεως συζήτηση στή νεοελληνική σκέψη. Ὄψεις τῆς φιλοσοφικῆς διερεύνησης ἀπό τόν 15° ὥς τόν 19° αἰώνα* (Ioannina 2002), 160–65.
76 See Vasilios A. Kyrkos, "Ὁ κορυδαλικός Νεοαριστοτελισμός καί οἱ φιλοσοφικές του συνδηλώσεις. Τό νόημα καί οἱ παρανοήσεις ἑνός φιλοσοφικοῦ ὅρου (Ἀριστοτελισμός)', *Κάτοπτρον Νεοελληνικῆς Φιλοσοφίας*, 3 (2016), 101–37.
77 See Manoussos I. Manoussakas, 'Αἱ ὁμιλίαι τοῦ Νεκταρίου Ἱεροσολύμων', *Κρητικά Χρονικά*, 7 (1953), 163–93 (pp. 168–69, footnote 24).

the Greek culture vis-à-vis the Western scientific advances of modern times. His perspective was a strong traditionalist one supporting the religious and cultural supremacy of the Greek Orthodox East exclusively on the basis of past achievements, given that all sciences had their origins from ancient Greece (ἀπὸ τῶν Ἑλλήνων). In a characteristic passage, he thus argued that one simply needed to look for every kind of scholarly/scientific knowledge, either religious or profane, in the writings of those who had lived before that era. In his view, this procedure was fully sufficient in order to draw from there all the true knowledge that one might have been seeking.[78] He also proceeded to attack and reject modern science in the figures of Copernicus and Galilei, because they had actually turned earth and heaven upside down and disseminated false knowledge. Nektarios' categorical conclusion was that the Orthodox had no need at all of such teachers and lessons, as they were fully self-sufficient and self-reliant, not least because of the exclusive authenticity of their past, including both the Orthodox tradition and the unparalleled ancient Greek intellectual heritage.[79]

The above example illustrates in an eloquent way the broader consequences of Orthodox traditionalism. For Nektarios, all knowledge without exception could be found in the past of the Greek Orthodox East, not in the misleading Western religious and scientific innovations. The past held thus a decisive and definitive superiority above the present and the future in his conceptual hierarchy and could not be superseded at all. Needless to say, such a regression towards the past and its authorities was uttered by Nektarios a few years before Isaac Newton was going to publish his *Philosophiae Naturalis Principia Mathematica* (1687). This attests to the huge gap dividing East and West around the end of the seventeenth century with regard to scientific standards. In addition, it can explain why this kind of excessive traditionalism rendered a Scientific Revolution in the Greek East a sheer impossibility. Finally, it suffices to mention the case of the Aristotelian Georgios Koressios (c. 1570–1659/60), instructor of Greek language at the University of Pisa (1609–15), who in 1612 initiated a scientific debate with a pioneer of modern science, Galileo Galilei, albeit to his ridicule.[80]

There are also further testimonies to the growing influence of Corydallic Aristotelianism in the Greek Orthodox world under the auspices of the official church. This can be discerned during the discussions and the related correspondence of the Eastern Orthodox Patriarchs in the early eighteenth century with the Non-Jurors — a group of Anglicans who in 1688 had split from the main Anglican Church because they denied allegiance to King William of Orange. It was about an exchange of ideas on religious issues and the potential agreement of union between

---

78 Anna Stef. Karamanidou, Νεκταρίου Πατριάρχου Ἱεροσολύμων Ἐπιστολές (1650–1672) (Thessaloniki: Barbounakis, 2019), p. 321: 'Ἀποκρινόμεθα ὅτι ἐξαρκεῖ πρὸς πᾶσαν ἐπιστημονικὴν γνῶσιν, τήν τε καθ' ἡμᾶς, καὶ τὴν ἔξω, ἐγκύπτειν ταῖς βίβλοις καὶ συγγράμμασι τῶν πρὸ ἡμῶν, κἀκεῖθεν ἐρανίζεσθαι τὴν περὶ παντὸς τοῦ ζητουμένου ἀλήθειαν.'
79 Karamanidou, Νεκταρίου, p. 322: 'Τοιούτων ἡμεῖς διδασκάλων καὶ μαθημάτων οὐ χρῄζομεν.'
80 See Nikolaos M. Stoupakis, Γεώργιος Κορέσσιος (1570 ci.–1659/60). Ἡ ζωή, τό ἔργο του καί οἱ πνευματικοί ἀγῶνες τῆς ἐποχῆς του (Chios: Omireio Pneumatiko Kentro, 2000); Benakis, Μεταβυζαντινή Φιλοσοφία, pp. 9–14.

the two sides, from which both were supposed to profit. It was in this context that the Non-Jurors in a letter of 18 August 1716 mentioned that they were specifically reviving 'the ancient education/knowledge' (τὴν παλαιὰν παιδείαν) in one of their proposals for a potential agreement with the Orthodox side.[81] It is not clear whether they were explicitly referring to the religious domain or not, but in all probability the point concerned the critical examination of traditional education and the entire corpus of knowledge bequeathed by the past as well as the necessary corrections or adjustments. This was, after all, a predominant attitude towards past knowledge and authorities in early modern times and later on in Western Europe. Interestingly enough, in their long answer from 18 April 1718, the Orthodox Patriarchs appeared to be annoyed by this point, because they had assumed that the Non-Jurors not only intended to teach them novel things in the profane realm, but also to change several things in the already irrevocably established church tradition. As a result, they found this proposal inacceptable and answered it in detail, showing once more unmistakably the Orthodox self-sufficiency and self-complacency in both religious and profane matters.

More specifically with regard to the latter: The Non-Jurors should not make — so the Orthodox side argued — the mistake of considering the Greek East as uninformed, uneducated and ignorant because of the political situation at that time. In fact, the Orthodox Patriarchs claimed to have a very satisfactory educational level, given that they possessed the writings of Aristotle and of other savants, as well as their commentators and interpreters; in addition, there were many schools in various cities and regions, in which the students were taught daily in Greek language both the divine lessons and the profane knowledge with a great investigative spirit and diligence. More importantly, the curricula followed the teachings of the Church Fathers in the religious domain, whereas in the philosophical/scientific realm they were based on Aristotle. All the more, the Orthodox appeared even ready to teach the Non-Jurors and contribute to their scientific enlightenment.[82] No doubt, this official legitimation of Corydallic Aristotelianism in the early eighteenth century was not done for the same reasons as Loukaris had done this in the early seventeenth century. It was the outcome of the usual traditionalist fermentations within Orthodox cultures,

---

81 Joannes Dominicus Mansi, Joannes Baptista Martin and Ludovicus Petit (eds), *Sacrorum Conciliorum nova et amplissima collectio*. Vol. 37. *Anni 1720–1735* (Paris 1905; Reprinted: Graz: Akademische Druck- und Verlagsanstalt, 1961), cols 383–94 (col. 385).

82 Mansi, Martin and Petit (eds), *Sacrorum Conciliorum*, cols 395–454 (cols 413, 415): 'Ἔχομεν παρ' ἡμῖν τὰς ἀριστοτελικὰς βίβλους καὶ ἄλλων σοφῶν καὶ τοὺς τούτων ὑπομνηματιστὰς καὶ ἐξηγητάς, καὶ σχολαί εἰσι παρ' ἡμῖν κατὰ διαφόρους πόλεις καὶ χώρας, ἐν αἷς αὗται διδάσκονται καὶ διαλευκαίνονται, ἐξ ὧν δυνάμεθα πλοῦτον σοφίας οὐκ ὀλίγον ἀρρύσασθαι [...] Ἀλλ' οἱ καλοὶ κἀγαθοὶ Βρεττανοὶ μὴ τοιαύτην ὑπόνοιαν ἐχέτωσαν περὶ ἡμῶν, ὡς δῆθεν ἀμοίρων διαμεμενηκότων παντάπασι τῆς ἀρχαίας ἐκείνης καὶ πατρίου καὶ ἐθάδος παιδείας, ἔν τισι δὲ σὺν θεῷ καὶ κρειττόνως ἢ παρ' ἄλλοις τισὶν εἰς ἔτι καὶ νῦν παρ' ἡμῖν διατηρουμένης. Ἀλλὰ μή τις ἡμᾶς τῶν μεμψιμοίρων οἰέσθω λέγοντας ταῦτα εἰκαίως ἐγκαυχᾶσθαι· τἀληθὲς καὶ γὰρ λέγομεν. Ἔχομεν γὰρ θεοῦ χάριτι καὶ εἰς ἔτι καὶ νῦν ἐν διαφόροις τόποις, ὡς εἴρηται, σχολὰς καὶ ἀκαδημίας, ἐν αἷς διδάσκονται καθ' ἑκάστην ἑλληνιστὶ καὶ μόνον τά τε ἐξωτερικὰ καὶ τὰ θεῖα μαθήματα μετὰ πολλῆς ἐρεύνης τε καὶ ἐπιμελείας, κατὰ τὴν τῶν πατέρων μὲν διδασκαλίαν ἐν τοῖς θεολογικοῖς, κατὰ δὲ τὸν Ἀριστοτέλην ἐν τοῖς φιλοσοφικοῖς.'

in which secondary, relative and contingent elements gradually acquired a similar normative significance exactly as the main religious components of the Orthodox tradition. Finally, the expressed intention of the Orthodox to teach the Non-Jurors in the scientific realm, as well as their self-sufficiency and apparent confidence reveal that they had lost touch with reality; even more so, as they were addressing a culture which had experienced the Scientific Revolution (*inter alia*, through the contributions of Isaac Newton) and was a harbinger of modern science through its university institutions (e.g., Oxford, Cambridge) and scientific associations (e.g., the 'Royal Society of London for Improving Natural Knowledge', founded in 1660).

What is striking, though, is the fact that Chrysanthos Notaras (c. 1655/60–1731), Patriarch of Jerusalem (1707–31), was deeply involved in the formulation of the above Orthodox answer. He was a very learned person with a superb scientific background, as he had studied in Western Europe (e.g., in Italy and in France) and was keenly aware of the scientific advances there in modern times.[83] Why did he choose then to support the above traditionalist position? Maybe this was due to the rules and restrictions imposed by the church diplomacy at that time. No doubt, Chrysanthos knew modern science very well, yet he kept a cautious, reserved and balanced stance on many matters and did not openly endorse all modern scientific positions. This mostly happened when he was addressing his Orthodox compatriots, who in his opinion were probably not ready to fully accept modern science. Such an ambivalent attitude is clear in his rather limited acceptance of the Copernican worldview, although he knew beyond doubt that this was already a scientifically established theory in Western Europe.[84] Chrysanthos kept this rather hesitant and neutral attitude in the Anthrakitis case in the 1720s as well, which will be treated in more detail below. Although he knew Anthrakitis personally and tried to help him at the beginning, he did not intervene actively later on in order to save him from the Patriarchal condemnation for teaching other philosophical systems than Aristotelianism.[85] Seen in this way, Chrysanthos could certainly not be characterised as an Orthodox traditionalist, yet his obvious ambivalence between the old intellectual establishment and modern science indirectly shows how powerful and resilient the traditionalist camp was at that time.

The same acceptance of Corydallic Aristotelianism by the church as the sole true, allowable and authoritative philosophical and scientific system can be clearly observed a few years later in the context of the condemnation of an Orthodox cleric, Methodios Anthrakitis (c. 1660–1736).[86] The aforementioned traditionalism developed thus further and was growing even stronger and influential with the passing of time, although there were also louder voices to abandon Aristotelianism

---

83 See Pinelopi Stathi, *Χρύσανθος Νοταράς, Πατριάρχης Ἱεροσολύμων. Πρόδρομος τοῦ Νεοελληνικοῦ Διαφωτισμοῦ* (Athens: Syndesmos ton en Athinais Megaloscholiton, 1999).
84 See Makrides, *Die religiöse Kritik*, pp. 45–50.
85 See Alkis Angelou, *Τῶν Φώτων. Ὄψεις τοῦ Νεοελληνικοῦ Διαφωτισμοῦ* (Athens: Ermis, 1988), pp. 25, 26, 32, 35 and 36.
86 Petsios, *Ἡ περί φύσεως συζήτηση*, pp. 231–45; Konstantinos Petsios, *Μεθόδιος Ἀνθρακίτης. Εἰσαγωγή στή Σκέψη καί τό Ἔργο του* (Ioannina 2006).

and endorse modern science (e.g., by the Prince Nikolaos Mavrokordatos in a work written between 1717 and 1718, which was however first published much later[87]). An early conflict between the established old and the new philosophical/scientific ideas had already taken place around 1716 in Thessaloniki between the monk Pachomios, a student of Anthrakitis, and the Aristotelian teacher Iannakos. Pachomios is even described as a reviler of Aristotle *par excellence* (ὑβριστὴς ἦν τοῦ Ἀριστοτέλους ἄκρος).[88]

A bit later, Anthrakitis himself was accused of introducing novel and dangerous philosophical and scientific ideas (e.g., Descartes, Malebranche) into the Greek school curricula, a fact that led to his condemnation by the Patriarchal Synod in Constantinople on 23 August 1723. The accusation was that he had abandoned Corydallic Aristotelianism, which had been already established in school curricula for a long time. This was regarded as a threatening innovation and a serious break with an almost sacrosanct tradition. Thus, in the condemnation text of 1723, it was clearly stated that Antrhakitis had abandoned the ancient tradition of the pious Orthodox teachers, which was kept up to that day; namely, to teach natural philosophy and other profane sciences according to the Aristotelian Peripatetic tradition.[89] The specific reference to the 'ancient tradition' makes the importance of this dimension in the overall church argumentation quite clear. *Antiquitas* was always a strong criterion for correctness in Orthodoxy, and accordingly a long-established tradition in the church was seen as something to be revered and be kept intact by later generations. Naturally, this concerns pre-eminently the religious domain, but it may also include any profane knowledge that for some reason was legitimised and enjoyed the church's support. Here it is about an all-encompassing, totalistic approach to the whole corpus of tradition, which does not distinguish between core and secondary elements and cannot proceed to a historicisation of its gradual articulation and construction across time. This is because it is not difficult to prove that Corydallic Aristotelianism has never been such an 'ancient tradition', but rather one that had been approved by the church through Patriarch Cyril Loukaris as late as the early seventeenth century. Yet, in the context of traditionalism, all this hardly matters, and contingent elements can be easily absolutised and thus immunised against any criticism, change, adjustment or overcoming.

The same traditionalist logic was repeated in the reinstatement of Anthrakitis by the Patriarchal Synod on 1 June 1725. There he was explicitly ordered to specifically teach solely Corydallic Aristotelianism, a 'common, usual and familiar' system that was being taught at that time at the Patriarchal Academy in Constantinople and

---

87 See Nikolaos Mavrokordatos, Φιλοθέου πάρεργα, ed. by Grigorios Konstantas (Vienna: Franz Anton Schrämbl, 1800), p. 54.
88 See Benakis, Μεταβυζαντινή Φιλοσοφία, p. 47.
89 Mansi, Martin and Petit (eds), *Sacrorum Conciliorum*, col. 235: 'Ἐπιδείξασθαι θέλων ἑαυτὸν νέον φιλόσοφον καὶ θεολόγον, ὅσα μὲν κατὰ παράδοσιν ἀρχαίαν οἱ εὐσεβεῖς τοῦ ἡμετέρου γένους διδάσκουσι καὶ διδάσκονται μαθήματα, ἐν μὲν τοῖς περὶ φύσεως λόγοις καὶ ταῖς θύραθεν ἐπιστήμαις, δηλαδὴ τὰ τῆς περιπατητικῆς φιλοσοφίας, ἐν δὲ τῇ θεολογίᾳ τὰς ἱερὰς βίβλους τῶν θεοσόφων Πατέρων τε καὶ διδασκάλων τῆς τοῦ Χριστοῦ Ἐκκλησίας, τούτων πάντων τὴν διδασκαλίαν καὶ ἀνάγνωσιν παρῃτήσατο καὶ ἀπεδοκίμασεν, ὡς οὐκ ἄξια κρίνας τῆς ἰδίας ἀμαθείας καὶ ψυχικῆς πωρώσεως.'

was regarded as fully harmless to the Orthodox doctrine. Aside from this, it was outspokenly prohibited to Anthrakitis and his students to teach any other 'unusual, unfamiliar and alien' philosophical system.[90] Besides, if his students were to teach somewhere or to undertake the leadership of a school, they had to ask permission from the church and get its approval, not only with regard to their Orthodoxy, but also in order to teach solely and exclusively Corydallic Aristotelianism (ζητῆσαί τε καὶ λαβεῖν ἄδειαν τῆς διδασκαλίας καὶ παραδόσεως μόνων τῶν τοῦ Κορυδαλλέως φιλοσοφικῶν μαθημάτων).[91] This policy is indicative of the strenuous efforts of the church to protect and preserve the traditionalist educational establishment under its control.

Once again, the above traditionalist statement makes evident the pervasive negative attitude against any novelties, especially the ones coming from outside (Western Europe), and the complacency with the familiar, established and conventional knowledge standards bequeathed by the past. Such a stance neglected or even ignored the originally 'alien' character of Corydallic Aristotelianism, given its genesis out of the spirit of Paduan Aristotelianism. In other words, it was far from a traditional system, but rather a novelty that had been approved by the church a few decades ago for specific reasons. Interestingly enough, there were several Greek students (e.g., Eustathios Nomikos, Nikolaos Stratigos, Demetrios Meradaris, Nikolaos Katsaitis) at the University of Padua in the first half of the eighteenth century, who had tried to save the prestige of Aristotelianism, either out of conservatism or of national pride. This was probably because the University of Padua since 1738 had introduced a chair of modern experimental philosophy by replacing one of the two chairs of Aristotelian philosophy.[92] As for Anthrakitis, in his apology (30 November 1723) he made clear that he was favouring no specific philosophical system as an absolute one (καμμίαν φιλοσοφίαν δὲν δέχομαι, οὔτε διὰ βεβαίαν ἔχω)[93] and that he preferred to choose the more pertinent in his view from the many existing ones. He also tried to de-legitimise the position of the church by arguing that every Church Father had a different philosophical preference, yet this did not lead necessarily to official accusations of heresy.[94] He thus reiterated his conviction that he was not condemned by the church as a bad Christian or for a deviation from the church doctrine, but because he preferred another

---

90 Eustathios Pelagidis, "Ἡ συνοδικὴ ἀπόφαση γιὰ τὴν ὁριστικὴ ἀποκατάσταση τοῦ Μεθοδίου Ἀνθρακίτη", *Μακεδονικά*, 23 (1983), 134–47 (p. 137): 'Μόνα τὰ ὑπὸ ἐξηγητῇ τῷ κυρῷ Κορυδαλλεῖ ἑρμηνευόμενα τῆς περιπατητικῆς φιλοσοφίας μαθήματα, τὰ καὶ ἐν τῇ πατριαρχικῇ σχολῇ ἐνταῦθα εἰς Κωνσταντινούπολιν παραδιδόμενα, καὶ μηδεμιᾶς ἐξ αὐτοῦ λύμης τῇ ὀρθοδοξίᾳ προστριβομένης. Ἐκτὸς δὲ τῆς διδασκαλίας τῶν συνήθων τοῦ κυροῦ Κορυδαλλέως αὐτοῦ συγγραμμάτων μηδεμίαν ἄλλην παράδοσιν ἀσυνήθους καὶ ξένης φιλοσοφίας τολμῆσαι ὅλως ποτὲ οὔτε τὸν ῥηθέντα Μεθόδιον, οὔτε τινὰ τῶν μαθητευσάντων αὐτῷ.'
91 Pelagidis, "Ἡ συνοδικὴ ἀπόφαση", p. 138.
92 See Aristeidis P. Stergellis, *Τὰ δημοσιεύματα τῶν Ἑλλήνων σπουδαστῶν τοῦ Πανεπιστημίου τῆς Πάδοβας τόν 17ᵒ καί 18ᵒ αἰ.* (Athens: Parnassos, 1970), pp. 35–36 and 68–72.
93 See Angelou, *Τῶν Φώτων*, p. 26.
94 Angelou, *Τῶν Φώτων*, p. 28: 'Πρὸς καὶ τοὺς Πατέρας βλέπομεν πῶς ὁ καθεὶς διάφορον ἐσπούδαζε φιλοσοφίαν. Δὲν ἠκούσαμεν ποτὲ νὰ ἐστάθη αἱρετικὸς εἰς Σύνοδον καὶ νὰ ἐλέγχεται διὰ αἱρετικὸς μὲ τὸ νὰ σπουδάζῃ τὴν τοῦ τάδε φιλοσοφίαν.'

philosophical system than the church-authorised Aristotelianism.[95] This absolutisation of Aristotelianism by the church and its consequences were also witnessed by others during the same period. Konstantinos Koumas (1777–1836) thus mentioned that any innovation in this matter appeared, as always, to be dangerous, given that the church considered any other philosophical system than Aristotelianism its enemy.[96] In fact, the Patriarchal Academy in Constantinople was a centre of Aristotelianism, which was preserved there with religious meticulousness and precision (διετηρεῖτο μετὰ θρησκευτικῆς ἀκριβείας).[97]

Given the growing contacts between the Greek Orthodox world and Western Europe in the course of the eighteenth century, it is no surprise to witness various such debates between traditionalist and progressive currents and actors in numerous domains, including in the religious one. The so-called Kollyvades conflict, which erupted on the Holy Mountain Athos in the 1750s and acquired further dimensions later on that rendered the intervention of the Patriarchate of Constantinople imperative, is a case in point.[98] As far as the scientific realm is concerned, there are several examples of such debates and conflicts. Especially several promoters of new scientific ideas intended to overcome Aristotelianism and pave the way for the introduction of modern science into the school curricula.[99] To this purpose, they used various strategies, such as to show the overall incompatibility between Aristotelianism and Christian theology in general and thus deprive Aristotelianism of its ecclesiastical approval, given that some Aristotelians at that time kept trying to bring Aristotelian ideas and Orthodox doctrine even closer. The related debate between the Newtonian Nikolaos Zerzoulis (c. 1710–73) and the Aristotelian priest-monk Dorotheos Lesvios in the 1740s vividly illustrates these developments, especially because Zerzoulis criticised sharply the extreme reverence Aristotle was still enjoying among many Orthodox as if he were infallible and even above the Christian tradition.[100] In this way, we may talk an 'Orthodox wave' against Corydallic Aristotelianism that was gaining momentum at that time. This new generation of clerics and scholars tried to show the relativity of this system and its necessary overcoming on the basis of new scientific data and exigencies. In all probability, these later critics were not familiar with the initial intentions of Patriarch Loukaris when he had approved and authorised it for the school curricula. They might have also not known exactly the intellectual roots and basic coordinates and

---

95 Angelou, *Τῶν Φώτων*, p. 26: 'Καταδικάζομαι λοιπὸν ὑπὸ τῆς Συνόδου ὄχι ὡς κακὸς Χριστιανός, ὄχι εἰς κάνένα δόγμα τῆς Ἐκκλησίας, ἀλλὰ πῶς φιλοσοφῶ διαφόρως ἀπὸ τοὺς Ἀριστοτελικούς.'
96 Konstantinos Koumas, *Ἱστορίαι τῶν ἀνθρωπίνων πράξεων*. Vol. 12 (Vienna: Anton von Haykul, 1832), p. 560: 'Ὁ νεωτερισμὸς ὅμως, καθὼς πάντοτε, ἐφαίνετο ἐπικίνδυνος. Παρὰ τὴν Ἀριστοτελικὴν φιλοσοφίαν πᾶσα ἄλλη ἐνομίζετο πολέμιος τῆς ἐκκλησίας.'
97 Theodoros M. Aristoklis (ed.), *Κωνσταντίου Α΄ τοῦ ἀπὸ Σιναίου ἀοιδίμου Πατριάρχου Κωνσταντινουπόλεως τοῦ Βυζαντίου βιογραφία καὶ συγγραφαὶ αἱ ἐλάσσονες ἐκκλησιαστικαὶ καὶ φιλολογικαί, καί τινες ἐπιστολαὶ τοῦ αὐτοῦ* (Constantinople: Proodos, 1866), p. 2.
98 See Ioannis Zelepos, *Orthodoxe Eiferer im osmanischen Südosteuropa: Die Kollyvadenbewegung (1750–1820) und ihr Beitrag zu den Auseinandersetzungen um Tradition, Aufklärung und Identität* (Wiesbaden: Harrassowitz, 2012).
99 For an overview, see Petsios, *Ἡ περὶ φύσεως συζήτηση*, pp. 273–371.
100 See Benakis, *Μεταβυζαντινή Φιλοσοφία*, pp. 33–72 and 79–88.

contours of this system. But they certainly knew that it was an outdated one that had to replaced and that it was not worth the official church support it was still enjoying.

An interesting case from this epoch concerns the aforementioned polyhistor cleric Voulgaris, who during his long educational activities in various cities of the Greek area under Ottoman rule tried to move beyond the established Aristotelianism and introduce new philosophical and scientific ideas from Western Europe. As a result, he faced serious problems by traditionalist teachers and the overall religious and social establishment (e.g., in Ioannina by the teachers from the Balanos family, who were in favour of Aristotelianism[101]) and was forced to leave both the schools and the places where he was employed. The last incident in the Greek area, before leaving it definitely for Germany and later for Russia, occurred in Constantinople where Voulgaris was active as a teacher at the Patriarchal Academy in the early 1760s. There he fell into disfavour with several Aristotelian circles, including Samuel Chantzeris (1700–75), the learned Patriarch of Constantinople (1763–68 and 1773–74).[102] Chantzeris was firmly attached to the Aristotelian philosophical system, which he considered almost infallible. Further, it was a mere impossibility for him to change this fundamental orientation in old age, as this was the only system that he had been taught in the past and had unconditionally endorsed.[103] Interestingly enough, he was critical of the Aristotelian traditions that had developed in Western Europe and were superseded by modern science and technology, which were also not deprived of his critique.[104] This is because he most probably intended to support the long and supposedly unbroken continuation of an indigenous Greek Orthodox appropriation of Aristotle in the footsteps of the early Church Fathers. Consequently, he argued that his own Aristotelianism was fully in congruence with the tradition of the divinely driven Church Fathers. For him, it was not at all coincidental that Basil of Caesarea, Gregory of Nazianzus and many other Church Fathers preferred and endorsed Aristotelianism rather than any other philosophical system. In his

---

101 See Ἡ Φιλοσοφία στά Γιάννινα. 250 χρόνια ἀπό τήν ἔλευση τοῦ Εὐγενίου Βούλγαρη στήν πόλη μας. Ἐπιστημονική Ἡμερίδα (Ioannina, 15 December 1993, University of Ioannina), published in Δωδώνη, 25/3 (1996), 9–78. Interestingly enough, Paduan Aristotelianism, disseminated by various Greek scholars in the Ottoman Empire, did also have an impact on the Ottomans and their 'natural philosophy'. The learned Esad of Ioannina, who translated the work *Commentarii lucidissimi in octo libros Aristotelis de physico auditu* of Johannes Cottunius (1577-1658) into Arabic, is a case in point. For more details, see B. Harun Küçük, 'Natural Philosophy and Politics in the Eighteenth Century: Esad of Ioannina and Greek Aristotelianism at the Ottoman Court', *Osmanlı Araştırmaları / The Journal of Ottoman Studies*, 41 (2013), 125–58. See also Harun Küçük, *Science without Leisure: Practical Naturalism in Istanbul, 1660–1732* (Pittsburgh: University of Pittsburgh Press, 2020).
102 See Vasilios K. Bakouros, Σαμουήλ Χαντζερής ὁ Βυζάντιος (1700–1775). Ἡ συμβολή του στήν πνευματική κίνηση τοῦ Γένους κατά τόν 18ο αἰ. (Athens: Prosopo, 2008); Agathangelos Siskos (ed.), Ὁ Πατριάρχης Σαμουήλ Χαντζερής καί ἡ κοινοτική ἐκπαίδευση στήν Πόλη (Constantinople: Romaiiki Koinotita Neochoriou, 2017).
103 Aristoklis (ed.), *Κωνσταντίου Α΄*, p. 359: 'Προστετηκώς ταῖς τοῦ Ἀριστοτέλους δόξας, ἀπταίστους ταύτας πρεσβεύων, ἀχωρίστως ταύταις προσκείμενος καὶ πολιὸν τῇ τριχῇ ἔχων τὸ αὐτό, ὃ ἐδιδάχθη φρόνημα, ἀπεστρέφετο τά παρ' Εὐγενίου παραδιδόμενα, ὡς νεωτέρας φρενὸς κυνήματα.'
104 Manouil Gedeon, 'Σαμουὴλ Χαντζερῆ, Πατριάρχου Κωνσταντινουπόλεως, ἐπιστολαὶ ἀνέκδοτοι', Ἐκκλησιαστικὴ Ἀλήθεια, 4 (1883/84) 143–48 (p. 146).

view, this had happened exactly because they had acknowledged the great veracity and potential of this system. If one thus compares — he continued — what these Fathers had considered as good and worth endorsing with the modern philosophical systems, then it is like comparing the sunrise with the sunset.[105] Chantzeris' opinion makes clear the strong influence of Orthodox traditionalism, inasmuch as he tried to construct an unbroken continuity of Greek Orthodox Aristotelianism since the time of the early Church Fathers. In such a context, historical details, nuanced approaches and necessary distinctions did not seem to play a role. For example, the Cappadocian Church Fathers of the fourth century were more influenced by Platonic ideas and less by Aristotle.[106] But such a historicisation did not matter much for Chantzeris, who simply wanted to establish and legitimise such a long Aristotelian chain for the Orthodox world, starting from late antiquity down to his own era. This incident shows the later changes that took place within the predominant church discourse about Aristotelianism in the context of Orthodox traditionalism. In the case of Chantzeris, thus, this discourse was explicitly connected to the authority of the Greek Church Fathers and accordingly legitimated.

It was against the background of this intellectual traditionalism that Voulgaris — a staunch supporter of the Orthodox tradition, but simultaneously also a liberal spirit — attempted to introduce a new natural philosophy according to his own eclectic method, following the criterion of correct reasoning and without compromising his Orthodox faith. Especially in his *Logic*, he wrote a critical overview of the development of the Greek intellectual tradition after the fall of Byzantium and observed that most scholars, aside from few exceptions, were following almost blindly Aristotelian ideas and refused to examine and endorse other perspectives, either older or modern.[107] Voulgaris was aware of the dangers posed by this kind of traditionalism, which unduly venerated antiquity as a whole and the achievements of the past, despite the fact that he also tried in the end to combine older traditions with the modern ones in the frame of his eclecticism.[108] The liberation from such a pervasive traditionalism, fuelled by the church and its fixation on past authorities, was also attempted by Voulgaris' students, such as by Iosipos Moisiodax (1725–1800), who was known for his severe

---

105 Gedeon, 'Σαμουὴλ Χαντζερῆ', pp. 146–47: ''Ο δ' ἀξιῶ καὶ λέγω ὡς οὐκ ἄν παρ' ἦν οἱ θεῖοι ἄνδρες ἄλλην αὐτὸς φιλοσοφίαν ἀσπασαίμην. Οὐ γὰρ ἄν Βασίλειοι καὶ Γρηγόριοι, καὶ τηλικούτων καὶ τοσούτων πατέρων θεοσόφων σειρὰ τὴν ἀριστοτελικὴν πρὸ πασῶν προὔκριναν δόξαν, καὶ ἠσπάσαντο, μὴ μέγα τι κατιδόντες ἐν αὐτῇ καὶ ἀληθές, κατ' ἐκεῖνο μάλιστα καιροῦ, ὅτε καὶ τὰ Δημοκρίτῳ καὶ τοῖς πολλοῖς φιλοσοφούμενα νεαλέστερα ἐπεχωρίαζον αὐτοῖς καὶ ἀκμαιότερα, καὶ τοῖς τότε ἐπιτηδειότερα φιλοσοφοῦσι [...] Καὶ τοῦτο οὐχ ὡς παραβάλλων τά καθ' ἡμᾶς λέγω, ἀλλὰ τὰ πάλαι παρὰ πατράσι καλὰ καὶ ζηλωτὰ πρὸς τά παρ' αὐτῶν νεοτευχούμενα, ὡς εἴ τις παραβάλλοι τὰς ἡλίου ἀνατολὰς πρὸς τὰς δύσεις.'
106 See Jaroslav Pelikan, *Christianity and Classical Culture: The Metamorphosis of Natural Theology in the Christian Encounter with Hellenism* (New Haven/London: Yale UP, 1993); George Karamanolis, *The Philosophy of Early Christianity* (Durham: Acumen, 2013).
107 Eugenios Voulgaris, *Ἡ Λογικὴ ἐκ παλαιῶν τε καὶ νεωτέρων συνερανισθεῖσα* (Leipzig: Breitkopf, 1766), p. 44: 'Οἱ πάντες (ἢν ἕνα τυχόν, καὶ δεύτερον ἐξέλοις) τὴν αἵρεσιν Περιπατητικοί, καὶ τῆς Ἀριστοτέλους ἑνὸς φωνῆς ἠρτημένοι, οὐδὲν δέ, ὃ μὴ τῆς ἐκείνου φρενὸς εἴρηται ἐπιγέννημα, οὐδὲ τὸ τυχὸν προσιέμενοι ἐν τῷ φιλοσοφεῖν, οὔτε παλαιόν, οὔτε νεώτερον.'
108 Voulgaris, *Ἡ Λογική*, p. 45.

social criticism.¹⁰⁹ He particularly tried to get rid of the outdated Aristotelianism and deprive it of the church support by introducing the new natural philosophy. He was also keenly aware of the intellectual situation in Western Europe at the end of the eighteenth century. There, aside from a few monastic schools (τὰ σχολεῖα τῶν μοναζόντων) where it is still taught, Aristotelianism was in his view in a moribund state and would certainly not last long.¹¹⁰ But unfortunately, the Greek Orthodox Aristotelianism of his era was a philosophical system, which considered all other philosophical traditions as ungodly or at least as causing and leading to ungodliness.¹¹¹

All in all, the proponents of new scientific ideas gradually enabled the transition to the modern scientific worldview at the end of the eighteenth and the beginning of the nineteenth century. However, despite critique, Corydallic Aristotelianism's influence still lingered on, especially through the circulation of manuscripts. Interestingly enough, two of Corydalleus' commentaries on Aristotle (Εἴσοδος Φυσικῆς Ἀκροάσεως κατ' Ἀριστοτέλην and Γενέσεως καὶ φθορᾶς περί κατ' Ἀριστοτέλην) were published posthumously in book form in Venice in 1779 and 1780 respectively, edited by the archimandrite Cyprian from Cyprus. Such a publication took place rather unexpectedly in an era when modern science was becoming stronger and influential in the Greek East. What is even more striking is that the introduction (Προθεωρία) to Corydalleus' above first volume stems from a then unpublished work of Voulgaris on natural philosophy entitled Τὰ ἀρέσκοντα τοῖς φιλοσόφοις, which followed the modern scientific standards. This book was published much later in 1805, but parts of it may have been circulating earlier in manuscript form. How can this rather paradoxical combination between a traditional and a modern scientific orientation may be explained? We do not know all the particular circumstances of this posthumous publication of Corydalleus' works, but this introduction may have been an attempt to bring the two philosophical-scientific strands together, namely that of Corydalleus (the older) and that of Voulgaris (the modern).¹¹² Was this an attempt to create a new paradigm of a mutual relationship between philosophy and Orthodoxy in general? As already mentioned, Voulgaris himself was eclectic in his philosophical and scientific preferences and tried (especially in his later years) to find compromises between old and new ideas, although he was an outspoken supporter of modern developments. There were also other attempts at that time to combine Aristotelianism with modern science and philosophy, such as the one by the Prince of Wallachia Alexander Ypsilantis (1726–1807) in 1776, aimed at reorganising the curriculum at the Princely Academy of Bucharest.¹¹³ Needless to say, there existed

---

109 See Paschalis M. Kitromilides, *The Enlightenment as Social Criticism: Iosipos Moisiodax and Greek Culture in the Eighteenth Century* (Princeton, NJ: Princeton UP, 1992).
110 See Iosipos Moisiodax, Ἀπολογία. Μέρος Πρῶτον (Vienna 1780), reprinted and edited by Alkis Angelou (Athens: Ermis, 1976), p. 24, footnote 1.
111 Moisiodax, Ἀπολογία, p. 5.
112 See Manolis Patiniotis, "Ὅταν ὁ Εὐγένιος Βούλγαρης προλογίζει τόν Θεόφιλο Κορυδαλλέα (Πρόδρομη ἀνακοίνωση)", Νεῦσις, 8 (1999), 171–77.
113 See Apostolos E. Vakalopoulos, Πηγές τῆς Ἱστορίας τοῦ Νέου Ἑλληνισμοῦ. Vol. 2 (1669–1812) (Thessaloniki: Etaireia Makedonikon Spoudon, 1977), pp. 345–47.

further possibilities of relating modern ideas with Orthodoxy, such as in the form of Newtonianism, which enabled a more 'pious natural philosophy' in congruence with the then scientific advances.[114] After all, Newtonian physics was taught by Voulgaris himself at the Athonias Academy on Mount Athos, as well as at the Patriarchal Academy in Constantinople.[115]

Be that as it may, we know for sure that Corydallic Aristotelianism did not die out, but continued to exert significant influence among the still existing proponents of the old scientific tradition, who kept vehemently opposing modern science. Considering that this took place even in the first decades of the nineteenth century, this renders the significance of such Aristotelianism and the overall impact of Orthodox traditionalism quite evident. The most characteristic case is perhaps that of the ardent Aristotelian Sergios Makraios (1734/40–1819), who was teaching for a long time at the Patriarchal Academy of Constantinople, also becoming its principal for a while. He is perhaps more widely known for attempting to refute the Copernican worldview through the use of Aristotelian cosmology and other ancient Greek theories as late as 1797.[116] Throughout his life, he remained a fervent follower of Aristotle, whose works he studied systematically, diligently and meticulously on the basis of his 'authentic commentator' Corydalleus, whom he highly valued.[117] His was a traditionalist orientation *par excellence* that was opposing all changes in both the religious and the profane domain. This is evidenced, among other things, in his last book of 1816, in which he outright condemned human vanity, because it never stays still and keeps looking for novelties, as the introduction of the Copernican worldview had amply demonstrated. In his view, it was human vanity that led to the conception of this worldview in the first place with catastrophic consequences for the entire universe. This was because the new cosmology mixed and confused everything in nature and created a lot of frustration by turning heaven and earth upside down and moving the fixed and immovable elements in the universe.[118] In the preface to the above book, Makraios appeared, however, as being more objective, given that he

---

114 See Efthymios Nicolaidis, 'The Greek Enlightenment, the Orthodox Church, and Modern Science', in *Enlightenment and Religion in the Orthodox World*, ed. by Paschalis M. Kitromilides (Oxford: Voltaire Foundation, 2016), pp. 49–62.
115 See Giorgos N. Vlahakis (ed.), Ἡ νευτώνεια φυσική καὶ ἡ διάδοσή της στὸν εὐρύτερο βαλκανικό χῶρο (Athens: Ethniko Idryma Erevnon, 1996); Manolis Patiniotis, 'Periphery Reassessed: Eugenios Voulgaris Converses with Isaac Newton', *The British Journal for the History of Science*, 40 (2007), 471–90.
116 See Makrides, *Die religiöse Kritik*, pp. 81–146.
117 Cf. Makraios' letter to Chrysanthos Aitolos from 9 March 1785 about the lessons he was teaching at the Patriarchal Academy: 'Ἐπ᾽ αὐτὸν τὸν φιλόσοφον [sc. Aristotle] σὺν ὀλίγοις διεκπονῆσαι διέγνων, συγχρώμενος τῷ λαμπροτάτῳ διδασκάλῳ, δαδούχῳ καὶ ὑπομνηματιστῇ γνησιωτάτῳ τοῦ φιλοσόφου [sc. Corydalleus]. Μετῆλθον ἄρα σὺν αὐτοῖς ἐπιστήσας τὸν νοῦν πανταχῇ, τοῦ Ἀριστοτέλους θηρώμενος καὶ διερμηνεύων.' See Vasilios Sfyroeras, 'Ἀνέκδοτοι ἐπιστολαί Σεργίου Μακραίου πρὸς Χρύσανθον τὸν Αἰτωλόν', Ἐπετηρὶς τοῦ Μεσαιωνικοῦ Ἀρχείου, 8/9 (1958/59), 191–200 (p. 199).
118 Sergios Makraios, Ἐπιτομὴ φυσικῆς ἀκροάσεως (Venice: Nikolaos Glykis, 1816), pp. 110–11: 'Ἡ κενοδοξία μέντοι τῶν ἀνθρώπων, ἥτις οὐδέποτε ἠρεμεῖ, οὐδὲ ἐμμένει τοῖς τεταγμένοις, ἀλλὰ συγχέει καὶ μετακινεῖν πειρᾶται καὶ τὰ ἀκίνητα, ἀνεμόχλευσε καὶ γῆν αὐτήν, καὶ τὸν οὐρανὸν συνετάραξε καὶ τὰ πάντα συνέχεεν.'

emphasised the need for attaining true knowledge beyond established authorities and personal preferences.[119] Did this mean that he also distanced himself from his previous blind Aristotelianism? It seems that this was more of a rhetorical strategy to increase his credibility, given that he kept supporting Aristotelianism and the old worldview throughout his book. After all, this was the intellectual legacy that he left at the Patriarchal Academy of Constantinople with his traditionalist orientations.[120] However, there were other teachers at the same Academy (e.g., Dorotheos Proios, c. 1765–1821), who were more familiar with modern science, which they tried to introduce into its curriculum.[121]

In the case of Makraios, we may observe once more a further development of the discourse about Aristotelianism in the frame of Orthodox traditionalism. For Makraios, the true discoveries in science had been made by the ancient Greeks, and this was his agenda in attacking modern science stemming from Western Europe. Here the emphasis was put on the glorious ancient Greek past, which Makraios claimed to continue somewhat in his own era, not on the legacy of the Greek Church Fathers, as in the previous case with Chantzeris. All these, however, were various facets and strategies of the aforementioned traditionalist context, created and fuelled by the church and its need to preserve the Orthodox tradition intact from any external threat or contamination. The main goal was to defend and legitimise the past as qualitatively superior over the present and the future, not only in the religious, but also in the profane domain. The particular strategies Orthodox traditionalists used to achieve this goal varied enough, as this became evident in the present section through the numerous diverse arguments adduced to support and authorise Corydallic Aristotelianism in the Greek Orthodox East as the *non plus ultra* philosophical and scientific system.

Concluding Remarks

This case study has hopefully illustrated the overall contours of the Orthodox traditionalism and its broader repercussions including those in the scientific realm. It also tried to explain the process through which this traditionalist milieu operates and defies change and innovation. It concerned the absolutisation of a relative worldview (Corydallic Aristotelianism) within the overall corpus of the Orthodox tradition, which was considered *e principio* sacrosanct and untouchable. As a consequence, this worldview was also finally considered instrumental for the preservation of this tradition. Hence, it could not be abandoned, and both the official church and Orthodox traditionalist actors defended it staunchly within the educational *status quo*

---

119 Makraios, Ἐπιτομή, pp. ια΄–ιε΄.
120 See Tassos Ath. Gritsopoulos, Πατριαρχικὴ Μεγάλη τοῦ Γένους Σχολή. Vol. 1 (Athens 1966), 427–44, and Vol. 2 (Athens 1971), 55–58.
121 See Styliani-Christina A. Apostolidou, Δωρόθεος Πρώιος. Ἕνας ἐπιφανής λόγιος τοῦ Νεοελληνικοῦ Διαφωτισμοῦ (Thessaloniki: Ostracon Publishing, 2016).

of the day. Aside from the specific, conditional needs of the church to introduce and approve it in the first place, this worldview became subsequently a central element closely associated with the Orthodox tradition. However, it was exactly this particular worldview that had been superseded in Western Europe by the advent of modern science a long time ago. This example can thus offer a glimpse of the reasons as to why a Scientific Revolution has not and could not have taken place in the Greek Orthodox East, as this had happened in Western Europe. The role of Orthodox Christianity in this context is, based on the evidence from the aforementioned selected sources, far from unimportant. It had contributed significantly to the emergence and establishment of a dominant traditionalist milieu for centuries since Byzantine times, which was against any innovation from the very beginning. Furthermore, this situation is not only valid to a large extent for the Greek Orthodox world under Ottoman rule, but can be also observed *mutatis mutandis* in other predominantly Orthodox cultures as well (e.g., in Russia up to the seventeenth century[122]). The fact that the Orthodox world had limited exposure to the project of modernity as a whole can further explain this uncritical fixation on the past and its veneration in various forms. Needless to say, all this does not only pertain to the rise of modern science, which could never happen as such in the Orthodox world, but to numerous other issues, both religious and non-religious, that are part of the rich, yet still controversial heritage of modernity.

---

122 Alexander Vucinich (*Science in Russian Culture: A History to 1860*, Stanford, CA: Stanford UP, 1963, 4) talked about '*the absolute conservatism of the Church, which consistently opposed intellectual innovations, either Western or native, was dedicated to a perpetuation of the dogma as formulated by early Byzantine writers. Latin, and everything written in it, was for centuries considered the devil's tool and an enemy of Orthodoxy. The budding sciences and sceptical philosophy, with their cumulative challenges to the sacred authority of theological dogmatism, did not find even a feeble echo in Russia*'. For further information, see William Francis Ryan, 'Science in Medieval Russia', *History of Science*, 5 (1966), 52–61; Colin Chant, 'Science in Orthodox Europe', in *The Rise of Scientific Europe, 1500–1800*, ed. by David Goodman and Colin A. Russell (Sevenoaks, Kent: Hodder & Stoughton, 1991), pp. 333–60.

DONALD A. YERXA

Science and Religion in Historical Perspective: Some Brief Thoughts from the Engaged Periphery*

▼ ABSTRACT Familiarity with the substantial historical scholarship of the interface between science and religion in the West is needed as scholars consider relations between science and religion in the Orthodox Christian world. Engaging this historical literature is, of course, essential for establishing a comparative framework of what is both common and unique to the Western and Orthodox contexts. It also gives rise to important questions, such as: What do we mean by 'science' and 'religion'? Are we able to offer a convincing narrative of the history of science and religion? Of what value is the specific science-and-religion experience of one society for another? Can we go beyond specific contexts, which certainly suggest areas of difference, to ascertain patterns of similarity?

This essay further argues that there has been lack of symmetry in the science-and-religion debate in the West. The 'traffic' on the science-and-religion conversational bridge in the Western context appears to be one-way. Or two-way to the extent that science has the right of way, and religion (especially traditional Christianity) is asked repeatedly to yield. Much of the science-religion conversation, especially as conducted by Protestant theologians, is in fact more of a monologue with theology either playing the role of what I would call a 'scientism referee' or of exploring creative ways — often termed

---

* I would not want to present myself as anything other than a generalist historian/editor who speaks from the engaged periphery of the science and religion conversation. I am indebted to Arlin C. Migliazzo who used the phrase 'engaged periphery' in the title of a recently published article: 'Fides, Historia, and the Conference on Faith and History at Fifty: Perspectives from the Engaged Periphery,' *Fides et Historia* 51:1 (Winter/Spring 2019): 36–46.

Donald A. Yerxa • Eastern Nazarene College

as 'finding space' — by which traditional Christian doctrines might be reconceived to fit better with the current scientific understandings. In the light of all this, we can hope that the Orthodox discussion might encourage more robust two-way traffic. To accomplish this what is needed is a greater recognition of the experiential and the mysterious side of theology and even science. Orthodoxy can play an important role in educating the West as to how mystery enhances our necessarily limited understanding of the cosmos and the divine, as well as ourselves.

Greater familiarity with the historical scholarship of the interface between science and religion in the West would be helpful for many Orthodox scholars.[1] Over the past few decades talented historians have provided a rich understanding of the past interactions of science and religion in the West. Several of them — including John Brooke, Ronald Numbers, William Shea, and Peter Harrison — have participated in the Science & Orthodoxy around the World Project (SOW). Their scholarship, among other things, has effectively demolished a number of stereotypical portrayals ('myths', if you will) that have surrounded past discussions of science and religion. In *Galileo Goes to Jail*, a very helpful volume edited by Ronald Numbers, several of these misunderstandings are discussed. They include:

That the mediaeval (Latin) church suppressed the growth of science;
That Galileo was imprisoned and tortured for advocating the Copernican theory of the earth's motion;
That the scientific revolution liberated science from religion;
That Thomas Huxley, 'Darwin's Bulldog', soundly defeated Bishop Wilberforce in their famous debate in 1860 over evolution and religion at the Oxford University Museum;
That the 1925 Scopes Trial in the United States represented a sound defeat of anti-evolutionism; and
That modern science has been the principal agent of secularisation in Western culture.[2]

By and large, these 'myths' are subsets of the 'greatest myth in the history of science and religion': the so-called 'conflict thesis'. The view that science and religion have been in a constant state of conflict undergirded the dominant narrative in the history of science that reigned virtually unchallenged for over a century until the latter decades of the twentieth century.[3]

---

1 To be sure, historians and public intellectuals in the West would also benefit from this scholarship.
2 From *Galileo Goes to Jail and Other Myths about Science and Religion*, ed. by Ronald L. Numbers (Cambridge, MA: Harvard University Press, 2010).
3 Numbers, *Galileo Goes to Jail*, p. 1.

No one has done more to discredit the conflict thesis than David Lindberg, Ronald Numbers, and John Brooke. (The latter two participated in the previous two Project SOW international conferences.) Lindberg and Numbers noted in an important anthology, *God and Nature: Historical Essays on the Encounter between Christianity and Science* (1986), that the past interactions of science and Christian faith were so 'complex and diverse' that they defied 'reduction to simple "conflict" or "harmony" [...]. Although instances of controversy are not hard to find, it cannot be said that scientists and theologians — much less science and Christianity — engaged in protracted warfare'.[4] Extensive historical research convincingly supported Lindberg and Numbers's conclusion, enabling them to reassert in 2003:

> [...] historical study does not reveal science and Christianity locked in deadly combat; nor does it disclose an interaction of unfailing support and mutual compatibility. The relationship between science and Christianity proves to be much more intricate and interesting than these traditional alternatives allow, richly varied and nuanced, thoroughly human, and imbued with the same complexity that we find in other areas of human experience.[5]

No serious discussion of the conflict thesis can omit the work of John Brooke, who — as a result of his influential *Science and Religion: Some Historical Perspectives* (1991) and subsequent writing — has been dubbed 'the slayer of the conflict thesis'. Brooke has helped to reshape the way a generation of scholars has viewed the interaction of science and religion.[6] His emphasis on the rich complexity of past engagements of science and religion utterly discredited the conflict thesis and, indeed, rendered all science-and-religion master-narratives suspect. Any attempt to uncover 'some timeless, inherent relationship' between an essentialised science and an essentialised religion cannot be substantiated by historical inquiry that takes historical and cultural contexts seriously.[7]

Historians of science and religion will find nothing new here. But the historiography I have briefly touched upon is essential for understanding the fundamental questions and issues related to science and religion that emerged

---

4 David C. Lindberg and Ronald L. Numbers, 'Introduction', in *God and Nature: Historical Essays on the Encounter between Christianity and Science*, ed. by Lindberg and Numbers (Berkeley: University of California Press, 1986), p. 10.
5 David C. Lindberg and Ronald L. Numbers, 'Introduction', in *When Science and Christianity Meet*, ed. by Lindberg and Numbers (Chicago: University of Chicago Press, 2003), p. 5.
6 Thomas Dixon, 'Introduction'; and Noah Efron, 'Sciences and Religions: What it Means to Take Historical Perspectives Seriously', in *Science and Religion: New Historical Perspectives*, ed. by Thomas Dixon, Geoffrey Cantor, and Stephen Pumfrey (Cambridge: Cambridge University Press, 2010), pp. 1 and 258.
7 Efron, 'Sciences and Religions', p. 249; and John Hedley Brooke, 'Science, Religion, and Historical Complexity', in *Recent Themes in the History of Science and Religion*, ed. by Donald A. Yerxa (Columbia: University of South Carolina Press, 2009), pp. 37–46.

in the West.[8] Moreover, I submit, engaging this historical literature is essential for establishing a comparative framework of what is both common and unique to the Western and Orthodox contexts.

§

Exploring a few questions provides more texture to my point.

First: Is emphasising complexity and context enough? Having demolished the conflict thesis, are we able to offer a convincing replacement narrative of the history of science and religion?

Historian of science Noah Efron, for example, doubts that 'merely multiplying the complexity of an account renders it better'.[9] Brooke and his colleague Geoffrey Cantor warned in their 1995–99 Gifford Lectures that preoccupation with particular contexts risks dissolving 'the great issues that have been debated under the banner of "science and religion" into the fragments of local history'.[10] Behind the specific issues at stake for historians of science and religion loom very important questions that cut to the core of contemporary historical inquiry. Does complexity, with its insistence on the local and the particular, necessarily run counter to efforts to synthesise and look for patterns? Can historians function without master historical narratives, even though they necessarily blur the particularities of context? A number of historians, including Numbers and Peter Harrison, have noted that there is room for generalisation and pattern-seeking in the history of science and religion, but I am not aware of any consensus on the contours of such a post-Brookean historiography.[11]

Second: What do we mean by 'science' and 'religion'?

So far, I have used the terms 'science' and 'religion' informally. But, as some historians of science have noted, this usage is imprecise and unsatisfactory because these terms have meant 'different things in different times and places'.[12] Few terms are more contested than 'religion'. The diversity of religious traditions and expressions,

---

[8] Recent additions to the literature addressing the conflict thesis include: *The Warfare between Science and Religion: The Idea That Wouldn't Die*, ed. by Jeff Hardin, Ronald L. Numbers, and Ronald A. Binzley (Baltimore: Johns Hopkins University Press, 2018); and James C. Ungureanu, *Science, Religion, and the Protestant Tradition: Retracing the Origins of Conflict* (Pittsburgh: University of Pittsburgh Press, 2019).

[9] Efron, 'Sciences and Religions', p. 250. See also Dixon, 'Introduction', p. 13.

[10] John Brooke and Geoffrey Cantor, *Reconstructing Nature: The Engagement of Science and Religion* (Edinburgh: T & T Clark, 1998), p. 25.

[11] See Peter Harrison, '"Science" and "Religion": Constructing the Boundaries'; and Ronald L. Numbers, 'Simplifying Complexity: Patterns in the History of Science and Religion', both in *Science and Religion*, pp. 23–49 and pp. 263–82, respectively.

[12] John Hedley Brooke and Ronald L. Numbers, 'Introduction: Contextualizing Science and Religion', in *Science and Religion around the World*, ed. by Brooke and Numbers (Oxford: Oxford University Press, 2011), pp. 3–4.

as Peter Harrison has noted, 'is too great to warrant speaking of religion in general as having some kind of unitary historical force'.[13] Similarly, there are a number of scientific disciplines with distinctive methods. Consequently, Brooke suggests that it would be better to speak of 'sciences' and 'religions'.[14]

Any serious discussion of the history of science and religion must now engage one of the most important books on the subject written in the last few decades: Peter Harrison's *The Territories of Science and Religion* (2015), based on his 2011 Gifford Lectures. He provides a convincing account of how the meanings of the terms 'religion' and 'science' have changed over time in such a way that made the conflict model of their relationship possible. 'The compartmentalization of modern Western culture that gave rise to these distinct notions of "science" and "religion"', Harrison contends, 'resulted not from a rational or dispassionate consideration of how to divide cultured life along natural fracture lines, but to a significant degree has been to do with political power — broadly conceived — and the accidents of history'.[15] He notes that the way the categories of science and religion emerged in the Western consciousness determines what we think about their present relationship. There are significant implications of Harrison's thesis that I'll discuss a bit later.

Third, and perhaps most to the point of Project SOW: Of what value is the specific science-and-religion experience of one society for another?

It would be a mistake to imply that the Western experience is normative, especially if we value historical and cultural context. Indeed, the importance of context is undoubtedly the basic premise of any comparative exercise. Once again, I refer to Brooke and Numbers: 'Science-religion dialogues have taken many forms. They have been conducted very differently in different times and places. There is no unique solution to problem of how to describe the place of the sciences in, or their bearings on, the world's religions'.[16] That said, we are still left with the problem of the relationship of the local and particular with the general.[17] Can we go beyond specific contexts, which certainly suggest areas of difference, to ascertain patterns of similarity? In this regard, the Project SOW is making a major contribution by enabling a more fruitful comparative analysis.

§

---

13 Peter Harrison, 'Religion, Innovation, and Secular Modernity', in *Religion and Innovation: Antagonists or Partners*, ed. by Donald A. Yerxa (London: Bloomsbury, 2016), p. 85.
14 John Hedley Brooke, 'Contributions from the History of Science and Religion', in *The Oxford Handbook of Religion and Science*, ed. by Philip Clayton and Zachary Simpson (Oxford: Oxford University Press, 2006), p. 297. See also Brooke and Numbers, 'Contextualizing Science and Religion', p. 4.
15 Peter Harrison, *The Territories of Science and Religion* (Chicago: University of Chicago Press, 2015), pp. 3–4.
16 Brooke and Numbers, 'Contextualizing Science and Religion', p. 19.
17 See David N. Livingstone, 'Which Science? Whose Religion?' in *Science and Religion around the World*, pp. 278–96, especially p. 292.

One final observation. At the first SOW international conference, I commented on what I perceived to be a lack of symmetry in the science-and-religion debate in the West. From my vantage point on the engaged periphery, I noted that the traffic on the science-and-religion conversational bridge in the Western context appears to be one-way. Or two-way to the extent that science has the right of way, and religion (especially traditional Christianity) is asked repeatedly to yield. It seems that some theologians are all too willing to appropriate the terminology and findings of science in accommodationist ways reminiscent of H. Richard Niebuhr's 'Christ *of* culture' approach.[18]

I should have been more measured in my assessment — noting, for instance, the valuable contributions from scholars such as Alister McGrath, John Polkinghorne, Andrew Briggs, and Roger Wagner. Still, much of the science-religion conversation, especially as conducted by Protestant theologians, strikes me as being a monologue with theology either playing the role of what I would call a 'scientism referee' or of exploring creative ways — often termed as 'finding space' — by which traditional Christian doctrines might be reconceived to fit better with the current scientific understandings. And I continue to have questions about this 'dialogue' — interesting and creative, yes; but constructive and meaningful, I'm not so sure.

In the February 2017 meeting, I expressed hope that the Orthodox discussion might encourage more robust two-way traffic. To accomplish this, I called for a greater recognition of the experiential and the mysterious side of theology and even science. And I suggested that a discerning embrace of mystery could be a means of addressing the asymmetry. Admittedly, mystery is often viewed as a 'science stopper', invoking it being akin to committing intellectual suicide. But surely, I argued, recognizing the limits of human understanding can serve to stimulate the further pursuit of knowledge.[19] If that is the case, then Orthodoxy could play an important role in educating the West as to how mystery enhances our necessarily limited understanding of the cosmos and the divine, as well as ourselves.

Since I voiced these views, I have encountered the work of Paul Tyson and Michael Hanby, who I believe offer ways that may well address the imbalance that concerns me. Tyson, a philosophical theologian and apologist for Christian Platonism, decries the fact that the West has accepted a grossly inadequate view of reality that is bereft of any transcendent grounds for everyday experiences of love, beauty, meaning, and the goodness of God. He does not accept the autonomy of knowledge from faith and challenges the notion that what counts for real knowledge is sealed off from

---

18 H. Richard Niebuhr, *Christ and Culture* (New York: Harper & Row, 1951), especially pp. 83–115. For a recent example of a group of Christian theologians advancing positions 'that create space and allow for creative dialogue and interaction with the relevant science', see *Finding Ourselves after Darwin: Conversations on the Image of God, Original Sin, and the Problem of Evil*, ed. by Stanley P. Rosenberg (Grand Rapids, MI: Baker Academic, 2018), especially p. 204.

19 In support of my argument, I mentioned a number of scholars, including Freeman Dyson, Steven Weinberg, Marcelo Gleiser, and Wilfred McClay. I would add to these Alister McGrath. See his *The Great Mystery: Science, God and the Human Quest for Meaning* (London: Hodder, 2018), especially pp. 105–19; and *The Territories of Human Reason: Science and Theology in an Age of Multiple Rationalities* (Oxford: Oxford University Press, 2019), especially pp. 182–202.

meaning, values, and the transcendent. It is impossible here to provide anything other than a crude impression of Tyson's sophisticated analysis. But I offer the following bold quotes from his *Faith's Knowledge: Explorations into the Theory and Application of Theological Epistemology* (2013) and *De-Fragmenting Modernity* (2017) as representations of his views:

> [...] the entire cultural pattern of modernity is one premised on the separation of faith from knowledge; beauty from truth; religion from science; objective facts from subjective values; power, wealth, and reality from morality, teleology, and meaning.[20]
>
> Where astonishment with being is the grounds of knowing, things look very different. Knowing grounded in the wonder that there is anything at all grounds knowledge in a value outlook of abundance and delight. Openness to wonder orientates the knower as being within a reality that the knower did not create, that the knower is gifted to be within, and where the knower is part of a meaningful cosmos. Wonder itself is a function of meaning. But wonder is not masterable such that the dialectic between the known and the unknown, between the immediacy and mystery, between the increase of knowledge and the increase in wonder is not overcome. And here true knowledge is inseparable from love, such that mere mastery can never be the final purpose of knowledge.[21]

Michael Hanby's *No God, No Science? Theology, Cosmology, Biology* (2013) has been hailed as an attempt to formulate 'a theologically grounded metaphysics of science'.[22] The book's stated purpose is 'to retrieve the Christian doctrine of creation *ex nihilo* from the distortions imposed upon it by the totalizing claims of positivist science', especially evolutionary biology. Hanby, a professor of religion and philosophy of science at the Catholic University of America, rejects the idea that a rapprochement of sorts can be reached between science and theology by simply urging each to mind its own business. But the question of what the respective business of science and theology is — and thus the question of how to distinguish their respective tasks — cannot be determined on theologically neutral grounds. As Hanby writes: 'Science cannot determine for itself its relation to theology [...] without effectively *doing* theology, without saying, explicitly or implicitly where to draw the line or how to characterize the difference between God and the world [...]'.[23] He explains:

> [S]cience is intrinsically related to theology because one cannot identify the object of scientific inquiry — namely, nature — without simultaneously

---

20 Paul Tyson, *Faith's Knowledge: Explorations into the Theory and Application of Theological Epistemology* (Eugene, OR: Pickwick, 2013), p. 189.
21 Paul Tyson, *De-Fragmenting Modernity: Reintegrating Knowledge with Wisdom, Belief with Truth, and Reality with Being* (Eugene, OR: Cascade Books, 2017), p. 107.
22 Paul Tyson's review essay of *No God, No Science? Theology, Cosmology, Biology*, http://www.academia.edu/7952808/Michael_Hanby_No_God_No_Science_ (accessed 15 November 2018).
23 Tyson's review essay of *No God, No Science?*; Ken Myers's interview of Hanby, May 2014, Mars Hill Audio Vol. 121, https://marshillaudio.org/catalog/volume-121 (accessed 28 October 2018).

distinguishing it from that which is not nature — namely, God — and without giving tacit specification to the character of this "not" [...]. [Moreover,] there is no retreat to an ontologically neutral 'methodological' standpoint in order to escape this relation.'[24]

If I read Hanby correctly, he is challenging the assumption of the modern academy that methodology dictates ontology. In an interview, Hanby has noted that 'there is always a tacit dependence upon something more than what a purely mechanistic explanation could account for'. He explains that he is attempting to call the sciences' attention to 'the wonder and mystery not simply that something came into being at some remote time out of nothing, but to the mystery of being right now [...] to the wonder that at this moment I occupy a time and space in the cosmos as a unique entity that will never be replicated, as novel, not simply reducible to what came before'.[25]

Lastly, I take heart that the 'After Science and Religion Project', sponsored by the Templeton World Charity Foundation, has been launched at the University of Queensland under the leadership of Peter Harrison and Paul Tyson. Distinguished participants in this project are being asked 'to re-think the way in which we conceive of science and religion and their respective territories'. The project is clearly inspired by Harrison's *Territories* argument that 'science and religion have been defined and constructed within a distinctive temporal and cultural context to perform separate (or competing) functions, and the way those natures and territories are defined have far reaching consequences'. I am hopeful that the projected publication of three books — two edited volumes (with the tentative titles of *Theology and Science: Towards a New Conversation* and *Theologians on Science: New Possibilities*) and a monograph (tentatively titled *Theology of Science*) by Paul Tyson — could alter the trajectory of the science-religion conversation in stimulating and productive ways.[26] Stay tuned.

---

24 Hanby, *No God, No Science?*, p. 19.
25 Myers interview of Hanby, Mars Hill Audio, Vol. 121.
26 The project's website can be found here https://iash.uq.edu.au/project/after-science-and-religion-rethinking-foundations-science-religion-discourse (accessed 2 January 2021).

IVAYLO NACHEV

Ecology and Environment from an Orthodox Perspective: Current Encounters in Bulgaria

▼ ABSTRACT The article examines current discussions on some of the global ecological challenges of our time among Orthodox Christian circles in Bulgaria, aiming to assess their role is in the overall debates in the country in this field. In order to explain the lack of a very active engagement of Orthodox Christians in Bulgaria, the specific discussions on ecology and the environment are put in the context of the recent history of the Eastern Orthodox Church in the country and some of the main challenges it faces in the contemporary world. The article looks in more detail at different positions of Bulgarian Orthodox thinkers and opinion leaders. The main focus of the article are two recent television debates which could illustrate growing awareness in the last few years about ecological issues and the willingness of some Orthodox Christians from various backgrounds to take a more active stance on a number of the acute ecological problems. The text analyzes as well the position of the Bulgarian Orthodox Church, the biggest religious organisation in the country, which noted the ecological problems in some of its official strategic documents that were published recently. The article also makes remarks on some of the reactions to international Christian engagements with the ecological challenges of our time. Noticing the quite limited number of Bulgarian publications which are solely dedicated to ecological questions, the article touches upon some of the theological dimensions of the views of Eastern Orthodox Christians. The article suggests that there exists a consensus on the significance of the current environmental challenges for society. In spite of the fact that the Orthodox perspective on environmental problems has been rarely promoted very actively so far, indications of growing interest and a willingness for a more active involvement suggest that the Eastern Orthodox view on environmental problems could play a more substantial role in future Bulgarian debates.

Ivaylo Nachev • Institute of Balkan Studies and Centre of Tracology at the Bulgarian Academy of Sciences

Environmental problems have become one of the key global challenges of our time and their impact seems to increase further in the twenty-first century. Issues such as climate change, loss of biodiversity, pollution of soil, water and air, logically are top priorities in world politics and public debates. There is hardly any community on earth which has remained unaffected and the prospects for the future do not seem much brighter. Given the scale of these challenges the solutions to such problems demand immense resources and mobilisation. In spite of the unpleasant situation opinions on ecological topics — not only on the possible measures but also on the need for global efforts — diverge on many occasions. In order to help in seeking solutions, various religious leaders have already engaged in efforts to become part of the dialogue on environmental issues and help protect the environment. Some of them stand out as leading figures in the debate on a global scale. In this respect, the 2002 common declaration of Pope John Paul II and the Ecumenical Patriarch Bartholomew on the environmental crisis could be mentioned. In this context, the topic has been slowly gaining more attention among Bulgarian Orthodox Christians during the last few years. The aim of this paper is to examine this process of increasing awareness among Orthodox Christian thinkers in Bulgaria. It will also seek to map the growing interest and willingness to take part in the debates, and also to highlight various positions in the context of current debates on ecology in the country.

It would be no surprise to note that the Orthodox perspective on environmental problems has been so far scarcely present in contemporary discussions about the environment in Bulgaria. A lack of traditions for active involvement in contemporary problems on the part of Orthodox Christians, especially as far as the official Church is concerned, can provide just a partial explanation. This comparative passivity among Eastern Orthodox circles is in contrast OR stands out against the background of an overall marked awareness of environmental problems which are generally high on the public agenda in Bulgaria (to what extent there are any successful measures is another question), with the discussions on ecological problems being mainly promoted by various environmentalist groups and activists. In this respect the text will address several main questions. Do the Bulgarian Orthodox Christians have something to say in this discussion? Do they want to take part in it? Could they contribute in a meaningful way to this major challenge of our time? Is this in any way impacting the main mission of the Church?

Although the Christian perspective has been rarely manifested so far, recently, an increasing interest can be observed in the importance of the relationship between human beings and their natural environment. A number of discussions which will be examined in this article suggest that the situation is changing and the Orthodox view might start playing bigger role in Bulgarian debates in the future. The article will look at opinions of Orthodox Christians from various backgrounds — academic circles, journalists and others. Special attention will be given to the institutional response by the mainstream Bulgarian Orthodox Church. The article also seeks to answer questions such as are there specific features in the Orthodox approach to ecology, who are the agents who facilitate the discussions and what are the ecological and environmental aspects which attract the most attention in the Bulgarian context.

The Eastern Orthodoxy in Bulgaria

But before continuing with the main subject some general notes are probably in order about the historical context and some specific features of the Bulgarian Eastern Orthodox milieu. Following a revival after the fall of the communist regime in 1989, Eastern Orthodoxy nowadays is the most widespread religion in Bulgaria, to which a large majority of the population officially belongs. According to the most recent available data of the 2011 census, more than three-quarters of the people who answered the question about religion declared themselves Eastern Orthodox Christians (this is equal to a total of some 4.4 million people). In addition, the current Bulgarian constitution defines Eastern Orthodoxy as the 'traditional' religion of Bulgaria. This official status and high rate of support (at least declarative) goes hand in hand with the fact that Eastern Orthodoxy is a religion with long traditions in Bulgaria dating back to the Christianisation of the country in the ninth century.[1] However, in addition to these official facts and the high level of declared religiousness there are many other factors at play. The impact of the communist regime that dominated the country and society in the period between 1944 and 1989 and the post-totalitarian (post-communist) context are among the key factors that should be taken into consideration.[2] Just as in many other spheres of public life, the fall of the communist regime brought about a new situation, one of a complex and sometimes very contradictory mixture of elements of continuity and change. The state-sponsored atheism was abandoned, including state institutions promoting this ideology (on many occasions called 'scientific atheism') that characterised the pre-1989 period. In spite of no longer being the only one that was promoted, the atheistic doctrine of that time has retained some influence. In addition, the totalitarian state had carried out systematic policies to marginalise the Bulgarian Orthodox Church as an institution and also this has its consequences up to the present day. As current research shows the public image of Bulgarian Orthodox Church has been to a great extent shaped during the communist period and it remains difficult to break away with this negative legacy.[3]

At the same time the Bulgarian Orthodox Church has undergone a period of dynamic changes; sometimes these transformations have had a quite contradictory

---

1 For an account of the interplay between state, society and Church in the long run see Nonka Bogomilova 'Main Stages and Facts in the History of State-Church Relations in Bulgaria', *Occasional Papers on Religion in Eastern Europe*, 4 (2015), 50–70.
2 For a brief overview of the pre-1989 context see: Daniela Kalkadijeva, 'The Bulgarian Orthodox Church and the Cold War', *Euxeinos*, 8 (2012), 5–12. The growing popularity of religion, of Eastern Orthodoxy in particular, seems a common phenomenon for a number of post-communist countries. For more on this aspect see Nonka Bogomilova, 'Reflections on the Contemporary Religious "Revival" Religion, Secularization, Globalization', *Occasional Papers on Religion in Eastern Europe*, 4 (2004), 1–10 (pp. 5–8). For a slightly different view on the level of religiousness, based on numbers of baptism and Church marriages, see Жоржета Назърска и Светла Шапкалова, 'Ниво на религиозност на православното население в България според данни от православните храмови регистри (1989–2014)', *Християнство и култура*, 9 (2015), 77–90.
3 М. Методиев, *Между вярата и компромиса: Българската православна църква и комунистическата държава (1944–98 г.)*, (София: Институт за изследване на близкото минало/ Сиела, 2010), p. 17.

character. On various occasions the efforts for change have been accompanied by internal personal conflicts of serious magnitude, including a schism resulting in the creation of an alternative synod in the late 1990s, undoubtedly, these controversies have not promoted any improvement of its public image. In addition to the current situation within the Bulgarian Orthodox Church, another important issue, and one in fact interrelated with it, is the real degree of religiousness and the actual character of religious consciences among people who declare themselves to be Eastern Orthodox. The often cited statistical data for a very high percentage of people belonging to the Eastern Orthodox Church can be in fact misleading. There are many uncertainties about these figures as many Bulgarians regard Eastern Orthodoxy as nothing more than a traditional component of culture and their national identity. Moreover, just a very small proportion of the people who declare themselves to be Eastern Orthodox are really devoted and practicing Christians who, to put it very straightforwardly, go to church every Sunday and are well aware of Christian teachings and dogmas, even some basic ones, and accept all the Christian fundaments. This phenomenon has been indicated by various sociological surveys and has been discussed by some critical voices among the clergy. So, for example, the European Values Study from 2008 found that less than 5% of the respondents in Bulgaria attend religious services every week. In addition, many respondents have fragmented views of Eastern Orthodoxy and even support views which are in contradiction with some core Christian dogmas.[4]

Orthodox Thinkers and the Bulgarian Orthodox Church on Ecology

This overall context partly explains the difficult emergence of ecological questions among the Bulgarian Eastern Orthodox circles. A first observation that should be taken into account is that the number of publications which are dedicated exclusively to ecological questions from an Orthodox perspective are very limited, and this applies to both scholarly and popular editions. Moreover, there are practically no thorough and more analytical texts on ecology from an Eastern Orthodox perspective. In view of the lack of comprehensive analytical works, the growing interest in the ecological topic could be observed in scattered passages in various books and articles. Even more important seems the appearance of the topic in different media programs which reach a wider audience. In respect to increasing interest in ecological issues, it should be noted that a recent edition of a television programme focussing on Christian perspectives to contemporary problems and a public debate were broadcast online, both in in 2018.

But first let's examine the official position of the Bulgarian Orthodox Church. Not being seen as a top priority in its ranks, the environmental issue is mentioned in some of its official documents. Included in a recently published strategy for foundational

---

4   Теодора Карамелска, 'Нагласите към религията в България според Европейското изследване на ценностите', *Християнство и култура*, 4 (2009), 31–34.

religious and cultural education, the problem of the 'the ecologic crisis' is listed among the most serious challenges of our time according to the Bulgarian Orthodox Church.[5] It is noteworthy hat among the other listed challenges, the ones which are put directly after the ecological problems are 'Problems related to the detachment of ethics, science and technique from the Christian values'. The question is further developed in the guidelines for application of this strategy of the Bulgarian Orthodox Church. The document notes 'an unprecedented increase in environmental problems nowadays', adding that the present 'social reforms, being deprived of a Christian basis, have in fact led to a system that legitimises […] social inequality and irresponsible exploitation of nature, which in turn causes new environmental and social problems …'.[6] However, with the exception of few mentions in these statements, in strategic documents the official church authorities have remained fairly passive in this respect. Apart from the two documents no other statements on specific occasions or issues have been published nor were there any other orchestrated measures taken to promote the Church's view on ecology and the environment. There are also no figures among the high-ranking clergy who have shown a pronounced and active involvement with the ecological issue. Yet, this comparatively inactive position should be assessed against the backdrop of the fact that the Bulgarian Orthodox Church generally avoids excessive involvement in most of the other public discussions on contemporary issues or problems which are generally perceived as contemporary and thus are not so directly related with the mission of Church.

Recent discussions in the Media

At the same time, some informal circles and people with Orthodox views seem much more active at this stage. The first of the abovementioned public discussions was a programme on national television, titled 'Man — master or housekeeper of nature?'. The two guests in the studio of the national broadcaster BNT were journalist Angel Ivanov and a cleric, Archimandrite Kasian.[7] A few more words should be said about Archimandrite Kasian who generally could not be considered as one of the most typical mainstream voices among Bulgarian Christians. Archimandrite Kasian is the founder and abbot of an Old Calendar monastery (the Kopilovski monastery near the town of Kyustendil, western Bulgaria), one which is not in communion with the official Bulgarian Orthodox Church (but the brotherhood is affiliated instead with the Church of the Genuine Orthodox Christians of Greece). In addition to all its other core actives, the monastic brotherhood is very active in producing agricultural products (not very typical as well for other monasteries in the country). The production of

---

5 Cultural and educational strategy of the Bulgarian Orthodox Church (Original title: Стратегия за духовна просвета, катехизация и култура на БПЦ), available at: http://bg-patriarshia.bg/index.php?file = strategies_1.xml.
6 The guidelines for application of the strategy are published at: http://bg-patriarshia.bg/index.php?file = strategies_2.xml.
7 The broadcast is accessible at: https://www.bnt.bg/bg/a/khristiyanstvoto-i-ekologiyata.

the monastic farm is aimed for both their own consumption and for the market, and most importantly the monastery strictly applies environmentally friendly methods for cultivating the land. Archimandrite Kasian himself is an interesting figure as he has a background in sciences, with degrees in geophysics and applied mathematics. According to his own account he did not pursue an opportunity to continue his studies in order to obtain a Phd in atomic physics, foreseeing the risks from the unmanageability and danger to humanity from nuclear energy plants. At this point in his life he turned to theological education and later to monasticism.

During the television programme Archimandrite Kasian emphasised the Biblical grounds for engagement of Christians with the ecological problems. He pointed out that this view specifically relates to the agricultural activities of the monastic brotherhood which he leads because all their activities are marked by great respect to the needs of the land that feeds people. Kasian argued that mankind has been lost in chasing just the material things and noted the extreme commercialisation in societies nowadays. He also argued that some technological improvements and advancements in various scientific spheres often have negative side effects. Sciences not only failed to solve problems but also brought mankind into a vicious circle, according to the Archimandrite. Intellectual and spiritual development lags behind and, for example, people today can hardly comprehend the full potential in texts of the Holy Fathers of the Church, he added. In his opinion measures to protect the environment are generally positive but people should not be forgotten either — 'there is ecology for everything but there is no ecology for the soul', he argued.

According to the other participant, the journalist Angel Ivanov, ecological thinking is an intrinsic aspect of Christian life. The Orthodox Christian perspective is that human beings should be responsible towards the creation of the Creator, they should not demand but be thankful, in his opinion. However, once the process of commercial exploitation of land starts this gratitude fades away. At the same time, one should think about bringing fruits not only in the physical but also in the spiritual sense. The two guests in the studio agreed that environmental topics attract wide attention nowadays but the voice of Christians is hardly heard in contrast to the visibility of opinions of secular environmentalist movements.

The second discussion presented a similar perspective and similar problems.[8] It should be noted that the two events were in no way related with each other as they had different organisers and the participants also differed (with the exception of journalist Angel Ivanov who took part on both occasions). This second recent public discussion, named 'Christianity and Ecology', included four speakers — three academic theologians and a journalist. The participants in the discussion were associate professor Mariyan Stoyadinov, assistant professor Smilen Markov and journalist Angel Ivanov. The moderator of the event was associate professor Kostadin Nushev. One

---

8 A video record of the discussion is available on the web site Pravoslavie.bg here: https://www.pravoslavie.bg/%D0%B1%D0%B8%D0%BE%D0%B5%D1%82%D0%B8%D0%BA%D0%B0/%D1%85%D1%80%D0%B8%D1%81%D1%82%D0%B8%D1%8F%D0%BD%D1%81%D1%82%D0%B2%D0%BE-%D0%B8-%D0%B5%D0%BA%D0%BE%D0%BB%D0%BE%D0%B3%D0%B8%D1%8F/.

of the key points which were highlighted by all participants was that in the Christian Orthodox view Man has a central position in the ecological debates. This implies that attention should be turned as well to our own thinking and behaviour. Another commented upon point was that Christian values genuinely suggest environmental awareness as nature is also God's creation. It was noted as well that discussions from an Orthodox Christian perspective need to be better informed and take into account the current level of scientific knowledge in the field of ecology and environment. The discussion also put forward the observation that younger generations engage readily with environmental causes. It was noted that if the Orthodox Church wants to reach the younger people it cannot neglect ecological questions. Yet, some of the participants mentioned separate elements in activist secular environmental movements which are not compatible with Orthodox values, including activism of vegan groups which often mainly seek provocation. There was consensus in the panel that the Orthodox perspective can contribute to finding solutions for the environmental problems. So, according to Mariyan Stoyadinov, the Church can significantly contribute to the formation of ecological thinking and consciousness and part of the Christian solution will be a more moderate consumption and gratefulness for all that is given to us.

Theological Approaches to Nature and Ecology

Based on these examples of recent public discussions that related Eastern Orthodoxy with ecology, it could be claimed that the dialogue between Orthodoxy and ecology might need to start from some terminological clarifications which should as well be well communicated with the broader public. As Pavel Pavlov, a Theology Professor at the Sofia University, argued in a conversation with the author of this article the Orthodox understanding of ecology is somewhat different from the mainstream secular ideas of ecology and environmental protection. The secular ecological vision, strongly influenced by leftish conceptions and leftish political agendas, puts strong emphasises on specific measures for protecting natural resources in his opinion. While this secular vision focusses, for example, on specific actions to keep water or air clean, the Orthodox vision on ecology is wide-ranging; it interprets ecology as a worldview question. Such a worldview approach would naturally prevent the misuses and destruction of various natural resources.

The Christian Orthodox view is based on substantial theological fundaments as it relates ecology with the Christian conception of the act of creation and the initial existence of an ideal world, according to Professor Pavel Pavlov. After Christ and redemption man was again saved from darkness. In the Christian vision on ecology in the centre stands man who has the duty to be a good householder of the world. The word householder or steward — '*домакин*', '*иконом*' — appears in most of the observed discussions on ecology in the Bulgarian context and thus can be considered as one of the key concepts in interpreting the Orthodox view. In addition to this theological argumentation, the Bulgarian discourse bases itself on an old written tradition, according to Professor Pavlov. In his opinion the Orthodox perspective on nature can be traced back to the ninth-century writer and scholar John the Exarch

(*Йоан Екзарх*), and his most notable work *Шестоднев* (Shestodnev, Hexameron) that provides a wide-range panorama of the existing knowledge on nature of his epoch.⁹

Echoes from the International Debate

As already noted, the ecological topic has not yet been subjected to thorough analytical examinations from an Orthodox perspective in Bulgarian scholarly or more popular publications. Along with several Bulgarian authors that touched upon the subject and the recent public discussions referred to here, a significant number of translated articles on environmental issues were published in various newspapers and journals. In that respect a noteworthy case is the speech of Ecumenical Patriarch Bartholomew, titled 'Creation and hesychia. The impact of the climate changes on the global and the regional politics', which was delivered at the main hall of the Bulgarian Academy of Sciences in November 2015. The patriarch, whose numerous initiatives in the field of ecology had earned him the pseudonym the "Green Patriarch", argued in his speech that he is concerned about the ecologic crisis because in his view there are no two ways to comprehend the world as religious and secular, adding that the care for social justice and human rights could not be separated from measures for a sustainable environment. In his opinion our relation to nature reflects our relations to other people and God. The point of view of the Orthodox Church to the environment is based on the fundamental principle that the world is created by God. In his speech the Ecumenical Patriarch Bartholomew also focussed attention on natural disasters that are being caused by climate change and affect most strongly the poorest regions in the world. In his opinion in these regions adaptation will not be sufficient and instead fundamental changes of the global politics should urgently be carried out. The concluding remarks of Patriarch Bartholomew argued that the crisis of our time is not in the first place environmental, but one which concerns the way in which we perceive and understand the world. In his opinion we treat our planet blasphemously precisely because we do not see it as a gift from God, failing to meet our duty to respect it and pass it to future generations. Following this official lecture aimed at academic public, the speech was published in several main Christian editions for the general public in the country.¹⁰ So this work could be counted, along with a number of other translated works, as one of the drivers of the environmental debate in Bulgaria during the last few years.

---

9   For a more detailed account on Orthodox perspectives to nature see Ivan Christov, 'Theological and scientific approaches to the contemplation of nature', in *Orthodox Theology and the Sciences*, ed. by Pavel Pavlov, Stoyan Tanev and George Dragas (Sofia: Newrome Press LLC, 2013), 68–94. For more details on John the Exarch Robert see Иван Дуйчев 'Естественонаучни знания в съчиненията на Йоан Екзарх', *Списание на Българската академия на науките*, 4 (1982), 36–47.
10 See, for example: Ecumenical Patriarch Bartolomew, 'Творение и исихия. Влиянието на климатичните промени върху световната и регионалната политика', *Двери на Православието*, 6 February 2016. Accessible on: https://dveri.bg/component/com_content/Itemid,100522/catid,281/id,22013/view,article/.

Opportunities for Dialogue

The current observations allow us to claim there exists a wide consensus among Bulgarian Orthodox Christians that the environmental challenges are of paramount importance to society. Moreover, there exist a number of thinkers who are of the opinion that the Orthodox perspective not only can, but also should, start playing a more active role in ecological debates. The examined cases in this article suggest that in general there is readiness from the Orthodox side to engage in ecological matters. Yet, this general openness combines with a lack of proactive engagement. The latter can be illustrated by the fact that Christian Orthodox circles have rarely initiated activities that promote their perspectives on ecology. While in media and academic circles there are a number of exceptions, the official Church representatives haven't so far engaged in such discussions. Another point is the lack of any dialogue with scientific experts who specialise in ecology. In addition, scientific advances and specific achievements are rarely mentioned by the Orthodox commentators and are rarely used as arguments in debates on ecological issues (as is the case with nearly all participants in the debates). From the other side, the neglect of Orthodox opinions and thought by scientific community is much stronger. Given the common goal for environmental protection, exchanges between religious and scientific circles in a field of common interest could be an excellent platform to engage more widely with other circles in society. It could be speculated further that if the Christian positions on ecology were better informed about the latest scientific developments in the field, their statements would gain a much stronger impact. Having said this, we do not doubt that the Orthodox perspective has significant potential, much of it unutilised yet, to build bridges on tough questions and in that way contribute to meet growing ecological challenges.

SANDY SAKORRAFOU

Science, Religion and Bioethical Issues in Greek Orthodox Journals

(1998 to the present)

▼ ABSTRACT The present paper constitutes a preliminary attempt to discuss the perception of medical bioethical issues, as this is made manifest in articles on euthanasia, organ donation/transplantation, brain death, and abortion in two well-known Greek Orthodox journals between 1998 — the year the Special Synodical Committee for Bioethics was founded — to the present. These journals are the following: *Hē drasis mas* (Ἡ Δρᾶσις μας), the journal of the [Greek] Christian University Student Action (Χριστιανική Φοιτητική Δραάση), and *Aktines* (Ἀκτίνες), the monthly periodical of the [Greek] Christian Union of Scientists. Both periodicals belong to two of the oldest and most renowned paraecclesiastical brotherhoods in Greece, they are among the oldest publications in print, and share a somewhat scientific orientation. Studied through the lens of the Orthodoxy-bioethics relationship for the first time, it becomes apparent that these periodicals may share the same interest in bioethical topics as the Synodical Committee for Bioethics, although their perception and intentions differ on certain points. In particular, the authors of the articles in these two Greek Orthodox journals, who are mainly physicians acquainted with the latest biomedical advances, feel that it is legitimate to participate in the contemporary public bioethical discourse in Greece. However, their perception of medical bioethical issues should be explored especially in the light of the concepts of 'true medicine' and the 'Christian physician,' as well as the authors' accompanying strong religious convictions. Their writing is shaped furthermore by their own motivation to express their insistence on the once-dominant paternalistic attitude in the physician-patient relationship. According to this, the practice of medicine is a special vocation governed by a well-developed 'ethical system', that is a combination of the Hippocratic tradition and Christian ethics. By virtue of their extensive training and experience physicians

Sandy Sakorrafou • National Hellenic Research Foundation

Orthodox Christianity and Modern Science: Past, Present and Future, ed. by Kostas Tampakis and Haralambos Ventis, SOC, 3 (Turnhout, 2022), pp. 63–82.
© BREPOLS ⁂ PUBLISHERS   10.1484/M.SOC-EB.5.130954

know what 'should' be done and only seek the 'good of the patient'. Consequently, other values and notions, such as the concept of the autonomy of the patient, are restricted or abandoned.

Introduction

During the late 1990s, the importance of biomedical achievements and their impact on everyday life, as well as the confusion they engendered among believers, led the Orthodox Church of Greece to conclude that it had to responsibly inform its flock about, and formally present its positions on, the emerging bioethical issues. For this reason, the Special Synodical Committee for Bioethics was created in November 1998 with the sole purpose of exploring and reflecting on these matters in consultation with the Church of Greece and guided by the Orthodox ethos, God's word, and the Patristic and ecclesiastical tradition.[1]

Even before the founding of the Committee, Greek Orthodox journals had attempted not only to inform their overlapping audiences on several bioethical issues but also to shape their opinion in the hope of placing ethico-religious principles at the core of ongoing secular discussions centred on these matters in Greece. As a rule, these journals are closely related to certain brotherhoods of theologians. Such organisations have always been independent of the Greek Church in terms of both their structure and their missionary activity, but they maintain cordial relations with it. Usually described as extraecclesiastical or paraecclesiastical, their publications are frequently pervaded by intellectualism with an emphasis on apologetics, delivering a rather popularising version of Orthodox theology.[2]

The present paper constitutes a preliminary attempt to discuss the perception of medical bioethical issues as this is made manifest in articles on the so-called 'culture of death'–specifically euthanasia, organ donation/transplantation, brain death, and abortion — in the following well-known Greek Orthodox journals between 1998 (the year of the Committee's foundation) to the present. These journals are *Hē drasis mas* (Ἡ Δρᾶσις μας, hereafter: *HDM*), the journal of the [Greek] Christian University Student Action (Χριστιανική Φοιτητική Δράση), and *Aktines* (Ἀκτίνες), the monthly

---

1   The Official Government Gazette of the Hellenic Republic, 261/A/20.11.1998, 'Περί συστάσεως, οργανώσεως και λειτουργίας της Επιτροπής Βιοηθικής της Εκκλησίας της Ελλάδος' [On the establishment, organisation, and operation of the Committee for Bioethics of the Church of Greece]. See also the official website of the Church of Greece: http://www.ecclesia.gr/greek/holysynod/commitees/bioethics/bioethics.htm.
2   Christos Yannaras, *Orthodoxy and the West*, trans. Peter Chamberas and Norman Russell (Brookline: Holy Cross Orthodox Press, 2006), pp. 217–50. For the paraecclesiastical organisations in Greece, see indicatively Vasileios Gioultsis, 'Κοινωνιολογική θεώρησις των θρησκευτικών αδελφοτήτων' [A Social View of the Religious Brotherhoods], in *Θέματα Κοινωνιολογίας της Ορθοδοξίας* [*Issues in the Sociology of Orthodoxy*], ed. by George Matzaridis (Thessaloniki: Pournaras, 1975), pp. 169–203; Amaryllis Logotheti, 'The Brotherhood of Theologians Zoe and Its Influence on Twentieth-Century Greece', in *Orthodox Christian Renewal Movements in Eastern Europe* ed. by Aleksandra Djurić Milovanović, Radmila Radić (Cham: Palgrave Macmillan, 2019 [2017]), pp. 285–302.

periodical of the [Greek] Christian Union of Scientists. These periodicals have been chosen principally because: (i) they belong to two of the oldest and most renowned paraecclesiastical brotherhoods in Greece; (ii) they are among the oldest publications in print; (iii) they have a somewhat scientific orientation; and (iv) they have never been explored through the lens of the Orthodoxy-bioethics relationship before. It is therefore interesting to read about the authors' views on the aforementioned bioethical topics and even to compare their opinions with the official positions of the Greek Orthodox Church. As will be shown below, while they may share the same interest in bioethical topics as the Synodical Committee for Bioethics, their perception and intentions differ on certain points.

The journal *HDM* was founded in 1961, initially as a newsletter of the Christian Student Action, the student section of the Association of Greek Orthodox Missionary Action 'St. Basil the Great', which works in turn under the spiritual guidance of the conservative 'Sōtēr' Brotherhood of Theologians. The journal regularly publishes popularising articles on major scientific topics with a view to educating the general public, but it mainly addresses university students and scientists. Over the years, the task of popularising bioethical issues has essentially been undertaken by one author in particular, Emmanuel Panagopoulos, a professor of Surgery, who demonstrates adequate knowledge of the topics and proceeds with theological critiques as he considers it necessary.

The journal *Aktines* was founded in 1938 by the Christian Union of Scientists. This union is a member of the collaborating Christian unions of the Internal Mission of Orthodox Association 'Apostolos Paulos', which works under the spiritual guidance of the 'Zōē' Brotherhood of Theologians. The journal principally addresses scientists and physicians, with a view also to educating the general public. It publishes popularised scientific articles on history, literature, philology, philosophy, social topics, Orthodox theology and religion. As will be shown below, preoccupied with medical ethics as they are, the authors with an interest in bioethical issues are usually cautious and modest in the articulation of their theological arguments.[3]

In both journals, the authors of the relevant articles are usually physicians or university professors in medical schools who regard bioethics as an extension, or a transformation, of medical ethics. They use a mixture of scientific and theological language; although the language is quite theological in orientation and expression, as the authors are addressing Christian believers, there is generally also a strong emphasis on scientific reasoning and language, since the audience consists of theologians, natural scientists, school teachers and university students. All the authors share some common objectives: (i) clarifying any uncertainties in clinical matters relating to certain bioethical issues, (ii) weakening secular bioethical arguments, and (iii) stressing the significance of the Orthodox Christian religion in the bioethical debate. Most importantly, they understand the contribution of the Christian religion to the creation of medical bioethics in the light of the concept of 'true medicine', and endorse

---

3 See the official website of the Christian Union of Scientists: http://xee.gr/aktines.html.

the image of the 'Christian physician' who acts as a reminder of the once-dominant paternalistic attitude towards medical practice.

The Context of the Greek Orthodox Bioethical Discourse: A Short Historical Review

As early as the 1930s, topics of a general bioethical character — such as life, health, disease, abortion, and conception control — appeared in books on Orthodox ethics. In the 1970s, a few works systematically addressed general bioethical questions and the Orthodox theological foundations of bioethics are sketched out. In the late 1980s, a variety of articles were written on topics related to Orthodox teachings on life and well-being, as well as on euthanasia, organ donation/ transplantation, abortion, and new reproductive techniques. In general, Orthodox writers did not consider bioethical issues to be unique, but rather intermingled with other aspects of human experience, based on the Orthodox Christian viewpoint that sees all life as existing under the care of God.[4] Until the late 1990s, Orthodox bioethics in Greece was an amalgam of various opinions expressed by Orthodox theologians, priests and physicians, and natural scientists. Those thinkers had developed their guidelines and principles in the context of the Orthodox Church tradition — liturgy, ascetical practices, canons and icons — and the Scriptures (though some are said to have been subject to certain western Christian influences).[5]

However, given the latest biomedical developments and the bioethical dilemmas that had emerged, it became clear that the Greek Orthodox Church had to formulate common positions on certain bioethical topics; requests had already been made in articles in both the aforementioned periodicals, for instance, on the occasion of an interorthodox conference on Bioethics and Orthodoxy in 1997.[6] In 1998, the Special Synodical Committee for Bioethics was established.[7] Since then, the Committee has published several reports and press releases on various bioethical topics.[8] As a result,

---

[4] *The Encyclopedia of the Eastern Orthodox Christianity*, ed. by John Antony McGuckin, 2 vols (Malden, MA: Wiley Blackwell, 2011), I, pp. 72–73.

[5] *Bioethics Yearbook, Theological Developments in Bioethics*, ed. by Andrew B. Lustig and Baruch A. Brody, 5 vols (Dordrecht: Kluwer Academic Publishers, 1988–97), I (1991), pp. 85–101; III (1993), pp. 117–31.

[6] Ch. L. Koulas, 'Βιοηθικά Διλήμματα και Ορθοδοξία' [Bioethical Dilemmas and Orthodoxy] (*Correspondence*) *Aktines*, no. 588 December (1998), 70–72; Emmanuel D. Panagopoulos, 'Βιοηθικά Διλήμματα και Ορθοδοξία (Εντυπώσεις από ένα συνέδριο)' [Bioethical Dilemmas and Orthodoxy (Impressions from a Conference)], *Hē drasis mas*, no. 355 February (1998), 66. (hereafter: *HDM*)

[7] The Committee is made up of nine members: besides a representative of the Church, there are three members who represent theology, three who represent medicine, and three who represent the law.

[8] See the official website of the Church of Greece: http://www.ecclesia.gr/greek/press/theologia/index.asp.

the formal Greek Orthodox bioethical discourse has developed in accordance with the guidelines and principles of the Church of Greece.[9]

In the journal *HDM*, the readers had the chance to learn about the Synodical Committee for Bioethics through the publication of the inaugural address delivered at the launching ceremony for the Committee by the Archbishop of Athens and All Greece Christodoulos in 1998.[10] Years later, the periodical would publish a reprint of an interview with the Chairman of the Committee, Nikolaos (Hatzinikolaou), Metropolitan Bishop of Mesogaias and Lavreotiki, in which readers read about the Committee's role in the contemporary bioethical discourse. In the interview, Nikolaos defines two kinds of bioethics: the bioethics of 'boundaries and constraints' and the bioethics of 'principles and directions'. The former is identified with secular bioethics, which sets certain boundaries in order to protect people in an endeavour constrained by the continuous progress of science and technology. The bioethics of 'principles and directions' is about finding the principles that liberate people, and for Nikolaos, this is precisely what the Committee does. In this case, the role of the Orthodox Church in the bioethical discourse is not to deliver certain decisions and impose them on believers, but to give directions within the Christian view of God and human being. In other words, the role of the Church is not to accept or refuse, to allow or prohibit, but rather to guide, support and forgive. Of course, Nikolaos understands that this assignment is not an easy one. There are certain bioethical issues that can be answered clearly by Christian teachings and others that need further investigation. He accepts that the Church should view the scientific discourse as an opportunity to articulate theological concepts in a contemporary manner, as was the case with philosophical discourse in the past. However, as he points out, the field of theological discourse is more extensive than the field of scientific discourse; the latter may prove insufficient to describe certain situations and concepts which are beyond the scope of reason. Even then, the Orthodox Church is not claiming to be stating a non-negotiable truth. According to Nikolaos, it may be acceptable for Orthodox Christians to review their stance on bioethical issues in light of the latest scientific accomplishments, but not their ethos. The Christian ethos is important for the Church; especially, as he argues, in a society where eugenics and euthanasia are promoted, while pain and disabilities are viewed as unacceptable.[11]

In the journal *Aktines*, the authors on bioethical topics are physicians and hence focus on the relationship between medicine and bioethics. As a rule, they refer to ethics or to medical ethics, describing either the philosophical discipline or the

---

9 It is noteworthy that the scholarly journal *Theologia*, founded in 1923 by the Holy Synod of the Church of Greece, has hosted only a handful of articles on bioethical issues. Although the journal does not necessarily convey the views of the Holy Synod and the theology academics who constitute the editorial board of the journal, when it comes to bioethics, it seems that, for the journal, it is the work of the Committee to form and declare the official position of the Church on the issues in question.
10 'Βιοηθική' [Bioethics], *HDM*, no. 366 March (1999), 110–12; no. 367 April (1999), 144–45.
11 Nikolaos Hatzinikolaou, 'Ζούμε σε μία ευγονική και ευθανασιακή εποχή' [Living in an Era of Eugenics and Euthanasia], *HDM*, no. 414 December (2003): 384–86; no. 415 January (2004), 22–24.

code of medical morality put forward by medical practitioners. However, there are a few references to the term 'bioethics', which describe it as a science that asks moral questions and emerged mainly in the context of contemporary medical practice (and the life sciences).

For Athanasios Avramides and Serafim G. Kastanakis, both professors of Pathology, the Hippocratic Oath demonstrates the ethical nature of medicine; the mission of medical research is to serve humanity. Hence, physicians should be sceptical about the application of the latest technological advancements in the medical context.[12] George Daikos, a professor of Pathology, refers to the need for contemporary medical education to be enhanced with the study of universal moral values (through the teaching of Humanities, the teacher's exemplar, etc.) in order for young physicians to practice a humanitarian kind of clinical practice. It is then of the highest priority to establish a sustainable and generally acceptable universal moral narrative that would determine the character of bioethics. For Avramides, Orthodox Christian bioethics seems a good suggestion, as was also argued by the philosopher and bioethicist Herman Tristram Engelhardt.[13] The so-called universal moral values could include, as Daikos suggests, autonomy/self-determination, justice, informed consent, the physicians' principle of 'Primum non nocere', and human rights (as they were introduced by the Christian religion and fully articulated in the Declaration of Helsinki, a statement of ethical principles for medical research).[14] Interestingly enough, these proposed values are partially identified with the four principles of bioethics, namely: respect for autonomy, justice, beneficence, and non-maleficence. The only opportunity for the reader to inform themselves about these is presented in a special issue of the journal *Aktines*. The issue, which is entitled 'Contemporary Concerns relating to Bioethics' contains the proceedings of the seventh medical meeting of the Christian Union of Scientists. In her welcome speech, physician Spyridoula Kyriakopoulou refers to the four principles as she delivers a quick definition of bioethics.[15]

Finally, George Maragos, a professor of Paediatrics, speaks about the complementary role played by medical deontology and its relation to the code of ethics. He also refers to the significance of the application of medical deontology in hospitals where the contemporary clinical practice has become more complex and presents numerous legal, deontological and ethical complications. He argues that the Code of Medical

---

12 Athanasios B. Avramides, 'Ιατρική και Ηθική (Ηθική στην ιατρική έρευνα και τις εφαρμογές της)' [Medicine and Morality (Morality in Medical Research and Its Applications)], *Aktines*, no. 644 October (2003), 256–59; Serafim G. Kastanakis, 'Η Άσκηση του ιατρικού λειτουργήματος κατά το ιπποκρατικό και χριστιανικό πρότυπο' [The Practice of Medical Vocation according to Hippocratic and Christian Exemplar], *Aktines* no. 772 November-December (2018), 210–16.
13 See Herman Tristram Engelhardt, *The Foundations of Christian Bioethics* (Exton, PA: Swets and Zeitlinger Publishers, 2000).
14 George Daikos, 'Η ιατρική παιδεία και οι ηθικές αξίες' [Medical Education and Moral Values], *Aktines*, no. 644 October (2003), 269–73.
15 Spyridoula Kyriakopoulou, 'Εναρκτήριος λόγος' [Welcome Speech], *Aktines*, no. 732 June (2012), 161–62.

Ethics and Deontology has certain positive effects, not only on the treatment strategies of physicians and nurses, but also on the general medical care of patients. Maragos also endorses the participation of clerics in hospital ethics committees; given that clerics pose the fundamental questions about life and death, but are also capable of shedding light on the patients' spiritual and ethical concerns, he believes this to be in the patients' best interest.[16]

Euthanasia and the Sanctity of Human Life

For the Greek Orthodox Church, euthanasia is the precipitation (with the help of a third party as an act [active euthanasia] or omission [passive euthanasia]) of the death of a human person who is suffering or going through an incurable and painful illness, who has remained conscious and expressed the desire to bring their life to an end.[17]

The authors in both journals adopt the above definition and explicitly express their concerns. Panagopoulos in the journal *HDM* argues that euthanasia is being promoted as a solution to the fast-growing population of elderly people, the so-called 'silver tsunami', given the related social pressures on the health system, economy, and society. He considers 'the so-called painless, easy and dignified death' an immoral practice that depreciates the value of human life. Any attempt to legalise it — he cites the questionable recent trend for public opinion polls — leads not only, he says, to the 'slippery slope' that ends with the killing of a patient with or without his/her consent, but also to a further dechristianisation of Western societies.[18]

His comments are in agreement with the views of the Greek Orthodox Church. For the Committee, euthanasia should not be considered a 'decent death', but a suicide-assisted death, a combination of suicide and murder. The so-called 'right to death', the legalisation of euthanasia, could be transformed into a threat to the lives of those who might be unable to meet the economic demands of their treatment, promoting not only a racist and eugenic rationale of youth and good health but also a kind of 'euthanasia tourism' in those countries where euthanasia is legal. In all cases, the Committee argues, any attempts to justify the practice of euthanasia are principally underlain by a materialistic, ephemeral perception of life and death in contemporary society, where health care is treated as a commodity, and terminally or severely ill patients are useless in terms of economic growth. In addition, critically ill patients may be desperate due to their physical discomfort, the pain, and the feeling that

---

16 George Maragos, 'Νοσοκομειακή Ιατρική και Ηθική' [Hospital Medicine and Ethics], *Aktines*, no. 644 October (2003), 260–64.
17 The basic positions on the ethics of euthanasia were published by the Special Synodical Committee for Bioethics in 2002, two years after the legitimisation of the practice of euthanasia in Holland and Belgium.
18 Emmanuel D. Panagopoulos, 'Ευθανασία: Λύση για το Ασημένιο Τσουνάμι' [Euthanasia: A solution to the 'silver tsunami'], *HDM*, no. 490 June-July (2011), 216–18.

they are a burden to other people. As a result, their decision in favour of euthanasia is very often made in a state of depression, when their minds are not lucid.[19]

In the journal *Aktines*, Avramides states that the term 'euthanasia' was originally associated with a good and quiet death or a glorious one for the homeland, or dying for one's faith in Christ; however, he considers the current meaning of the term to be a degradation of the original notion. It now refers to ending the life of a person who suffers from an irreversible and dangerous illness with the help of a third party. Then, he describes six types of euthanasia: active (willing or unwilling), passive (withdrawal of medical treatment), eugenic (concerning children who are found to be suffering from certain disabilities during prenatal procedures), social (racial, sexual, and national), the euthanasia that deliberately hastens the end of an unwanted life, and 'Christian euthanasia'. In the case of the latter, death is not simply a biological but also a spiritual event; the believers pray for a Christian end to their life, which will be painless, blameless and peaceful; they trust God to end life when the time comes.[20]

Daikos refers to the patient's informed consent on the occasion of the legalisation of euthanasia in Holland. He notices that although, according to legal guidelines, euthanasia is acceptable if the patient who makes the request explicitly consents to it in full consciousness, quite a large number of cases of euthanasia and assisted suicide are undertaken without the patient's consent. As he sees it, this is due to the inefficiency of the principle of patient autonomy[21] — often, a patient is not well or fully informed before they take a life-affecting decision, as well as, the lack of essential support for dying people and, mainly, the technological capability for considerably extending life expectancy through artificial support. The latter is generally said to delay the agony of death and the physician should therefore be able to make a discretionary decision informed by love and compassion about what is best for the patient. However, for Daikos, physicians have no right to prolong death, just as they are not in a position to terminate life.[22]

What may seem to be a bold suggestion can be said to mirror the Church's position on the consequences of the latest technological developments in medicine and the role of the physician as an instrument of God in the service of human beings. Specifically, a physician is permitted ethically not to employ an aggressive means of

---

19 Bioethics Committee, 'Basic Positions on the Ethics of Euthanasia (6.11.2002)', (Athens: The Holy Synod of the Church of Greece, 2002), Articles 21–22, 28–30, 37. Retrieved 6 June 2019 at http://www.bioethics.org.gr/03_b.html#4#4.
20 Athanasios B. Avramides, 'Ευθανασία και Ευθανασία' [Euthanasia and 'Euthanasia'], *Aktines*, no. 740 July-August (2016), 235–38. See also Athanasios B. Avramides, *Euthanasia* (Athens: Akritas Publications, 1995).
21 According to Bioethics, for a medical intervention to be considered 'ethical', medical practitioners have to respect a patient's autonomy in thought, intention and action when making decisions on health care matters. This marks a gradual shift away from a paternalistic approach towards a client-centred approach in which the patient plays a more active role in his/her own life and death.
22 George K. Daikos, 'Ευθανασία' [Euthanasia], (*Correspondence*), *Aktines*, no. 617 January (2001), 34–35.

extending the life of a dying patient when this does not relieve or heal.[23] Nevertheless, as the Church admits and Avramides points out,[24] the physician's mission is to save human life and to be patient. It should always be borne in mind that an unexpected advance in treatment of a disease, a possible error in the medical assessment, or even a miraculous development may occur.[25]

The argument against euthanasia is further enhanced by an examination of the related concept of 'quality of life', which has been used largely in arguments in favour of euthanasia, and which refers to the aforementioned 'decent death' or 'right to death'. 'Quality of life' usually refers to a person's emotional, social, and physical well-being, their intellectual capability, and their ability to perform the ordinary tasks of living within a community. Panagopoulos, in the journal *HDM*, disputes 'quality of life' as a subjective and arbitrary concept, a product of a highly materialistic society with a focus on the economy and limited resources. He then dismisses it as an ideological concept that actually denies the value of human life, especially given the presence of certain mental or physical disabilities, and promotes a culture of death. Panagopoulos agrees with the Church that 'quality of life' should be replaced by the core Christian principle of the sanctity of human life.[26]

Echoing the thesis of the Greek Orthodox Church, Panagopoulos points out that human life is a gift from God. It is unique, priceless and sacred; these properties are due to the creation of the human person in God's image.[27] For the Greek Orthodox Church, any attempt to define life in human terms (restricted by the human will, thought, decision, or capability) strips life of its sanctity. Humans have been created by divine grace as immortal; since their body and soul are made in an unbroken unity, biological life alone can never define what humans are. At death, the human body dissolves, but the eternal human soul is preserved to be united with the resurrected body. Thus, the significance of present life depends on the possibility of *theōsis* ('deification') and of salvation through redemption. For all these reasons, according to Christian teachings, neither the duration of life nor the moment of death can be defined in terms of human rights. In any case, the Orthodox Church does not recognise the right of self-efficiency. The value of human life is considered absolute and fully protected, independent of the agent's will or the quality of his/her life.[28]

In the journal *Aktines*, professor of Surgery Vasileios Kekēs also highlights the significance of the concept of the 'sanctity of human life', though in a less

---

23 Bioethics Committee, 'Basic Positions on the Ethics of Euthanasia (6.11.2002)', Article 15.
24 Athanasios B. Avramides, 'Η ευθανασία ... υπό νέα δοκιμασία' [Euthanasia ... Under a New Trial] (*Correspondence*), *Aktines*, no. 619 March (2001), 98–99.
25 Bioethics Committee, 'Basic Positions on the Ethics of Euthanasia (6.11.2002)', Article 18.
26 Emmanuel D. Panagopoulos, 'Πολιτισμός θανάτου. Από την ιερότητα στην ποιότητα της ζωής' [A Culture of Death: From Sanctity to Quality of Life], *HDM*, no. 478 April (2010), 150–52.
27 Emmanuel D. Panagopoulos, 'Υπάρχει ζωή που δεν αξίζει να βιωθεί;' [Can Life not be Worth Living?], *HDM*, no. 395 January (2002), 12–13; idem 'Ευθανασία. Πορεία σε ολισθηρό και χωρίς τέλος κατήφορο' [Euthanasia. A Slippery Slope without End], *HDM*, no. 545 January (2017), 20–22.
28 Bioethics Committee, 'Basic Positions on the Ethics of Euthanasia (6.11.2002)', Articles 4–10, 31.

theological way. Quoting from an article entitled 'Sanctity and Organ Donation's Societal Value'[29] in the *Bulletin*, the official publication of the American College of Surgeons, he argues that: 'individual sanctity is an essential component of humanness with deep roots in culture, religion, and law. Indeed, an individual's sanctity transcends even death, persisting in the minds of those who knew or know of the decedent'.[30]

Organ Donation/Transplantation and the Definition of 'Brain Death'

The topics of organ donation/transplantation and brain death are considered to be interconnected and both are thoroughly investigated in the two journals. In the aforementioned article by Kekēs, the readers are informed about the types of organ transplants and the chances of transplant rejection. The author, following on from the article in the *Bulletin*, elaborates on the obstacles to organ donation and the problems pertaining to the acceptance of brain death. The readers learn that, in accordance with the 'dead donor' principle, vital organs should be taken only from dead patients, while the retrieval of vital organs for transplantation should not lead to death. Moreover, brain death became compatible with the dead donor rule when it was codified by the Uniform Determination of Death Act, which was drafted in 1980 in the USA. The Act states that: 'an individual, who has sustained either irreversible cessation of circulatory and respiratory functions, or irreversible cessation of all functions of the entire brain, including the brain stem, is dead. A determination of death must be made in accordance with accepted medical standards'.[31] However, as the author notices, the ambiguity in brain death and the possibility of reversing a cardiac death puts the determination of death in question. The author is cautious and modest; he does not further explore any religious concerns about organ donation/transplantation or brain death, as he does not consider himself an expert. Instead, he quotes a few concerns from the book *Freedom and Responsibility: A Search for Harmony — Human Rights and Personal Dignity* by Patriarch Cyril of Moscow.[32]

Kekēs' article is found in the aforesaid special issue of the journal *Aktines* under the title 'Contemporary Concerns relating to Bioethics'. In the same issue, Apostolos

---

29 Michael R. Marvin, Kenneth M. Prager, Max V. Wohlauhel, and James G. Chandler, 'Sanctity and Organ Donation's Societal Value', *Bulletin of the American College of Surgeons*, 97 (1) (2012), 12–23.
30 Vasileios Kekēs, 'Μεταμοσχεύσεις οργάνων. Μήνυμα ζωής ή βιασμός της Δημιουργίας' [Organ Transplantation. Message of Life or Violation of Creation?], *Aktines*, no. 732 June (2012), 178–84 (p. 181).
31 Kekēs, 'Μεταμοσχεύσεις οργάνων', p. 181.
32 Patriarch Cyril of Moscow *Freedom and Responsibility: A Search for Harmony — Human Rights and Personal Dignity* (London: Darton, Longmann and Todd, 2011). The goal of the book is to articulate an Orthodox Christian perspective on human rights and dignity, freedom, and responsibility, vis-à-vis the Western secular humanist concepts.

Nikolaidis, Professor of Sociology of Religion, authors an article based on his book *From Genesis to Genetics* (2006), in which he presents several theological and ethical concerns relating to organ donation/transplantation. One of these concerns is that, while the Church anticipates that medical practitioners will come up with an exact and final definition of brain death, it refers to a brain-dead person not as a 'dead person' but as 'a brain-dead patient'. He also argues that if the practice of organ donation leads to a person's death, then it is justified theologically to speak of it in terms of murder. As for the perception of organ donation as self-sacrifice, a concept introduced by the Church, Nikolaidis realises that this may sound awkward to some believers, especially when the presumed consent of the brain-dead donor is questionable. Of course, as he points out, additional ethical questions may arise concerning issues such as the free consent of the donor, the donor's altruistic and Christian motives, as well as the problem of the commercialisation of human organs for transplantation.[33]

In a long article in the journal *HDM*, Panagopoulos adopts a more hostile attitude towards the concept of 'brain death'. Before the Uniform Determination of Death Act in 1980, there was the 1968 report of the Ad Hoc Committee of Harvard Medical School which set out to examine the definition of brain death. It was this report that led to the introduction of the new criteria for pronouncing death based on total and irreversible cessation of all brain function. In that case, artificial ventilation was allowed to be suspended for brain-dead bodies without the fear of legal punishment against medical practitioners, and organs could be safely removed for transplantation from these bodies while circulation continued.[34]

Panagopoulos accuses the aforementioned clinical definition of brain death of clearly serving the purposes of organ transplantation and medical cost saving. He justifies his argument on the basis of a 1997 scientific article that exposed the motives behind the report that declared a non-functioning brain to be the fundamental sign of death.[35] His intention is to show that, despite it being in common use, the concept of 'brain death' remains incoherent in theory and confused in practice; the debate on how brain death should be defined and whether the medical standards are valid continues. For him, the concept of 'brain death' is a controversial topic, and while it is legally acceptable, it is not morally so. In addition, the vague definition of 'brain death' proves that a conceptually coherent account of death is still forthcoming. Thus, according to Panagopoulos, the concept of 'brain death' is a social and clinical

---

33 Apostolos B. Nikolaidis, 'Θεολογικά και Ηθικά Ζητήματα ως προς την Υποβοηθουμένη Αναπαραγωγή και τις Μεταμοσχεύσεις' [Theological and Ethical Concerns on Assisted Reproduction and Organ Transplantations], *Aktines*, no. 732 June (2012), 185–98. On the commercialisation of human organs, see Emmanuel D. Panagopoulos, 'Η ανήθικη ηθική της αγοροπωλησίας ανθρώπινων οργάνων' [The Unethical Morality of the Commercialisation of Human Organs], *HDM*, no. 492 October (2011), 302–04.

34 On the criteria for pronouncing brain death, see indicatively Gary S. Belkin, *Death before Dying* (Oxford: Oxford University Press, 2014); Winston Chiong, 'Brain Death', in *The Routledge Companion to Bioethics*, ed. by John D. Arras, Elizabeth Fenton, and Rebecca Kukla (London: Routledge, 2018), pp. 462–73.

35 Giacomini, M., 'A Change of Heart, or a Change of Mind? Technology and its Redefinition of death in 1968', *Social Science and Medicine* 44 (10) (1997), 1465–82.

construction which is highly convenient for the procurement of transplantable organs and the withdrawal of life support.[36]

In 1999, the Synodical Committee of Bioethics drew up the official document on the ethics of transplantation in order, on the one hand, to contribute to the understanding of the various problems arising from transplantations, and, on the other hand, to encourage all potential donors to take more responsible decisions. According to the Committee, the document 'is not an indisputable ecclesiastical text; rather, its publication seeks to initiate a debate on the issue of transplantations. However, we believe that it maintains the accuracy of scientific and clinical reality and safeguards the relevant basic principles of Orthodox anthropology. The text is explicit, provides guidance, embraces man as an image of God, and bears witness to the Orthodox Christian ethos'.[37]

In Article 12, the Church of Greece maintains that it not only respects but also trusts medical research and clinical actions. The Church could therefore espouse the internationally accepted view that brain death is identified with the irrevocable biological end of a person. Brain death in this case constitutes 'a final and irreversible destruction of the brain and a state of total loss of sense and consciousness. In the state of brain death, the respiratory function is maintained only artificially, and the termination of artificial ventilation leads to an almost immediate interruption of the heart's function'.[38]

In a rare instance of disagreement, the Synodical Committee for Bioethics is criticised for being hasty. Avramides in *Aktines* argues that the Committee has accepted the controversial definition of brain death as the irrevocable biological end of a human person without first answering medical or theological questions on the determination and nature of death, such as where is the centre of life, is the heart the centre of life, where is the soul, when does the latter finally depart from the human body, etc.[39]

Panagopoulos in *HDM* notes that the Committee lapses further into medical and theological error when it claims in Article 13, that the 'artificial support of respiration succeeds in temporarily retarding the process of decomposition of the body, but not the departure of the soul'.[40] For him, artificial ventilation only prolongs life in a

---

36 Emmanuel D. Panagopoulos, 'Η απομυθοποίηση του εγκεφαλικού θανάτου. Από την καθιέρωση στην αμφισβήτησή του' [The Demystification of Brain Death: from its acceptance to its being called into question], *HDM*, no. 364 January (1999), 34–36; no. 365 February (1999), 64–66; no. 366 March (1999), 108–10; no. 367 April (1999), 142–44.
37 Bioethics Committee, 'Basic Positions on the Ethics of Transplantations (10.12.1999)' (Athens: The Holy Synod of the Church of Greece, 1999). The English translation was retrieved on 6 June 2019 at http://www.bioethics.org.gr/en/Transplantations4 l.pdf.
38 Bioethics Committee, 'Basic Positions on the Ethics of Transplantations (10.12.1999)', Article 12.
39 Athanasios B. Avramides, 'Ιατρική και Ηθική (Ηθική στην ιατρική έρευνα και τις εφαρμογές της)' [Medicine and Morality (Morality in Medical Research and Its Applications)], *Aktines*, no. 644 October (2003), 256–59.
40 Bioethics Committee, 'Basic Positions on the Ethics of Transplantations (10.12.1999)'. Avramides also discusses this article and other points that Panagopoulos examines, see Athanasios B. Avramides, 'Μεταμοσχεύσεις και Βιο-ιατρική Ηθική' [Transplantation and Bio-Medical Ethics], *Aktines*, no. 638 February (2003), 33–37.

biological body; it does not suspend its decomposition. He holds that brain death is not an event, but a process that leads progressively to death.[41] During brain death, the human organism under life support is considered to be alive still, because the soul is still within the body. Such an argument is built on fundamental theological presumptions: (i) a human person is a psychosomatic entity; (ii) the unity of body and soul (*symphyia*) is a mystery that cannot be analysed scientifically; (iii) the beginning of biological life from the moment of conception is due to the mystery of the unity of body and soul; and (iv) the centre of human physical, intellectual and mental activities is not the brain but the soul.[42] He even attempts to justify scientifically these theological presumptions by reference to an article by D. Alan Shewmon, the leading critic against the criterion of total brain death, who concluded from a meta-analysis that 'the phenomenon of chronic brain death implies that the body's integrative unity derives from mutual interaction among its parts, not from a top-down imposition of one "critical organ" upon an otherwise mere bag of organs and tissues'.[43] For Panagopoulos, a brain-dead patient is actually a living soul who is dying, not a dead person. The dying person has not lost their physical, intellectual or mental existence; their personhood status is not determined by any medical diagnoses, but by divine providence.

By focusing on the brain death issue rather than organ transplantation, both of the above comments by Avramides and Panagopoulos fail to grasp the main point: namely, that the organ donation of brain-dead patients, as well as the conscious decision of a healthy person to offer his/her organs to a suffering person, is viewed by the Greek Orthodox Church as an act of love and altruism, in accordance with Orthodox Christian teachings and the Orthodox ethos.

By pointing out the significance of one's self-sacrifice, the Committee does not consider the donation of a human body as an act of suicide or euthanasia. Life is a gift from God that is given to humans so they can offer it in return with love.[44] The ethical problem of transplantations, therefore, relates more to the respect and expression of free will than to a scholastic determination of brain death: 'even if brain-death is not identified with the final separation of the soul from the body, as some people claim, when someone wishes to offer their organs, along with their organs they would also offer their life'.[45]

The Church of Greece is philanthropic towards the recipient, but respects and recognises the role of the donor as more important. The spiritual benefit of the donor

---

41 On death being considered not as a sudden, violent and quick event, but as a process, see also Dimitra Kanaloupiti, Pinelopi Michalakopoulou, 'Ο θνήσκων ασθενής' [The Dying Patient], *HDM*, no. 485 January (2011), 14–16.
42 Emmanuel D. Panagopoulos, 'Η συμφυΐα του σώματος και της ψυχής. Βιοηθικές επισημάνσεις' [The Unity of Body and Soul. Bioethical Notes on the Union of Body and Soul], *HDM*, no. 499 May (2012), 178–79; no. 500 June (2012), 206–07.
43 D. Alan Shewmon, 'Chronic "Brain Death": Meta-Analysis and Conceptual Consequences', *Neurology* 51 (6) (1998), 1538–54.
44 Bioethics Committee, 'Basic Positions on the Ethics of Transplantations (10.12.1999)', Article 9.
45 Bioethics Committee, 'Basic Positions on the Ethics of Transplantations (10.12.1999)', Article 10.

is thought to be greater than the biological gain of the recipient. Of course, according to the Committee, the donor must be informed and voluntarily consent ('conscious consent') to the removal of their organs, in case they are diagnosed as brain-dead in the future. Most notably then, organ donation/transplantation is regarded primarily as an opportunity to transmit the Christian ethos of mutual love, communion, and self-sacrifice to society.[46]

Abortion

The authors of the abortion-related articles share the same position: abortion is considered to be premeditated murder, as the human embryo bears the 'image' of God and has the moral status of a person from the moment of conception.[47] This is in agreement with the official position of the Church of Greece, which does not recognise abortion as an individual right. For the Church, abortion is an ethically unacceptable act, and its legalisation, directly or indirectly, is a deviation from moral and social norms.[48]

For Panagopoulos in *HDM*, pro-abortion legislation such as the newer abortion law 1609/1986 on the artificial termination of pregnancy in Greece[49], or the UN Committee's declaration of abortion as a human right for women, is regarded as biased and immoral. It neglects the rights of the unborn child by denying the personhood of the embryo, and promotes the killing of innocent human life in the name of woman's welfare and rights in regard to her body and her life. Specifically, the UN Committee's declaration of abortion authorises medical abortion in cases of sexual assault, rape, incest, and situations in which the continued pregnancy endangers the mental and physical health of the mother. Nevertheless, for Panagopoulos, the mental health of a woman is jeopardised by abortion, as has been shown — he argues — in a study[50] purporting to reveal a causal link between abortion and subsequent mental health

---

46 Bioethics Committee, 'Basic Positions on the Ethics of Transplantations (10.12.1999)', Articles 5, 15, 18–21.
47 Emmanouel Panagopoulos, Ἡ υπόσταση του εμβρύου στην αρχή της ζωής του' [The Status of the foetus at the beginning of its life], *HDM*, no. 774 December (2009), 383-86; Ioannis K. Aggelopoulos, 'Ηθικοδογματική θεώρησις των εκτρώσεων' [An Ethico-Dogmatic Account of Abortion], *Aktines*, no. 776 July-August (2019), 129–134.
48 Bioethics Committee, 'Δελτίο τύπου για τις εκτρώσεις (04/04/2003)' [Press Release on Abortion] (Athens: The Holy Synod of the Church of Greece, 2003). The press release was issued on the occasion of report No. A5–0020/2003 (on aid for policies and actions on reproductive and sexual health and rights in developing countries), which was voted in by the European Parliament in 2003.
49 On women's right to abortion according to the Greek Penal and Civil Codes and the Greek Constitution, see Dimitrios D. Filolaos, 'Τεχνητή διακοπή της κυήσεως: Δικαίωμα ή έγκλημα;' [Artificial Terminations of Pregnancy: A Right or A Crime?], *Aktines*, no. 616 December (2000), 345–55; Maria Goula, 'Η άμβλωση υπό το πρίσμα του Δικαίου' [Abortion in the light of the Law], *Aktines* no. 781 May-June (2020), 100–06.
50 Priscilla K. Coleman, Catherine T. Coyle, Martha Shuping and Vincent M. Rue, 'Induced Abortion and Anxiety, Mood, and Substance Abuse Disorders: Isolating the Effects of Abortion in the National Comorbidity Survey', *Journal of Psychiatric Research* 43 (2009), 770–76.

problems.[51] However, this study has been dismissed by the scientific community as invalid.[52] A similar point is made by the gynaecologist-obstetrician Zoe D. Siasou in *Aktines*, where she refers to the controversial *Post Abortion Stress Syndrome*[53] and discusses not only the physical but also the so-called mental effects (guilt, anxiety, depression, suicidal thoughts, etc.) of abortion on a woman's health. It should be noted that the aforementioned lack of concern for women's rights to their body and their mental health after an abortion seems to recall a basic position of the Greek Orthodox Church: 'The basic function of the female body to which the entire female existence is directed is the reproductive function. The woman exists anatomically, physiologically and sentimentally for the embryo, the pregnancy and childbearing'.[54]

Siasou also makes an attempt to investigate the causes of abortion. According to her, unwanted pregnancies are most often due to: (i) ignorance of contraception or omitting to use of it (contraception is not included in the Greek state health care system), (ii) sexual activity at an early age, (iii) a lack of proper sex education, (iv) financial or social problems in the case of a couple confronting an unexpected pregnancy, (v) being a single parent, and (vi) the negative impact of having an unwanted pregnancy on a woman's professional life. It is only in a minority of cases that pregnancy is terminated due to (vii) genetically disabilities found during prenatal testing. To deal with the problem of abortion, the author suggests that more should be done to update family planning on contraception and provide proper education to adolescence aimed at abstaining from sex. However, the readers should not misunderstand her intentions. Siasou does not recommend the adoption of a certain state health policy on family planning and sex education; she rather seems to endorse Greek Orthodox Church's precepts on personal responsibility towards family, society, and — mainly — embryonic life.[55]

It is finally noteworthy that because they do not provide a rigid theological argument, these authors usually make an appeal to the emotions in order to convince their audiences. They accompany their articles either with an image of a fully-grown crying baby or a haunting image of an embryo. Sometimes, a pro-life argument is built on descriptions of an eight-week-old foetus as a perfect little human person or encouraging readers to watch the controversial 1984 anti-abortion film *The Silent*

---

51 Emmanuel D. Panagopoulos, 'Έκτρωση: Γυναικείο δικαίωμα στην υγεία ή φόνος;' [Abortion: A Woman's Right to Health or Murder?], *HDM*, no. 495 January (2012), 22–24 (pp. 23–24).
52 Julia R. Steinberg and Lawrence B. Finer, 'Examining the Association of Abortion History and Current Mental Health: A Reanalysis of the National Co-morbidity Survey Using a Common-Risk-Factors Model', *Social Science and Medicine* 72 (2011), 72–82.
53 The name *Post Abortion Stress Syndrome* has been given to the psychological after-effects of abortion, based on Post Traumatic Stress Disorder (PTSD). The term has not been accepted by the American Psychiatric Association or the American Psychological Association. In fact, pro-choice advocates accuse their counterparts of making up PASS in order to further their political agendas.
54 Bioethics Committee, 'Basic Positions on the Ethics of Assisted Reproduction (11/1/2006)' (Athens: The Holy Synod of the Church of Greece, 2006), Article 12.
55 Zoe D. Siasou, 'Το πραγματικό κόστος μιας έκτρωσης' [The Real Cost of Abortion], *Aktines*, no. 763 May-June (2017), 83–87.

Scream,[56] which shows the ultrasound video of a midterm abortion, thus promoting the image of the uterus as a 'sanctuary' for a foetus, not part of a woman's body and persona.

'True Medicine' and Bioethics

As medical experts, the aforementioned authors regard themselves as best placed to comment on the medical details of bioethical issues and to stress the ambiguity and vagueness of clinical matters. Moulded by Orthodox Christian theological education and practice, however, their perceptions of bioethical issues — such as those described above — are conceived in the light of the concept of 'true medicine'. This concept coincides with the concept of 'true science', which is also usually adopted in these Greek Orthodox journals. According to this concept, science is 'true' when it is consistent with the Bible and the Patristic tradition. Only then is it in harmony with Orthodox Christian beliefs.[57] Similarly, therefore, medicine is 'true' when it is based on a combination of the Hippocratic and Christian views of the patient as a person, a psychosomatic entity, and an image of God; 'true medicine' is not considered to be simply the science of repairing the human body, but rather the art of healing the human person in an inseparable union of body and soul. In this case, medicine and the Orthodox Christian religion are considered to be complementary: medicine loses its true orientation without ethical Christian values, while the Orthodox Christian religion may use the latest medical achievements in a contemporary articulation of theological discourse.

'True science' is considered moral in its practice, as it is produced by 'true scientists', people with strong Christian beliefs which manifest themselves through their work and with a set of ethical virtues.[58] Concomitantly, 'true medicine' is considered the product of 'Christian physicians' who emphasise the physician-patient relationship and prioritise their professional integrity and virtuous behaviour in line with the Christian ethos; they act out of philanthropy and love and are not motivated by self-interest and the rules of the marketplace. Of course, as Kuhse and Singer note, such thinking is in no way strange to medical practitioners, given that physicians have been reflecting for centuries on the qualities the 'virtuous physician' should possess, particularly in relation to their patients. These reflections have usually been connected to current religious teachings.[59]

---

[56] The film was narrated by Dr. Bernard N. Nathanson, a physician, co-founder of the National Association for the Repeal of Abortion Laws (now NARAL Pro-Choice America) in 1969, who became a pro-life activist.

[57] See more in Sandy Sakorrafou, 'Science and Orthodox Christianity: Perceptions of Their Relationship in Greek Christian Journals (1980–2010)', *The Journal of Religion* 100 (2) (2020), 232–67.

[58] See Sakorrafou, 'Science and Orthodox Christianity'.

[59] Helga Kuhse and Peter Singer, 'What is Bioethics? A Historical Introduction', in *A Companion to Bioethics*, 2nd edn, ed. by Helga Kuhse and Peter Singer (West Sussex: Wiley-Blackwell, 2009), p. 6.

The concept of 'true medicine' and the portrait of the 'Christian physician' are thoroughly explored in the journal *Aktines*, since a great number of Christian Union of Scientists members are physicians. For them, the dominant model of 'true medicine' is the 'medicine of the whole person' introduced by Paul Tournier in the 1950s. This 'holistic' medicine, a mixed Hippocratic/Galenic approach enhanced by Christian anthropology, considers the patient as a physical, mental, and emotional unity in relation with others and God and it is thought to promote a deeper understanding of the work and the mission of the physician.[60]

As Michalis T. Miligkos, a cardiologist, points out, 'true medicine' is determined not only by the decent, humble, honest, prudent, unselfish, and companionate personality of the physician, but also by his/her steady and persistent faith in Christian values in practising medicine out of love and care for human beings, not for his/her personal financial gain; being a physician is a vocation.[61] For him, a Christian physician combines a deep Christian faith with a prudent urge to philosophise on life (following Hippocrates and Galen) and to enrich his/her knowledge of medical research and clinical practice. As Miligkos notes, both philosophy and medicine comprehend the human being as a unique psychosomatic and intellectual entity, and contemporary biomedicine underscores this understanding still further as a unity between matter, spirit, and soul.[62]

Thrasyboulos Ketseas, a physician himself, even attempts to offer some guidelines to those who consider themselves to be Christian physicians. As he notes, a Christian physician has a series of responsibilities towards patients, including: (i) making a diagnosis, applying the best treatment strategy, and praying for them. A physician should also recommend praying to a patient, as the importance of prayer in healing, the author assures us, is confirmed;[63] (ii) deterring future parents from having an abortion. The Christian physician should inform them that an abortion at any stage in the pregnancy is considered to be premeditated murder, making the parents killers and the physician who assists their accomplice. As Ketseas underlines these guidelines

---

60 See Michalis Th. Miligkos, 'Εις μνημόσυνον Paul Tournier. Η Ιατρική της Προσωπικότητας στην Ελλάδα' [In Memory of Paul Tournier. The Medicine of the Whole Person in Greece], *Aktines*, no. 624 October (2001), 242–47; idem, 'Είκοσι έτη από τον θάνατό του. Paul Tournier, ενας βαθιά ανθρώπινος γιατρός' [Twenty Years since His Death. Paul Tournier. A Deeply Humanitarian Physician], *Aktines*, no. 675 November (2006), 275–76; idem, 'Paul Tournier, 12.5.1898–7.10.1986', (*Correspondence*), *Aktines*, no. 724 September-October (2011), 264; Kastanakis, 'Η Άσκηση του ιατρικού λειτουργήματος κατά το ιπποκρατικό και χριστιανικό πρότυπο'.
61 See also Vasileios Kekēs, 'Ιατρική: Λειτούργημα-Αποστολή' [Medicine: Vocation-Mission], *Aktines*, no. 644 October (2003), 265–68.
62 Michalis Th. Miligkos, '"Όταν οι γιατροί στοχάζονται ... (από την Ιπποκρατική σκέψη ως τη γνώση του γονιδιώματος)' [When Physicians Contemplate ... (From Hippocratic Thought to Knowledge of the Genome), *Aktines*, no. 618 February (2001), 41–49. A similar point is presented in his later article; see 'Ιατρική Φιλοσοφούσα', *Aktines*, no. 644 October (2003), 251–55.
63 Miligkos also refers to the importance of spirituality and prayer for patients' healthcare needs; see Miligkos, '"Όταν οι γιατροί στοχάζονται ...', p. 44. See also George D. Maragos, 'Το πνευματικό ιστορικό του ασθενούς στην ιατρική πράξη' [The Spiritual Record of the Patient in Medical Practice], *Aktines*, no. 621 May (2001), 150–51.

accord with certain convictions shared by the members of the Christian Union of Scientists. The Union is against the practice of euthanasia, which is incompatible with the Christian perception of human life and is cautious about how 'brain death' is practically defined or how it may relate to organ donation/transplantation. It has also declared its opposition to the legal decriminalisation of abortion in Greece since it recognises the embryo as a living person.[64]

Conclusions

Bioethics is an interdisciplinary inquiry involving medicine, biology, genetics, pharmacology, law, sociology, ethics and theology.[65] The role of religion and theology in the emergence and evolution of bioethics has proved controversial. Some accounts claim that theologians and religiously-oriented philosophers have made a significant contribution to the 'renaissance in Medical Ethics' and the creation of bioethics. These accounts also argue that the field of bioethics, once dominated by religion and medical traditions, has now become secularised and is thus now shaped primarily by philosophical and legal concepts; as a consequence, they argue, the public discourse on bioethics now emphasises secular rather than religious or theological themes.[66] Other accounts do not exaggerate the historical role of religion and theology. According to them, it was not theologians who principally shaped the conceptual framework of bioethics, but rather cultural and social changes such as the inhumanity of the medical treatments forced on patients during the 1960s, the civil rights and anti-war movements of the same period, and the need to reach a consensus about certain issues in the public sphere. Therefore, such accounts imply that the character of the public discourse on bioethics has been secular from the start.[67]

Regardless of the role of religion in bioethics' origins, what now attracts more attention is the role of religion and theology in public bioethics. In general, the public debate on bioethics has a secular character and is aimed at 'consensus building' on legislation and public policy considered in terms of individual rights and liberties. This consensus is expressed in an appropriate public language, which is considered to be neutral, secular, and rational. Theologians and Christian-oriented writers either adopt the terms of the public language when arguing

---

64 Thrasyboulos B. Ketseas, 'Christian Physicians' [Γιατροί Χριστιανοί], *Aktines*, no. 725 November (2011), 288–90; no. 726 December (2011), 313–15. Avramides also refers to a humanitarian model of medicine, see Athanasios B. Avramides, Ιατρική της Ανθρωπιάς [The Humanitarian Medicine] (Athens: Tinos, 2009).
65 Evangelos D. Protopapadakis, (2018) 'Γιατί Βιοηθική;' [Why Bioethics?], *Bioethica* 4 (1) (2018), 2–4.
66 Callahan, Daniel 'Religion and the Secularization of Bioethics', *The Hastings Center Report* 20 (4) (1990), 2–4; Scott B. Rae and Paul M. Cox, *Bioethics: A Christian Approach in a Pluralistic Age* (Grand Rapids, MI: W. B. Eerdmans 1999), pp. 1–5.
67 Bonnie Steinbock, 'Introduction', in *The Oxford Handbook of Bioethics*, ed. by Bonnie Steinbock (Oxford: Oxford University Press, 2007), pp. 1–11; Kuhse and Singer, 'What is Bioethics?', pp. 3–11.

about public matters, 'translating' their religious commitments into moral terms that are acceptable to all or reject such 'translation' as useless. Those who reject 'translation' believe that it neither properly conveys theological convictions nor gains any significant influence for theology in the public realm. Moreover, they disagree with the dominant narrative that the 'secular' sphere is neutral; all participants in the bioethical public discourse inevitably come from diverse communities with different identities.[68]

It could be said that the Orthodox theological discourse does not openly challenge the secular character of the consensus in public bioethics but promotes the use of religious narratives and language as equal to other moral traditions. Bioethical principles are viewed principally as secular articulations of traditional Christian positions on life, death, etc.; as a result, all bioethical issues are, methodologically speaking, the subject of study and research for the Orthodox Church. In particular, the thought and methodology of the Church Fathers are said to contribute to the development of bioethics by bringing forward the message of Orthodox ethos and morality, as well as enriching the discourse through the theological ecclesiastical understanding of the human person, society, and values. In this case, theologians have to promote deliberation and more active participation of the religious community in pursuing Christian values on specific bioethical matters.

The Orthodox theological discourse has moved into the realm of public bioethics in Greece, largely through the appropriation of scientific argumentation and the status that accompanies its expertise:[69] there are several scientists from different academic disciplines on the Special Synodical Committee for Bioethics, and even its chairman has a strong scientific background. Hence, it was not only theologians and religious 'authorities' that felt it was fundamentally legitimate to participate in the contemporary public bioethical discourse in Greece but also the authors of Greek Orthodox journals, such as *Aktines* and *HDM*, who are mainly physicians acquainted with the latest biomedical advances. These authors have regularly published popularising articles on bioethical topics using a more or less religious language for matters they comprehend primarily as medico-ethical.

That being the case, most of these authors focus primarily on the physician-patient relationship and fail to recognise that long-established medical ethics are not sufficient to meet current biomedical challenges. As mentioned above, it is especially in the light of the concepts of 'true medicine' and 'Christian physician', as well as the authors' accompanying strong religious feelings, that their perception of medical bioethical issues should be explored.[70]

---

68 Lisa Sowle Cahill, 'Can Theology Have a Role in "Public" Bioethical Discourse?', *The Hastings Center Report* 20 (4) (1990), 10–14; idem, 'Theology's Role in Public Bioethics', in *Handbook of Bioethics and Religion*, ed. by David E. Guinn (Oxford: Oxford University Press, 2006), pp. 37–55.
69 See also Evangelos Ch. Chaniotis, 'Aspects of the Contribution of Church of Greece and Orthodox Theology in the Developments of Bioethical Dialogue', *Bioethica* 2 (2) (2016), 69–82.
70 Cahill, 'The Role of Theology in Public Bioethics', pp. 37–55.

As medical experts, these authors assign primary importance to the medical ambiguities contained in these matters and consider themselves to be capable of deciding what is best for society. They also feel competent to play the role of theologians in the public sphere; since the discussion of bioethical challenges is conducted in scientific terms, they are also more familiar with science/medicine than theologians. Furthermore, as members of the Greek Orthodox congregation, they regard themselves as bearers of the common Orthodox morality, since they believe that the majority of Greek citizens consider themselves to be active Orthodox Christians.[71]

In addition, they seem to share a common motivation: acting as a reminder of the once-dominant paternalistic attitude towards medical practice. According to this, by virtue of their extensive training and experience, physicians know what 'should' be done; they only seek the 'good of the patient' and the practice of medicine is a special vocation or calling governed by a well-developed 'ethical system' that is a combination of the Hippocratic tradition and Christian ethics. Consequently, the aforementioned authors leave no room for the expansion of other values and notions, such as the concept of the autonomy of the patient. They do not accept that the cessation of life can also be an expression of one's right to life, while abortion could equate to a woman's right to control her body and her life. However, it is questionable whether their participation in the bioethical debate in Greece has had any impact beyond the restricted circle of their religious audience, which is closely related to the unions and brotherhoods mentioned above.

---

71 For the models of public bioethics, see John H. Evans, 'Who Legitimately Speaks for Religion in Public Bioethics?', in *Handbook of Bioethics and Religion*, pp. 61–79.

MARIA BOURI

Medicine, Suffering and Death: Palliation and the Ethics of Caring for Those we cannot Cure

▼ ABSTRACT The ethical challenges faced by medicine and bioethics concerning the care of patients with life-limiting and incurable conditions, although identified years ago, still remain current. Despite increasing concern about death and dying in modern medicine, remarkable technical capacities to relieve symptoms, and dedicated palliative care services, persistent suffering remains a reality while health professionals are left in perplexity on how to care when cure is not possible. Scholars from the fields of philosophy of medicine, moral philosophy and theology joined the dialogue on complex dilemmas faced by contemporary medicine and their views illuminated core elements of the ethics of caring for severely ill and dying patients; however, a broader narrative to encompass, activate and potentially extend their profound insights is still pending. Contribution of Orthodoxy in current dialogue on bioethical issues, especially those arising from patients' suffering in the face of severe illness and death, remains sparse, mainly focusing on discussions of and positions on euthanasia and artificial prolongation of life. Orthodox theologians and other scholars have underlined the differences between Western and Eastern Christianity in relation to bioethical debates and, in particular to moral issues pertaining to the care of critically ill patients; however, it seems that relevant quest and dialogue need to become more profound and systematic, to focus on core notions, issues and questions raised by western philosophers, theologians and bioethicists, while it is equally important this discussion reaches health care professionals. Fundamental beliefs of Orthodox theology, including the notion of *prosopon*, the prominence given to spiritual death, and the primacy of active presence over logical explanations of suffering and evil, may re-orient the dialogue into new and largely unexplored perspectives, while a promising and meaningful alternative might be provided for understanding ethical dilemmas, attitudes and caring practices in the face of suffering and death.

Maria Bouri • University of West Attica

A. Setting the Scene: Suffering, Bioethics and the Humanities

Medicine's constitutional foundation has been the mission to liberate people from pain, suffering, disease and premature death. Whereas as a science, medicine has to display omnipotence, even by denying the powerfulness of death itself, during clinical practice vulnerability and fatality are omnipresent, as people still suffer and eventually die from untreatable life-limiting illnesses.[1]

Nowadays, increasing numbers of people, mostly adults but also children, diagnosed with chronic debilitating diseases, such as cancer, AIDS, various metabolic, neurologic and respiratory problems, achieve an increased survival due to advanced medical support and biotechnological progress; however, the majority of these conditions are not curable and patients are in need of symptomatic care and palliation only.[2] Yet, it is increasingly recognised that contemporary medicine has not succeeded in responding to the magnitude of distress and the full range of needs experienced by those patients who stand outside the realm of its triumphs.[3] Research data have showed a significant burden of suffering experienced by chronically and terminally ill people (even for those cared for in high technology settings), patient dissatisfaction regarding care delivery, and clinicians' avoidant behaviour prevailing when a fatal diagnosis is made.[4] Suffering has been attributed by patients to their feelings of powerlessness and hopelessness, of being fragmented and objectified, struggling for their perspectives to be heard and their needs to be covered, while dying patients experience isolation, helplessness, meaninglessness, loss of control, loss of self, worthlessness, existential loneliness, and a sense of disrupted and incomplete biography.[5]

---

1 A paradox lies at the very core of medicine: an effort to accept death when a particular patient's death is unavoidable and concurrently rejecting death 'as a matter of principle for a research ambitious medicine' [Daniel Callahan, 'Death: the distinguished thing', *Hastings Center Report (Special Report)*, 35 (2005), p. S6]. This 'medical schism', involving both a return to 'tame death' through palliation, and to 'conquer death one disease at a time', draws medicine in two contradictory directions, inevitably expressed at patient's bedside [Daniel Callahan, 'Death, mourning and medical progress', *Perspectives in Biology and Medicine*, 52 (2009), p. 108].
2 Katherine E. Sleeman, Maja de Brito, Simon Etkind, Kennedy Nkhoma, Ping Guo, Irene J. Higginson, Barbara Gomes, and Richard Harding, 'The escalating global burden of serious health-related suffering: projections to 2060 by world regions, age groups, and health condition', *Lancet Global Health*, 7 (2019), pp. e883–e892.
3 Mildred Z. Solomon, 'Modern dying: from securing rights to meeting needs', *Annals of the New York Academy of Sciences*, 330 (2014), pp. 105–10.
4 Megan Best, Lynley Aldridge, Phyllis N. Butow, Ian Olver and Fleur Webster, 'Conceptual analysis of suffering in cancer: a systematic review', *Psychooncology*, 24 (2015), pp. 977–86; Joanne Wolfe, Holcombe E. Grier, Neil Klar, Sarah B. Levin, Jeffrey M. Ellenbogen, Susanne Salem-Schatz, Ezekiel J. Emanuel, and Jane C. Weeks, 'Symptoms and suffering at the end of life in children with cancer', *New England Journal of Medicine*, 34 (2000), pp. 326–33.
5 Fredrik Svenaeus, 'The phenomenology of suffering in medicine and bioethics', *Theoretical Medicine and Bioethics*, 35 (2014), pp. 407–20; Noelia Bueno-Gómez, 'Conceptualizing suffering and pain', *Philosophy, Ethics and Humanities in Medicine*, 12 (2017), 7; Eric J Ettema, Louise D. Derkesen, and Evert van Leeuwen, 'Existential loneliness and end-of-life care: a systematic review', *Theoretical*

In medical literature, the gold standard for conceptualisation of suffering is Eric Cassel's definition of suffering as a state of severe distress that threatens the integrity and intactness of the person; during the ultimate personal injury that serious illness and impending death imply, the wholeness and individuality of the person are broken down, the central purpose of the ego disappears, self-conflict arises and attention withdraws from the world back to the self.[6] This definition of suffering suggests that its sources are external to the self of the sufferer, favouring thus a functional approach towards its identification through familiar methods used for measuring physical symptoms. Consequently, patients' suffering levels and their responses to severe illness are detected and 'scored' though diverse questionnaires, listed as adaptive or maladaptive adjustments, and various interventions are planned to positively affect 'outcomes'.[7] When the alleviation of suffering is not possible, various practices and assumptions are employed by clinicians so as to escape the reality of suffering, usually through denying or sentimentalising it, or objectifying it by ascribing its relief to a certain 'skill' exhibited by specialists in the helping professions.[8]

Interestingly enough, much of the suffering reported in current medical literature is characterised as 'unnecessary', as it should and ought to be relieved given the available material and human resources.[9] On the contrary, it seems that medicalisation and isolation of the severely ill and dying patients by modern healthcare system as well as lack of full conceptualisation of suffering by clinicians, eventually add to patients' anguish and distress.[10]

Medicine and Bioethics, 31 (2010), pp. 141–69; Govert den Hartogh, 'Suffering and dying well: on the proper aim of palliative care', *Medicine, Health Care and Philosophy*, 20 (2017), pp. 413–24; Dianne Fochtman, 'The concept of suffering in children and adolescents with cancer', *Journal of Pediatric Oncology Nursing*, 23 (2006), pp. 92–102; Maria Bouri, 'Glimpses into their worlds: exploring the suffering of seriously ill and dying children' (Unpublished master's thesis, Swansea University, 2007).

6 Eric J. Cassell, *The nature of suffering and the goals of medicine*, 2nd edn (Oxford: Oxford University Press, 2004), pp. 29–45.
7 For example, see: Hartogh, 'Suffering and dying well', pp. 417–20, where reference is made to the method of determining one's 'suffering score' on the 'distress thermometer'.
8 Dawson S. Schultz and Franco A. Carnevale, 'Engagement and suffering in responsible caregiving: on overcoming maleficence in health care', *Theoretical Medicine*, 17 (1996), pp. 189–207.
9 Mia Berglung, Lars Westin, Rune Svanstrom, and Annelie Johansson Sundler, 'Suffering caused by care-patients' experiences from hospital settings', *International Journal of Qualitative Studies in Health and Well-being*, 7 (2012), pp. 1–9; Maria Arman, Arne Rehnsfeldt, Lisbet Lindholm, Elizabeth Hamrin, and Katie Eriksson, 'Suffering related to health care: a study of breast cancer patients' experiences', *International Journal of Nursing Practice*, 10 (2004), pp. 248–56; Hadi Karsoho, Jennifer R. Fishman, David Kenneth Wright, and Mary Ellen Macdonald, 'Suffering and the medicalization at the end of life: the case of physician-assisted dying', *Social Science and Medicine*, 170 (2016), pp. 188–96.
10 Alicia Krikorian and Juan Pablo Román, 'Current dilemmas in the assessment of suffering in palliative care', *Palliative and Supportive Care*, 13 (2015), pp. 1093–1101; Ben A. Rich, 'Pathologizing suffering and the pursuit of a peaceful death', *Cambridge Quarterly of Healthcare Ethics*, 23 (2014), pp. 403–16; Karsoho and others, p. 190; Berglung and others, pp. 4–7.

Concurrently, oncologists, intensivists and other health professionals suffer high costs of caring for incurable patients: according to relevant research, clinicians experience 'burnout syndrome', 'compassion fatigue', 'secondary traumatic stress disorder', grief reactions due to repeated losses of patients, and feelings of failure and frustration of being unable to 'save' their dying patients.[11] Health professionals' fear of death has been reported to negatively affect provision of care[12] while acceptance of death by health personnel is considered as a basic requirement for providing humane care to incurably ill, regarded either as an attitude towards death which could be taught, or as a subjective state achieved by self-reflection and increased self-awareness.[13] Yet, no educational programme has been appraised to positively impact on all dimensions of 'death attitudes', promote acceptance or decisively support clinicians achieve a certain state of enhanced self-consciousness which would both 'arm' and 'shield' them in the face of death and dying.[14]

Although alleviation of suffering has been the most fundamental ethical principle in medicine and unnecessary suffering a strong motivation for the development of bioethics itself,[15] inquiries about the nature and meaning of suffering have largely been marginalised in bioethics debates.[16] Bioethics developed as a field during the

---

11   Margo M. C. van Mol, Erwin J. O. Kompanje, Dominique D. Benoit, Jan Bakker, and Marjan D. Nijkamp, 'The prevalence of compassion fatigue and burnout among healthcare professionals in Intensive Care Units: A systematic review', *PLoS One* 10 (2015), e0136955; Vitor Parola, Adriana Coelho, Daniela Cardoso, Anna Sandgren, and João Apóstolo, 'Prevalence of burnout in health professionals working in palliative care: a systematic review', *JBI (Joanna Briggs Institute) Database of Systematic Reviews and Implementation Reports*, 15 (2017), pp. 1905-33; Patrick Meadors, Angela L. Lamson, Mel Swanson, Mark White, and Natalia Sira, 'Secondary traumatization in pediatric healthcare providers: compassion fatigue, burnout, and secondary traumatic stress', *Omega (Westport)*, 60 (2009-10), pp. 103-28; Connie M. Ulrich, Ann B. Hamric, and Christine Grady, 'Moral distress: a growing problem in the health professions?', *Hastings Center Report*, 40 (2010), pp. 20-22.
12   Lena Peters, Robyn Cant, Sheila Payne, Margaret O'Connor, Fiona Mcdermott, Kerry Hood, Julia Morphet, and Kaori Shimoinaba, 'How death anxiety impacts nurses' caring for patients at the end of life: a review of literature', *Open Nursing Journal*, 7 (2013), pp. 14-21; Rachel A. Rodenbach, Kyle E. Rodenbach, Mohamedtaki A. Tejani, and Ronald M. Epstein, 'Relationships between personal attitudes about death and communication with terminally ill patients: How oncology clinicians grapple with mortality', *Patient Education and Counseling*, 99 (2016), pp. 356-63.
13   Camilla Zimmermann, 'Acceptance of dying: a discourse analysis of palliative care literature', *Social Science and Medicine*, 75 (2012), pp. 217-24.
14   Efficiency has been proved for communication skills training programs aiming to advance technical aspects ('steps') of the process of breaking bad news and decision-making. See also: Maria Bouri, 'Educating health professionals on pediatric palliative care' (Unpublished doctoral thesis, National and Kapodistrian University of Athens, 2017).
15   Svenaeus, 'The phenomenology of suffering in medicine and bioethics', p. 408; Ronald M. Green and Nathan J. Palpant, *Suffering and bioethics* (New York: Oxford University Press, 2014), pp. 1-12; Albert R. Jonsen, ed. 'The birth of Bioethics' (Special Supplement), *Hastings Center Report*, 23 (1993), pp. S1-S15.
16   Barry Hoffmaster, 'Understanding suffering', in *Suffering and bioethics*, ed. by Green and Palpant, pp. 31-53; Jeniffer L. Gibson and Ross G. Upshur, 'Ethics and chronic disease: where are the bioethicists?', *Bioethics*, 26 (2012), pp. II-IV.

1960s and several prominent theologians, along with philosophers and scientists, joined the emerging dialogue on the moral implications of modern developments in medicine and healthcare.[17] Drawing from the long traditions of religious communities on reflecting on life, sufferings and death, theologians provided the first ethical critiques of modern medicine by bringing the person of the patient and the illness experience to the foreground.[18] Yet, the influence of the field of theology in elaborating the conceptual framework of bioethics has been modest, despite its constant presence into early debates.[19]

Gradually, a transition took place, which is considered decisive for the marginalisation of suffering by bioethics: from 'thick' substantive questions on the meaning of human illness raised in the early days, to 'thinner', more formal approaches, shifting thus from ends to means so as to fit with the purposes of a secular and rationalistic medicine.[20] As bioethics adopted methods of logical reasoning and rational justification, evidence-based approaches soon entered the field, and the focus turned on achieving 'solutions for moral problems in an impartial, unprejudiced, and non-culturally biased way', by balancing 'advantages and disadvantages in the search to justify one particular ethical option. The objective of this type of argumentation was not an absolute and definite answer for moral problems, but rather a coherent and rational way of problem-solving.'[21] What emerged was a moral language of rights, pluralism, and strategies for achieving consensus as well as an imperative 'to push religion aside' moving in the direction of 'regulatory ethics'.[22] In this context,

---

17 David Callahan, a Catholic theologian, has been the basic founder of *The Hasting Center of Bioethics*, in 1969 (the first of its kind in USA) and the person who basically shaped its Catholic perspective. Fletcher, an Episcopal theologian (his book *Morals and Medicine* was published in 1954), focused on truth telling and the care of dying, on personalism and the rights of the patients, their freedom and authority. In 1970, another theologian, Methodist Paul Ramsey, in his book *The Patient as a Person*, discussed the effects of modern medicine in modifying the moral dimensions of the physician-patient relationship which he viewed as a covenant one, shaped by a shared purpose: attainment of cure. For a detailed reference to the contributions by representatives of various theological traditions, see: David Smith, 'Religion and the roots of the bioethics revival', in *Religion and medical ethics: looking back, looking forward*, ed. by Allen Verhey (Grand Rapids: Eerdmans, 1996), pp. 9–18. It should be noted the absence, in these early debates, of scholars from Orthodox Christianity.
18 Jeffrey P. Bishop, 'The dominion of medicine: Bioethics, the human sciences, and the humanities', in *To fix or to heal: patient care, public health, and the limits of biomedicine*, ed. by Ana Marta Gonzalez and Joseph E. Davis (New York: New York University Press, 2016), pp. 263–64.
19 Pascal Borry, Paul Schotsmans, and Kris Dierickx, 'The birth of the empirical turn in bioethics', *Bioethics*, 19 (2005), p. 57 & p. 59.
20 Raymond De Vries, 'Good without God: Bioethics and the sacred', *Society*, 52 (2015), pp. 439–40; Bishop, 'The dominion of medicine: Bioethics, the human sciences, and the humanities', pp. 267–68.
21 Borry and others, 'The birth of the empirical turn in bioethics', pp. 59–60.
22 Daniel Callahan, 'Why America accepted Bioethics', in Jonsen, ed. 'The birth of Bioethics', pp. S8-S9. According to Callahan, 'bioethics is a native-grown American project' (cited in Jonsen, p. S3) and modern bioethicists depicted characteristically American concerns and secularised reflections about the rights of individuals, fairness and equity in access to benefits with resolution of moral problems to rely on regulations, guidelines, and 'monitoring, regulatory bodies', p. S8.

reference is made to suffering regarding dilemmas on euthanasia or withdrawing and withholding futile interventions.[23]

The most influential driving force towards this direction was the four-principle (autonomy, beneficence, justice and nonmaleficence) approach to bioethical debates launched by Beauchamp and Childress in their book *Principles of Biomedical Ethics*, first published in 1978.[24] These mid-level principles (i.e. which require no foundational grounding, teleological or ontological commitments) predominated as they provided the best means to negotiate moral arguments without entailing theological or metaphysical input.[25]

Furthermore, bioethics centred upon and also contributed to the formation of the 'autonomy paradigm', characterised by 'an individualistic moral perspective in which the promotion of individual autonomy and the protection of individual interests are the paramount ethical goals', and based on both the 'medical model' of illness-as-a-threat to individual self and the 'contractual view' of the physician-patient relationship wherein independent rational agents set up contractual agreements with the shared purpose to fight disease.[26] Nevertheless, the autonomy paradigm has been proved inadequate for the situation of persons with chronic debilitating conditions: the evolving and transformational nature of chronic illness, discerned by various limitations, support needs and interdependency, calls for re-conceptualising conventional view of autonomy as freedom and independency from limits and constraints and as affirmation of protective boundaries between self and others.[27] Moreover, during the deteriorating course of incurable conditions, patients often experience a gradual loss of rationality and competency; therefore, according to predominant discourse in which moral agency is identified with rationality and self-definition, they seem to lose their status as moral agents. The necessity for a bioethics of chronic illness (and possibly for a bioethics of dying), continues to be relevant.[28]

In parallel, around the 1970s, two initiatives from within medicine attempted to 're-humanise' its technological and reductionist focus by re-orienting the dialogue on human persons and their experiences of illness and suffering.[29] In this prospect, the psychiatrist George Engel introduced the 'biopsychosocial model' as a comprehensive paradigm of health care, incorporating the social, psychological, and behavioural dimensions of illness, patients' values and perspectives.[30] The expectation had been that if health professionals could accommodate a wider view of the human being,

---

23 Svenaeus, 'The phenomenology of suffering in medicine and bioethics', p. 408; Hoffmaster, 'Understanding suffering', pp. 31–53.
24 Tom L. Bauchamp and James F. Childress, *Principles of Biomedical Ethics*, 5th edn (Oxford: Oxford University Press, 2001).
25 Bishop, 'The dominion of medicine: Bioethics, the human sciences, and the humanities', pp. 271–72.
26 Bruce Jennings, Daniel Callahan and Arthur Caplan, 'Ethical challenges of chronic illness', *Hastings Center Report*, 18 (1988), p. S3, p. S8.
27 Jennings and others, 'Ethical challenges of chronic illness', p. S11-S12.
28 Gibson and Upshur, 'Ethics and chronic disease: where are the bioethicists?', pp. II–IV.
29 Bishop, 'The dominion of medicine: Bioethics, the human sciences, and the humanities', pp. 273–74.
30 George Engel, 'The need for a new medical model: a challenge for biomedicine', *Science*, 196 (1977), pp. 129–36.

including relevant research from the social sciences on the meaning of illness, medicine would be better situated to meet patients' needs in a holistic and ethical way; however, almost over forty years after its presentation, and although it seems appropriate for the context of chronic care, acceptance and implementation of this model remain limited.[31]

The medical humanities movement has been a second attempt to bring forth humanism in medicine, having as its guiding principle that employing humanities in medical education would become the means for ethical and high-quality care, centred on the lived experience of patients and their experiences, including suffering.[32] Specifically, cultivating the capability of future doctors to 'see suffering' has been a fundamental incentive for this movement, assuming that departing from 'mechanisms' and causal explanations could foster empathy, reflection, trustworthiness and sympathetic understanding of patient's actual experiences.[33] Research, however, indicates that training in medical humanities has rather focussed on improving the skills of doctoring and advancing future physicians' 'professionalism': 'incorporating medical ethics and humanities teaching into medical education allows each learner to enhance his or her abilities of observation, introspection, reflection, and critical thinking. These skills better enable learners to become caring health care professionals, with sophisticated, clinically responsive insight into the suffering of patients and a willingness to selflessly ameliorate patient suffering'.[34] Indeed, while humanities programs have been helpful in promoting professionals' understanding of patients' illness experience and suffering, how this comprehension could be transferred to clinical practice remains obscure.[35]

In summary, the ethical challenges faced by both modern medicine and bioethics regarding prevention and alleviation of suffering experienced by patients living with chronic life-limiting and incurable conditions, although identified years ago, still remain current.[36]

---

31 Derick T. Wade and Peter W. Halligan, 'The biopsychosocial model of illness: a model whose time has come', *Clinical Rehabilitation*, 31 (2017), pp. 995–1004.
32 Jane Macnaughton, 'Medical humanities' challenge to medicine', *Journal of Evaluation in Clinical Practice*, 17 (2011), 927–32; Tristram H. Engelhardt Jr., 'Bioethics and the philosophy of medicine reconsidered', in *Philosophy of Medicine and Bioethics. A twenty-year retrospective and critical appraisal* ed. by Carson A. Ronald and Chester R. Burns (Dordrecht/Boston/London: Kluwer Academic Press, 1997), pp. 88–89.
33 Rita Charon, 'To see the suffering', *Academic Medicine*, 92 (2017), pp. 1668–70; Bishop, 'The dominion of medicine: Bioethics, the human sciences, and the humanities', pp. 276–77.
34 David J. Doukas, Laurence B. McCullough, Stephen Wear, Lisa S. Lehmann, Lois LaCivita Nixon, Joseph A. Carrese, Johanna F. Shapiro, Michael J. Green, and Darrell G. Kirch, for the Project to Rebalance and Integrate Medical Education (PRIME) Investigators, 'The challenge of promoting professionalism through medical ethics and humanities education', *Academic Medicine*, 88 (2013), p. 1626.
35 Andrea Schwartz, Jeremy S. Abramson, Israel Wojnowich, Robert Accordino, Edward J. Ronan, and Mary R. Rifkin, 'Evaluating the impact of the humanities in medical education', *The Mount Sinai Journal of Medicine: A Journal of Translational and Personalized Medicine*, 76 (2009), pp. 372–80.
36 Jennings and others, 'Ethical challenges of chronic illness', pp. S1–16.

B. The Paradigm of Palliative Care and some Limitations

Palliative care largely developed as a discipline during the last twenty-five years with the aim of facing, in an organised manner, all the novel issues that arose in caring for people with life-limiting and terminal diseases, mainly by focusing on care and quality of life when cure is unattainable.[37] Having a religious background in both Eastern and Western traditions (even the etymology *pallium*- 'omophor' points to the symbolisation of the Good Shepherd carrying the rescued lamb on His shoulders), today it is almost entirely secularised.[38] A fundamental element of the definition of palliative care has been the perception of the patient not only as a physical, but also as a psychosocial and spiritual being; spiritual care in particular has been a central constituent of palliative care, presumably due to its religious roots, highlighted by Cicely Saunders (the leading founder of the field) through her concept of *total pain* comprising the biological, emotional, social and spiritual aspects of suffering.[39]

In the context of life-threatening illness, spiritual or existential pain and distress serve as synonymous terms for suffering, while clinicians' engagement with patients' 'spiritual health' is considered an essential prerequisite for the holistic treatment of suffering.[40] Nevertheless, despite construction of numerous spiritual questionnaires, reviews show lack of conceptual clarity and a wide variance in the ways spirituality is operationalised.[41] Qualitative analyses of palliative care patients' views on spirituality often produce complicated categories such as 'achievement of ontological multidimensional connectedness', or show abstract outcomes to be accomplished by delivering 'spiritual care', such as 'spiritual conversion', 'discovery of one's (true) self' or 'consent returning back to nature' wherein one truly belongs.[42] Moreover,

---

37 David B. Morris, 'The cloak and the shield: a thumbnail history of palliation', *Illness Crises & Loss*, 6 (1998), pp. 229–32.
38 Mark Taubert, Helen Fielding, Emma Mathews, and Ricky Frazer, 'An exploration of the word "palliative" in the 19th century: searching the BMJ archives for clues', *BMJ (British Medical Journal) Supportive & Palliative Care*, 3 (2013), pp. 26–30.
39 Cicely Saunders, 'The evolution of palliative care', *Patient Education & Counselling*, 41 (2000), pp. 7–13.
40 Best, 'Conceptual analysis of suffering in cancer', p. 984; Mako Caterina, Kathleen Galek and Shannon R. Poppito, 'Spiritual pain among patients with advanced cancer in palliative care', *Journal of Palliative Medicine*, 9 (2006), pp. 1106–13.
41 Karen E. Steinhauser, George Fitchett, George F. Handzo, Kimberly S. Johnson, Harold G. Koenig, Kenneth I. Pargament, Christina M. Puchalski, Shane Sinclair, Elizabeth J. Taylor, and Tracy A. Balboni, 'State of the science of spirituality and palliative care research. Part I: Definitions, measurement, and outcomes', *Journal of Pain and Symptom Management*, 54 (2017), pp. 428–40; Tracy A. Balboni, George Fitchett, George F. Handzo, Kimberly S. Johnson, Harold G. Koenig, Kenneth I. Pargament, Christina M. Puchalski, Shane Sinclair, Elizabeth J. Taylor, and Karen E. Steinhauser, 'State of the science of spirituality and palliative care research. Part II: Screening, assessment, and interventions', *Journal of Pain and Symptom Management*, 54 (2017), pp. 441–53.
42 Daniel P. Sulmasy, 'Spiritual issues in the care of dying patients. "… It's Okay between me and God"', *JAMA: The Journal of the American Medical Association*, 296 (2006), pp. 1385–92; Particia Boston, Anne Bruce, and Rita Schreiber, 'Existential suffering in the palliative care setting: An integrated literature review', *Journal of Pain and Symptom Management*, 41 (2011),

assessments and interventions attempt to diagnose spiritual well-being (or the lack of it) while excluding views not aligning with its current operational definition so as 'the very language of spirituality has to be transformed into the language of psychosocial coping, which fits nicely into the metaphysics of efficient causality.'[43] Specific psycho-spiritual entities thus emerge such as the 'demoralisation syndrome' referring to patients whose suffering is primarily caused by existential distress, a 'syndrome' described in palliative and hospice settings as a maladaptive response to imminent death.[44]

Palliative care professionals aim at responding to patients' needs on all dimensions of illness by employing different 'clinical frameworks' so as a *good death* to be achieved.[45] They should be able to recognise the various psychological stages that dying patients go through (described by Kübler-Ross in the 60s[46]), as well as to teach, help, facilitate, and enable their patients to cope efficiently, show resilience and finally reach a state of acceptance for impending death and letting go of life. Indeed, conveying acceptance was among the most frequent caring interventions identified in studies, one which is supposed to contribute to a dignified exit, a basic element of *good death* in the palliative care setting.[47] However, a widely accepted definition of *good death* has not been reached despite increasing efforts by researchers to locate its attributes,[48] and the quest for *eu-thanasia*, in its literal meaning, remains unaddressed. What seems to prevail is the model of *aware dying* (proposed by Glasser and Strauss[49] years ago), which is not only a modern psychological ideal, but also a necessity for a prevalent pattern relying on open discussions for the efficient 'management' of the dying stage

---

pp. 604–18; Mathieu Bernard, Florian Strasser, Claudia Gamondi, Giliane Braunschweig, Michaela Forster, Karin Kaspers-Elekes, Silvia Walther Veri, Gian Domenico Borasio, and SMILE Consortium Team, 'Relationship between spirituality, meaning in life, psychological distress, wish for hastened death, and their influence on quality of life in palliative care patients', *Journal of Pain and Symptom Management*, 54 (2017), pp. 514–22; Seyedeh Zahra Nahardani, Fazlollah Ahmadi, Shoaleh Bigdeli, and Kamran Sltani Arabshahi, 'Spirituality in medical education: a concept analysis', *Medicine Health Care and Philosophy*, 22 (2019), pp. 179–89.

43   Bishop P. Jeffrey, 'From anticipatory corpse to posthuman God', *The Journal of Medicine and Philosophy: A Forum for Bioethics and Philosophy of Medicine*, 41 (2016), p. 687.
44   Rich, 'Pathologizing suffering and the pursuit of a peaceful death', pp. 407–08.
45   Ezekiel J. Emanuel and Linda L. Emanuel, 'The promise of a good death', Supplement 2 *Lancet*, 351 (1998), pp. SII21–29. Authors claim that in the developed world, a good death is feasible and propose an assessment tool ('framework for a good death') to assist clinicians achieve their patients' good death and lessen their suffering during their dying trajectory. According to this framework, suffering is 'diagnosed' either by poor conditions and outcomes in all or nearly all of tool's 'modifiable' dimensions or by identifying 'overwhelmingly bad experience' in 1–2 of these dimensions (pp. SII 22–23).
46   Elisabeth Kubler-Ross, *On death and dying* (New York: Scribner, 1969).
47   Zimmermann, 'Acceptance of dying', pp. 217–24.
48   Emily A. Meier, Jarred V. Gallegos, Lori P. Montross-Thomas, Colin A. Depp, Scott A. Irwin, and Dilip V. Jeste, 'Defining a good death (successful dying): literature review and a call for research and public dialogue', *The American Journal of Geriatric Psychiatry*, 24 (2016), pp. 261–71.
49   Barney G. Glaser and Anselm L. Strauss, *Awareness of dying* (Chicago: Aldine Publishing Company, 1965).

through practices which make this process easier, smooth and quiet, not only for the dying and family but also for the care providers and the health system in general.

When ethical dilemmas arise in end-of-life care, 'traditional' bioethics principles seem almost inapplicable.[50] Autonomy needs to be modulated against both the fragility of the individual and the prospect for maintaining personal integrity while being dependent on others; thus, autonomy in the palliative context assumes a relational character not included in its established meaning.[51] Yet, attainment of autonomy in palliative care is considered to be best served through an 'ethical' framework comprising a list of best interests, wishes, choices, preferences, and other concerns expressed by patient and family, to be fulfilled.[52] Furthermore, within the rhetoric of palliative care, the dignity of individual patients is identified with the accomplishment of their wishes about how and where (if not when) they choose to die; however, end-of-life decision-making highlights the conceptual vagueness over the notion of human dignity, which is unattainable when it is limited to self-determination and self-government. Occasionally it is assigned to choices rooted in patient's autonomous rights, or even used in 'euthanasia laws' labeled as 'Death with Dignity' acts.[53] Different dying-with-dignity and autonomy ideals are therefore formulated depending on various views and choices expressed by all parties involved — social, medical and human[54] — whereas the definition of 'unbearable suffering', a pivotal criterion for legal practice of euthanasia in some countries, remains intangible and variable.[55]

It has been posited that palliative care ethics cannot rely on normative ethics principles because dying patients are considered to enter into a 'liminal state' where normative concepts do not necessarily apply.[56] In this context, practical wisdom is regarded as the most appropriate ethical concept for responding to complex and multilevel end-of-life questions and dilemmas, as it can provide the necessary skills

---

50 Hillel Braude, 'Normativity unbound: liminality in palliative care ethics', *Theoretical Medicine and Bioethics*, 33 (2012), pp. 107–22; Simon Woods, 'Respect for persons, autonomy and palliative care', *Medicine, Health Care and Philosophy*, 8 (2005), pp. 243–53.
51 Braude, 'Normativity unbound', pp. 109–15.
52 Woods, 'Respect for persons, autonomy and palliative care', pp. 243–53.
53 Kathryn Proulx and Cynthia Jacelon, 'Dying with dignity: the good patient versus the good death', *American Journal of Hospice and Palliative Care*, 21 (2004), pp. 116–20.
54 Jeannette Pols, Bernike Pasveer, and Dick Willems, 'The particularity of dignity: relational engagement in care at the end of life', *Medicine, Health Care and Philosophy*, 21 (2018), pp. 89–100.
55 Donald van Tol, Judith Rietjens, and Agnes van der Heide, 'Judgment of unbearable suffering and willingness to grant a euthanasia request by Dutch general practitioners', *Health Policy*, 97 (2010), pp. 166–72. Study's findings showed that the majority of Dutch doctors interviewed (n = 113) were willing to make an exception of the rule that physical symptoms should consist a necessary condition for suffering to be characterised as intractable, implying that euthanasia could be equally practiced in cases of 'existential kinds' of suffering.
56 Braude, 'Normativity unbound', pp. 107–22. Having been developed in the transitional space between dominant medical technologies and compassionate care, and blurring the boundaries between life and death, palliative care provides an appropriate context for the anthropological concept of liminality which signifies biological and social transition. Braude supports that this may explain why formulation of a systematic ethics of palliative care remains difficult.

to face uncertainty and navigate the antithetic boundaries implied by liminality. For others, this skill is essential for palliative care clinicians in order to locate patients' 'psychological good' which cannot be quantified, and therefore identified as straightforwardly as their 'medical good'.[57]

Critiques of the palliative care movement claim that although rooted in attempts to apply comprehensive and compassionate care to the end of life, it has resulted in the medicalisation of the dying process and the separation of dying persons from the broader community, increasing thus instead of alleviating their suffering.[58] Palliative medicine, by rendering a person's psychological, spiritual and social contexts relevant to medical practice, where they can be measured, assessed and managed by specialised experts, has been transformed into 'biopsychosociospiritual' medicine, potentially serving as a *pall*, a death shroud, covering over death and dying and 'making them palatable through palliation'.[59]

Elimination of suffering is considered a basic element of the 'normative' conception of dying well prevailing within the palliative care context.[60] Correspondingly, various instruments and interventions have been formulated with the purpose of detecting and assessing suffering in the face of death, which is 'specific' for the palliative care setting.[61] This functional approach rests on the ideal of a patient who is enabled to die in peace because both his physical symptoms and other dimensions of suffering are under full medical control, while deviations from this ideal are perceived as defects to be repaired; family support and spiritual care are also considered to serve this purpose whereas 'monitoring' by specialists extends beyond death, to the mourning period.[62]

Acceptance of death is viewed as another means through which death can be managed and controlled in the palliative care context. The acceptance–denial dichotomy is instrumental in the palliative care discourse on dying, which invites patients to participate in the planning of their death, and by offering psychological assistance to those 'who do not comply': dying persons and their families are approached 'as individuals who deny death, and as being capable of transformation through acceptance, with help from empathetic health care workers',[63] who 'know' death and dying by being experienced in measuring its 'goodness' and 'success'.[64]

Despite various inconsistencies and limitations, favourable outcomes have been detected for palliative care provision in terms of symptom relief, psychological

---

57 Braude, 'Normativity unbound', pp. 110–16. Author uses the Aristotelian notion of *phronesis* to denote practical prudence in resolving complex decision–making issues in the palliative care setting.
58 Karsoho and others, 'Suffering and the medicalization at the end of life', pp. 188–96.
59 Jeffrey P. Bishop, 'The palliating gaze' in *The anticipatory corpse: medicine, power, and the care of the dying*, ed. by Jeffrey P. Bishop (Notre Dame: University of Notre Dame Press, 2011), pp. 253-78.
60 Hartogh, 'Suffering and dying well', p. 421.
61 Krikorian and Román, 'Current dilemmas in the assessment of suffering in palliative care' pp. 1094–95.
62 Hartogh, 'Suffering and dying well', p. 418.
63 Zimmermann, 'Acceptance of dying' p. 223.
64 Bishop, 'The palliating gaze', pp. 258-64.

distress and spiritual well-being.[65] It is particularly in the palliative care context that both professionals and patients came to realise the distance between scientific progress and human reality, to acknowledge that care does not coincide with cure, that doctors have been trained to cure and patients come to health settings in order to be cured, unprepared to face their mortality, in a cultural milieu that denies death and celebrates youth and longevity. Yet, quests for meaning, value and alleviation of suffering remain unresolved while consensus has not yet been reached on the role clinicians should play in supporting their incurable and dying patients. Enormous efforts to bring about 'death with dignity', including the provision of hospice and palliative care, and improving end-of-life education for health professionals, have achieved only mixed success.[66] A paradox might thus be identified: increasing concern about death and dying, remarkable technical capacities to relieve symptoms and improve care, dedicated palliative care services and yet persistent suffering of dying patients, adults and children alike.

In summary, palliative care practice appears to involve complex moral issues and dilemmas not straightforwardly compatible with the dominant conceptualisations of bioethics.[67] Despite the apparent moral imperative motivating the practice of palliative care, its development has not been accompanied by an equally clear and coherent body of ethical framework; however, it seems that no bioethical models, rules or theories might be applicable in this context before there is an understanding of both the moral experience of vulnerability and the ethical underpinnings of the appeal for assistance and 'palliation.'

C. Morality and Mortality in Medicine: Views from Philosophy, Theology and Ethics

Scholars from the fields of philosophy of medicine, moral philosophy and theology joined the dialogue on ethical issues faced by contemporary medicine.[68] Writers in

---

65 Betty R. Ferrell, Jennifer S. Temel, Sarah Temin, Erin R. Alesi, Tracy A. Balboni, Ethan M. Basch, Janice I. Firn, Judith A. Paice, Jeffrey M. Peppercorn, Tanyanika Phillips, Ellen L. Stovall, Camilla Zimmermann, and Thomas J. Smith, 'Integration of palliative care into standard oncology care: American Society of Clinical Oncology clinical practice guideline update', *Journal of Clinical Oncology*, 35 (2017), pp. 96–112.
66 Callahan, 'Death: the distinguished thing', p. S5.
67 Henk ten Have and David Clark, 'Conclusion: ethics and palliative care', in *The ethics of palliative care. European perspectives*, ed. by Henk ten Have and David Clark (Buckingham: Open University Press, 2002), p. 235.
68 In this section, reference will be made to some key figures who participated in the first decisive debates in the field of bioethics [see for example the contributions of Alasdair MacIntyre, Tristram Engelhardt, Stephen Toulmin, Edmund Pellegrino, and Stanley Hauerwas in *Knowledge, value and belief*, ed. by H. Tristram Engelhardt Jr. and Daniel Callahan, Volume II: The foundations of ethics and its relationship to science (New York: The Hastings Center, 1977)]. Some of the views of Charles Taylor were also included due to their pertinence to the ethics of medicine [see for example: Franco A. Carnevale and Daniel M. Weinstock, 'Questions in contemporary medicine and

(and founders of) the field of philosophy of medicine in the early 80s, such as Toulmin, Pellegrino and Thomasma, turned to philosophical concepts that could inform clinical practice with attributes capable of providing answers to moral dilemmas, including those inherent in the care of severely ill and dying patients. They recognised the limitations set by principle-based ethics, being too abstract and remote from 'the contextual and experiential complexity of clinical decision-making, and too conductive to an overly rationalistic, quasi-legalistic ethics that overemphasises quandaries and stifles compassion and moral creativity', arguing that intractable suffering arose due to healthcare actions that neglected a holistic and patient-centered approach.[69]

Stephen Toulmin questioned the discrepancy between the dogmatism of 'rules' and 'principles' in theoretical ethics and the relativism of various personal 'value systems' inherent in particular clinical circumstances.[70] Concurrently, David Thomasma and Edmund Pellegrino focused on the therapeutic relationship between physician and patient, as both a context and a source for the right and good decision which could relieve suffering and heal the patient. While in current bioethics, the prevailing notion of autonomy had placed ultimate authority for decisions at the end of life under the control of the patient, these thinkers attempted to examine the philosophical underpinnings of the doctor-patient relationship so as to derive from the therapeutic interaction itself the principles and virtues which would guide best its moral ends.[71] In this line, Pellegrino supported the view of patients as *persons*, opposing their current perception as organs, statistics, consumers, or agents-participants in the 'negotiated contract model' of the decision-making process.[72]

Advocating the internal morality of medicine and focusing on the moral agent rather than the moral act, these scholars turned attention from general to professional ethics, being aware that 'the traditional benign and respected image of the physician as both moral and technical authority has been replaced by the physician as protector, facilitator and advocate of the self-determination of the

---

the philosophy of Charles Taylor: an introduction', *The Journal of Medicine and Philosophy: A Forum for Bioethics and Philosophy of Medicine*, 36 (2011), pp. 329–34]. Finally, Paul Ricoeur's thoughts on the dying phase are also discussed given their relevance to end of life care [Ds Frits de Lange, 'Affirming Life in the Face of Death: Ricoeur's *Living Up to Death* as a modern ars moriendi and a lesson for palliative care', *Medicine, Health Care and Philosophy*, 17 (2014), pp. 509–18]. Nevertheless, extensive reference to all prominent figures from the fields of philosophy, ethics and theology who profoundly influenced bioethical debates, exceeds the scope of this article. It should therefore be noted that the background of all scholars discussed in this section is Western Christianity, with the exception of H. Tristram Engelhardt who entered the Orthodox Church in 1991.

69 Edmund D. Pellegrino, 'Toward a virtue-based normative ethics for the health professions', *Kennedy Institute of Ethics Journal*, 5 (1995), p. 266.
70 Stephen Toulmin, 'How medicine saved the life of ethics', *Perspectives in Biology and Medicine*, 25 (1982), pp. 748–49.
71 David C. Thomasma, 'Establishing the moral basis of medicine: Edmund D. Pellegrino's philosophy of medicine', *The Journal of Medicine and Philosophy: A Forum for Bioethics and Philosophy of Medicine*, 15 (1990), pp. 246–54.
72 Pellegrino, 'Toward a virtue-based normative ethics for the health professions', pp. 265–68.

patient.'[73] In contrast to a 'nomological method of moral reasoning' in which explanation and decision-making is analogically deduced from theory, within the healing relationship, the good of the patient becomes the primary moral end.[74] In this teleological approach, orientation is towards the ends and purposes of the relationship within which some agreement on a *telos* is feasible, while the degree to which decisions and actions of the moral agents (physicians and patients) approximate these ends, determines their moral value. Therefore, the good of the patient should be considered as much 'more than simple medical good; it includes patient's perception of good — material, emotional, or spiritual'; nevertheless, when cure is not possible, physicians should be able 'to care for and help the patient to live with residual pain, discomfort, or disability.'[75]

Supporting thus the practical rather than 'theoretical' ethics, these scholars introduced the virtue tradition in medicine aiming to define the virtuous physician by drawing on the Aristotelian-Thomist notion of virtue and its relationship to the ends of human life.[76] By concentrating on the primacy of the good over the right in particular instances, they underlined the *phronetic* character of medical practice and suggested a focus on the virtues which foster good practical judgment.[77] The Aristotelian concept of *phronesis* was thus called upon to designate the caregiver's prudence to discern the concrete particularities of challenging situations, including ambiguity and uncertainty, inherent elements of all moral decision-making in end of life. Concurrently, this form of practical wisdom presupposes awareness of both the limitations of one's knowing and the fragility of all solely human goodness.[78] Certain virtues exercised by medical practitioners (*phronesis*, compassion, justice, fidelity to trust, among others) were regarded as the cultivated dispositions which would impart the capacity to heal, while their possession would define the good and virtuous practitioner.[79]

---

73 Edmund D. Pellegrino and David C. Thomasma, *The virtues in medical practice* (New York/Oxford: Oxford University Press, 1993), pp. 54–55.
74 David C. Thomasma, 'What does medicine contribute to ethics', *Theoretical Medicine*, 5 (1984), p. 271.
75 Pellegrino and Thomasma, *The virtues in medical practice*, pp. 52–53. Authors underline that 'if it were merely a matter of technical correctness, of medical good alone, the major moral principle would be competence' (p. 53).
76 Pellegrino, 'Toward a virtue-based normative ethics for the health professions', pp. 253–77.
77 Pellegrino and Thomasma, *The virtues in medical practice*, pp. 51–61. Authors emphasise the significance of the virtue of 'temperance' for end of life care, as it enables physicians to 'shepherd' medical technology to 'good human aims, instead of "playing God"' (pp. 124–25).
78 Eric B. Beresford, 'Can phronesis save the life of medical ethics?', *Theoretical Medicine*, 17 (2009), p. 223. According to Beresford, (pp. 210–11): 'the phronetic character of medical practice has served to underline the inadequacy of a model of moral reasoning that assumes that right actions can be deduced with certainty from uncontroversial and unambiguous first principles.' Author concludes that *phronesis* might even save the life of bioethics, as it enables physicians to discern the dangers inherent in any moral reflection which fails to recognise the limits of one's own perspective (p. 223).
79 Pellegrino, 'Toward a virtue-based normative ethics for the health professions', pp. 268–70. It is of note that the Christian virtues of faith, hope and love (caritas), were later added to the list, as these 'supernatural or theological' virtues would perfect 'natural virtues' and enhance the healing

These scholars introduced humanities programs in medical schools, aiming to foster the appropriate values of virtuous and *phronetic* physicians;[80] however, they acknowledged that any pursuit of virtues should be linked to a broad, although still missing, theory of the good.[81] Concomitantly, they re-oriented the dialogue on moral issues in medicine from theory to the clinical reality of the physician-patient relationship, being very critical about practices supposed to preserve the objectivity of clinical judgment, such as distancing and disengagement from patients' suffering, attitudes considered to block building a healing relationship and promoting restoration despite adversity.[82]

Disengaged care has been criticised by Charles Taylor, who posited that the objectified gaze of modern science, although essential for scientific discovery, transforms the nature of caring from an authentic form of human action into mere technical production.[83] Caring for the stranger experiencing illness and loss is challenging in current health settings since the value of caring is hidden by more powerful claims of efficiency and efficacy of skillful technological interventions. Furthermore, caring practices become paradoxical in a culture that characteristically limits the definition of human dignity to autonomy and independence, further blocking sympathetic and engaged care.[84]

Modernist forms of care practices not only entail but also require 'disengagement' of the caregiver as human person from the patient's situation of illness; however, detached care can advance bioethical problems instead of resolving them, as caregivers fail to understand patients' experiences, distress, meanings and perspectives.[85] Rather, for Taylor, medical ethics and moral decision-making can be largely facilitated if professionals comprehend 'what is going on' in this person's life as a whole, advocating

---

potential of the physician, by dictating the (Christian Catholic) way of living his life and practicing medicine, see: Edmund D. Pellegrino and David C. Thomasma, *The Christian virtues in medical practice* (Washington: Georgetown University Press, 1996).

80 Edmund D. Pellegrino, 'The humanities in medical education: Entering the post-evangelical era', *Theoretical Medicine*, 5 (1984), pp. 253–66; Thomasma, 'What does medicine contribute to ethics', pp. 267–77.
81 Beresford, 'Can phronesis save the life of medical ethics?', p. 221.
82 Edmund D. Pellegrino, 'Medical ethics in an era of bioethics: resetting the medical profession's compass', *Theoretical Medicine and Bioethics*, 33 (2012), pp. 22–23.
83 Charles Taylor, *Sources of self. The making of the modern identity* (Cambridge: Harvard University Press, 1989), trans. by Xenophon Komninos (Athens: Indiktos, 2007), pp. 237–61. Taylor supported that disengagement consists an important characteristic of the identity of 'modern self' while he pointed to 'moral sources' as a motivation with the potential to empower engagement in meaningful caring practices (pp. 263–302).
84 Patricia Benner, 'Formation in professional education: an examination of the relationship between theories of meaning and theories of self', *The Journal of Medicine and Philosophy: A Forum for Bioethics and Philosophy of Medicine*, 36 (2011), pp. 342–53.
85 Dawson S. Schultz and Franco A. Carnevale, 'Engagement and suffering in responsible caregiving: on overcoming maleficience in health care', *Theoretical Medicine*, 17 (1996), p. 193. Taylor discerned between 'sympathetic care' as foundational element of engaged care, in contrast to the 'disengaged nature of various sentimentalist and cognitive forms of care that is given primacy in modern medicine (of which "empathic" care is a variation)' (p. 207).

thus an interpretive or hermeneutic conception of medical practice.[86] The process of interpretation, through the exercise of what Taylor calls 'strong or radical evaluation', becomes an ethical pursuit itself as it involves radical questioning and reflecting on the quality of person's life and the kind of being this person is or would like to be, rather than weighting competing desires and choices or deducing from principles or rules.[87] Taylor also criticised modern moral theory for its universalistic assumptions which disregard how historical socio-cultural 'horizons of meaning' shape conceptions of the good. Accordingly, any framework regarding 'right reason' in medical decision-making is already shaped by larger narrative discourses, including unarticulated notions of the good which the ends of medicine entail.[88]

Engagement with and not avoidance of patient's suffering, could be achieved though the physician's active involvement in the dialogical process of interpreting the illness experience.[89] Narrative knowing (radically different from scientific-technical knowing) involves empathetic understanding of both the patient as person and patient's lived experience of affliction, suffering and loss, all prerequisites for the care which will promote healing even if cure is not feasible.[90] Taylor's thought provides a counterforce to the prevailing procedural discourse of modernity — which fosters bureaucratised and commercialised conceptions of care and which fails to acknowledge the creative structure of all medical and ethical understanding — thus advocating the prospect of medical ethics as an interpretive ethics of care.[91] Furthermore for Taylor, current medicine cannot guide clinicians to face the moral dilemmas inherent in the care of suffering patients: health professionals, in order to be able to help, heal, and sustain such a challenging practice, need to embody and enact the inherent meanings of being member participants in practice communities oriented to a common 'supreme good' acting compassionately on behalf of others.[92]

But physicians, as MacIntyre has claimed, no longer support patients in achieving any commonly shared good, but instead help them attain their 'self-prescribed' personal

---

86 Charles Taylor, Franco A. Carnevale, and Daniel M. Weinstock, 'Toward a hermeneutical conception of medicine: a conversation with Charles Taylor', *The Journal of Medicine and Philosophy: A Forum for Bioethics and Philosophy of Medicine*, 36 (2011), p. 443.
87 Dawson Stafford Schultz and Lyndia Victoria Flasher, 'Charles Taylor, phronesis and medicine: ethics and interpretation in illness narratives', *The Journal of Medicine and Philosophy: A Forum for Bioethics and Philosophy of Medicine*, 36 (2011), pp. 401–04. According to authors (p. 403), 'the outcome of radical evaluation reflects neither simply the patient's will (patient autonomy) nor the will of the physician (beneficence) but is an expression of the reciprocal relation that stands in balance between them.'
88 Carnevale and Weinstock, pp. 330–33. Authors claim that 'Taylor's conception of moral life provides a promising alternative for understanding ethical concerns in medicine, in the midst of significant discontent with prevailing bioethical models' (p. 331).
89 Schultz and Flasher, 'Charles Taylor, phronesis and medicine', pp. 401–04.
90 Schultz and Carnevale (pp. 193–95) have launched the term 'clinical phronesis' to describe medical responsibility engendered by engaged care-giving, based on Taylor's idea of 'radical evaluation': clinical phronesis is viewed as a qualitative appraisal concerning the worth of the desirable characteristics of medically proper care.
91 Schultz and Flasher, 'Charles Taylor, phronesis and medicine', pp. 401–04.
92 Benner, 'Formation in professional education', p. 344.

ends. Given the absence of a broader narrative unity characterising contemporary society, physicians (and patients alike) have no sources from which to obtain the moral resources to respond in a meaningful way to ethical dilemmas in clinical settings; therefore, coupled with the current loss of the medical profession's moral credit, patients themselves must become their own moral authorities.[93]

While in *After virtue* MacIntyre supported that practice itself is discerned by 'goods internal' to its constitutive activities, a view pertinent to medical practice as well,[94] he noted that nowadays there exists no 'moral authority to whom we can hand over judgment' as to how internal goods such as health, protection of life and freedom from pain, 'are to be related to one another, which is to have priority over which, and how they are related to other human goods'.[95] Grounding morality, he argued, in a reason that departs from traditions, has failed and led to moral fragmentation since in the absence of a collective teleological framework, any pursuit of morality becomes meaningless.

Similarly, contemporary medicine has lost inherent shared moral ends, those evaluative criteria that govern both the achievement of specific goals of the practice and the development of physicians' creative skills and abilities for their accomplishment. In this prospect, the inquiry is how physicians will be sustained to bridge the gap between 'what *can* be done for this patient?' and 'what *should* be done for him', and since medicine remains unable to discern between the two, physicians are left in perplexity.[96] Indeed, shared decision-making models within current medicine[97] presuppose that there is no objective, knowable reality of human flourishing to which physicians can aspire the care of their patients; therefore, the optimal end remains each patient's subjectively articulated 'life-project'. Rational and empirical methods of reasoning are increasingly employed so that various individual projects are fulfilled, while the role of the clinician is shifting 'from *virtuous helper* to *risk manager*'.[98]

Furthermore, MacIntyre emphasised that all human beings are dependent on others as the frail nature of humanity calls for an 'ethos of solidarity' involving acknowledgement of both the virtues which render people independent and those that enable them to recognise reliance on others. He noticed that the meaning

---

93 Jon Tilburt, 'Shared decision making after MacIntyre', *The Journal of Medicine and Philosophy: A Forum for Bioethics and Philosophy of Medicine*, 36 (2011), p. 154.
94 Thomas A. Long, 'Narrative unity and clinical judgment', *Theoretical Medicine*, 7 (1986), pp. 75–76.
95 Alasdair MacIntyre, 'Patients as agents', in *Philosophical Medical Ethics: Its nature and significance*, ed. by Stuart F. Spicker and H. Tristam Engelhardt Jr. (Dordrecht-Holland/Boston USA: D. Reidel, 1977), p. 210.
96 Long, 'Narrative unity and clinical judgment', p. 85.
97 Exemplified by the prevailing model of 'enhanced autonomy' (proposed by Quill and Brody) which encourages patients and physicians to actively exchange ideas, explicitly negotiate differences, and share power and influence to serve the patient's best interests. See: Timothy E. Quill and Howard Brody, 'Physician recommendations and patient autonomy: finding a balance between physician power and patient choice', *Annals of Internal Medicine*, 125 (1996), pp. 763–69.
98 Tilburt, 'Shared decision making after MacIntyre', pp. 150–53.

of human vulnerability towards biological and mental dangers has not been comprehended from the greatest part of moral philosophy, stressing that western philosophy exhibits a denial of human incapability and dependence, forgetting the bodily (and thus vulnerable) dimension of human existence.[99] In his standpoint, it is precisely the fact of mutual fragility and dependency that characterise both the human condition and the caring clinical relationship, which should form the basis of restoring the role of virtuous practitioners and attaining shared decision-making in morally complex situations.[100]

However, in MacIntyre's view, virtue ethics requires a reasonably determinate conception of the good of human life conceived as unity achievable if the moral agent understands one's actions as part of a broad narrative sequence.[101] Furthermore, this narrative should not be considered a static 'state of affairs' but one that implies recognition that the meaning of a particular life facing vulnerability and adversity lies in the context 'of a larger moral history in which death and suffering are not merely negative deprivations', should they have a significance in the context of a broader narrative.[102]

Indeed, for MacIntyre 'what makes the problems of medical ethics irresolvable in our culture is the lack of any shared background of beliefs which could provide a context for moral reasoning by providing a view of human nature and society'.[103] He described moral premises in moral arguments as 'incommensurable', since they are no longer structured by any coherent, shared metaphysical conception; however, too much 'incommensurability' of moral frameworks across patients and clinicians, blocks achievement of a common perspective and what remains is patients' individual 'life-plans', including schedules for the end of their lives.[104] In the absence of a coherent narrative in which autonomy and self-government, as well as dependence and reliance on others can be balanced, then clinical medicine, however scientifically well-founded, cannot enhance patient's well-being in the face of serious illness and disability, but only incidentally.[105]

It is in medicine where Hauerwas finds the most pertinent example of MacIntyre's account of moral practice, arguing that medicine is in its fundamental nature a

---

99 Alasdair MacIntyre, *Dependent rational animals: why human beings need the virtues* (London: Bloomsbury Academic, 1999) trans. by Maria Daskalaki (Athens: Koukkida, 2013). Author pointedly remarks that, in the context of philosophy, sufferers are discussed only as recipients of philanthropy from the part of (rational) moral agents.
100 Tilburt, 'Shared decision making after MacIntyre', p. 167.
101 Earl E. Shelp, 'Introduction', in *Virtue and medicine. Explorations in the character of medicine*, ed. by Earl E. Shelp (Dordrecht/Boston/Lancaster: D. Reidel, 1985), p. XII.
102 Alasdair MacIntyre, 'Can medicine dispense with a theological perspective on human nature?', in *Knowledge, value and belief*, ed. by H. Tristram Engelhardt Jr. and Daniel Callahan, p. 39. MacIntyre criticised most teleological doctrines which conceive the true end for man as a 'state of affairs', while Christian teleology, as in Augustine or Aquinas, supports that in this life 'we are always in via', implying a notion of moral progress wherein ethical choices attain their meaning.
103 MacIntyre, 'Patients as agents', pp. 211–12.
104 Tilburt, 'Shared decision making after MacIntyre', pp. 158–59.
105 Long, 'Narrative unity and clinical judgment', pp. 78–82.

'moral art', one of the few remaining areas with substantive ends, a practice with internal goods and standards of excellence wherein the virtues can be cultivated and embodied.[106] Distancing from deontological and consequentialistic moral decision-making, Hauerwas argued that human beings can only face the complexity of concrete moral dilemmas if the focus is relocated from conduct to 'character' considered as 'the basic moral determination of the self'.[107] Formation of a moral character is derived from a broader narrative placing the self in relation to a good from which a person's moral disposition and accompanying virtues gain meaning. Such a narrative is imperative for the field of medical ethics so as to guide the development of an ethos sufficient to support the often conflicting values and ends inherent in the practice of medicine.[108]

Hauerwas characterised medicine as a 'tragic profession' since it reflects the limits of our own existence; concurrently, it is exactly its practice under the conditions of finitude which provides a powerful paradigm of moral task: to continue to do the right thing, to care for this immediate patient, even when there is no assurance for any kind of 'success'.[109] Yet, modern medicine, he remarked, has become too noisy in order to cover the silences of illness and death, centred on the denial of vulnerability and mortality, and rendered a means to overcome our fragility, while in its essence it is a practice of learning to live with our frailty and finitude. Furthermore, current confidence in technical rationality, claiming that the good can only be determined in accordance with 'reason', cannot impart the necessary skills for such care because it cannot deal adequately with the limits of life. This predominant discourse within medicine results in clinical inconsistencies to which patients are subjected in a collective effort to avoid facing the limitations of man's existence; if clinicians fail to comprehend this fact, the potential of moral destructiveness is increased as caring is confused with curing, resulting in 'unintended inhumanities' which may inadvertently increase suffering although aiming to relieve it.[110]

Since medicine is necessarily involved in tragic choices, Hauerwas contended that a substantive story is needed to sustain and give direction to medical care without which technology serves as a substitute, allowing to further delay decisions of life and death.[111] The Christian story is central for him as a meaning context rich enough to enable physicians and patients to deal creatively with the evil of illness and death and the fragility of human life. While the field of bioethics has traditionally

---

106 M. Therese Lysaught, 'Hauerwas and the redemption of bioethics', in *Unsettling arguments: a Festschrift on the occasion of Stanley Hauerwas's 70th birthday*, ed. by Charles Robert Pinches, Kelly S. Johnson, and Charles M. Collier (Oregon: Cascade Books, 2010), p. 156.
107 Thomas W. Ogletree, 'Character and narrative: Stanley Hauerwas' studies of the Christian life', *Religious Studies Review*, 6 (1980), p. 25.
108 Stanley Hauerwas, 'On medicine and virtue: a response', in *Virtue and medicine. Explorations in the character of medicine*, ed. by Earl E. Shelp, pp. 353–54.
109 David Burrell and Stanely Hauerwas, 'From system to story: an alternative pattern for rationality in ethics', in *Knowledge, value and belief*, ed. by H. Tristram Engelhardt Jr. and Daniel Callahan, pp. 139–40.
110 Ogletree, 'Character and narrative', p. 29.
111 Burrell and Hauerwas, 'From system to story', p. 139.

assumed an 'ontology of conflict' regarding life and death dilemmas, theology, he believes, can provide an alternative rooted in the central Christian practices of forgiveness and reconciliation.[112] He claimed that if Christian convictions have any guidance to provide as how to comprehend and respond to suffering, and how to be present to one another despite human vulnerabilities, this can be done 'by helping us to discover that our lives are located in God's narrative — the God that has not abandoned us even if we or someone we care deeply about is ill.'[113] An ethos is therefore needed in medical practice to 'sustain the effort to care in the face of death', an ethos which Hauerwas finds in the context of a caring community able to absorb the destructive terror of the evil of suffering and death and to support health professionals care for those they cannot cure. This can be accomplished mainly by *being there*, 'for it is not easy matter to be with the ill, especially when we cannot do much for them other than simply being present'[114]; to be truly present with others in suffering and death requires a commitment rooted in a concrete understanding of both the meaning of suffering and the limitations of human nature.[115]

For Hauerwas, medicine needs the church as a 'political space', not specifically as a source for moral commitments but rather as a resource of values and practices necessary to support clinicians in instances of ambiguity, uncertainty, death and dying. In the absence of the church, 'medicine cannot help but dominate our lives', becoming a powerful practice without end, without context, without any wider community to give it purpose.'[116] His view is that the yet unanswered question, 'how ought religion speak to medical ethics', should be transformed to the question 'how does the church speak to the practice of medicine', how to be truly present for weakened people, and that 'to believe that such a presence is what we can and should do entails a belief in a presence in and beyond this world'.[117] Yet, Hauerwas's question remains open on

---

112 Lysaught, 'Hauerwas and the redemption of bioethics', p. 168.
113 Stanley Hauerwas, *Naming the silences. God, medicine and the problem of suffering* (Michigan: William. B. Eerdmans, 1990), p. 67. Hauerwas highlighted this point by making explicit reference to current attitudes towards children's suffering: he argues that we tend to 'abandon' children to the institutional means we have of buying time, which is medicine, so that they may get the chance to 'create' a life-narrative since we believe that they do not possess one. This act looks as the only alternative 'as long as we refuse to believe that we are all, adults and children alike, born into a narrative not of our own making' (p. 126). Therefore, what bothers us even more about childhood suffering is that it makes us face our deeper suspicions that all of us lack a life story which would make us capable of responding to illness in a meaningful way.
114 Stanley Hauerwas, 'Salvation and health: why medicine needs the church', in *Theology and Bioethics: exploring the foundations and frontiers*, ed. by Earl E. Shelp (Dordrecht: D. Reidel, 1985), p. 223. For Hauerwas, medicine as a moral practice draws its essence from the extraordinary moral commitment of a society to care for the ill, and even more, for its incurable and dying members.
115 Stanley Hauerwas, *Suffering presence: theological reflections on medicine, the mentally handicapped, and the church* (Notre Dame: University of Notre Dame Press, 1986).
116 Lysaught, 'Hauerwas and the redemption of bioethics' p. 164. According to the author (p. 165), 'if the church were fully to embody the identity to which Hauerwas calls it, separate institutions [for the dying, i.e. hospices] might not be necessary.'
117 Hauerwas, 'Salvation and health: why medicine needs the church', pp. 205–24.

what kind of church it must be to welcome, care for, nurture and sustain those in medicine and society who are the weakest and the more vulnerable as well as those committed to their care: 'to be Christian is to be part of a community through which I am trained to die early. What difference that training might make for the hierarchy of goods and authority of which medicine partakes [...] remains one of the most interesting questions before us'.[118]

These concerns are intensified in a world such as that described by Engelhardt, who attributed the crisis of secular morality and bioethics to the loss of moral foundations and the absence of a canonical moral vision.[119] He argued that in Western bioethics there has been an almost absolute rejection of traditionally religious, especially Christian, accounts of moral obligations, and morality is produced through rationality and discursive human reason. In this secular context, reference to God is replaced by philosophical rational reflection; however, moral philosophy constantly being socially, historically and culturally determined, has not succeeded in firmly comprehending the nature of good and right or in providing specific normative guidance. Therefore, in the absence of either God or a moral rationality, morality and bioethics are intractably plural, shattering into numerous perspectives, leaving patients with what agreement and consent can justify, while moral choices are consequently reduced to life-style choices.[120]

Engelhardt observed that in post-modern culture, the trend is towards privatisation of religious commitments into a complex range of religious-aesthetic sentiments whilst religion has become a privatised pursuit of perfection.[121] All meaning is therefore devalued and demoralised, placed fully within the horizon of the finite and the immanent and what dominates is the language of human rights and death-with-dignity, exercised by *persons*, which for secular morality are those who are self-conscious, rational and able to give consent. So today, for responding to ethical dilemmas and resolving suffering, all that is needed is what Engelhardt calls 'freedom of permission', implying tolerance of self-determined choices, applied in peace and without disturbing others. But, he remarks nobody will be able, 'outside of a particular moral tradition, ideology, religion, or content-full political perspective, to assign any general secular value to the particular choices or structures [...] created through the peaceable consent of those involved.'[122] While Engelhardt acknowledged the unavoidability of affirming a secular pluralistic ethic, he emphasised both the relative poverty of that ethic and the significance of membership in a community of substantive shared moral beliefs. In his book *After God: Morality and bioethics in*

---

118 Stanley Hauerwas, 'Why I am neither a communitarian nor a medical ethicist', in 'The birth of Bioethics', ed. by Albert R. Jonsen, p. S10.
119 H. Tristram Engelhardt Jr., *The foundations of Christian Bioethics* (Lisse: Swets & Zeitlinger Publishers, 2000), trans. by Polyxeni Tsaliki-Kiosoglou (Athens: Armos Books, 2007), pp. 176–87.
120 H. Tristram Engelhardt Jr., *After God: Morality and bioethics in a secular age*, trans. by Polyxeni Tsaliki-Kiosoglou [Mount Athos (Agion Oros): Holy Great Monastery of Vatopedi, 2018], pp. 103–08.
121 H. Tristram Engelhardt Jr., 'Christian bioethics in a post-christian world: facing the challenges', *Christian Bioethics: Non-Ecumenical Studies in Medical Morality*, 18 (2012), pp. 110–11.
122 Engelhardt, 'Bioethics and the philosophy of medicine reconsidered', pp. 95–96.

a secular age, he reminds us that traditional Eastern Christianity embodies such a community, being an encounter with God and not a lifestyle preference or another self-constructed meta-narrative.[123]

Engelhardt drew attention to the fact that differences in theology between Western and Eastern Christianity are reflected in disparities between traditional and post-traditional accounts of bioethics and relevant conceptualisations of the meaning of suffering.[124] In Orthodoxy, the focus is on the immediate personal relationship with a personal God, unmediated by a system, either called morality or ethics, and activated by turning from oneself to God, which is not achieved through discursive, rational reflection or intellectual contemplation but through repentance and pursuit of holiness.[125] Consequently, health care professionals cannot accompany patients in the face of suffering and the threat of death in a 'humane fashion' if they ignore the need for patients' spiritual preparation and readiness for repentance to meet God.[126] And when the suffering of a terminal illness is intractable, rather than resorting to suicide or euthanasia, Christians should accept suffering as an opportunity for forgiveness and for emulating the example of Christ. This perspective advocates a morality of dying and death inaccessible by rational argument alone, and regards dignified death as the one positioned in the prospect of personal fulfillment and not the one that is controlled by medical technology up to the last moment.[127]

For Engelhardt, the possession of a 'God's eye perspective' by Orthodox Christian bioethics provides a knowledge of reality independent of all social constructions, offering thus a foundation that secular bioethics is deprived of. Without God, founding morality on an 'objectively true' perspective in order to rank moral principles and guide decision-making, means that people are isolated within the finite bounds of human nature and the endless plurality of moral perspectives. The ultimate 'cure' for suffering and untreatable disease can only be found through redemption and returning whole-heartedly to God, pointing thus to a theological ethics grounded in Christianity's grace-transforming way of life.[128]

The presence of any guiding perspective is disregarded by Ricoeur, who supports that the evil of suffering and death are not to be comprehended, tamed, and rendered acceptable through rational explanations — human beings should rather act against evil, not provide an *exegesis* for it.[129] In his final work, *Living up to death*, he claims that the inner perception of someone approaching the end of life is driven by the

---

123 Engelhardt, *After God: Morality and bioethics in a secular age*, pp. 402–09.
124 H. Tristram Engelhardt Jr., 'The Orthodox Christian view of suffering', in *Suffering and bioethics*, ed. by Green M. Ronald and Nathan J. Palpant, pp. 249–51.
125 H. Tristram Engelhardt Jr., 'Why ecumenism fails: taking theological differences seriously', *Christian bioethics: Non-Ecumenical Studies in Medical Morality*, 13 (2007), pp. 28–35.
126 Engelhardt Jr., 'Christian bioethics in a post-Christian world: facing the challenges' p. 95.
127 H. Tristram Engelhardt Jr., 'Physician-assisted death: doctrinal development vs. Christian tradition', *Christian Bioethics: Non-Ecumenical Studies in Medical Morality*, 4 (1998), pp. 119–20.
128 Engelhardt, *The foundations of Christian Bioethics*, pp. 365–417.
129 Paul Ricoeur, *Le Mal. Un défit à la philosophie et à la théologie* (Genève: Labor et Fides, 2004), trans. by Giorgos Grigoriou (Athens: Polis Editions, 2005), pp. 62–70.

impetus of life and not by the imminence of death. In this primacy of natality over mortality, *dying to live* becomes the main theme, opening up a space of possibility beyond impossibility, as nothing can be taken for granted up until the very last second.[130] 'Living up to death' means for Ricoeur 'living against death' in the sense of negating death's victory so that life continues in others, through others and for others, a fact which entails a *kenosis* of self-interest rather than a struggle for the individual appropriation of death.[131] In this context, fear of death does not indicate anxiety concerning the cessation of existence, but rather a deep concern of not having been *born* in vain: evil is 'to be annihilated, to be no-bodied', it is not 'to die'.[132]

Ricoeur refers to the testimony of palliative care physicians who notice the 'internal grace' of the dying person, a grace which he regards as the 'emergence' of the Essential, a term-symbol for the indescribable presence of transcendence.[133] The awareness of being-in-witness of someone 'living up to death' leads clinicians to exercise a gaze other than that of an objective external observer: the gaze of compassion, an integration of understanding and friendship.[134] Accompanying, he believes, is the most adequate word to denote this 'being with' the other, an experience unmediated by language codes, only accessible in the caring relationship.[135] What palliative care doctors witness by accompanying their patients is not an image or figuration of death but an affirmation of life, a move from the time of agony to an initial glimpse of the Essential, which has at its core a sense of living in the midst of dying.[136]

It is in this disapproval of one's self-attachment that space is opening up to grace and hope, or to the 'eternal present of divine concern', a mobilisation of the deepest resources of life under the light of the Essential.[137] This can be exemplified in the context of Ricoeur's notion of the *economy of the gift*, which depicts his dialectical comprehension of the relation of the human with the divine and the resultant moral relation of the self and the other: the good and the right are integrated only on the theological grounds of humanity's encounter with God, implying an ethics of unfolding human transformation in relation to the divine.[138] In this perspective, God

---

130 Morny Joy, 'Paul Ricoeur on life and death', *Philosophy and Social Criticism*, 37 (2011), p. 251.
131 Richard Kearney, 'Ricoeur: dying to live *for others*', *Philosophy and Social Criticism*, 37 (2011), p. 223.
132 de Lange, 'Affirming Life in the Face of Death', p. 514.
133 de Lange, 'Affirming Life in the Face of Death', p. 512.
134 Christopher Yates, 'Refiguring the essential word: the work of the imagination in Ricoeur's late apprenticeship', *Philosophy and Social Criticism*, 37 (2011), p. 231.
135 de Lange, 'Affirming Life in the Face of Death', p. 513. Indeed, the French word 'accompagnement' translated as 'support or presence, a way of being with others, and a willingness to stand by each other', denotes both solidarity and autonomy, departing thus from focus on the Anglo-American principle of autonomy and its rights-based, individualistic conception, see: Marie Gaille and Horn Ruth, 'The role of "accompagnement" in the end of life debate in France: from solidarity to autonomy', *Theoretical Medicine and Bioethics*, 37 (2016), pp. 473–87. However, authors note that this notion although 'originally reserved to describe palliative care' it was later employed to 'justify the right to terminal sedation at a patient's request' (p. 484).
136 Yates, 'Refiguring the essential word', p. 231.
137 Yates, 'Refiguring the essential word', pp. 233–34.
138 John Wall, 'The economy of the gift: Paul Ricoeur's significance for theological ethics', *The Journal of Religious Ethics*, 29 (2001), pp. 235–37.

is regarded as a dynamic potency expressed as a 'surplus', an enabling God rendering human beings more capable of an increasingly abundant existence, so as to allow for rebirth into more being, even in the eyes of imminent death. Consequently, the 'work of mourning' is considered as a conscious effort at *refiguration*, as an *ascesis* of our habitual self, departing from false symbolic structures and conceptualisations, seeking a new genesis, even when time seems limited and remaining life short. Therefore, to refigure the matter of death and dying gains the meaning of undergoing a transfiguration of *living*, valuing thus human existence in this world rather than orienting it towards the spiritual consolations of a life after death.[139]

Ricoeur's thoughts on the dying trajectory seem to restore the religious dimension in end-of-life care, resisting the privatisation of spirituality and locating it in the common experience of the care relationship.[140] His views can enrich the ethics of caring practices for dying persons, setting as essential foundations both discarding of the belief that death is simply a 'natural' part of life and understanding the vulnerable autonomy of human beings.[141] He reminds us that human beings are fragile and their efforts to establish autonomy are being continuously threatened in their fulfillment by human vulnerability, a dialectical course that never leads to fixed normative positions.[142]

For Ricoeur, it is one's openness to and availability for the Essential which joins the dying person to the others, and bridges the gap between the imminence of death and the broader community.[143] 'Affirming life' as a major value in palliative care may be realised exactly in this togetherness: the Eucharistic giving of one's life becomes thus an affirmation of the gift of life (a gift received so as to be passed to others), a perspective in absolute contrast with current prevailing anxiety about personal survival until or even after death. Therefore, instead of considering dying as an individual struggle for combating death, Ricoeur points to the Eucharistic celebration of sharing of one's love for life with others, suggesting that only this can transcend death as it implies an understanding that in the vulnerable relationality between mortal human beings exists the only possibility for overcoming the evil of suffering and death.[144]

D. Turning East: Open call for Orthodox Theology and Anthropology

The aforementioned thinkers (among others) illuminate different aspects of the ethics of caring for severely ill and dying patients, while to some extent their views appear

---

139 Joy, 'Paul Ricoeur on life and death', pp. 249–53.
140 de Lange, 'Affirming Life in the Face of Death', p. 512.
141 van Nistelrooij Inge, Petruschka Schaafsma and Joan C. Tronto, 'Ricoeur and the ethics of care', *Medicine, Health Care and Philosophy*, 17 (2014), pp. 488–90.
142 Theo L. Hettema, 'Autonomy and its vulnerability: Ricoeur's view on justice as a contribution to care ethics', *Medicine, Health Care and Philosophy*, 17 (2014), pp. 493–98.
143 Kearney, 'Ricoeur: dying to live *for others*', pp. 224–25.
144 de Lange, 'Affirming Life in the Face of Death', pp. 512–15.

to converge; however, it seems that a broader narrative or world view to encompass, activate and even extend their profound insights is still pending.

More specifically, a moral vision on how to respond to and alleviate the suffering of chronically ill, incurable and dying patients is yet missing.[145] Secular bioethics is particularly limited in adequately responding to human suffering in the face of human finitude, as it cannot express a unique, universally binding, moral standpoint from which to truly know the nature of the right, the good and the virtuous.[146] As Hauerwas has poignantly remarked, theories developed in the context of medical ethics and bioethics are 'not rich enough for us to understand why we should care for those we cannot cure'.[147] As Engelhardt has explained, in the absence of a definite moral point of view by secular bioethics, all attempts to grasp the meaning of human suffering so as to authoritatively guide medical decision-making are inevitably reduced to socially and culturally conditioned preferences regarding life and death styles.[148] By advocating a plurality of frameworks, visions and strategies, current bioethics debates rather contribute to confusion than assist clinicians to substantially help their patients.[149] Contemporary moral discussions, as MacIntyre has emphasised, are embedded in a cosmopolitan background isolated from traditional cultures and religions and devoid of a shared ethics to provide a common moral compass; accordingly, secular morality and modern bioethics are inherently ambiguous, irreducibly plural and necessarily contingent.[150]

Therefore, current medicine and bioethics are unable to offer a meaningful conception of and response to suffering, beyond merely descriptive accounts of this experience; indeed, numerous descriptions of suffering (experienced by severely ill patients and caregivers alike) have been proposed but no model or theoretical framework has been helpful in providing meaning and guidance for facing the ethical dilemmas and the suffering which incurable and ambiguous conditions imply. Concomitantly, virtue ethics and different patient-centred caring practices rooted in the 'autonomy paradigm' have not succeeded in relieving patients' suffering or supporting both patients and clinicians to deal with human frailty and mortality in a meaningful way. On the contrary and as the aforementioned thinkers have stressed, medicine's assumed virtues can quickly be turned into vices when they lack a scheme or a narrative based on deeper beliefs about the true nature and end of human life.[151]

---

145 Gibson and Upshur, 'Ethics and chronic disease: where are the bioethicists?', p. 111.
146 Mark J. Cherry, 'Human suffering and the limits of secular bioethics' in *Suffering and bioethics*, ed. by Green M. Ronald and Nathan J. Palpant, pp. 346–47.
147 Hauerwas, 'Why I am not a communitarian nor a medical ethicist', p. S10.
148 Engelhardt, *The foundations of Christian Bioethics*, pp. 161–276.
149 Mark J. Cherry, "The scandal of secular bioethics: what happens when the culture acts as if there is no God?', *Christian bioethics: Non-Ecumenical Studies in Medical Morality*, 23 (2017), pp. 89–92.
150 Thomas D. D'Andrea, *Tradition, rationality, and virtue: the thought of Alasdair MacIntyre*, 2nd edn (New York: Routledge, 2016).
151 Stanley Hauerwas, 'Must a patient be a person to be a patient?', *Journal of Religion, Disability & Health*, 8 (2004), p. 118. As shown in preceding section, MacIntyre, Hauerwas, Taylor and Engelhardt have explicitly raised this point.

Philosophers and other scholars within the Western tradition seem to expect religion to illuminate the impasse which this dialogue currently faces, as 'integration with religion would allow bioethics to move from the realm of the extraordinary to the ordinary, to consider the inevitable, everyday, ordinary problems of living and to see the need to respond to those problems as part of the moral responsibility of the medical community'.[152] Theology and religion are thus considered a source which might provide medicine its proper *telos*: 'it might be that only theology [...] can teach us to listen rightly to the call of the other, which is also a call of the Other [...] only theology can satiate our desires to rightly engage the mystery of being in suffering'.[153] But how this might be accomplished, remains to be identified;[154] furthermore, expectations of theology and religion seem to centre on the provision of another unequivocal canonical morality as a firm basis for making valid moral judgements in response to suffering and death.[155]

Contributions of Orthodoxy to the current dialogue on bioethical issues, especially those arising from patients' suffering in the face of severe illness and death, remains sparse,[156] and mainly focuses on discussions of and positions on euthanasia and artificial prolongation of life.[157] Engerhardt, Orthodox theologians and other scholars have underlined the differences between Western and Eastern Christianity in relation to bioethical debates and particularly to moral decisions regarding the care of critically ill and dying patients.[158] Fundamental beliefs of Orthodox theology,

---

152 De Vries, 'Good without God', p. 441.
153 Jeffrey P. Bishop, 'Beginning at the end: liturgy and the care of the dying', *Christian Bioethics: Non-Ecumenical Studies in Medical Morality*, 23 (2017), p. 78. Bishop himself (who entered Orthodox Church in 2010) turned to Devine Liturgy as a set of practices and rituals that bring people together, supporting that therapy for medicine's malaises lies in communities as contexts which re-integrate what has been shattered by dualisms and reductions of modernity (p. 79).
154 Apart from De Vries ('Good without God', p. 438-47), hopes put on theology and religion and to Christianity in particular, are expressed by numerous thinkers, indicatively: Taylor (*Sources of self*, p. 836), Pellegrino and Thomasma in their book *The Christian virtues in medical practice*, while the final phrase of Bishop's book, *The anticipatory corpse: medicine, power, and the care of the dying* is 'Might it not be that only theology can save medicine?' (p. 313); however, how theology could actually be a way out for medicine and what this would mean for the relief of suffering of severely ill and dying patients, ultimately remain unanswered.
155 Cherry, 'Human suffering and the limits of secular bioethics', p. 338.
156 As presented by Rev. Iuliu-Marius Morariu, 'Bioethics in the discussions of the Pan-orthodox Synode from Crete (2016)', *Astra Salvensis-revista de istorie si cultura*, 7 (2016), p. 252: 'Unfortunately, despite the importance of bioethics for nowadays society, in the papers of the Pan-Orthodox Synod that took place in 2016 in Crete, it is only a little topic in a bigger list of subjects.'
157 Hierotheos (Vlachos) Metropolitan of Nafpaktos and Agios Vlasios, *Bioithiki kai biotheologia (Bioethics and Bio-theology)*, 2nd edn (Livadia: Holy Monastery of the Birth of the Theotokos, 2010); Nikolaos Koios, *Bioithiki. Synodika keimena Orthodoxon Ekklision (Bioethics. Synodal documents of Orthodox Churches)* (Athens: Hellenic Center for Biomedical Ethics/Stamoulis, 2007).
158 See, for example: Cherry (2017), Delkeshamp-Hayes (2006), Engelhardt (2000, 2007, 2014/2018), Harakas (1999), Hatzinikolaou (2003), Hierotheos (2010), Skouteris (2005), Smith (2001). For a detailed review on the contributions of Orthodox theology to bioethical debates, see: Evangelos Ch. Chaniotis, 'Aspects of the contribution of Church of Greece and Orthodox Theology in the development of bioethical dialogue', *Bioethica*, 2 (2016), pp. 69–82.

including the notion of *prosopon*, the prominence given to spiritual death, and the primacy of active presence over logical explanations of suffering and evil (only to mention a few) if profoundly investigated may re-orient the discussion into new and largely unexplored perspectives, while a promising and meaningful alternative might also be provided for understanding ethical dilemmas, attitudes and caring practices in the face of suffering and death.

The concept of person in medicine and bioethics has been used primarily as a permissive notion with the purpose to protect the individual patient from the pitfalls of experimental medicine, specifically in the context of chronic and incurable illness where 'the shortcomings and limitations of an individualistic conception of the person become particularly apparent'.[159] Furthermore, while the idea of the 'person' can act as a moral restraint for some of the excesses of medical technology, its parameters often exclude, rather than include, people with disabilities, infants and people with severe brain injury, given that they are deprived of their rationality and decision-making capacity.[160]

In Orthodox anthropology, man is not viewed as a static, 'closed', autonomous and self-sufficient individual but as a dynamic reality determined by its relations with God; *prosopon* is the true substance of human being created in the image and likeness of God. To be made in the image of God means that man is free from necessity and is capable of being liberated from any natural power so that one's potential is activated for achieving *theosis* (deification) which is the true realisation of one's *prosopon*.[161] While the notion of the individual identifies man with nature as a confirmation of and adherence to the physical self (*philautia*), *prosopon* has the potentiality to transcend natural borders and to be fully expressed in denial of being-for-oneself (*kenosis*) and in seeking wholeness in unity with God.[162] Moreover, contrary to the conception of the individual as a self-sufficient and self-contained entity isolated from others, the conceptualisation of a person in the Orthodox Church is absolutely anti-individualistic, formed in accordance with Holy Trinity where no person is self-centred and remote but always existing in relation; *prosopon* becomes thus a relational category and the human being in its highest and truest form of existence is understood as a social entity, fulfilled only in communion with other human beings.[163]

---

159 Jennings and others, 'Ethical challenges of chronic illness', p. S8.
160 Tyler Tate and Robert Pearlman, 'What we mean when we talk about suffering — and why Eric Cassell should not have the last word', *Perspectives in Biology and Medicine*, 62 (2019), pp. 95–110.
161 John Meyendorff, *Byzantine theology-Historical trends and doctrinal themes* (New York: Fordham University Press, 1983/1979), trans. by Rev. Paylos Koumarianos & Basilis Tsagalos (Athens: Indiktos, 2010), pp. 297–307.
162 Vladimir Lossky, *Essai sur la théologie mystique de l'Eglise d'Orient* (Paris: Aubier, 1944), trans. by Stella Plevraki, 6th edn (Thessaloniki: Ekklisiastiko Idryma 'Evaggelistis Markos', 2007), pp. 136–67.
163 John Zizioulas Metropolitan of Pergamon, 'The meaning of being human — a theological approach', in *Science, technology and human values. International Symposium Proceedings*, ed. by Loucas G. Christophorou and Constantinos Drakatos (Athens: The Academy of Athens, 2007), pp. 302–03. As Zizioulas reminds us 'even suffering and death as forms of evil owe their appearance to the fact that in exercising freedom the human being refuses to accept the Other, God being the Other par excellence' (p. 300).

Furthermore, for the Orthodox view, being in the image of God is distinct from any particular human characteristic and condition; persons are not discerned by qualities or capacities of any kind, but by their uniqueness in the absolute sense of the term.[164] This inherent value in each person signifies true dignity, and persons are valued irrespectively, or rather including, malfunctioning or disabled body, mind or both.[165] In this context, human dignity is put in a different perspective from Catholic Christian thought,[166] as it is not a target to be achieved through particular moral actions and choices, but is already inherent in every human being.

This perspective of person as *prosopon* already puts on a totally different basis western conceptions of the suffering individual who, for healing to be realised, must maintain self-control, restore self-boundaries and intactness of actual self. On the contrary, in the case of *prosopon*, purpose shifts from the return to habitual self and immersion in nature to transcendence of nature, from integrity of self to completeness of being; primacy is thus given to potential and not actual, autonomous and detached self.[167] In this prospect, autonomy is viewed as man's liberation from dominance by worldly concerns, from what distracts and distorts him from his ultimate purpose in activating likeness to God, whereas defending autonomy implies both protecting confinement in natural limits and negating continuous exodus from man's finite existence towards true being. Therefore, aspects of suffering such as broken individuality, powerlessness, loss of self-government and self-determination, which are thought to establish its negativity in Cassel's definition, might be desired tasks in favour of accomplishing wholeness in deification.[168]

Indeed, the Orthodox Christian views of suffering contrast in many ways with those of Western Christianity and other religious traditions.[169] In Orthodox Christianity,

---

164 It may be understandable now why spirituality cannot be grasped within numerous questionnaires — God is personal and the uniqueness of the personal relationship with Him, a distinguishing mark of Orthodox theology, cannot be generalised and formulated in questionnaires and surveys.
165 Andrew Lustig, 'The Image of God and human dignity: a complex conversation', *Christian Bioethics: Non-Ecumenical Studies in Medical Morality*, 23 (2017), pp. 317–34.
166 Daniel P. Sulmasy, 'Death and dignity in Catholic Christian thought', *Medicine Health Care and Philosophy*, 20 (2017), pp. 537–43.
167 Thomas J. Bole, 'The person in secular and in Orthodox-Catholic Bioethics', *Christian Bioethics: Non-Ecumenical Studies in Medical Morality*, 6 (2000), pp. 97–100.
168 Cassel's model of suffering has been criticised [e.g.: Bueno-Gómez (2017); Tate and Pearlman (2019)] as his notion of intactness presupposes a normative definition of self already challenged by psychoanalysis and meta-modernity, while by asserting meaning-making to the 'person' and disease to the biological body, he finally shatters the holistic view of patient he struggles to maintain. Moreover, his model ignores that all major monotheist religions set an objective teleology as human end-purpose, to which the meaning of suffering is inevitably linked, irrespectively of the individual's subjective determination.
169 Stanley Samuel Harakas, *The Orthodox Christian tradition: religious beliefs and healthcare decisions, Religious traditions and healthcare decisions handbook series* (Chicago: Park Ridge Center for the Study of Health, Faith, and Ethics, 1999), p. 3. In relevant literature, Jewish and Roman Catholic views seem to prevail. For the Jewish tradition, suffering is conceived as a problem of ethics and of response; society, medicine and science have to respond to suffering through acts of justice. According to the Roman Catholic view, the awareness of suffering can have a salutary role in a

suffering is considered as potentially vital for salvation, if understood and accepted in the framework of spiritual growth toward God-likeness within which suffering is considered part of divine economy to awaken human beings and re-orient them towards their ultimate purpose.[170] This view of sufferer as embodying acceptance of the limits and finitude of the self, enduring evil and integrating this experience towards divine orientation, lies in absolute opposition to modern conceptions of suffering defined as not having control, not feeling worthwhile or valued, and living a life deprived of meaning and purpose. However, although pain and suffering are seen as opportunities for spiritual progress, they are not absolutely necessary prerequisites for it, nor do they exist for paying off any debts.[171] While the Orthodox Church recognises the inevitability of pain, suffering and death, it identifies no intrinsic value in them; in contrast, Western Christianity places suffering 'within an economy of sin, propitiatory punishment, and salvation, in which suffering plays a central role in paying off a penalty, namely worldly punishment due to sin.'[172]

Furthermore, given that *theosis* involves the totality of the person, both soul and body, the human body is not discarded in Orthodoxy but constitutes an essential element of our existence, participating in the sanctification of man and included in deification.[173] As a permanent and fundamental aspect of human nature as a whole, the body shares in the God-likeness, and consequently man is responsible for caring for its well-being.[174] This view calls for a caring attitude that would join all forces and mobilise all resources for relieving and palliating every aspect of pain and discomfort, under the purpose of preserving and respecting the body's sanctity; therefore, medical care is not simply aimed at restoring the functioning of a biological organism, but

---

moral agent's life, leading both to repair of a faulty condition that suffering points to and to the development of virtues necessary for this reparative task. See: Scott J. Fitzpatrick, Ian H. Kerridge, Christopher F. C. Jordens, Laurie Zoloth, Christopher Tollefsen, Karma Lekshe Tsomo, Michael P. Jensen, Abdulaziz Sachedina, and Deepak Sarma, 'Religious perspectives on human suffering: Implications for medicine and bioethics', *Journal of Religion and Health*, 55 (2016), pp. 159–73 (p. 171).

170 Jean-Claude Larchet, *The theology of illness* (trans. by John & Michael Breck), (New York: St Vladimir's Seminary Press, 2002), pp. 55–68.

171 Jean-Claude Larchet, *Dieu ne veut pas la souffrance des hommes* (Paris: Editions du Cerf, 1999), trans. by Cristos Koulas (Athens: Editions En plo, 2016), pp. 148–54. At this point, it could be noted that the original meaning of the English word 'redemption' is 'a buying back, releasing, ransoming', see: Online Etymology Dictionary, https://www.etymonline.com/search?q = redemption.

172 Engelhardt, 'The Orthodox Christian view of suffering', pp. 250–55. Engelhardt underlined the central spiritual therapeutic focus of suffering in Orthodoxy, due to the fact that 'suffering can waken us out of an absorption in ourselves and in the affairs of the world' (p. 254). It is of note that the original meaning of the word 'suffering' in English language had been 'undergoing of punishment, affliction, etc.', probably connected to the notion of a sinful body pleading for forgiveness and redemption, a meaning which resonates with the link between sin, suffering and punishment in Western Christianity. See: Online Etymology Dictionary, https://www.etymonline.com/search?q = suffering.

173 Kallistos Ware, Bishop of Diokleia, *The Orthodox Church* (Middlesex: Penguin, 1993), trans. by Joseph Roilidis (Athens: Akritas, 1996), p. 368.

174 Allyne L. Smith Jr., 'An Orthodox Christian view of persons and bodies', in *Persons and their bodies: rights, responsibilities, relationships*, ed. by M. J. Cherry (London: Kluwer Academic Publishers, 2002), p. 104.

also at offering optimal conditions which could facilitate the whole patient's spiritual growth as a psychosomatic entity, at every moment, including the end of life.[175] Maybe this view could alter high percentages of under-treatment of pain and other physical aspects of suffering in contemporary health care settings.

Medicine in the Christian context, just like disease and suffering, also serves as a means for man's spiritual purpose; physicians ought to be able to recognise that illness and the threat of death are relevant to the individual patient's spiritual situation, and thus strive to facilitate the patient's growth to holiness.[176] An Orthodox Christian understanding of medicine should acknowledge 'medicine's role for supporting what is at stake 'behind' patient's medical problems'[177] and if medical personnel becomes aware of this, then they should both cultivate and direct all of their potential to guide their curing and caring efforts so as to encourage their patients in gaining access to a profound dimension of their lives towards their ultimate aim; physicians should therefore be able to view each patient not as a human being who is dying but as a human person whose purpose is not to become dead.[178]

Human flourishing towards *theosis* entails the acquisition of virtues; although the theme of virtues in Eastern Christian thought has not been extensively discussed,[179] their conceptualisation differs from western theology and consequently from western philosophy. According to Maximus the Confessor, virtues exist in order to synchronise our existence to our *telos*, to predispose us to the experience of radical love — a divine gift already within us — while in western theology, virtues are inserted as a supernatural order between God and creation; therefore, virtues are not actually acquired but manifested as the true intentions of God's will for created nature.[180] Similarly, *grace* is not a kind of reward for the virtuous human beings, neither the cause of man's virtues; it is the cooperation between God's grace and man's free will (*synergia*) upon which human life is continuously transformed in a mysterious way not transposed to the logic realm.[181] This perspective contrasts with views of the aforementioned philosophers, who envisage the pursuit of virtues as prerequisites to achieving one's *telos* of moral

---

175 Philip LeMasters, 'The practice of medicine as *theosis*', *Theology Today*, 61 (2004), p. 174.
176 LeMasters, 'The practice of medicine as *theosis*', p. 174. For the author, physicians 'should attend with care to the kind of bioethical guidance that can direct medicine toward the ultimate end of *theosis*' (p. 178).
177 Corinna Delkeskamp-Hayes, 'Why patients should give thanks for their disease: traditional Christianity on the joy of suffering', *Christian Bioethics: Non-Ecumenical Studies in Medical Morality*, 12 (2006), p. 218.
178 Konstantinos Skouteris, *Bioithiki kai to ethos tis Orthodoxias (Bioethics and the ethos of Orthodoxy)* http://www.bioethics.org.gr/BioethicsOrthodoxy.pdf (2005), p. 5.
179 Perry T. Hamalis and Aristotle Papanikolaou, 'Toward a Godly mode of being: Virtue as embodied deification', *Studies in Christian Ethics*, 26 (2013), p. 273.
180 Hamalis and Papanikolaou, 'Toward a Godly mode of being', pp. 271–80. Authors conclude (p. 280) that: '... the study of the tradition of thinking on virtue in Easter Christian thought could also reveal new ways of conceptualizing classical problems in virtue theory, new insights into the dynamics of virtues' development, as well as new contexts of applied ethics'.
181 Lossky, *Essai sur la théologie mystique de l'Eglise d'Orient*, p. 234; Ware, *The Orthodox Church*, p. 350.

perfection, while limited consideration is given to the spiritual maturation of the person and the diachronic developmental character of individual ethical transformation.[182] Although virtue ethics is considered most compatible with Orthodoxy by emphasising the importance of one's character and habits of action, prioritising the person's overall *ethos* over the ethics of particular acts, and underlining the role of the community in virtuous character formation,[183] no virtue theory can be substantial without incorporating individual ethical and spiritual maturation.

Moreover, the human being's divine potentiality has not been a decisive background in morality debates in western bioethics while Orthodox bioethical discussions highlight exactly this element of metamorphosis and unity with God. In opposition to the fully informed individual, man is motivated to accept *agnosia*, the unknowable depth of things,[184] and to understand that *telos* is not *gnosis* of but unity with God.[185] Accordingly, salvation is not realised through theoretical knowledge of 'absolute truth' but through orientation towards an end purpose, which is the achievement of *theosis*, a dynamic rise initiating from current life.[186] Perhaps it is at this point where *phronesis* has a place by enabling clinicians to recognise the risks inherent in any moral reflection based on discursive philosophical analyses and rational arguments, unable to welcome *agnosia* and acknowledge the limits of man's knowing potential as well as the fragility of all merely human reasoning.

Death in Orthodoxy is understood as the rupture of the body-soul unity, a sound manifestation of man's fragility and frailty resulting from the differentiation of man's will from the life-giving God's will.[187] However, despite the fact that death is conceived as a consequence of the fallen and broken condition of Creation, this does not minimise its tragedy:[188] death remains an evil and its fear is understandable and reasonable. This view of death contradicts with various psychological approaches and interventions that concentrate on lessening fear of death, promoting acceptance and attitudes that 'tame' death.

---

182 Raphael Cadenhead, 'Corporeality and *askesis*: ethics and bodily practice in Gregory of Nyssa's theological anthropology', *Studies in Christian Ethics*, 26 (2013), pp. 281–99. Cadenhead discusses MacIntyre's understanding of practice within an account of narrative with focus to its *telos* as a realisation of man's quest of good and wherein the virtues are considered as means enabling persons to achieve practice's inherent goods.
183 Perry T. Hamalis, 'Eastern Orthodox Ethics', in *The International Encyclopedia of Ethics*, ed. by Hugh LaFollette (Oxford: Blackwell Publishing, 2013), p. 1527.
184 As Cherry has remarked in 'Human suffering and the limits of secular bioethics' (p. 338): 'To face the challenges of human suffering in an age of life-sustaining therapies, one must come to terms with the limits of human knowledge …'. Cherry entered Orthodox Church in 2001.
185 Lossky, *Essai sur la théologie mystique de l'Eglise d'Orient*, p. 46.
186 Meyendorff, *Byzantine theology*, pp. 470–78.
187 Nikolaos Loudovikos Fr., *Orthodoxia kai Eksychronismos-Byzantini exatomikeysi, kratos and istoria stin prooptiki tou Evropaikou mellontos (Orthodoxy and modernization — Byzantine individualization, state and history in the perspective of the European future)* (Athens: Armos, Books, 2006), p. 172.
188 Harakas, *The Orthodox Christian Tradition*, p. 9.

Furthermore, death for Orthodoxy is above all a spiritual reality, to which it is possible for somebody to belong while still being alive; true death is spiritual death, the necrosis of internal human being and the negation of the potential for restoration of man's true nature.[189] Church Fathers emphasise remembrance of death as an existential prompt for man to live his life in fullness;[190] with death we are called to undertake our existence and to *die alive*. In this prospect, death fear might be conceived as agony in the face of assuming the responsibility to fully activate one's divine potential when time is limited, or as the sad realisation of an unlived life, consumed and not lived in its essence. Even when death is imminent, fullness and completeness are still possible given man's divine potential, a fact which opens up a space of potentiality beyond impossibility, where nothing can be taken for granted up to the very last second. Maybe this is the miracle we clinicians pray for, for our patients, and family members for their love ones.

The Orthodox Church teaches that preparing for death is primarily a spiritual responsibility and in order to attain as much of the journey towards deification as possible, even prolonging life by all means may be viewed as an appropriate and not futile practice. Concurrently, the postponement of death and the avoidance of suffering should not become all-consuming projects and medical technology should not evolve into an idol of worldly self-preservation at all costs; instead, the overriding consideration is that Christians remain on target, using therapies to preserve and enhance life in ways that are consonant with growth in holiness. Because of this transcendent focus, traditional Christian end-of-life decisions will often engage concerns alien to secular medical decision-making and cause conflicts with the moral expectations of physicians who are not aware of this spiritual orientation.[191]

In Easter Orthodox bioethics, medical morality is not governed by the causistical application of a natural law, but it is the pursuit of *theosis* which determines content and purpose of morality. Therefore, Orthodox ethics is not concerned fundamentally with getting people to obey rules or to embody creditable virtues; instead, the focus is 'on changing oneself so as to turn from oneself to God' and primary significance is given to person's overall ethical comportment, rather than to the

---

189 Nikolaos Hatzinikolaou Fr., 'Prolonging life or hindering death? An Orthodox perspective on death, dying and euthanasia', *Christian Bioethics*, 9 (2003), p. 194.
190 Anestis G. Keselopoulos, *Ek tou thanatou eis tin zoin. Theologiki proseggisi stis prokliseis tis bioithikis (From death to life. Theological approaches to bioethical challenges)* (Thessaloniki: Pournaras, 2009), pp. 137–42.
191 H. Tristram Engelhardt Jr. and Ana Smith Iltis, 'End-of-life: the traditional Christian view', *Lancet* 366 (2005), p. 1048. An example can be found in the study of van Tol and others, 'Judgment of unbearable suffering and willingness to grant a euthanasia request by Dutch general practitioners', pp, 166–72, who reported that 'euthanasia request confronts doctors with a dilemma: either to uphold the duty to respect life or to uphold the duty [to] relieve suffering [i.e. by practicing euthanasia]' (p. 171), suggesting that these two duties, in the absence of a spiritual focus which could unite them, can only be considered as antithetical, a dilemma which imposed considerable psychological and moral burden on physicians in this study.

morality of distinct acts, a view very distant from the Law and the Judgment.[192] In circumstances where complex dilemmas arise, Orthodoxy provides no generalised commandments and rules to pronounce the right and the wrong action; rather, 'the enlightment and grace of God is reflected on each specific person',[193] comprising the source of the most appropriate decision and action. Considerations regarding moral rights, values and virtues are visualised in the perspective of the pursuit of holiness in union with God, while the focus is relocated from acting rightly and justly to what promotes and facilitates man's spiritual progress: excessive attention to general principles can even divert one's commitment to the personal context of communion with God.[194]

Indeed, Orthodox ethicists consider deeply the particular personal situation for which moral guidance is required. While Catholic teaching employs the law of double-effect to assess the moral ramifications of actions with varying effects, Orthodox authors focus on the comprehensive spiritual impact on and meaning for those involved with the action in question. In this perspective, even euthanasia can be envisaged as the problem of wholeness, meaning and value of our psychosomatic biological life, rather than as a matter of choice.[195] In cases of ambiguity and insurmountable dilemmas, the notion of *economia* (dispensation) might be called in, acknowledging that insisting on the letter of the law might hinder one's journey towards wholeness, authorising an exception to rules, and aiming to the avoidance of the greater harm that would result from strict application of the canon.[196] Moving from the universal to particular conditions, also calls for employment of *diakrisis* or *discernment*, a virtue through which norms are interpreted and applied to the specific context in whatever way promotes the growth to *theosis* of the unique *prosopon* involved.[197] *Diakrisis* might be a notion able to enrich and transform conceptualisations of what constitutes good ethical decision-making process in the face of complex clinical dilemmas.

As mentioned above, theologians and philosophers have noticed that accompanying seriously ill and dying patients also requires the presence of a compassionate community to support purposive endurance of suffering by locating it within a broader context offering coherence and understanding. Orthodox Ecclesia, by uniting the human with the divine element and preserving memory as a collective act, could become this supportive milieu. This view shatters any reality of loneliness and isolation currently reported by dying patients, and responds to the evidence that requests for the right to die do not necessarily express autonomy but rather loneliness and fear of dying alone and abandoned by others.[198]

---

192 LeMasters, 'The practice of medicine as *theosis*,' pp. 179–80.
193 Hatzinikolaou, 'Prolonging life or hindering death?', p. 187.
194 Engelhardt, *The foundations of Christian Bioethics*, pp. 219–76.
195 Loudovikos, *Orthodoxia kai Eksychronismos*, pp. 143–54.
196 Meyendorff, *Byzantine theology*, pp. 195–99.
197 Hamalis, 'Eastern Orthodox Ethics', pp. 1533–34.
198 Berna van Baarsen, 'Suffering, loneliness, and the euthanasia choice: an explorative study', *Journal of Social Work in End-of-Life and Palliative Care*, 4 (2009), pp. 189–213.

These perspectives may re-orient the dialogue from an ethics of death and dying, to an ethics of life, from the prevailing model of *aware dying* to a prospect of *aware living* and *alive dying*. In this context, 'affirmation of life in the face of death', a core value of palliative care, can be understood as caring for patients *living* up to death[199] with true cure conceived as metamorphosis of whole human being and retrieval of one's position in the trajectory towards *theosis*.[200] Consequently, what determines quality of life in the face of suffering and imminent death might be man's adherence towards this end purpose, rather than controlling every aspect of the dying process and preserving autonomy or a self-invented vision of dignity.[201]

E. Conclusions

Under the light of the above considerations, caring for patients we cannot cure, gains the meaning of accompanying persons, *being with* them and supporting them to unfold, build and advance their potential self. Such a caring practice, by bringing caregivers into the immediate presence of the patient's affliction, involves an inescapable element of suffering, a readiness to face without recoil the presence of our own affliction, our own fragility and fatality. This view re-directs the whole discussion away from assessing adaptive and maladaptive adjustments and detecting coping resilience as the ideals for both patients dying in peace and acceptance, and clinicians showing positive 'death attitudes'. To discern the place of suffering in the context of moral growth and re-orientation towards man's ultimate purpose, calls for an ethics of engaged presence rather than an ethics of principles.[202] Should this view prove to be fruitful, it may assign an entirely new meaning to the healing relationship and humane care, which philosophers of medicine have tried to define.

From the preceding discussion we might conclude that novel perspectives and understandings provided by Orthodox theology and anthropology might put on a totally different basis current discussions regarding the ethics of caring for incurably ill and dying patients and clinicians' responses to suffering. Palliative care, pointing to a 'paradigm shift' within contemporary medicine from mastery and control to *being with* the suffering other, before it is assimilated in mainstream medicine and becomes a new *ars moriedi*, could provide the ideal context to raise, face and systematically examine these concerns.[203] Themes briefly touched upon here, deserve

---

199 Ricoeur's thesis of the primacy of natality over mortality can be discerned here.
200 Dominique Beaufils Fr., *Ta foi t'a sauvé: Approach orthodoxe de la maladie et de la mort* (Paris: Desclée de Brouwer, 1996), trans. by Polyxeni Tsaliki-Kiosoglou (Athens: Parrisia, 2017), pp. 223–33.
201 Keselopoulos, *Ek tou thanatou eis tin zoin*, p. 119.
202 Braude, 'Normativity unbound', p. 116. Hauerwas' suffering presence is echoed here.
203 As ten Have and Clark conclude '… palliative care is more than another healthcare context in which moral issues emerge. It is an incentive for philosophers, theologians and ethicists generally to evaluate the notions and models of present-day bioethics itself' (p. 250), ten Have and Clark, 'Conclusion: ethics and palliative care', in *The ethics of palliative care. European perspectives*, ed. by Henk ten Have and David Clark, pp. 232–52.

to be discussed thoroughly by Orthodox theologians and philosophers, along with doctors, ethicists, philosophers of medicine and others; dialogue needs to become more detailed and systematic and more importantly, to focus on core notions, issues and questions raised by western philosophers, theologians and bioethicists, while it is equally important this discussion to reach health care professionals. And then it may be revealed that it is not fear of death and sense of failure that shape both our attitudes to death and caring for the dying, and our inability to effectively respond to suffering patients, but it is our *spiritual pain*, helpless as we feel in front of death, having turned to numerous 'goods' proved to be infertile to aspire us and sustain our caring practices over and above curing, hopeless as we stand, sensing though that the evil of death and suffering *should not* become immortal.

GAYLE E. WOLOSCHAK

Teaching about Science and Religion in the Seminary

▼ ABSTRACT Few Orthodox seminaries engage in teaching about science and religion. This is particularly surprising because Orthodox do not usually have concerns at the science-religion interface, and therefore engagement should be routine and without difficulty. Engagement of science and religion in the form of dialogue and discourse at the course level is particularly valuable although some confrontational concerns may be raised. Engagement could revolve around several major topics especially environmental issues since these have been championed by the Ecumenical Patriarch. In addition, discussion could also include areas such as bioethics, evolutionary biology, anthropology, and others. Some general points to be considered in designing such teaching and discussion experiences with science and religion include the following: (1) each discipline must be truthful to itself; (2) the disciplines themselves are very broad, making it difficult for one person to represent the entire field (e.g., a biblical scholar cannot necessarily reflect upon Patristics; a biologist cannot easily reflect upon physics; etc.); (3) discussion must be open to a wide range of scholars including theologians, scientists, pastors, philosophers, historians, and others; (4) one can find a richness in inter-faith dialogue on science-religion particularly environmental topics where a commonness is often found. In general, the goal of science-oriented lectures is not so much to have pastoral or theology students understand every aspect of the scientific question at hand, but rather it is to allow the students to experience the science as a spectrum of complex opinions and gain perspectives on how the science weighs in on the controversies. In an age with increasing technological advancement, future pastors and priests must be prepared for a life in a world that questions science

Gayle E. Woloschak • Northwestern University

on the one hand but wants to use every technological advance on the other. In developing science-religion programs at seminaries, consideration should be given to a more integrated approach: instead of having selected courses designed for exploring environmental science and religion, one idea is to integrate the science into the curriculum itself so that it is not treated as something separate but rather as an integrated whole.

Introduction

At the recent Halki III Summit (held in June 2019) on the Environment conducted by His All-Holiness the Ecumenical Patriarch Bartholomew, much discussion was held on teaching about environment and ecological concerns at Orthodox (and other) seminaries. The sad realization was that while Patriarch Bartholomew is known as the 'Green Patriarch', very few Orthodox seminaries have programs in ecological awareness from an Orthodox perspective. If one expands this to examine science and religion programs at Orthodox seminaries, these are equally limited in number for most curricula. A few have programs in bioethics, and one or two lectures in a theology course might be related to the topic, but these are rare and not specifically directed toward the science-religion interface. In some courses on Biblical studies, discussions of Genesis also include comments on evolution and express some approaches toward compatibility between the two.

Why should Orthodox seminaries engage in courses of this type? The answer to this is based in some of the same reasons for which any seminary would engage in them: because our students are taking courses that make them question how the world works; because science and technology is having a broad influence on life and life's choices; because the world's climate is changing and solutions are an ethical concern that the Church should speak about; and others. Nevertheless, Orthodox seminaries in particular should also reflect upon the theology that influences our attitudes toward environment, evolution, and other similar topics at the science-religion interface. This theology will have an influence not only on the Orthodox but also on the broad Christian community which would benefit greatly from the Orthodox articulation of this theology. Continued reflection and development of theological perspectives on scientific questions (such as environment, evolution, anthropology, and others) is desperately needed, and Orthodox seminaries are perhaps one environment where this can take place in a surrounding that ensures openness, honest reflection, and discussion.

At several different seminaries: St Vladimir's Orthodox Theological Seminary, Lutheran School of Theology Chicago and Pittsburgh Theological Seminary (Presbyterian) I teach wide-ranging science-religion interface classes. These include a variety of topics including Epic of Creation (about evolution), Future of Creation (about the environment), Bioethics, Theology and Science, and Theology and Evolution. In the past I have reflected upon the difficulties of being an Orthodox

Christian in a scientific community[1], and this may be at the root of my interest in bridging the two fields. All the same, I have found many other Christian communities open to science-religion dialogue while the Orthodox Church and particularly Orthodox seminaries have been ambivalent about the topic. This paper will deal with the question: how can we introduce science discussions into the theological (and pastoral) community?

Most often, the goal of science-religion dialogue is to bring scientists and theologians to the table to discuss topics of common interest. These topics can be wide-ranging including the origins of life, evolution, bioethics, genetic engineering, and more. My teaching at the Zygon Center for Religion and Science (housed at and a part of the Lutheran School of Theology at Chicago) has taught me that this dialogue (and classes that are engaged with these topics) should follow several considerations: (1) each discipline must be truthful to itself; (2) the disciplines themselves are very broad making it difficult for one person to represent the entire field (e.g., a biblical scholar cannot necessarily reflect upon Patristics; a biologist cannot easily reflect upon physics; etc.); (3) discussion must be open to a wide range of scholars including theologians, scientists, pastors, philosophers, historians, and others; (4) one can find a richness in inter-faith dialogue on science-religion particularly environmental topics where a common-ness is often found. Students participating in these classes for these talks however are even more important. They are the ones who may be able to reach other people from their parishes and communities and through that make the greatest impact on preservation of the environment.

Specific Courses in Science and Religion for Pastors and Priests

For any course that address issues at the science-religion interface, particularly those about the environment, it is important to engage future pastors into thinking about the science itself. This can be done in several ways. As an example, I will discuss the courses on environment established at the Lutheran School of Theology at Chicago. Scientists who can speak engagingly and at a level that non-scientists can understand are invited to explain the science that provides a basis for understanding environmental questions. This is important because it provides an opportunity for future pastors to discuss their own doubts about the science behind the environmental concerns. That is to say — any scientist giving a lecture on environmental biology will inevitably be asked about climate change and auxiliary topics regardless of whether that theme was mentioned in the class at all. For example, on environmental concerns, one popular question revolves around asking whether humans are responsible for global climate

---

[1] Gayle Woloschak, Perspectives from the Academy: Being Orthodox and a Scientist. in *Eastern Orthodox Christianity and American Higher Education: Theological, Historical and Contemporary Reflections*, ed by Ann Bezzerides and Elizabeth Prodromou, (Notre Dame: University of Notre Dame Press, 2017).

change or whether it is part of natural changes of planet Earth that are cyclic in nature. Similarly, scientists who work in evolutionary biology will be asked about proofs for evolution, questions of how we know how early life started, etc. Scientists then answer these questions and explain to the group why they believe what they believe.

Why is it so important to have scientists involved directly in these courses? Priests and pastors will reach a large number of people in their parishes. Offering them the opportunity to have all of their questions addressed directly by the science is one approach to 'convincing' them that climate change is human-caused or that evolution is the unifying theory for all of biology. Putting scientists in the room with theology students with open time for questions and discussion is probably a better approach to convincing students that there are truly climate change issues than assigning them to read a textbook on the topic. The ability of the pastors and theological students to directly engage the scientists in this environment is valuable and often life-changing for them.

There are often many challenges with selecting scientists who can and are willing to interact with future pastors. The scientific community is not friendly toward religion in general. A Pew survey of scientists documented that only 50 per cent of scientists believe in some type of supreme being, but that among them many are not drawn to organised religion of any type.[2] The study did not probe the reasons for these responses among scientists. Considering the volubility of some anti-religion oriented scientists, it is probably not surprising that the majority of scientists who are believers show no more than tepid religiosity. Peer pressure in science exists just as it does in other areas of life; thus, those who are vehement in their opinions create a climate where persecution in many small ways can prevent others from complete honesty. Anti-religion prejudice has shown itself in many ways in my own personal experiences and my experiences with students and others in academia. While most speakers in these science-religion programs who are recruited are believers, at times, acknowledged atheist scientists who are willing to engage the religious community have been selected to speak to provide diversity and to reflect a more complete representation of the scientific community. This perhaps seems contradictory to Orthodox thinking where one might want exclusively Christian speakers, but there is value in actually representing the community as it is instead of trying to showcase specific speakers who are perhaps not experts on the topic but are of the correct theological background.

The goal of science-oriented lectures is not so much to have pastoral students understand every aspect of the scientific question at hand, but rather it is to allow the students to experience the science as a spectrum of complex opinions and gain perspectives on how the science weighs in on the controversies. For example, it is not

---

2   The results of a Pew Research Center survey of scientists and the general public done in 2009 indicate that 33 per cent of scientists believe in God, 18 per cent believe in a higher power of some sort although not God, 41 per cent don't believe in either, and 7 per cent refused to answer. David Masci, "Scientists and Belief," *Religion and Science in the United States*, November 5, 2009, Pew Research Center, Washington, DC, http://www.pewforum.org/2009/11/05/scientists-and-belief/.

expected that students will be prepared to explain in detail why changes in emission of greenhouse gasses lead to global climate change or how molecular biology be used to support evolution; it is expected that they will be able to absorb the concepts and feel comfortable in the presence of others who are discussing it. As such, testing of scientific knowledge is not of as much value in a theological context as testing of applications of the knowledge. Can you write a sermon for Earth Day? Can you develop a program for youth ministry oriented toward the environment? Can you help the parishioner who is stuck on a literal reading of Genesis 1 as the scientific story for human origins?

Another approach that can be used to engage the science is to have the students experience it directly. With the increased access to bioinformatics tools and data it is relatively simple to stage a 'crowdsourcing' experiment in the classroom. Students are briefly taught how to use computational tools such as BLAST and resources such as GenBank and the Protein Data Bank. The task given to the whole class then is to compare genetic information from different animal species. This exercise is set up to show the similarity of life at the molecular level despite the apparent variety of life among different species. It is in part a problem of biology, evolution and even species relations. Students are given a specific 'problem': to evaluate whether gene (and protein) sequences for the same gene (or protein) among different species are more similar when species are evolutionarily similar to each other. Through this exercise, the students absorb the sense of the abundance of information in publicly available datasets on the National Institutes of Health (NIH) National Center for Biotechnology Information website[3]. They also recognize that, while molecular similarities between closely related species are high, they are not absent when a gene of the same function is compared between species as different as millimetres-long pond dwellers and humans. Students often claim that this work with actual genetic information about relationships of organisms helps them understand the unity of life better than any textbook could. I have heard from a few students who years later continue to use this exercise with young adult groups as a learning experience.

Visits (field trips) to scientific laboratories have also been used to provide an entry for pastoral students into the scientific world. For environmental classes we have often toured the environmental radiation laboratories (which I direct) at Northwestern University[4] or the large synchrotron called the Advanced Photon Source at Argonne National Laboratory[5] in the Chicago suburb of Lemont, IL where significant environmental (and other research) is on-going. On a recent visit this past semester, one student told me that on his way to the National Laboratory he had a bad attitude and thought that such a class would be a waste of time; during the course of the visit he became awestruck by the instrumentation and the vast capabilities of the facility. A week later he said that he had never been so engaged by science before and talked about how he had begun searching for more information

---

3 The site can be found here https://www.ncbi.nlm.nih.gov/.
4 The Woloschak Lab website can be found here: http://janus.northwestern.edu/wololab/.
5 The Argonne National Laboratory Advanced Photon website is: https://www.aps.anl.gov/.

and reading about synchrotron websites. While this degree of 'excitement for science' is not a necessary outcome for these visits, and other classmates were not equally struck by the experience, they all had a realisation that science can be appreciated on its own merit and that understanding its basics is within the reach of everyone. Accepting that immersion into science is not something foreign but part of human experience is of great value.

To provide balance in these science-religion classes, theologians and other religious scholars (such as biblical and liturgical scholars) are invited to provide theological reflections on the topic of environment and humanity's place in it. They provide a perspective that can be useful in a pastoral setting and the lectures are designed to provide support for those students who may wish to engage the topic in their own parish settings. Special emphasis is placed on the need for pastors to understand their own parish communities. If the parishioners are not ready to deal with environmental questions or evolution it should be a solemn duty of a pastor to work to open their hearts in a way that can lead them toward the acceptance of environmental concerns. This may take weeks, but often takes far longer. I had one student who herself was very concerned about the environment, but was assigned as a pastor to a parish in South Dakota in the US. Interestingly, this parish had an oil well with a drill on the site and the parish community supported itself financially with this oil well. She realised that trying to convince them that green forms of energy should be used over gasoline or oil was not likely to be the first thing she should mention on her initial visit to the parish. She resolved to work with the parishioners on environmental concerns slowly and at first introducing more distant concepts that might in time make the community more receptive to environmental concerns. Her first success was at eliminating styrofoam cups and replacing them with non-disposable coffee mugs. Because this choice is more environmentally conscious this helped the parish think about environmental issues differently. Even with this minor increase in self-awareness, one can hope that the prayers of this community would bring them closer to Christ. As a parish community grows more in the life of Christ, the more environmentally aware and concerned that group becomes.

Similarly, another student was being sent to a parish in the Deep South where the majority of the parishioners were heavily anti-evolution. The pastor knew that to bring up the issue publicly would probably cause his dismissal by the parish, so he decided to avoid the topic altogether until an opportunity arose. An opportunity did arise during his second year there. While the older parishioners were deeply entrenched in their views, teenagers and young adults were supportive of evolution; some were threatening to leave the Church altogether because of their parish's views about evolution. This forced the pastor to deal with the question publicly, and when he then took a stand in favour of evolution, it was very much welcomed by much of the parish community because of the fact that their youth were leaving over science-religion issues. In general, the older parishioners' minds were not opened by the pastor, but they were opened by their own young people and the firm stand they were willing to take on the issue. What the youth argued was that evolution was true, it was a scientific reality, and that a Church based in truth could not disagree with scientific truth. This reasoned thinking changed parishioners' minds; the pastor later acknowledged that his experiences in seminary discussing evolution from a theological perspective helped him respond appropriately in his own parish.

Other courses in the curriculum can also contribute to development of a strong religion-science perspective. Elsewhere, the relationship between evolution and ecology has been discussed in detail.[6] The link between ecology and evolution has long been recognised in academic circles; many universities have a single department of evolution and ecology, and studies in one discipline generally require coursework in the other. The two topics are usually viewed as two different sides of the issue of organism-environment interaction, with evolution studying the interaction from the perspective of the population over time and ecology examining this same interaction from the perspective of the environment over time. There are numerous examples of how environment affects evolution and how organisms affect environment. Furthermore, evolution and ecology are tightly linked, and separation of the two only leads to an inadequate understanding of nature and an inappropriate orientation toward the environment. Evolution as a concept should be acceptable to Orthodox Christians, particularly in light of the fact that Orthodox generally do not accept a literal understanding of Genesis. Acceptance of evolution, ecology and the ancient faith tradition should all facilitate a more balanced relationship of humanity with the world that surrounds us. Life evolved for the specific conditions one finds on planet Earth, and any breaking of this relationship (by space travel, for example) requires construction of an Earth-mimicking environment to allow for humans to subsist. This link between the evolution and environment is emphasised especially in classes at the Lutheran School of Theology at Chicago where two science-religion classes are designed to complement each other: Epic of Creation (which is a course about evolution) and Future of Creation (which is a course about environment) are each offered for a semester every other year. Most students take these two courses in consecutive years allowing them to better explore these relationships.

Because it is important for future pastors to be aware of environmental attitudes of other religious traditions, courses on the environment also include at least one session that engages different faith traditions. This is usually done as a panel discussion where believers of different faiths (Christian, Jewish, Muslim, Buddhist, Hindu) are invited into the classroom not so much to talk about their faith tradition as a whole but about ecological perspectives from each tradition. What is most interesting about these sessions is that as the speakers engage each other in discussion, their reverence for environment becomes apparent. While the actual faith for each tradition is of course different, the perspectives on human engagement with the natural world are often similar. Thus, ecology and environmental concerns can become a uniting issue among the various faith traditions and can be used as a strong force to fight the greed

---

6 Gayle Woloschak. 'Perspectives on Orthodoxy, Evolution, and Ecology'. in *Toward an Ecology of Transfiguration: Orthodox Christian Perspectives on Environment, Nature, and Creation*, ED by John Chryssavgis and Bruce Folz (NY: Fordham University Press, 2013) pp. 263–75.

and selfishness associated with deniers of global climate change in the world today. His All-Holiness Patriarch Bartholomew has himself taken the message of ecological conservation to other faith traditions in a variety of different situations. Engagement on other science-religion topics may be more challenging because of differences among faith traditions about evolution, bioethics, and others.

Practical aspects of environmental conservatism in faith-based groups are also emphasised throughout the lectures. The interaction with particular faith groups that are working to increase environmental awareness into their communities has been of great value to the pastoral students. For example, a Jewish community located in close proximity to the seminary hosts a vegetable garden on their grounds. Interested members of the congregation tend to the garden on a schedule that they have devised, and vegetable products are shared with a local homeless shelter and among the congregants who work the garden. This use of otherwise 'dead space' for production of crops that can be used by those in need is both 'green' and economical. A trip to visit this gardening congregation has spurred on similar activities from students who went on to pastor parishes of their own in several cases.

The concern that often arises for pastoral students when considering the practical aspects of the community engagement is that working just within their community and 'in the parish garden' may not be enough to create a needed change in climate agenda. To explore possibilities for broader activity, politically engaged faithful are also invited to lecture or participate in discussion panels. Some activists from religious groups who lobby at the state or US capital have spoken to the group about their efforts to change legislation, etc. Equally, several students attend rallies and shared their experiences with the rest of the group. For some of the LSTC students, ability to take this course of action is reassuring and rewarding. For others, the most important message of the course is that mutilating the environment is bad for the body and soul both of parishioners. Therefore, if pastors are care-takers of the parishioners of their flocks, helping their parishioners to care about ecology is important for that alone. As one grows in the spiritual life, care for everything in the world, in nature, all creatures becomes important. Care for the environment becomes an aspect of Christian life and not an optional addendum. His All-Holiness Patriarch Bartholomew has expressed it as follows: 'The fundamental criterion for an ecological ethic is not individualistic or commercial. It is deeply spiritual. For, the root of the environmental crisis lies in human greed and selfishness. What is asked of us is not greater technological skill, but deeper repentance for our wrongful and wasteful ways. What is demanded is a sense of sacrifice, which comes with cost but also brings about fulfillment. Only through such self-denial, through our willingness sometimes to forgo and to say "no" or "enough" will we rediscover our true human place in the universe.'[7] Elsewhere he states: 'It is a qualitative element of our faith that we believe in and accept a Creator who fashioned the world out of love, making and calling it "very good". Tending to and caring for this creation

---

[7] Ecumenical Patriarch Bartholomew, *Encountering the Mystery: Understanding Orthodox Christianity Today* (NY: Doubleday Books, 2008), p. 66.

is not only a political whim or social fashion. It is a divine commandment; it is a religious obligation. It is no less than the will of God that we leave as light a footprint on our environment."[8]

Expanding Courses

So far, this article dealt with courses that are specifically designed to engage science and religion, particularly on the topic of the environment or evolution, however, in a non-Orthodox setting. In the same context, in recent years, new approaches have been designed to better integrate the sciences into the seminary curriculum. Instead of having selected courses designed for exploring environmental science and religion, one idea is to integrate the science into the curriculum itself. Several such programmes have developed in recent years involving scientists in the planning of the curriculum and picking out those places in the course where discussion of science might be warranted. For example, a course examining liturgics might examine portions from Liturgy that point to environmental care. A course on biblical studies might select some texts that can be understood from an evolutionary context. These integrative approaches have been initiated recently, but a few of the examples that have been attempted appear to be quite successful.

One of the topics that has been most challenging has been a discussion of miracles (in classes of Theology, Biblical Studies, Liturgy, and so many others) and how they are understood in a scientific context. These types of courses open up a large range of discussions and permit pastoral students to reflect on questions they themselves face (and that they expect their parishioners to discuss) about how we accept concepts of miracles today. There is value in discussing areas of perceived inconsistency between science and religion.

It should be noted that none of the approaches listed in this article are designed to be strictly for science classes but rather could be used in the context of any trans-disciplinary class between the sciences and the humanities. Certainly for religion and science a broad array of controversial topics could be considered including genetic engineering, ethics of stem cells, use of genetically modified crops, and others. In addition, similar approaches are used in many universities for Science in the Arts classes, Science and the Humanities, and others. Despite this broad interest, the courses themselves are usually limited by the fact that while these humanities disciplines are engaging science, science is not really engaging them. It will take some time for such openness to be developed. All the same, inclusion of scientists in planning the course and perhaps giving a few lectures will help introduce the science as it is and not as others perceive it.

Finally, it is needful to acknowledge that a primarily Orthodox course on science and religion of environment would also need to include activities dedicated to prayer and contemplation of the world, perhaps even meditation in nature, away from the

---

8   Ecumenical Patriarch Bartholomew, *Encountering the Mystery*, p. 114.

classroom. This could provide the students with stores of strength and resilience to the challenges that increasingly face all who have an abiding love for Earth and its creatures.

Road to the Future

Science is becoming a part of every day life in many ways: medical care, technology, environmental issues that are in every day's newspapers, and more. Is science-theology discussion a mandatory requirement for seminary education? Certainly not every pastor can have a fundamental knowledge of scientific disciplines and how they work; one can argue that complexities of science are not well-suited to a seminary education. Nevertheless, pastors should not fear science, and courses that engage science can be useful to help in navigation of difficult and complex questions.

It is clear that science and technology is changing the world at a rapid pace; options that were not available even five years ago are available to parishioners today who are trying to decide how best to use these advances. For example, twenty-five years ago, when a couple was childless the only question they faced was should we adopt or not. About twenty years ago, the choices changed: should we have in vitro fertilization, should we have surrogate mothers? About two years ago, the questions expanded and now include should we have a boy or a girl, what color eyes and hair do we want the baby to have, and so much more. Soon with genetic engineering technology such as CRISPR applied to the eggs or sperm or the early embryos, even more questions will be included in the array of questions facing couples seeking parenthood. It is certain that these reproductive questions will expand to include even new technologies unimaginable today. The priest or pastor who has engaged science-religion issues in seminary may not be as averse to discussion of these topics as the pastor who has had no experience in dealing with these questions. In addition, one approach that has worked successfully in several parishes has been the development of parish pastoral teams that might include physicians, scientists, nurses, and others who can work with the priest to address these complex issues as they arise.

Based on the above discussion, in an age with increasing technological advancement, it is essential to prepare our seminarians for a life in a world that questions science on the one hand but wants to use every technological advance on the other.

One of the examples of a course that has been successful at Lutheran School of Theology is the Advanced Seminar in Religion and Science. This course is open only to senior students (as well as those that obtain special permission) and graduate students. A topic is chosen that is timely and that changes each year to move with the science and the interests of the community. This is a seminar course, so students are expected to make presentations and the faculty leader is permitted to bring in speakers.

Steps toward a program for development of an Orthodox seminary program might include development of tools to be used for course curriculum development, resources that might be used from such a course, and a listing of programs that might be good examples which could serve as a training ground for seminary students.[9] It is also advisable that each seminary have a seminary greening program that might include seminarians and others carrying out gardening projects, composting, water and electrical conservation programs, and others. Resources for successful programs would also be useful, including for example programs for green gardening or bee-keeping from Orthodox monastic communities, many of which have been involved in such work for centuries.

Summary

In summary, this paper points to the need for additional programs in science and religion for Orthodox seminaries where educating the pastors may lead to educating the faithful. Some key points I was hoping to make in this discussion are as follows:

The science-religion discussion requires a broad level of engagement that includes scientists, theologians, pastors, historians, artists, and more.

It needs to be recognized that no one disputant has all of the knowledge of the community they represent. Theologians are not biblical scholars, biologists are not physicists. There are limitations to the engagement.

Each discipline must remain true to itself reflecting the best most current knowledge of the time.

Actual engagement of science by pastoral students is often beneficial in gaining a better understanding of the field.

Environmental concerns can often be a bridge uniting various very different faith traditions.

Not all parishes, parishioners (or pastors for that matter) are at the same level of spiritual development and therefore may approach these issues differently.

There is a link between ecology and evolution at the level of the science; acknowledgement of this can lead to a clearer understanding of the relationship between organisms and their environment.

There is a need for love for the world as a domain of our stewardship that inspires repentance and motivates spiritual and material change.

Seminary curricula should encourage the development and inclusion of science-theology courses for future pastors.

Seminary programs should consider including practical approaches and considerations.

---

[9] An example is the St John Monastery, based near Thessaloniki, that sponsors programs in seed banking, bee keeping, gardening, and others.

KIRILL KOPEIKIN

Science and Theology: The Prospects for Fruitful Mutually Beneficial Cooperation

▼ ABSTRACT The main scientific problems of our time — the hard problem of consciousness, the problem of completing the second quantum revolution and the problem of the 'great silence' of the Universe — can be solved by turning to theological tradition. The fact is that modern physics builds a model of the world through the introduction of numerical values. These values allow us to compare the elements of the real physical world with mathematical objects — numbers. This mapping exists in the process of realising procedures of measurement, which is a study of the relation of one physical element to another. Thus objective science describes the world not as it is 'in itself', but only via the projection of different elements of the world on devices of measurement. The physical theories that result from this practise are thus theories of relations. By virtue of the 'relativity' of mathematical (structural) theories, the physical theories are opened up to substantive interpretations. The uniqueness of the current situation is that today we seem to have reached the limits of structural knowledge. 'Deeper' structures of the Universe that could be accounted for in the formal language of mathematics are not there. Thus it follows that the structures of the Universe that we can observe now are fundamental, ontological. But does this achievement mean that we have reached the limits of knowledge? Not at all! Further movement is possible in the direction of filling the mathematical syntactic structure with semantic existential content. As science originated as the study of the text of the Book of the World, complementary to that of the Bible, then when one searches for the semantic interpretation of the mathematical structures revealed by science it is reasonable to turn to the Bible as a source of meanings for filling formal mathematical structures of the physical world. The problem of interpreting (mathematical) texts is a hermeneutic problem

Kirill Kopeikin • St. Petersburg Theological Academy, St. Petersburg State University

and, therefore, traditionally theological. It is logical to presume that the correspondence between the internal mathematical ('psychical') model and the external physical world is not limited to only the structural similarity but can be extended to the ontological sphere. This will make it possible to create a new conceptual 'two-dimensional' language. Such a language would allow us to describe both the objectivity of the 'external' physical world — quantum world and the world of the Universe as a whole — and the subjectivity of the 'inner' psychical world.

D'où venons nous? Que sommes nous? Où allons nous? — *Where do we come from? What are we? Where are we going?* — such is the name of one of Paul Gauguin's (1848–1903) most famous paintings, one which he considered to be the culmination of his creative work. Indeed, no one can regard such questions with indifference. They are the questions theology seeks to answer. And they are the principle questions set forth by science. These days science, especially natural science, and primarily physics, are supposed to bring about practical results, to create advanced technologies and to open up new prospects for financial investment. But this is not what is most important. Well-known American physicist, Nobel Prize winner Richard Feynman (1918–98) argued that 'Physics is like sex: sure, it may give some practical results, but that's not why we do it'. One of the twentieth-century's leading physicists, Erwin Schrödinger (1887–1961) argued that the principle aim of science can be laid out in the words of the Delphic oracle: Γνῶθι σεαυτόν — *'Know thyself'*.[1] Schrödinger was convinced that none of the Sciences separately, but only all of them together, could resolve the main issue: to answer the question of man's place in the Universe and the meaning of his existence.

Cosmology as the main science

Just such a universal science combining different fields of knowledge, is, in essence, what cosmology is. It's object of investigation is the Universe, *Universum* — 'all that is'. As Karl Popper (1902–99) wrote, all science is essentially cosmology as it sets forth the problem of understanding the world in general, a problem which includes understanding ourselves and our knowledge of the world as entities which are a part of this world.

And here arises the problem, named 'the Great Silence of the Universe', or the Fermi paradox, stated in 1950 by the preeminent physicist Enrico Fermi (1901–95),[2] an American physicist of Italian origin. The so-called Copernican principle states that the Universe has no privileged locations. The Earth is thus not unique and in space

---

1 Erwin Schrödinger, *Science and Humanism* (Cambridge: Cambridge University Press, 1996).
2 Eric M. Jones, *"Where Is Everybody?" An Account of Fermi's Question* (Los Alamos: Los Alamos National Laboratory, 1985).

there should be plenty of star systems and planets with conditions that are similar to ours. This principle has been amply supported by recent discoveries of exoplanets. Thus nothing should prevent the origin of life and emergence of intelligence in other places in the Universe in the same manner as it has done on earth. Since the Universe is about fourteen billion years old, somewhere in space there must exist a technological civilisation far superior to ours; yet, for some reason, it has not been observed. The *SETI (Search for Extra-Terrestrial Intelligence)* project has not found anything that resembles signals from extraterrestrial civilisations after more than 50 years of searching. 'The great silence' of the Universe suggests that there is something fundamentally important about the Universe that we do not understand. 'The great silence of the Universe, the Fermi paradox, is not just a crisis of individual physical theories (like General Relativity or the Grand Unification Theory), it is a crisis of civilisation', so Vladimir Lipunov (Владимир Липунов), Professor of Astrophysics and Stellar Astronomy of the Physics Department at Moscow State University, has argued.[3]

One of those who tried to resolve the Fermi paradox, the Russian Victoriy Schwartzman (Викторий Фавлович Шварцман, 1945–98), was one of the more forward-thinking astrophysicists of his time. When his country was still under the thrall of Soviet materialism he asserted that the greatest challenge lies not in receiving the signal but in understanding that what we have received is a message. From his point of view, the problem of the search for life in the Universe is not merely a technological one that can be solved by increasing the sensitivity of the receiver or the time span of observations. It is, in fact, a cultural problem. He argued that, perhaps we are already seeing what could be called the *signal*, but we cannot interpret it as a message. The thing is that, as Schwartzman noted, the essence of the cultural message is inseparable from the message's form.[4] In cultural studies this fact is formulated in the form of Marshall McLuhan's (1911–98) aphorism '*The medium is the message*'[5]. The message of Gauguin's painting *D'où venons nous? Que sommes nous? Où allons nous?* is not only *who* and *what* is depicted on it but *how exactly* it was done. The message of the Universe to man is inseparable from the form of the message, Schwartzman believed. The identification of this form as having a meaning that is invested in the content of the message is, according to Shwartzman, the most important problem of all human culture. Indeed, only by understanding the message of the Universe, can we understand the world in which we live, and the place that world occupies.

It is noteworthy that when, in 2005, the journal *Science* marked its 125th anniversary with twenty-five questions which were considered the most pertinent for the beginning

---

3 Владимир Липунов, *От Большого Взрыва до Великого Молчания* [*From the Big Bang to the Great Silence*] (Москва: Издательство АСТ, 2018).
4 Викторий Шварцман, 'Поиск внеземных цивилизаций — проблема астрофизики или культуры в целом? [The search for extraterrestrial civilizations — the problem of astrophysics or culture in general?]', *Проблема поиска жизни во Вселенной: Труды Таллинского симпозиума 7–11 дек. 1981 г.* [*The problem of finding life in the Universe: Proceedings of the Tallinn Symposium, 7–11 Dec. 1981*] (Москва, 1986), p. 236 <www.pereplet.ru/text/shwartzman.html>.
5 Marshall McLuhan, *The Medium is the Massage: An Inventory of Effects* (Penguin Books, 1967).

of the third millennium. Characteristically, the first question was *What is the Universe Made of?* and the second, *What is the Biological Basis of Consciousness?*[6] Despite their apparent heterogeneity, these two questions are extremely close to each other.

Indeed, the first question relates to the fact that most of the world is a 'unknown thing'. As it has turned out the 'normal', or baryonic, matter known to us represents less than 5% of the mass of the Universe. The remainder is the so-called 'dark matter' and 'dark energy' about which we know almost nothing. If one stops to consider this it is shameful! Claims that physics and cosmology are exhaustive descriptions of the Universe are questionable when through them we understand less than 5% of reality.

The hard problem of consciousness

The second question relates to the so-called 'hard problem of consciousness', as David Chalmers lightly termed it.[7] Its essence lies in the following: we traditionally understand the world to be made up of the totality of material *bodies*. Yet in the world *of material bodies* there is, in fact, no place *for the psychical*. Indeed, in contrast to objectively existing 'bodies', consciousness is subjective, we *live it*. And it is completely incomprehensible how the subjective could appear in the objective world. Chalmers formulated the main question related to the problem of consciousness in the following manner: Why do objective processes in the brain not 'plunge into darkness' but are 'accompanied' by subjective experience? If the brain could process the incoming information and transform it into action without any subjective experience, then why should subjectivity be needed at all?

Another difficulty is connected with the fact that the psychical, in distinction from the physical, is always *directed* to something *intentionally*. If a physical body simply *exists*, then consciousness is always *about something*: I think about something, I experience something for some reason, that is the cause of my disturbance. But if the brain and neurons are physical bodies how could they generate the subjectivity and intentionality inherent in the human psyche? One of the most influential contemporary American philosophers, John Searle asked: 'How ... can atoms in the void represent anything?'[8]

It is thus clear that we first must answer questions about the nature of the Universe and consciousness so as to answer those most important questions: *Where do we come from? What are we? Where are we going?*

John Searle, considered to be a 'living classic in the philosophy of mind', proposes that the basic orientation of philosophy of mind over the last seventy-five years has been manifestly wrong. In Searle's opinion, Cartesian dualism and materialistic

---

6 Charles Seife, 'What is the Universe Made of?', *Science*, 309 (2005), p. 78; Greg Miller, 'What is the Biological Basis of Consciousness', *Science*, 309 (2005), p. 79.
7 David Chalmers, 'Moving forward on the problem of consciousness', *Journal of Consciousness Studies*, 4, № 1 (1997), pp. 3–46.
8 John Searle, *Minds, Brains and Science* (Cambridge, Massachusetts: Harvard University Press, 1984), p. 16.

monism are equally wrong. Dualism, according to Searle, does not agree with the modern scientific view of the world, whilst materialistic monism, despite its obvious inability to resolve the problem of consciousness, is the most widely held view. Yet this is rather more for reasons of a psychological character. Persistent attempts to solve the problem of consciousness were undertaken in the context of a materialist paradigm, not for scientific but for 'ideological' reasons — fear of the possibility of admitting the reality of 'the psychical' is only one step away from accepting the reality of 'the spiritual'.

Today colossal resources are being devoted to brain research and the 'hard problem' of consciousness. A number of large projects have been launched. Among these must be mentioned the American *BRAIN Initiative*, the European-led *Human Brain Project*, the Japanese *Brain/MINDS*, and the eponymous *China Brain*. But the answer to the question of what consciousness is and how it might be related to brain function has yet to be given. This search is being taken along the path of finding the 'material substrate' of consciousness — a search which, according to Searle and a number of other prominent researchers, is utterly misled. And the cost of failure is very high: expenditures on brain research projects are in the billions of dollars and such false starts are turning out to be very costly for their investors!

I am convinced that describing psychical reality demands a fundamentally new approach — a view 'from the inside' that is typical to theological discourse.

The prominent Russian mathematician, Professor Igor Shafarevich (Игорь Ростиславович Шафаревич, 1929–2017), noted that the question of the possibility of a computer simulation of the brain activity is, in fact, a restatement of the question about the materiality of the Universe.[9] Since the middle of the twentieth century, researchers have been promising that *AI* would be around the corner, 'in the next ten years'. The chronic failure of all these attempts attests to the fact that our materialistic notions about the Universe are patently false. Only by widening the scope of scientific investigation and including theological discourse into its orbit shall we be able to overcome the materialistic 'blinders' that pose to the study of consciousness an objective obstacle.

It is noteworthy that the famous American physicist of Russian origin Andrei Linde (Андрей Дмитриевич Линде) thinks that consciousness may be as fundamental as space, time and matter. Furthermore, the problem of consciousness may be closely connected with the problem of the birth, life and death of the Universe itself.[10]

More than half a century ago, the prominent American mathematician, physicist and Nobel laureate Eugene Wigner (1902–99) noted the close relationship between these two problems — the problems of physical reality and the problem of consciousness. He argued that physics and psychology represent the two most important disciplines

---

9   Игорь Шафаревич, *Один народ, одна страна, и один Бог, и одна Церковь* [*One people, one country, and one God, and one Church*] <https://pravoslavie.ru/4531.html>.
10 Andrei Linde, *Particle Physics And Inflationary Cosmology*, p. 232 <https://arxiv.org/pdf/hep-th/0503203.pdf>.

that together shape a mutually complementary picture of the world. Physics accounts for an objective world external to the perceiving subject, psychology the reality of the internal world. He is convinced that a complete image of the Universe requires that both of these views be in agreement.[11] Wigner hoped that in future physics and psychology would be combined into one deeper discipline, and today we can hope to arrive at the realisation of his aspirations.

Just such a holistic view of the Universe where the objective language for describing the external physical world was organically combined with the subjective language describing internal mental reality was the project of two of the twentieth century's most influential scientists: the physicist and Nobel laureate Wolfgang Pauli (1900–95) and the founder of analytical psychology Carl Gustav Jung (1875–1961). After more than a quarter-century of collaborative research, Jung and Pauli concluded that the physical and psychic are two interrelated properties (two 'aspects') of a single entity lying at the base of the whole of reality.

Adherents to this perspective, called *neutral monism*, include such thinkers as Benedictus de Spinoza (1632–67), William James (1842–1910) and Bertrand Russell (1872–1970), the aforementioned Carl Gustav Jung and Wolfgang Pauli, and contemporary adherents such as John Searle and David Chalmers. Unfortunately, Pauli's untimely death in 1958 prevented him from completing his work with Jung. Today the problematics Jung and Pauli together brought to the fore have been receiving more and more attention.[12] The groundwork they laid may be one of the 'points of growth' in interdisciplinary research programmes in physics, cosmology, psychology and theology.

---

11   Eugene Wigner, 'The Limits of Science', *Proceedings of the American Philosophical Society*, 94 (1950), pp. 422–27.
12   Kalervo Vihtori Laurikainen, *The Message of the Atoms: Essays on Wolfgang Pauli and the Unspeakable* (Heidelberg: Springer 1997); *Atom and Archetype: The Pauli/Jung Letters, 1932–95*, ed. by C. A. Meier and translated by David Roscoe (Princeton, NJ: Princeton University Press, 2001); Suzanne Gieser, *The Innermost Kernel: Depth Psychology and Quantum Physics* (Heidelberg: Springer, 2004); David Lindorff, *Pauli and Jung: The Meeting of Two Great Minds* (Wheaton, IL: Quest Books, 2004); Arthur I. Miller, *Deciphering the Cosmic Number: The Strange Friendship of Wolfgang Pauli and Carl Jung* (New York: Norton, 2009); Harald Atmanspacher and Hans Primas, *Recasting Reality: Wolfgang Pauli's Philosophical Ideas and Contemporary Science* (Heidelberg: Springer, 2009); Charles Paul Enz, *No Time to be Brief: A Scientific Biography of Wolfgang Pauli* (Oxford: Oxford University Press, 2010); Arthur I. Miller, *137: Jung, Pauli, and the Pursuit of a Scientific Obsession* (New York: Norton, 2010); Kirill Kopeikin, 'По следам Юнга и Паули в поисках соприкосновения физического и психического миров' ['In the Footsteps of Jung and Pauli in Search of a Contact Between the Physical and Mental Worlds'], in *Известные и неизвестные открытия XX века* [*Known and Unknown Discoveries of the Twentieth Century*] (St Petersburg: Publishing House of the St Petersburg State University, 2016, pp. 85–97; *The Pauli-Jung conjecture: and its impact today*, ed. by H. Atmanspacher and C. Fucks (Exeter: Imprint Academic, 2014); Massimo Teodorani, *Synchronicité: le rapport entre physique et psyché de Pauli et Jung à Chopra* (Cesena: Macro éditions, 2015); *L'arrière-monde ou l'inconscient neutre: psychologie des profondeurs et physique quantique selon C. G. Jung et W. Pauli*, ed. by Bruno Traversi (Avion: Ed. du Cenacle de France, 2018).

Hermeneutics of the Book of Nature

What sort of language could be built that would be able to organically combine an objective means of describing the physical world and the subjective, personal means of describing psychical reality? Here we can say that the most characteristic feature of the objective language of science comes to our aid. The fact is that modern physics builds a model of the world through the introduction of numerical *values*. These values allow us to compare the elements of the real physical world with mathematical objects — *numbers*. This mapping exists in the process of realising procedures of *measurement*, which is a study of the relation of one physical element to another. Thus objective science describes the world not as it is 'in itself', but only via the *projection* of different elements of the world on devices of measurement. The physical theories that result from this practice are thus *theories of relations*. By virtue of the 'relativity' of mathematical (structural) theories, the physical theories are opened up to substantive *interpretations*.

The 'minimalist' interpretation of classical physics is a materialistic one. Indeed, Kant's careful analysis of the prerequisites of modern European science showed that, from the Modern period onward, the metaphysics of nature has transformed into a *metaphysics of matter*. Until the early twentieth century, the materialistic interpretation of physics had been confirmed. But after the emergence of the theory of relativity and, especially, quantum mechanics, the situation radically changed.

In classical physics the concepts of mass, space, time and force seemed intuitively clear (although thanks to relativity it was found that this is not so). In quantum mechanics the mathematical representation of reality is a wave function or state vector. Despite the tremendous predictive efficiency of quantum mechanics we have absolutely no understanding of the *physical* reality that must correspond to this *mathematical* construct. It is a scandal! Almost a hundred years have passed since the development of quantum mechanics and what it is actually 'about' we still do not know. This was the reason why the leading Russian physicist and the Nobel laureate, Prof. Vitaly Ginzburg (Виталий Лазаревич Гинзбург, 1916–2009) regarded the matter of interpreting nonrelativistic quantum mechanics among the 'three great problems of modern physics'; until these questions are explained 'we can be sure about nothing'.[13]

The uniqueness of the current situation is that today we seem to have reached the limits of structural knowledge. For this there are two confirmations: both theoretical and experimental. The theoretical basis that we have reached the limit of structural knowledge was given by eminent Russian mathematician Professor Ludwig Faddeev (Людвиг Дмитриевич Фаддеев, 1934–2017). He proved that, from a mathematical point of view, the revolutions of quantum mechanics and of the special theory of relativity in physics are deformations of unstable algebraic structures into stable ones

---

13 Vitaly Ginzburg, 'On Superconductivity and Superfluidity (what I have and have not managed to do), as well as on the "physical minimum" at the beginning of the XXI century', *Physics Uspekhi*, 47 (11), (2004), 1155–170 (pp. 1169–170).

with the parameters of deformation $\hbar$ and $1/c^2$. 'Thus we are led to an important conclusion: whereas the change of classical mechanics into the quantum one is fully justified, we have no reasons to predict any change of the latter in the future'[14]. The stability of the mathematical structures of quantum mechanics and the theory of relativity means that equilibrium has been reached and further movement along the former path of searching for deeper and deeper structures is impossible.

The experimental confirmation of the achievement of the limits of structural knowledge is that quantum mechanics testifies to the impossibility of the detecting deeper structures. The eminent Irish physicist John Bell (1928–99) reflecting on the Einstein-Podolsky-Rosen paradox in 1964 wrote of certain inequalities which, if experimentally confirmed, would conclusively decide whether there are or there are not local hidden parameters that are observable[15].

The technical capabilities of the 1960s and 70s did not yet allow for such experiments to be designed. Subsequently, a number of experiments, the most decisive of which was a 1982 test led by the French experimental physicist Alain Aspect, showed a clear violation of Bell's inequalities. This completely unexpected result means that not only are we unable to discover the deeper structure of the Universe due to inadequate technical capabilities or because of a lack of energy — these deeper structures *simply do not exist*.

Famous American physicist Henry Stapp claims that 'Bell's theorem is the deepest discovery of science', and eminent American physicist and philosopher Abner Shimony (1928–2015) asserts: 'The philosophical significance of Bell's Inequalities, in my opinion, is that they permit a near decisive test of those world views which are contrary to that of quantum mechanics. Bell's work made possible, therefore, some near-decisive results in experimental metaphysics'. The winner of the 2009 Templeton Prize, Bernard d'Espagnat (1921–2015), agrees with Shimony that we have seen in the tests of Bell's inequalities 'our first steps in the elaboration of an experimental metaphysics'[16].

The violation of Bell's inequalities means that we have reached the limits of structural knowledge. 'Deeper' structures of the Universe that could be accounted for in the formal language of mathematics are not there. Thus it follows that the structures of the Universe that we can observe now are fundamental, ontological. But does this achievement mean that we have reached the limits of knowledge? Not at all! Further movement is possible in the direction of examining the content of these ontological structures by studying the process of their emergence.

Let me explain. As is well known today, modern science arose in the context of the conception that the Bible is the first Book of God and Nature the second.

---

14 Ludwig Faddeev, 'A Mathematician's View of the Development of Physics', *Proceedings of the 25th Anniversary Conference — Frontiers in Physics, High Technology and Mathematics 31 October — 3 November 1989*, ed. by H. A. Cerdeira, S. O. Lundqvist (Singapore: World Scientific Publishing Co, 1990), pp. 238–46.
15 John Bell, 'On The Einstein — Podolsky — Rosen Paradox', Physics, 1, № 3 (1964), pp. 195–200.
16 Bernard d'Espagnat, 'Toward a Separable "Empirical Reality"?', *Foundations of Physics*, 20, № 10 (1990), p. 1172.

Between them there can be no contradiction as they have been composed by one and the same Author. Furthermore, as one of the founding fathers of modern science, Francis Bacon (1561–1626), argued, study of the Book of Nature can be the key to a deeper understanding of the Bible.

What has research into the second Word of God given us? The principal conclusion of natural science, first formulated by Galileo, is as follows: the Book of Nature is written in the language of mathematics. But most importantly, as Galileo noted, when a person begins to describe the world with the help of mathematics, his knowledge becomes equal to the knowledge of God. It is truly extraordinary! It is mean, that the 'ideal' mathematics gives the most true description of physical reality And that it is mathematics that can give the key to the Bible. But what is mathematics and what is its nature?

Mathematics as a Universal Language

Among the many views on the nature of mathematics, one can identify two extreme positions. The first and, arguably, the most widespread is that mathematics is the result of abstracting from reality. The second view is, rather, the one more typical of working mathematicians: the amazing 'flexibility' of mathematical constructions requires us to propose that they actually exist, but exist in some sort of 'ideal' realm. Unfortunately, neither of these opposing views allow for the explanation of the status of mathematical objects. They also make it impossible to understand the causes of 'the unreasonable effectiveness of mathematics' in describing physical reality.

A sober look at mathematics inevitably leads to the conclusion that mathematical objects exist in our psychic reality, in the human mind. In this sense mathematics is 'subjective' and 'ideal' — in the real physical world there is no mathematics. On the other hand, mathematics is universal in the sense that it is the same for all entities employing it. Indeed, the above mathematical properties apply to all persons regardless of ethnic or religious affiliation. In this sense mathematics is 'objective'. However, mathematics does not exist in the 'head' of those who work with it. It is generated through effort, sometimes great effort. It is logical to presume that the universality and 'objectivity' of mathematics testify to the fact that the (psychical) forces which created mathematical reality are the same in all people.

By 'objectifying' mathematics we alienate it from ourselves and 'deaden' its. But one may try to look at mathematics not just as a static construction that exists outside of time, but to examine the process of its generation in the psyche of the mathematician-creator and thus fill it with a 'living', dynamic, and 'psychical' content.

How would this be possible? Investigating the process by which mathematics is generated in the mind of its creator extremely difficult. The fact of the matter is that we are merged with our psyche, we cannot go beyond its boundaries and regard it from the outside. But we can look at the traces that the dynamics of psychic life leave behind. As has already been said, this is firstly that mathematics is at once 'subjective' (located in psychical reality) and 'objective' (by virtue of its universal application). Secondly this is the sacred texts, the Bible among them. The Bible can and should be viewed not so much as a story about *events*, but as a narrative about the history of mankind's 'internal' world, and thus as story about the nature of the human soul. When the biblical narrative is taken as a cosmological theory or mythological history it actually amounts to a projection of the psyche's archetypal structures. Of course this is the case with all sacred texts. Our appeal to biblical narrative is due to the fact that modern science arose in the context of the European intellectual tradition, a tradition rooted in the biblical worldview.

The Bible begins with the Six Days of Creation, the story of God creating by means of His word out of nothing — *ex nihilo*. If the Bible is a Revelation, than this means that the Creator shows us his view of the Universe. If mankind wants to understand this text, he must attempt to put himself in the position of the creator, *in the image and likeness* of He who made him. Is there something in human experience that can be compared with creation *by the word*, creation *ex nihilo*? Of course, any literary, or poetic creativity is creation by word. But this is yet still creation 'out of something' — out of the accumulation of life experience, emotions, and the like. The only creation familiar to me that takes place 'out of nothing' is, indeed, mathematics!

Admittedly, initially mathematics arose out of certain practices that were, in some sense, 'experimental'. Along the course of this 'experimental' construction of mathematics, ideal mental objects were created. They began to live their own lives, ever striving toward 'pure', ideal knowledge. The 'pure' creation of mathematics sought by the 'perfect' mathematician is a withdrawal from any of the concepts arising from interaction with external reality. In fact, the 'pure creation' of mathematics is synonymous with the creation '*ex nihilo*'.

A mathematician beginning his creation with 'pure' mathematics rejects all the external and turns his own consciousness to the void as it arises in his soul. The very statement of the problem of the awareness of this purity gives birth to the idea of 'nothing' which is no longer 'nothing' but which is a certain 'something', namely the *empty set ∅*. The creation of *the empty set ∅ is out of nothing* indeed is the first act of creation. The French philosopher Alain Badiou emphasises the exclusiveness of this act: in distinction from all other axioms the axiom that attests to the existence of the empty set clearly postulates that its *existence* is the existence of *nothing*[17].

Subsequent acts in the creation of the mathematical universe are not creation out of nothing, but acts built upon previous mathematical constructs. This work is done by the mathematician by acts conceived through his creativity and free will according to certain laws, laws enabled through the structure of the *forces* of his soul. In all likelihood, the nature of these (psychical) forces that create mathematical reality are, as has been noted, the same for all people. Only in this way may one account for how 'subjective' mathematics can be so universal and universally valid.

The mode of action of these forces is described in the language of set theory, which is the foundation of modern mathematics. Thus one may pose the question: to what extent do these forces not only have structure but also content? To answer this question one can compare the acts of creation in the mathematical universe with the dynamics of the Six Days of Creation. We can appeal to an existential reading of the Genesis narrative in the 'mathematical' context of the creation of mathematics

---

17 Alain Badiou, *L'Être et l'Événement* (Paris: Seuil, 1988).

by the word of mathematician-Creator *ex nihilo*. Thus we will be able to fill out the mathematical syntactic structure with semantic existential content and create new conceptual 'two-dimensional' language. Such a language would allow us to describe both the objectivity of the 'external' physical world and the subjectivity of the 'inner' psychical world. I would term such a project *Mind T(h)e(chn)ology*.

The Universe as the ψυχή of God

Let us recall the theological context that gave birth to modern scientific thought: man is created *in the image and likeness* of God the Creator, and therefore able to understand His creation and to build suitable models of reality. It is logical to presume that the correspondence between the internal mathematical ('psychical') model and the external physical world is not limited to only the structural similarity but can be extended to the ontological sphere.

This shocking suggestion finds in itself an unexpected confirmation. The famous American psychologist Donald Hoffman from University of California, Irvine, believes that the reason why the problem of consciousness still defies solution that we are starting off with the wrong premise: we believe that reality is what we see, i.e. it consists of physical 'bodies'. In fact, he argues, what we see is only the 'interface reality' and not reality itself. He maintains that the reason for the failure of neuroscience to explain the nature of human consciousness is that neuroscientists and philosophers have ignored the progress made in fundamental physics. 'And then [neuroscientists] are mystified as to why they don't make progress. They don't avail themselves of the incredible insights and breakthroughs that physics has made. Those insights are out there for us to use'[18].

What sorts of insights regarding the fundamental nature of the Universe occurred in the twentieth century? In 1905 Albert Einstein published the article 'Does the Inertia of a Body Depend on its Energy Content?' There Einstein concludes that the 'mass of a body is the measure of its energy-content', which suggests what is perhaps the most famous formula of all physics: $E_o = mc^2$. If you consider it, the implications of this formula are staggering. Mass, in fact, represents a measure of matter. Being substance, matter exists by itself. Matter and its measurement — mass — is an absolute value. Physics has discovered that matter converts into energy. Energy is a characteristic, not a substance but a *process*. Furthermore, energy relies on a system of references and thus cannot be a characteristic of a substance. Nor can mass be a characteristic of a substance since it is equivalent to energy. Thus all substantial (materialistic) philosophy lies in ruins. That matter (as a substance) does not exist — is the main conclusion that can be drawn from the special theory of relativity!

Quantum mechanics was to become the next colossal breakthrough in our comprehension of the nature of *ultimate reality*. George Greenstein and Arthur Zajonc, authors of the book '*The Quantum Challenge: Modern Research on the Foundations of Quantum Mechanics*', have emphasised that the quantum universe forces upon

---

18   Donald Hoffman, 'Conscious Realism and the Mind-Body Problem', *Mind & Matter*, 6(1) (2008), pp. 87–121.

us a radical revision in our conception of the physical world, a revision which has by no means been achieved[19]. Before it was believed that the whole was made up of 'objectively existing' physical 'bodies' that obeyed immutable natural laws. In examining the universe we uncover the laws that govern these bodies. Indeed we may so 'delicately' observe nature so as to make no disturbances in the system under observation. But in quantum mechanics the situation turned out to be completely different. It is even impossible to 'spy' on the behaviour of a given system when measuring its parameters radically changes its behaviour. This is clearly demonstrated, for example, in delayed-choice experiments. They leave behind the impression that the particles examined are 'conscious' of the fact of their observation, that they have a psychical property. Hoffman, who calls himself a 'conscious realist', makes the same claim. He says that the reality represents the totality of acts of consciousness — something like Leibniz's monadistic universe. And it is not only Hoffman that thinks so. Erwin Schrödinger, Roger Penrose, David Chalmers — all are inclined toward the concept of panpsychism.

Such a strange conclusion can easily be understood in a theological context. As has already been stated, modern science arose on the basis that the world is the Book of God, compliment to the Bible. Yet if the world is the book of the Creator, a book He composed, then what type of ontological reality does it have? What conclusion can we draw in attempting to make sense of contemporary science in the substantive context of its origins, the context of Biblical Revelation? Opening the Bible to the Book of Genesis presents us with God's creation of the world out of nothing though His very Word. In the Niceo-Constantinopolitan Creed, God is called the Creator, Ποιητής, literally, the *Poet* of the Universe. If the world is a text, then *where* does it exist? When Tolstoy composed *War and Peace*, where did his creation come from? Without a doubt, in his internal reality, in the reality of his psyche (ψυχή)!

If we at once are giving logical sense to all that is clear to us thanks to the 'elements' of the *poetry* of the Book of Nature, and we can also recall the theological context from which the formulation of modern science came, then we will have to arrive at an unambiguous conclusion: 'The world is the ψυχή of the Creator', 'For in Him (ἐν αὐτῷ) we live and move and have our being' (Acts 17.28). The Universe is ψυχή of God in this sense that, firstly, the world does not consist of dead 'matter', but a living and logos-endowed fabric of existence, and, secondly, God needs no 'organ' in order to touch the world. He has *immediate* access to it just as we have immediate access to our ψυχή.

The presumption of a psychical nature to being opens the way to resolving the problem of interpreting quantum mechanics as well as to the completion of the 'second quantum revolution', a movement which is extremely relevant in today's world.

Now the EU is launching another project the *Quantum Technology Flagship*.[20] In an attempt not to fall behind America and China, in 2018 it intends to initiate an initiative

---

19 George Greenstein and Arthur Zajonc, *The Quantum Challenge: Modern Research on the Foundation of Quantum Mechanics*, (Jones & Bartlett Publishers, 2005).
20 <https://ec.europa.eu/digital-single-market/en/policies/quantum-technologies#Article>.

in quantum technologies with a billion euros of financing.[21] This could place Europe on the cusp of a 'second quantum revolution' and lead to a radical transformation of the sciences, industry and society. The essence of a 'second quantum revolution' consists in mastering the effects associated with the possibility of manipulating single quantum objects. This should lead to a new technological breakthrough, in particular, the creation of quantum computers, absolutely protected channels of quantum communication, supersensitive quantum sensors, etc. Two years earlier, the *Quantum Europe 2016* conference in Amsterdam[22] adopted the *Quantum Manifesto*.[23] This formulates a general strategy intended to set Europe as the avant-garde of the second quantum revolution.

George Greenstein and Arthur Zajonc, authors of *The Quantum Challenge: Modern Research on the Foundations of Quantum Mechanics*, note that quantum mechanics arose and developed not as a description of *reality*, but as a description of *the results of observations*. This recalls Ptolemy's geocentric system: perfectly explaining the observable movement of the planets from earth, but not the physical reality. Achieving a breakthrough in quantum information technologies, establishing an effective means of quantum cryptography and quantum computers knowing only quantum formalism is about the same as launching an artificial satellite from Earth using the Ptolemaic system. In this connection, the question arises: is the 'Copernican revolution' possible in the microcosm?

I am certain that a 'Copernican revolution' in the world of sub-atomic particles will become possible by resorting to the biblical tradition that presents its view of the 'interior' of being[24]. As already mentioned, this will create a new conceptual 'two-dimensional' language, capable of describing not only the 'external' structure of the Universe, but also its internal dynamics.

The surprisingly deep correspondence of the mathematical ('psychic', 'internal') model of the Universe to the outside world compels us to pose the question not only about the structural, but also about the ontological nature of this correspondence. Remembering the philosophical and theological context in which modern European scientific investigation arose, it is logical to assume that the correspondence between the internal 'psychic' mathematical model and the external physical world is not limited to their structural likeness, but can be extended into the realm of ontology. This allows one to resolve the problem of the interpretation of nonrelativistic quantum mechanics and move from a description of the *results of observations* to a description of *reality itself*. This approach allows us to include psychic reality in the scientific picture of the world and to complete the second quantum revolution. I would term such a project *Quantum T(h)e(chn)ology*.

---

21 <https://www.nature.com/news/europe-s-billion-euro-quantum-project-takes-shape-1.21925>.
22 <https://qutech.nl/quantumeurope/>.
23 <https://qutech.nl/wp-content/uploads/2016/05/93056_Quantum-Manifesto_WEB.pdf>.
24 Kirill Kopeikin, 'The Orthodox Tradition and a Personal View on the Universe "from Within"', *Orthodox Christianity and Modern Science: Tensions, Ambiguities, Potential*, ed. by Vasilios N. Makrides and Gayle E. Woloschak, SOC, 1 (Turnhout, 2019), pp. 237–46.

The Glass Bead Game with the Universe

The presumption of the psychical nature of being opens up the way to resolving the problem of the 'Great Silence of the Universe'. Once we view the Universe as the ψυχή of the Creator, and that we exist as a part of His psyche, we must radically transform the discourse that relates our understanding of the world. The first thing that comes to mind is that the large-scale structure of the universe is remarkably similar to the structure of the brain.

Furthermore, as has already been stated, physical theories are *theories of relations*, which are open to content-full *interpretation*. As science originated as the study of the text of the Book of the World, complementary to that of the Bible, then when one searches for the semantic interpretation of the mathematical structures revealed by science it is reasonable to turn to the Bible as that which lies at the foundation of the three Abrahamic religions — Judaism, Christianity and Islam. The concept of the project *Universal T(h)e(chn)ology* is that one must apply an art interpretation to the fundamental laws of the universe as they are observed from the study of the Book of Nature in the context of the biblical, Abrahamic tradition. This project resembles the *Game* as described by the famous German writer and Nobel laureate Hermann Hesse (1877–1962) in the novel *The Glass Bead Game* (*Das Glasperlenspiel*, 1943). If the fundamental laws of the Universe as observed in science 'speak' in the language of culture (as Carl Gustav Jung and Wolfgang Pauli tried to do in the mid-twentieth century), then scientific theories which have been 'instruments of influence' on the external world will become the means by which the world — and thus, in a sense, the Creator Himself — answers us and thus affects our inner world. This will be the longed-for 'signal from space', the 'language of the stars', of which the *budetlyanin* Velemir Khlebnikov (Велемир Хлебников, 1885–1922) dreamt, one of the brightest representatives of this futurist direction of thought that has been given the name 'Russian cosmism'[25].

A fundamental change in our understanding of the Universe and of our means of interacting with it allows us to resolve yet another vital issue — that of developing new methods of harmonising the human psyche by expanding its resources and enhancing its cognitive capabilities. These days this issue is becoming more and more important owing to ever-increasing psychological burdens, the ever-increasing flow of information, the increase in the number of psychological diseases, and the growth in life expectancy and its attendant risks of neurological disorders. According to assessments of the World Heath Organisation, one out of every four individuals has suffered at least once in their life from a psychological illness. On a yearly basis three hundred million people suffer from depression and eight hundred thousand commit suicide. The annual loss to the global economy owing to mental illness amounts to one trillion US dollars (€860 billion). The development of new methods to aid in the harmonisation of the human psyche will set the groundwork for the effective

---

25 George M. Young, *The Russian Cosmists: The Esoteric Futurism of Nikolai Fedorov and His Followers* (New York: Oxford University Press, 2012).

use of human potential and permit, at least in part, for the resolution of a whole set of these problems.

It seems to me that three of these research projects I have proposed — *Mind T(h)e(chn)ology*, *Quantum T(h)e(chn)ology* and *Universal T(h)e(chn)ology* — are quite able to fit into the contemporary scientific mainstream and can become a 'point of growth' for a renewed, fruitful interaction between theology and science.

ALEXEI NESTERUK

Humanity as the Central Theme of the Dialogue between Theology and Science

▼ ABSTRACT This paper promotes the view that the terms of the dialogue between Orthodox theology and science cannot be symmetric, because the dialogue is hiddenly theologicaly commited because both its terms have origin in human life. The dialogue is treated as representing an open-ended hermeneutic of the human condition. Then a question arises of the value and sense of such a hermeneutics and how the dialogue advances the explication of the mystery of man. The paper demonstrates that unlike classical philosophical and theological anthropology (positive religion), the advance in the dialogue initiates a new approach to the explication of the human condition based in the idea of self-affectivity of life, which has explicitly theological connotations. Thus the dialogue between theology and science is intrinsically maintained within a certain theological obviousness related to the fact of human life.

Introduction

This paper is the continuation and development of my approach to the dialogue (mediation) between Christian Orthodox theology and modern science presented in previous contributions to the SOW volumes.[1] Here is the summary of these discussions.

---

[1] A. Nesteruk, Philosophical Foundations of Mediation/Dialogue between (Orthodox) Theology and Science. In *Orthodox theology and Modern Science: Tensions, Ambiguities, Potential*. Ed. by V. Makrides and G. Woloschak (Brepols Publishers, 2009), pp. 97–121; A. Nesteruk, The Dialogue between Theology and Science in View of an Irreducible Ambiguity in Hermeneutics of the Subject. In *Orthodox Chjristianity and Modern Science: Theological, Philosophical, Scientific and Historical Aspects of the Dialogue*. Ed. by C. Knight and A. V. Nesteruk (Brepols Publishers, 2021), pp. 73-93.

Alexei Nesteruk • University of Portsmouth

Orthodox Christianity and Modern Science: Past, Present and Future, ed. by Kostas Tampakis and Haralambos Ventis, SOC, 3 (Turnhout, 2022), pp. 147–166.
© BREPOLS PUBLISHERS   10.1484/M.SOC-EB.5.130958

1) The dialogue between theology and science must rely on a rigorous philosophical demarcation between theology and science, determining the spheres of experience proper for use by both theology and science, so that the objectives of bringing them into correlation can only be stated after such a demarcation has been effected. We proposed the philosophical argument that the basis of the difference between the *givens* of experience of either of the world (in science) or the Divine (in theology), lies in the phenomenality of these *givens*. In the sciences these *givens* are related to physical substance and biological formations, making possible the representation of experience in the phenomenality of objects, whereas in theology one implies the *givens* within the phenomenality of events, that is the *modi* of phenomenality originating in particular concerns of subjectivity related either to its embodiment in the material environment, or to the foundations of its own contingent facticity. The essence of events, as a breaking into being of that which is beyond the worldly causality and that which is metaphysically impossible, is that they predetermine and redefine all possibilities of existents and it is in this sense that events can be assigned a 'primary' meta-ontological status. The more a phenomenon takes place in its phenomenality as an event, the more it doubts its metaphysical modus of being, for its sheer possibility follows from its metaphysically understood impossibility. Speaking of events relevant to theology one implies such events as creation of the world out of nothing, the Incarnation of the Word-Logos of God in flesh, the Resurrection etc. These events resist the possibility of their non-contradictory comprehension (in a metaphysical sense) preventing the formulation of their identity status (on the ground of the principle of contradiction), that is, in different words, they challenge classical ontology and its definition of being. The phenomenon of man related to every human person has a similar status of events. The same can be said about the dialogue between theology and science. Indeed, the dialogue between science and theology does not have any metaphysical necessity but acquires its specific concreteness in the events of hypostatic life incorporating reason and free will that cannot be deduced on the grounds of worldly causality and ontology. We advocate the view that the dialogue between theology and science represents an event-like phenomenon related to life's self-affective manifestation (expressed, for example philosophically, through the paradox of subjectivity[2]). Correspondingly, the interpretation of the dialogue demands a new philosophy that deals with the phenomenon of man understood as an event of life having a 'meta-ontological' status, blessing and justifying the possibility of a philosophical and scientific knowledge of the world, as well as the facticity of theology itself.

The immediacy of the *given* in theology understood as communion,[3] entails that this theology cannot acquire a metaphysical form (that is a form conditioned by ontological considerations), thus it demands the extension of philosophy beyond

---

2   See A. Nesteruk, *The Sense of the Universe. Philosophical Explication of Theological Commitment in Cosmology* (Minneapolis: Fortress Press, 2015), pp. 136–61.
3   See e.g. A. Nesteruk, *Light from the East: Theology, Science and the Eastern Orthodox Tradition* (Minneapolis: Fortress Press, 2003).

metaphysics. Philosophy has to incorporate into its scope the *givens* originating from such aspects of the human experience, that is such phenomena as birth, love to the other, the self-affectivity by one's own flesh and hence by the flesh of the universe, the perception of events of communion etc., that is, those *givens* which cannot be presented in the phenomenality of objects. These phenomena, by evading the rubrics of the metaphysical and transcendental description, cannot receive any straightforward scientific interpretation. However, if one needs to relate (hermeneutically) these phenomena to those ones which are described by the sciences, one has at least to attempt to apprehend them philosophically. Here theology constitutes a challenge for philosophy: the latter, under the condition that the *givens* of communion are taken as a new form of rationality and knowledge, must be extended beyond its traditional metaphysical and transcendental scope. Such an extension of philosophy brings it to a purely empirical sphere, by disregarding a basic transcendental question of what can be known and what cannot (that is a priori conditions of knowledge). By being empirical because of its *dependence on the transcendent*, theology of communion precedes philosophy by formulating new challenges for philosophy in the conditions when the metaphysical and transcendental matrix of thinking cannot be employed anymore. It is in this sense that one can talk of a rationality of theology (which is beyond metaphysics and transcendental delimiters) in a more complicated sense than that of philosophy. The same can be said of theology in its 'dialogue' (mediation) with the special scientific disciplines: theology points out that there is the transcendent foundation of the contingent facticity of the human world (constituted by the sciences), whose presence is 'sensed' as an incredible unknowability of the world, but not in the sense of a lack of knowledge or time to apprehend it, but in the sense of an intuitive excess of the universe in any instant of human life, where this life reveals itself as a 'bedazzling event' of presence of light of the *Life* from the Word (the Word Who was with God and Who was God). By asserting that theology 'precedes' philosophy and hence philosophical rationality in the sciences we admit that the relation between theology and science cannot be symmetric, so that the 'dialogue' must not be understood as a dialogue between two independent human activities. The 'primacy' of theology implies that the 'interaction' between theology and science (effected in the 'dialogue') is theological *per se* so that the terms of this 'interaction' are not independent parts of the pre-existent existential relationship between them. If theology, by the manner of its inherence in the fact of the human existence, is intrinsically present in any philosophical and scientific insights on the world and life, one can claim that all scientific activity is imbued with theology, that is, there is a hidden *theological commitment* which pertains to philosophy and science.

2) Since both theology and science originate in one and the same human phenomenon, the 'dialogue' between them can be understood as an attempt to maintain an existential equilibrium between two attitudes to the human existence, expressed by philosophers in numerous ways under the generic name of the paradox of subjectivity. The duality in the hermeneutics of the subject[4] expressed

---

4   See Nesteruk, 'Philosophical Foundations of Mediation/Dialogue between (Orthodox) Theology and Science'.

in this paradox and which is transparent in the dialogue between theology and science, receives its elucidation from the basic aspect of man's existence understood theologically as its creaturehood: man exists physically through communion with God by the fact of his createdness, but he does not 'possess' himself entirely in the world because the conditions of *communion through grace*, that is the conditions of salvation for eternity, are not part of the world.[5] Indeed, by detecting his ambivalent position in the world in the paradox of subjectivity, man discovers himself in the conditions of incapacity of understanding the contingent facticity of such a paradox as a characteristic descriptor and delimiter of his embodied consciousness. Through attempts to find a metaphysical ground for himself, man instead produces an infinite hermeneutics of the predicament of his duality thus sensing that any specific and historically concrete means of enquiry into the sense of himself by himself cannot be justified, so that man remains unknowable to himself. Here, an inerasable Divine image in man invokes the latter to seek for God's help and thus following that God, who once descended in the world to teach man about his creaturehood in order to be deified. Theology encounters the sciences (and philosophy) in order to release man from an intellectual impasse of unknowability and to invite him to learn (from his archetype in Christ) that in spite of his creaturehood, he remains in communion and has a potential to achieve the union with God.

3) Since the paradox of subjectivity reflects a particular way of articulating man's unknowability by himself, the dialogue between theology and science (aiming to 'resolve' the paradox) represents an open-ended hermeneutics of the human condition with a purpose of explicating this condition. Since the riddle of this unknowability cannot be resolved in terms of metaphysical concepts, the dialogue between science and theology cannot hope to achieve anyl 'reconciliation' of theology and science which would imply a modification of the human condition. The moral tension between man's created condition in flesh and its Divine image, together with the capacity of receiving grace of deification, retains the dialogue active and alive always and forever, just confirming a simple existential truth that both — science and theology — originate in one and the same man, created in communion with God, but living in a moral tension between the sense of its created finitude and longing for the unconditional and the infinite.

The Phenomenological Reversal in the Attitude to the Dialogue between Theology and Science

The next question which one must discuss is: what is the goal of an open-ended hermeneutics of the human condition undertaken in the dialogue between theology and science? More precisely: a) where does the necessity (if such exists) for such a dialogue follow from?; b) what is the value of this dialogue? The first question attempts to tackle an alternative: either the dialogue is a contingent happening in the history

---

5   J. Zizioulas, *Communion and Otherness* (London: T&T Clark, 2006).

of humanity and hence does not have any deep ontological foundation (there is no necessity for such a dialogue in order to survive physically), or, alternatively, the dialogue is the result of some hidden propensity in the human condition making it inevitable and hence necessarily subordinated to the logic of the human affairs. If the dialogue is a contingent happening in history, the question about its value and purpose has no philosophical sense. If the situation is opposite and the dialogue pertains to the human condition, one has then to explicate what the value and purpose of such a dialogue is in the context of the explication of the human condition philosophically. Invoking the idea of purpose, it must not imply such a teleology when the achievement of the purpose (goal) stops the whole project antecedently leading to this purpose. Rather, in line with Kant's idea of formal purposefulness[6], one speaks of purpose as a regulative ideal for the dialogue to take place at all without formulating the purpose as a 'material' end as if, for example, theology and science would be reconciled. If we assert the open-endness of the dialogue as a hermeneutics of the human condition, this implies, by definition, that there is no end in this activity of mediation between theology and science as soon as man exists. In this case the *telos* of the dialogue is not that which could be described as a final state in the ongoing mediation between theology and science leading their interaction to the standstill. In view of this the underlying motivation of the dialogue is the enquiry into man's sense of itself, understanding in advance that the *telos* of this dialogue (that is answering the perennial question 'What is man?') cannot be achieved at any stage of man's historical development. Such a vision of the sense of the dialogue retains a basic puzzle: what is the ultimate foundation for the dialogue, that is, what is the ultimate foundation of that subject who runs the dialogue and produces the hermeneutics of its own condition? Saying it differently, the very hermeneutics of the human condition is taking place in the conditions of unknowability of the contingent facticity of this condition and its hermeneutics. In this sense, even if one introduced the *givens* of theology and religious experience into the scope of one's rationality, so that human beings compare it with the natural sciences' stance on the sense of humanity, the basic philosophical question 'What is man?' (what is that immediate centre of the *givenness*, that is of disclosure and manifestation of life and the reality of the universe) remains unanswered.

Since the hermeneutics of the human condition involves both theology and science, or, to put it more accurately, the immediate conscious experience of the mystery of life and createdness on the one side, and physical and biological embodied existence, supplemented by theoretical models of life and the universe, on the other side, such a hermeneutics has already implied that the *givens* of theology, as the *givens* of the 'rational' apprehension of human existence, are present, so that the dialogue and corresponding hermeneutics cannot be conducted from an 'outside' position, surpassing both theology, philosophy and science. Correspondingly, since theology is present in the dialogue as an already given fact, to say that the dialogue imbued with theology is biased, that is relevant only to believers, would be unwise and naïve,

---

6   I. Kant, *Critique of Judgment*, § 10.

because the contingent facticity of the dialogue depends on the facticity of humanity, that is forming such a realm of experience which cannot be disentangled from the living presence of humanity as a primary sense-forming event. In this sense the dialogue between theology and science not only provides one with the hermeneutics of the human condition, but, first of all, it manifests life of humanity understood in an absolute sense as existence *par excellence*. Sceptics and naturalists, apologists of the physical reductionism pretend to consider the human phenomenon in the phenomenality of objects by losing the insight that anyone who enquires into the sense of this phenomenon and the sense of the dialogue already subsists in this life.

The oblivion of this inward presence of life, removing the predicament of a human person as mediating between the poles of the finite and infinite, does not allow one to understand that it is this mediation as the propensity of life in general that makes it possible to produce the synthesis of the object which is both a matter of a scientific discourse and immediately experienced existence, articulated meaning and primordial *givens*.[7] At the same time, on its noetic pole, the dialogue between theology and science, as the mediation between the infinite and the finite, represents such a practical synthesis of the person, who is at once an existent (in rubrics of the worldly) and the end (the goal for the worldly realm to be articulated by man), who realises the scale of disproportion with the universe and thus the originary fragility of human reality[8] (expressed through the paradox of subjectivity).

One term of the paradox asserts that man is a natural result of the universe's evolution according to physical causation. The second term asserts freedom in man who is capable, because of this freedom, of synthesising all aspects of knowledge of the universe and positioning himself above nature, that is above physical causation. Man unconsciously (that is in a non-intentional consciousness) performs an instantaneous synthesis of the past and present of the universe, that synthesis which *de facto* manifests to man himself his presence in the universe. The universe precedes him and continues to permeate him as if the planet Earth, the solar system, Milky Way and the entire universe were the inorganic body of his individual consciousness and transcendental ego. Being a part, man unknowingly (unconsciously) contains the whole universe in the same way as he is not aware of his tissues, muscles and blood (unless he is wounded and bleeding). The material whole, the universe is inside man even if he is not aware of it. In view of this, the original ego which experiences the paradox of subjectivity is simultaneously present in three ways: 1) as an actual and immediate presence taken at the beginning as the ground of any articulation; 2) through the indefinite cosmic, geological and historical past which constantly operates unconsciously, but which in some circumstances becomes to be known as real; 3) through the anticipation of the future by unfolding the sense of its own past as humanity's infinite task. The human fragility is exactly here: the mystery of the ambivalence between a uniquely functioning ego and belonging to the universal intersubjectivity, between the split in intentionalities directed to the world and to

---

[7] P. Ricoeur, *Anthropology* (Malden, MA: Polity Press, 2016), p. 197.
[8] P. Ricoeur, *Anthropology*, p. 197.

the sense of life, between being the internal world (part of the world) in the external whole, and vice-versa, containing the world, that is being the external world, remains unsolved. It seems that to overcome the formulated philosophical impasse one has to invoke some ideas of the trans-empirical and even trans-worldly dimension of human existence.

Edmund Husserl, when he mentions the paradox in his *Crisis*[9], is aware that the paradox can be 'resolved' through an appeal either to metaphysics or positive religion. For phenomenology both ways are unacceptable and he formulates its task: 'For the philosopher ... the juxtaposition "subjectivity *in* the world as object" and at the same time "conscious subject *for* the world", contain a necessary theoretical question, that of understanding how this is possible. The *epoché* (phenomenological reduction), in giving us the attitude above the subject-object correlation which belongs to the world ... leads us to recognise, in self-reflection, that the world that exists for us, that is our world in its being and being-such, takes its ontic meaning entirely from our intentional life.'[10] If 'I' and the world are considered as intentional immanence, they cannot be isolated into separate material or spiritual being of their own. The subject transforms the world into the phenomenon insofar it detects the world's essential truths. Intentionality constitutes the truth of the world and history as this happens in the sciences by departing from actual concrete man. Then the paradox of subjectivity becomes the contradiction between what *is* (but has no meaning), and that which reveals and will become the meaning of that which has been and will be. As agents of intentional operations we are not mere object-men, but rather operative and active subjects constituting the meaning of the world consciously or unconsciously. In this case the original ego can either be an actual human individuum, or unconscious presence within it of the past of the whole physical universe. Since actual humanity longs for its self-constitution through the explication of its own sense as true and having meaning, the goal of such a constitution is transcendental intersubjectivity while it reveals itself in distinct material human beings. Every particular man becomes an objectification of the transcendental ego as that intentional tension (caught in the paradox) that lives in him. The functioning of ego is unique because it is present in every subject which is simultaneously transcendental intersubjectivity. It is in this sense that when the paradox is formulated one starts from the ego in the first person and then proceeds to the intersubjective constitution of the world and man himself. Husserl writes: '... each transcendental "I" within intersubjectivity (constituting the world ...) must necessarily be constituted in the world as a human being; in other words, that each human being "bears within himself a transcendental "I".'[11] Thus the paradox is the unceasing movement of subjectivity between two indicated poles, that is, an open-ended hermeneutics of the human condition as a dialogue between the egocentric presence in himself and intersubjectively constituted decentred world in entirety of its parts, present and future. The movement between the hermeneutic

---

9   E. Husserl, *Crisis of the European Sciences* (Evanston: Northwestern University Press, 1970), p. 178.
10 E. Husserl, *Crisis of the European Sciences*, pp. 180–81.
11 E. Husserl, *Crisis of the European Sciences*, p. 186.

of man as related to its empirical incarnation in rubrics of space and time on the one hand, and the hermeneutic of man as a particular realisation of transcendental subjectivity which cannot be presented in the phenomenality of objects (and hence has roots in the world of freedom), forms that teleological inevitability in the human condition through which one attempts to formulate the sense of the human existence as its infinite task. Being intrinsically teleological in a formal sense[12], the human condition remains inexplicable for man himself. It is because of this that philosophy, in order to overcome its impasse in answering the question 'What is man?', has to either invoke theology, or to change itself in order to appropriate the mystery of the human ambivalent existence as the *given* to which neither the ideas of metaphysics or positive religions apply. This means that it is this mystery that must initiate a philosophical research in such a way that does not resolve this mystery but advances an explication of its sense, and hence indirectly constitutes the sense of humanity. The dialogue between theology and science — an open-ended hermeneutics of man standing at the crossroads of the world and that transcendental foundation which makes humans able to articulate the world intersubjectively — thus contributes to the constitution of the sense of humanity.

The major fact of the human experience is that humanity can articulate things radically beyond its macroscopic life-world. By articulating the universe from micro-scales of its quantum proto-state to the scales of the whole visible cosmos, creating schematic images of the universe, human beings transcend not so much the macroscopic conditions of their embodiment on Earth, but rather the epistemological limits of their practical life. The universe as a whole, as well as many objects from the unseen realm, are posited by humanity as belonging to the intelligible domain, that is, as ideas. This cognitive capacity of abstracting from empirical reality cannot as such be explained by means of physics and biology: one cannot give any deduction of how the twenty centimetres of the physical brain, subordinated to the physical laws, generate a conscious capacity to transcend the scales of its physical space and time in order to produce an 'instantaneous' synthesis of the universe. The contingent facticity of both, the empirical world, as well as that of the noetic cosmos of ideas, remains unaccounted for through human knowledge which has to satisfy itself with the sheer *givenness* of the latter. Thus there is another empirical fact that human beings mimic the composite structure of the whole realm of existence, the physical and intelligible. The paradox of subjectivity expresses this fact. Then, if the predicament of the paradox reflects the basic structure of being, any attempted resolution of the paradox, which would aim to resolve the problem of the human condition, would imply the resolution of the mystery of the dual structure of all being. Coming to this point and referring to the philosophers of the past, one could suspect that this perennial problem could put an end to any further philosophising. For to enquire into the sense of being from a particular contingent position in it would only demonstrate an unrestrained ambition of the human intellect which must be disciplined through an exercise of humility reminding this humanity of how transient

---

12 See our reference above to Kant's *Critique of Judgement*.

and fragile its existence is. Indeed, if human nature resembles the dual nature of the universe making potentially possible its instantaneous synthesis in every particular person (since this synthesis includes the synthesis of this person itself), one cannot extract this person from the universe and 'look' at it as if the universe would be an external object. This means that all philosophical and theological methods based on the natural attitude (in a phenomenological sense) will fail at dealing with grasping the ultimate sense of human persons. The required change of attitude will mean the radical inversion of the problem of the human condition (and hence the sense of the dialogue between theology and science), by stopping any attempts of its philosophical and theological resolution once and forever.[13] But this will require, in order to shed light on the mystery of the human existence, either to adhere to a theological narrative, historically inhered in the Bible, or, alternatively, to make an inversion in answering the question 'What is man?' by interpreting this very question and the open-ended sequence of possible responses to it as constitutive for the phenomenon of humanity.

Thus if the phenomenon of man is considered as lying in the foundation of the contingent facticity of the dialogue between theology and science, the goal and value of this dialogue can only be explicated through further insights into the perennial question 'What is man?' There are two possible ways of formulating such an explication:

1) A vast theological hermeneutics (positive religion in Husserl's sense) of the sense of human freedom and rationality as originating in the 'image of God'. In this case the 'resolution' of the paradox of subjectivity, as well as the 'reconciliation' of science and theology could be treated as biased on the grounds of the conditions of faith which deviate from the conventional delimiters of experience and knowledge of objects. In other words, such a 'resolution' of the paradox (as well the stance on the dialogue between theology and science) would be a priori theologically committed simply because the philosophical mediation between theology and science would be based on the *givens* of theology. Here all examples of theological anthropology would do, however one should remember that all models of humanity are constructed in the natural attitude as if one object (man) depends on another metaphysical foundation (God).

2) The second option is linked to the overcoming of the natural attitude with respect to the phenomenon of man by starting with the problem of the facticity of consciousness as the irreducibility of communion with God where the notions 'consciousness' and 'God' effectively become synonymous. Here the discourse changes its direction towards treating the phenomenon of humanity as a saturated phenomenon, whose metaphysical tackling becomes impossible whereas its event-like phenomenality necessitates the appeal to theology in a radical sense, by linking the very essence of humanity to communion with God as self-affective Life.

---

13 According to Karl Jaspers. 'We cannot exhaust man's being in knowledge of him, we can experience it only in the primal source of our thought and action. Man is fundamentally more than he can know about himself K. Jaspers, *Ways to Wisdom* (New Haven: Yale University Press, 1954), p. 63.

It is the second way of explicating the sense of the question 'What is man?' that is advocated by us (employing some ideas from a phenomenological philosophy oriented towards theology).

The Phenomenon of Man Through the Self-Affectivity of Life

For a sceptical scientist or for an atheist, as well as for a secular phenomenological philosopher it would be problematic to accept that the truth of man has its foundation in God, for any reference to the Divine would imply transcendence, principally impossible in science and prohibited by phenomenology: 'God' as a transcendent reference must be reduced, so that any judgement about it ontological status is suspended.[14] However a theologically insightful mind would press a point that the very reduction as well as the functioning of consciousness would be impossible at all if the reference to the source of its contingent facticity would be eidetically removed. One could suspect here a return to metaphysics postulating a certain ground of the facticity of consciousness through a relation God-man. However, one can avoid such a leap towards metaphysics by claiming that the *sheer manifestation of consciousness as its self-affectivity* is itself a different expression of that which humanity names God. What is asserted is that any hypothetical (phenomenological) reduction of God in consciousness would imply the cessation of functioning of consciousness itself, that is the cessation of the human phenomenon. It is this impossibility of a reduction of God in all conscious human activity, including the dialogue between theology and science, that explicates the sense of that which we call philosophically 'theological commitment.'

One may give a comment on the sense of that which is implied in 'theological commitment'. According to Husserl the invocation of the notion of God implied transcendence with respect to consciousness itself, so that Husserl's next step was to *reduce* the thus affirmed God and to remove the subject of the Divine from the phenomenological project. However, as was admitted by later phenomenological thinkers, the major problem with such a procedure is that it does not discern between God as a mental construction which is subject to any possible operation of consciousness, such as reduction, for example, and the living God of faith whose presence in consciousness is exactly that principle which makes this consciousness possible at all and whose suspension leads to the cessation of consciousness creating thus an existential contradiction. Jean-Luc Marion writes in this respect: 'Husserl submits what he names "God" to the reduction only in so far as he defines it by transcendence (and insofar as he compares this particular transcendence with that, in fact quite different, of the object in the natural attitude); and yet in Revelation *theo*-logy, God is likewise, indeed especially, characterised by *radical immanence to*

---

14 One can point to Husserl, who in his *Ideas I* (§ 58) subjected God to reduction, bracketing it and depriving it of any trans-conscious status (E. Husserl, *Ideas Pertaining to a Pure Phenomenology and to a Phenomenological Philosophy. First Book* (Dordrecht: Kluwer Academic Publishers, 1998)).

consciousness, and in this sense would be confirmed by a reduction.'[15] Thus the theological commitment is the position which, while admitting the possibility of a phenomenological reduction of any particular object of knowledge, refuses any reduction of God, placing God in the foundation of that consciousness which is responsible for theology, philosophy and science.

What follows from this line of thought is that a new theological turn in modern phenomenology points towards a possibility of understanding God as a principle of existence of consciousness, conscious life and hence of the world as articulated by intelligent beings. God and life become inseparable through conscious life's self-affectivity. By introducing self-affectivity as the principle of Divine manifestation Michel Henry, de facto, extends this principle to human life. According to him: 'The concept of self-affection as life's essence implies its acosmic character, the fact that being affected by nothing other, nothing external or radically foreign to the world, it comes about in itself in the absolute sufficiency of its radical interiority — experiencing only itself, being affected only by itself, prior to any possible world and independently of it.'[16] However, unlike God, human beings experience their own self-affectivity without being able to understand its factual presence as well as the foundation of this facticity. Here the formulated human predicament effectively provides a dynamic 'definition' of man: "As far as I am me, I affect myself; I am myself the affected and what affects it, myself the "subject" of this affection and its content. I experience myself, and constantly, in that, the fact of experiencing myself constitutes my "Me". But I have not brought myself into this condition of experiencing myself. I am myself, but I myself have no part in this "being-myself": I experience myself without being the source of this experience. I am given to myself without this givenness arising from me in any way. I affect myself, and thus I self-affect myself — that is, it's me who is affected and I am so by myself, in the sense that the content that affects me is still me — and not something else, such as the affection felt, touched, willed, desired, thought, and so forth. But this self-affection that defines my essence is not my doing. And thus I do not affect myself absolutely, but, precisely put, I am and I find myself self-affected.'[17]

By invoking a theological terminology, human self-affectivity is hypostatic (personal), but enhypostasised not by man himself. Every man comes into existence in the already enhypostasised condition. The source of this enhypostasisation is the acosmic self-affective life itself, named by God.

Leaving aside theological elucidations of how to describe that agency which enhypostasises man's self-affectivity in the framework of positive religions, the philosophical question remains as to how express this givenness of self-affectivity

---

15 J.-L. Marion, *Being Given. Toward a Phenomenology of Givenness* (Stanford: Stanford University Press, 2002), 242–43 (see also a footnote 4 at p. 343).
16 M. Henry, *I am the Truth. Toward a Philosophy of Christianity* (Stanford: Stanford University Press, 2003), p. 105.
17 M. Henry, *I am the Truth*, p. 107.

to man himself. What is implied here is a phenomenological description of those phenomena that are more immediate and close to man's existence, those phenomena that exclude any a priori positioning of them in rubrics of the discursive capacity of reason. First of all one refers to the self-affectivity of the body by the body, that is the sense of flesh as a mediator between life in the body and the surrounding world. To be in a body is to be affected by that physical environment where such a body functions. In this sense to experience self-affectivity of life through a body means to experience self-affectivity of life through belonging to the whole universe. The paradox of human subjectivity receives its new formulation as the perception of self-affectivity by the world (as belonging to it and the impossibility of existing without it), which proceeds from the originary self-affectivity of the fact of living. As man's existence is affected by the worldly realities through the body, the sciences are explicating how this happens by articulating the physical conditions of the very possibility of bodily self-affectivity. The sciences articulate the conditions of the facticity of the self-affectivity of man in physical terms without explaining the contingent facticity of these conditions themselves (which remain an intrinsic part of the self-affectivity of the acosmic life incarnated in the matter of the world). Creation of the world can also receive its new interpretation as a modus of the self-affectivity of God (as life) in its outward expression as creation of the world. Correspondingly, humanity is involved in this self-affectivity through being created by God, as well as through His incarnation in flesh.

The incarnation of God in human flesh created by this God, manifests that God is also self-affected by that which he has created, that is by the flesh of the world. That which is created by God enters in the condition of self-affectivity of God because God descended into the world becoming the incarnate Christ. This 'second-stage' self-affectivity of God by its own flesh originates in the 'initial' self-affectivity of God as Life expressed outwardly in Life's creation of the world out of itself. In this context the world can be treated as the manifestation of the self-affectivity of God as Life, confirmed through the affectivity of the incarnate God by the conditions of the world (birth of Jesus, Christ's teaching, his suffering and death on the Cross). Being subjected to the conditions of flesh which was created by the Logos, Christ the Logos in flesh was affected by the conditions of his own creation. And this is the self-affectivity of God the incarnate which plays an archetypical role in understanding the self-affectivity of human life.

On the one hand Christ as fully human, was affected by the cosmological and geographical conditions in space, ecological and biological specificity, by historical circumstances and by being surrounded by contingent people. But all these so to speak material conditions were ultimately imposed on Jesus Christ by Himself, being the Word-Logos, who predisposed fully human Jesus Christ to these conditions through creating the world. But if the world was created as the outward expression of the initial self-affectivity of God-Creator, this world must have some inherent signs of this self-affectivity. For Christ this self-affectivity can be expressed through the paradox of the Incarnation. On the one hand, being in human flesh in one particular location in the universe, which is rather special for the Incarnation to take place, Christ as a human being is affected by the world. On the other hand, being the Creator of the universe, Christ-Logos is present (theogenically) everywhere in the universe through the fact that all pieces and moments of the universe comprise their unity as being created by the Christ-Logos (the self-affectivity of God has an acosmic character). Being locally on Earth, Christ is affected by Himself, for his human existence on Earth is sustained only because the whole structure of the universe is adjusted to the fact of existence of human life on Earth. The integrity and unity of the universe is thus locally manifested on earth as a theological-topological isomorphism between the whole universe and Earth, as an element of the instantaneous synthesis of the universe as Christ's self-affectivity through creation of this universe. This self-affectivity of the Logos-Christ does not require any reference to the ultimate cause of this self-affectivity, because it is self-generated, so to speak, self-caused. Correspondingly in Christ, who as fully human experienced his human-self affectivity, but in the Ipseity of the hypostasis of the Logos, this self-affectivity of Christ-man and Christ-God do coincide. The paradox of the Incarnation, cascading towards the paradox of human subjectivity in Christ, did not cause in him any anxiety and despair in understanding the sense of the human, because it is the Logos-Christ who created his own humanity through his Divine self-affectivity.

The tension between the specific spatial location of the human Christ and his hypostatic presence everywhere in the universe as God was a particular manifestation of the Logos-Christ's self-affectivity, expressed not only in terms of space, but in terms of the initial conditions of the universe and physical laws which were responsible for providing the conditions on Earth in which the body of the Incarnate Logos (as well as his mother) became possible. The same conditions are necessary for the existence of other human beings. Thus the self-affectivity of God expressed through his Incarnation is ultimately responsible for the existence of all of humanity. By the same token one can claim that for us, humans, the phenomenon of humanity that experiences the paradox of subjectivity becomes an expression of self-affectivity as an inherent characteristic of the living condition of being contingent upon the self-affectivity of acosmic Life, and it is this human self-affectivity that becomes a source of anxiety and moral tension between the finite physical life and potentially infinite consciousness encoded in the dialogue between theology and science, so that this dialogue itself becomes an outward expression of this self-affectivity.

The self-affectivity of man experienced through the paradox of subjectivity can be explicated through the twofold perception of space. Correspondingly the terms of the dialogue between theology and science can also be qualified as a different attitude to spatial perception of their phenomena. If one suspends the already formed natural attitude with respect to space and considers a genesis of spatiality as a certain form of relation to the world formulated from within the developing subjectivity, one realises that space understood in a mundane sense appears as generated from the event of life. For example, if one looks at a child's entrance into this world in the act of birth, from the external point of view his life depends on the world's conditions and in this sense is open to the world's invitation to exist. The main existential factor in this initial mysterious non-separatedness between a child and the world is the early sensual consciousness of the other, the mother who through love inaugurates in a child the sense of space. Space appears as a mode of relationship, in which, on the one hand, a loving human being manifests itself as a pre-conscious ecstatic reference, whereas on the other hand the same human person is caught in consciousness as the other supplemented by the spatial attributes of this otherness expressed in terms of extended (and measurable) space. This dialectical 'standing in front of' and 'standing apart from' in personal relation is an existential fact which cannot receive any further foundational justification. Its contingent facticity is an historical event of emergence of personhood through being affected by that 'standing apart from' that creates a spatial dimension of this relationship.

Knowledge of other persons is possible either through 'standing in front of' or 'standing apart from' and implies the intuition of space either as inseparable presence or absence. This is related not only to other human beings, but also to knowledge of nature as the reality of the other. One can admire the grandeur of the visible universe by experiencing it either through the personal 'opposite' of ecstatic reference (that is as presence) or as the opposite measured through spatial dimensions (that is as absence; remote objects). In this dichotomy the presence of the personal ecstatic reference to the other, its fundamental irreducibility from sensible experience and personal consciousness, predetermines the intuition of space as a definite form of experience. Here the 'I' that cannot give an account for the facticity of its personal ecstatic reference to the world, is formed by this reference (self-affectivity) which is projected in consciousness as a form of 'standing apart', that is of space. Thus the perception of space can be considered as self-affectivity through the intrinsic inseparability between humanity and the world, the self-affectivity which is implanted through being created in the world and in the Divine image. Space becomes a vehicle of human involvement in the world through hypostatic differentiated embodiment which makes possible the relationship with the world's objects as well as other persons.

The language of ecstatic reference to (communion with) the world and other persons implies a phenomenological attitude because the space of personal relationship is unfolded from within events of life. In this attitude the very notion of the outer world originates from within the boundaries of the same personal relationship and thus the making of the world an abstract and independently existing object can originate only from within the condition when the very personal relationship to the world receives a status that is similar to the status of all other objects. The world as a personal 'opposite' of ecstatic reference is perceived in the dialogue between humanity and the world as some *other*, hypostatically subsistent in every 'I' of this humanity. The representation of the relationship with the world in the phenomenality of objects consists in that the world becomes a passive object of observation and study, from which the sense of belonging to it is removed. The world becomes an 'object', and the personal space of 'standing in front of' the world transforms into a sheer 'standing apart from' the world in space as measurable and controlled extent. Space is presented in the phenomenality of objects when the relationship with the world is transferred into the sphere of pure thought which thinks this relationship but does not experience it (thus a reflective thinking entails an exit from experience of self-affectivity). It is in the conditions of the breakdown of the initial unity between subject and object (experienced as self-affectivity) that the representation of space acquires more and more geometrical, measurable character associated with the boundaries of things (as objects), that fill in the universe.

Scientific cosmology for example thinks of space exactly this way, where the measure of space is determined by its capacity to contain astronomical objects. Despite such a vision of the universe in the phenomenality of objects, the experience of *placelessness* of the universe (that is, the experience of the universe through an ecstatic personal reference) remains irreducible (self-affectivity). This 'standing in front of' the universe as the personal 'opposite' is free from its actual physically infinite extent, and thus remains indeterminate in the limits of scientific thinking rooted in the category of quantity as well as mundane geometrical intuitions of spatial hierarchy in terms of 'closer' and 'far,' 'here' and 'elsewhere,' 'right' and 'left,' etc. In this sense the universe as a term of personal relationship manifests its sheer *presence*, but such a presence that cannot be described in terms of place. The latter represents one term of the paradox and a theological counterpart to the vision of the world from the dialogue between theology and science.

In both cases, either through experience of belonging to the universe, or through experience of its absence because of the impossibility of circumscribing the universe in forms of thought, this experience determines the space of personal relationship as a certain indeterminacy of 'standing in front' of the universe (as non-extended and non-measurable), objectifying the working of the self-affectivity of life. Space as relationship thus signifies the modality of life; existential events of movement towards the other as manifestations of the basic foundations of being of humanity. However, this movement towards the other is not self-evident and is taking place only in the conditions of awareness of space as a potential threat of 'standing apart,' that is separation, if that movement towards the other and 'standing in front' of the universe ceases to function as elements of life (when self-affectivity degrades towards sheer affectivity and passivity of a subject). Here is a dialectics of space which finds its characteristic expression in the dialogue between theology and science: space is always capable of being transformed from the condition of personal relationship (which is de facto affirmed in theology) into a soulless form of separation and quantitative measurement (in science) if life of a hypostatic embodied subject is treated as determinism of biological survival, and the universe, instead of being a participant in the relationship (being a cause of affection of humanity), becomes an impersonified background of existing, whose contingency (as the lack of self-affectivity) not only cannot be comprehended, but, in fact, cannot be even detected (as in the sciences).

However, the intuition of the universe as the created wholeness always functions as that invisible background for the natural attitude and implies such a relationship of 'standing before' when all extensional plurality of experience is reduced to null in the event of ecstatic relationship towards the universe's creator.[18] There is a double

---

18 As an example of this one can point to the Anaphora in the Divine Liturgy, or to the prayer for the whole world of monks living in reclusion and 'beyond' the world, and contemplating the whole being from the cell of their solitude.

meaning hidden in this event: the ecstatic personal relationship with respect to God (self-affection) precedes any consciousness either of his presence or absence in the universe and thus of consciousness of presence or absence of the universe as created totality. The existential reality of God and the world, created by him, are defined through the immediate proximity of the relationship so that the very person and its subjectivity, not being able to verbalise and objectivise this relationship, is constituted by this relationship in a 'non-objectivised space' (the elusive self-affectivity of human life is itself constituted by life's relation to God).

It is this non-extended and non-measurable intimate 'opposite' of the personal relationship that constitutes space as relation. The universe as 'noema' of the Divine intention 'stands before' God without any extension; however this 'standing before,' as relation, tends to be expressed in the human perception of God as extended space. On the one hand there is no space between God and the world (God abides in creation without any spatial connotation); on the other hand, as embodied creatures in the extended universe, human beings experience their relationship with God and his creation in the modality of space. On the one hand man manifests himself in the placeless totality of its own articulating hypostasis (its self-affectivity, that is when the world is present through the imitation of the Logos-given capacity); on the other hand, as functioning corporeity (i.e. as embodied being), man feels himself isolated in the world of dividing extension (passivity of being affected by space).

Since such a dual perception of space is unavoidable in the created condition, what is left to humanity is to find its archetype in which the 'standing before' and 'standing apart' in the relationship between the world and God, man and God, and man and the world, is overcome by the Divine humanity of Jesus Christ. The transcendent foundation of the extended space and time of the universe is present and immanent within this world in such a way that we encounter its transcendence through the incarnate Christ who, while being in this world manifests its transcendence as the Logos that reaches out infinitely beyond the whole created world. To acquire the sense of the unity of all extended space as an instant of the Divine love, not intellectually through the instantaneous synthesis of the universe in human consciousness, but existentially, one must exert a synthesis of mediation between divisions in creation and then between the world and God. The Orthodox tradition calls this way of spiritual ascent *deification*. To grasp the sense of the universe as a whole, including all of its space and time one needs to 'acquire' the mind of Christ when one comes to truly know the things of the universe and the sense of its space. It is here through such desired deification that the intellectual tension between the instantaneous synthesis of the universe in a theological mode of thinking is mediated with the divided and extended world of objects which is a subject of scientific knowledge. One could imagine that the tension between the terms of the dialogue between theology and science could be removed on the moral level (thus lifting up the drama of such a dialogue) by asserting the proper sense of humanity responsible for both theology and science, humanity understood, as we saw, within a radical theological stance. However in no way would this imply the overcoming of ontological differences between the acosmic self-affective Life, that is the Divine, and that which is created through this self-affection as its contingent outcome. The moral tension in the human condition detected in the dialogue between theology and science can be overcome with no intention and no possibility of changing its created nature.

The Dialogue Between Theology and Science as a Mediation Between Different Phenomenalities of the World in Man

The paradox of subjectivity, as a reflection upon the position of humanity in the universe becomes an obstacle in asserting humanity's centrality in the sense of disclosure and manifestation of the universe. By holding the image of the universe as a whole, human transcendental subjectivity, its 'I', experiences a disagreement between the phenomenon of the universe expected to appear in the manner of ordinary objects (in science) and the 'I's' subjective experience of the universe through sheer belonging to it (in theology). Consequently, the 'I' cannot constitute the universe as an 'object' whose concept would agree with the conditions of experience of the universe through ecstatic reference of standing in front of it. One has here the intuitive saturation by the universe which imposes itself by excess, that makes this universe present, but invisible and incomprehensible. The universe appears as a saturated phenomenon which resists any regard with respect to itself as an object: it engulfs the subjectivity of the 'I' to such an extent that any attempt of the universe's constitution is suspended. The universe is *visible* (in its particular pieces and moments) but it nevertheless cannot be *looked at*. It is this feature of visibility as presence and at the same time the impossibility of gazing at it that characterises the saturated phenomenon Of the universe which de facto constitutes humanity itself. Then the dialogue between theology and science can be interpreted as an attempt to balance two different phenomenalities in one and the same subjectivity: an event of communion with the universe versus its representation through extended in space objects. This reflects the situation with the sense of the human condition, when man (as the center of disclosure and manifestation) appears to himself as unable to be presented in the phenomenonality of objects(reducinig humanity to ots organismic existence) .

The unknowability of man by himself can be expressed as his incapacity to formulate his position in the physical universe, as a condition of not being able to adapt to and to be at home in the world, once again expressed in the dialogue between theology and science. In analogy with Jean-Francois Lyotard,[19] the meeting with the world as belonging to it, that is when the world appears as a saturated phenomenon can be described as a return back to the condition of infancy, for as infants, humans are helplessly exposed to a strange and overwhelming environment while lacking the ability to articulate what affects them. By reducing this analogy to the bodily functions, the universe as saturated phenomenon deprives the body of its attunement to the universe. In a trivial sense there is the body's contingent, and

---

19 J.-F. Lyotard, *The Inhuman. Reflections on Time* (Cambridge/Oxford: Polity, 1991), p. 4.

literally free-flying, position in the space-time of the universe so that it is 'displaced' and hence is not attuned to the universe. This condition of not being attuned to the universe signifies a gap between sensibility and the possibility of mental articulation or linguistic expressibility in situations when human beings meet saturated phenomena. The universe is received through the 'I's' sight as pure donation which cannot be caught as complete in rubrics of thought at any given moment of time. One can say that to wrestle with the saturated phenomenon of the universe is to be in constant despair of chasing its escaping presence which constantly reminds the 'I' of the unclarified nature of its created finitude. The 'I', unable to constitute the phenomenon of the created universe as a whole, experiences itself as being constituted by this phenomenon through inescapable creaturely participation: the 'I' is being constituted by the universe as if the 'I' is being gazed at by the universe. However the 'I' is constituted by the universe only in the sense that both the 'I' and the universe are enhypostasised by their hypostatic otherness in an intrinsically co-inherent way, when one cannot exist without the other (self-affectivity of man is a part of the universe). By being in the universe the 'I' does not have (it simply cannot have) any dominant point of view over the intuition of the universe as an expression of the very fact of life. The universe as a saturated phenomenon engulfs subjectivity by removing its parts and spatial extension. In a temporal sense, the universe is always already there, so that all events of subjectivity's life unfold from the donating event of the universe as constantly coming into being, in which the unforeseeable nature of every consequent moment entails the unending historicity and unpredictability of existence. In a spatial sense, the contingency as concrete factuality of an event of appearance of the 'I's' life, which is not foreseeable and phenomenologically hidden from the 'I's' comprehension, makes its position in the universe *out of tune* leaving the human 'I' with no place in the universe. Its 'place' is its sheer facticity and any constitution of the universe's space by the modalities of the human will reduce the universe to its limited phenomenality, the phenomenality which is not; for the universe is the saturated phenomenon indivisible according to quantity, unbearable according quality, unconditioned according to relation and irreducible to the 'I' according to modality.[20]

Thus we see with a new force that the tension between the worldly experience as communion (the universe as a saturated phenomenon) and that of the world as a manifold of extended objects de facto underlies the essence of the dialogue between theology and science that deals with two complementary phenomenalities of the universe which, by the fact of their origin in one and the same human being, have to be in a constant critical attitude to each other, by determining the sphere of their legitimate application with no claims for the priority of one with respect to another and even less with no intention to overcome their difference. The universe as a saturated phenomenon enters the proper givens of theology because of being commensurable with the human life by the fact of their creation by God. Scientific

---

20 J.-L. Marion, 'The Saturated Phenomenon', in *Phenomenology and 'The Theological Turn': the French Debate* (New York: Fordham University Press, 2000), p. 211.

cosmology, by dealing with the universe as the constituted world of physical objects, enters the hermeneutic of the human condition by inserting into the latter the hermeneutics of the universe (as the necessary condition for humanity as well as for both of the hermeneutics). One can say that the ongoing enquiry into the sense of the dialogue between theology and science forms an endless intertwining hermeneutics of experience of living in the universe as communion (and a saturated phenomenon) and an outward constitution of the universe as extended space and time in cosmology. Such a working of the phenomenologically dualistic human subjectivity (explicitly present in the dialogue) contributes to the hermeneutics of the human condition in general pointing to the irreducible and primordial facticity of the self-affective life as being the unity of flesh (as materialised consciousness) and mind (as spiritualised matter).

Conclusion

Ultimately, the dialogue between theology and science explicates a fundamental problem of consciousness, the problem of mind and body as the fundamental unknowability of man by itself. Theology makes an ontological claim of *Imago Dei* by referring the latter to the unknowable and infinite God. The sense of God can arise from within the human subject, but its infinite predicates which reflect the fundamental human unknowability of God yet have an ontological sense. Thus the problem of mediation between theology an science as such has ontological overtones relating humanity to God through the idea of the Image. Then the riddle of humanity, its ultimate mystery is transferred to the teaching of creation of the world and man out of nothing. In a way the hard problem of consciousness becomes a different form of expression of that which is radically unknown: humanity as created by God out of nothing. This observation entails that if the latter, that is, *creatio ex nihilo* is invoked in the context of the modern scientific man in his dialogue with science as a reference point, this problem acquires some 'ontological' dimension in spite of the initial conviction that it cannot be solved ontologically. Then ther question is: what kind of ontology is needed to preserve the integrity of human beings as part of the natural world, as well as the integrity of the natural world in the presence of human existence? One might suggest the following answer: one needs a creational ontology that understands the world as *flesh*, created with intrinsic structures and with the power to unfold, to produce and to bring forth, a being constantly becoming, in which the human is a particularly rich intertwined pattern, a being woven in the prison of the flesh by a productive power made and sustained by God the creator, and hence, ultimately created by God *ex nihilo*. As such a world unfolds in life and human consciousness, these things all turn back on the world and in this way actualizing more of its inherent potentiality. Such a world has its integrity precisely as creation *and* creative, and human beings precisely as integral parts of this creative creation, of which they are also the co-creators. All these metaphysical statements imply that there is a creative principle of self-affective Life that is in the foundation of all. And it is the manifestations of this Life that humanity detects as its own hard problems related to understanding of what is humanity and what is its sense of existence. By asking why life in men acts in that way as it acts, by creating that consciousness which interrogates itself about its own functioning duality in the world, man manifest through himself this life and implicitly answers the hard question: its consciousness is split in itself and capable of enquiring into the facticity of this split because he is alive.

DORU COSTACHE

Theological Anthropology Today: Panayiotis Nellas's Contribution*

▼ ABSTRACT Being deeply interested in bridging theological anthropology and contemporary scientific culture, Panayiotis Nellas undertook a profound assessment of patristic antecedents. He was convinced that the patristic tradition holds the solution to his quest, as quite a few of the early Christian and Byzantine theologians engaged with the knowledge of their time. From the patristic tradition he learned that the human mystery is irreducible to any one definition and that, in its complexity, the human phenomenon requires multidisciplinary decoding. It is for this reason that, after identifying the highlights of theological anthropology, he proceeded to translate the traditional wisdom into the vocabulary of contemporary disciplines and views. This includes scientific and philosophical terms. He recorded his findings in his masterpiece, Ζῶον θεούμενον (the deified animal), which constitutes the object of my analysis. I study his insights under three headings, 'Complexity', 'Holism', and 'The integration of theology and science'. The first section outlines his articulation of the human phenomenon as complex and multilayered. The second section considers his interdisciplinary approach, by which he proved that the human mystery reveals its content only through a corresponding approach, namely, when looked at through the multifocal lens of several disciplines and perspectives. The third one focuses upon the elegant articulation of theological insights in Nellas's anthropological thinking, which takes as its starting point the analogy of the icon. The scientific analysis of the icon's material does not affect its theological dimension and use.

---

* This paper was written during my honorary associateship with the Department of Studies in Religion, the School of Letters, Art and Media, the Faculty of Arts and Social Sciences, the University of Sydney (2017–23), being based on research undertaken both there and at St Cyril's Coptic Orthodox Theological College, a member institution of the Sydney College of Divinity.

Doru Costache • The University of Sydney, Sydney College of Divinity

Orthodox Christianity and Modern Science: Past, Present and Future, ed. by Kostas Tampakis and Haralambos Ventis, SOC, 3 (Turnhout, 2022), pp. 167–182.
© BREPOLS ❧ PUBLISHERS   10.1484/M.SOC-EB.5.130959

> In like manner, theological anthropology remains unaffected by the scientific exploration of human nature. My study brings to the fore Nellas's traditionally grounded solution in regard to bridging theology and science, which proves that the current warfare paradigm is not the only way ahead. But his greatest contribution, I posit, is the fact that, in so doing, that is, by showing an alternate route leading away from the battlefield, his solution frees believers of fear — fear of science, of research, of technological advancements, and of critical thinking. In addition, his solution shows that the ethical values can be reaffirmed within the context of a new theological anthropology whose scientific implications do not hinder its spiritual valences.

Contemporary scientific anthropology, with its naturalistic or materialistic outlook, challenges the way Christians represent the human phenomenon on a number of levels. A case in point is that evolutionary anthropology totally disregards humankind's aspect as God's privileged creation whose supernatural condition transcends biology. From the evolutionary perspective, humankind merely is the side effect of random natural occurrences, the fortunate outcome of biological necessity. No other glory awaits us, to paraphrase Steven Weinberg's famed statement, apart from the satisfaction of realizing how unimportant we are.[1] No values are perennial, objective, or divine. Our entire axiology draws on subjective — human, all too human — aspirations meant to conceal our pointless existence. Right and wrong, virtue and sin, holiness and villainy bear no significance outside our consciousness. C. S. Lewis characterised this worldview[2] as 'the great myth of our century with its gases and galaxies, its light years and evolutions, its nightmare perspectives of simple arithmetic in which everything that can possibly hold significance for the mind becomes the mere byproduct of essential disorder'.

Many Christians detest this undignified picture which relativises the traditional ethical values that focus upon humankind's supernatural condition. Their concerns increase when they consider cosmology's boundless universe deprived of centre and missing any qualitative landmarks — a universe in which, according to Stephen Hawking's last book, posthumously released, there is no place for God's presence whatsoever.[3] An infinite universe, furthermore, where, as Alexandre Koyré had it, the values and the meanings become untenable.[4] Lost in the infinite universe, or perhaps the multiverse, the human being is no longer the royal inhabitant of the centre and the first citizen of a purposeful cosmos. Instead, humankind dwells

---

1   See Steven Weinberg, *The First Three Minutes: A Modern View of the Origin of the Universe*, updated edition (New York: Basic Books, 1993), pp. 154–55.
2   C. S. Lewis, *Perelandra* in *The Space Trilogy: Out of the Silent Planet — Perelandra — That Hideous Strength* (London: HarperCollins Publishers, 2013), p. 290.
3   Stephen Hawking, *Brief Answers to Big Questions* (London: John Murray, 2018), pp. 23–38.
4   Alexandre Koyré, *From the Closed World to the Infinite Universe* (Baltimore: The Johns Hopkins Press, 1957), pp. 275–76.

on a little rocky planet that orbits a yellow dwarf star situated at the outskirts of a typical galaxy within the local cluster, adrift in the immensity of an unimaginably vast expanse. Against this backdrop, whether evolutionary anthropology is correct or not, no significance can be ascribed to the human being and its aspirations.

Initially, when they realised the implications of the new worldview, many Christians, western and eastern alike, reacted against all things scientific.[5] Nothing could be agreeable to them, from the heliocentric system and the evidence of natural processes to the paleontological proofs of an Earth older than previously believed, and evolution, as well as, more recently, the infinite universe and its expansion. To this day, terrified by the prospect of pointlessness, even certain Orthodox Christian milieus seek refuge behind the walls of biblical and patristic literalism, actually the supernaturalistic anthropology of the Middle Ages.[6] Traditional anthropology lends support to these values, indeed, but within the framework of contemporary scientific culture the Christian axiology these milieus defend collapses together with the supernaturalist foundations upon which it is built.

Another approach holds the solution for this ongoing impasse, making possible the reaffirmation of Christian values even within contemporary culture. The author whose contributions interest me, Panayiotis Nellas (1936–86), exemplifies the opposite of the panicked reactions described above. Not being prone to reductionist thinking, he courageously redrafted Christian anthropology within the parameters of contemporary science. As Aidan Nichols observed, his primary purpose was to revive 'patristic anthropology for his own contemporaries',[7] not to repeat its main arguments as they were posited in late Antiquity and the Middle Ages. It was a matter of translating the traditional Christian categories into the language of modern anthropology. The outcome of his arduous undertaking is a realistic and multifaceted depiction of the human being, biological as well as theological, personal and social,

---

5 See on this the essays gathered in *Reading Genesis after Darwin*, ed. by Stephen C. Barton and David Wilkinson (Oxford University Press, 2009). See also Andrew J. Brown, *The Days of Creation: A History of Christian Interpretation of Genesis 1:1–2:3*, History of Biblical Interpretation 4 (Blandford Forum, UK: Deo Publishing, 2014), esp. pp. 167–279.

6 Recent scholarship identified a range of 'traditionalist' responses to modern scientific culture. Doru Costache, 'The Orthodox Doctrine of Creation in the Age of Science', *Journal of Orthodox Christian Studies* 2/1 (2019): pp. 43–64, esp. pp. 43–48. Christopher C. Knight, 'Natural Theology and the Eastern Orthodox Tradition', in *The Oxford Handbook of Natural Theology*, ed. by Russell Re Manning (Oxford University Press, 2013), pp. 213–26, esp. pp. 213, 223–24. Andrew Louth, *Introducing Eastern Orthodox Theology* (London: SPCK, 2013), pp. 74–78. Vasilios N. Makrides, 'Orthodox Anti-Westernism Today: A Hindrance to European Integration?', *International Journal for the Study of the Christian Church* 9/3 (2009), pp. 209–24. See also the studies reunited in *Orthodox Constructions of the West*, ed. by George E. Demacopoulos and Aristotle Papanikolaou, Orthodox Christianity and Contemporary Thought (New York: Fordham University Press, 2013).

7 Aidan Nichols, *Light from the East: Authors and Themes in Orthodox Theology* (London: Sheed & Ward, 1999), p. 171. To my knowledge, Nichols's is the single extensive analysis of Nellas's book available in English (*Light from the East*, pp. 170–80). See also the far briefer accounts of Paul M. Collins, *Partaking in Divine Nature: Deification and Communion* (London: T&T Clark, 2010), pp. 81–82, and Andrew Louth, *Modern Orthodox Thinkers: From the Philokalia to the present* (London: SPCK, 2015), pp. 191–93.

distinct from the cosmic array yet consubstantial with it, natural and yet called to attain a state above nature. Formulated against the backdrop of contemporary science, his anthropological views lend substance to the traditional ethical values and, beyond them, to the glorious figure of humankind called to holiness and deification.

Of the nuanced portrait of the human being in his masterpiece, Ζῶον θεούμενον ('deified animal'),[8] I focus upon the aspects of complexity, holism, and the integration of theology and science.[9] By and large, his contribution is analogous to Pierre Teilhard de Chardin's (1881–1955) in the west.[10] A comparative analysis of their approaches falls outside the scope of my study. What I wish is to show that by integrating contemporary science and Christian anthropology, Nellas's input illustrates a superior way of handling matters, free of the fear and of the reductionism pertaining to the reactions mentioned above. His synthesis is a most efficient way of promoting the traditional values in terms intelligible to contemporary culture. I do not draw explicit conclusions regarding morality and the values, but my approach suggests ways ahead in that direction.

Complexity

Nellas was equally dissatisfied with the materialism of scientific anthropology and the popular representation of human nature as soul and body. Both are immanentist approaches that consider human nature within itself. That said, while sharing immanentism in common, they illustrate two opposite forms of reductionism, monistic and dualistic, respectively. Neither paints a full portrait of humankind.

In turn, Nellas proposed a complex perspective, namely, a theocentric, christological, and 'iconic' anthropology that assesses the human phenomenon through a transcen-

---

8 Herein I use a recent edition of this work: Παναγιώτη Νέλλα Ζῶον θεούμενον: Προοπτικὲς γιὰ μιὰ ὀρθόδοξη κατανόηση τοῦ ἀνθρώπου (Ἀθήνα: Ἐκδόσεις Ἁρμός, 2000). An English translation of the work is available: Panayiotis Nellas, *Deification in Christ: Orthodox Perspectives on the Nature of the Human Person*, trans. Norman Russell, Contemporary Greek Theologians 5 (Crestwood, NY: St Vladimir's Seminary Press, 1987). Throughout, I refer to both the original and Russell's translation. For quoted passages I use the original Greek version, giving my own translation, but I also indicate the corresponding pages in Russell's translation. The original title of the work is the abbreviation of a sentence towards the end of Gregory the Theologian's *Oration* 38.11.22–24: ζῶον ... θεούμενον. The edition I use throughout is *Grégoire de Nazianze: Discours 38–41*, ed. by Claudio Moreschini and Paul Gallay, Sources chrétiennes 358 (Paris: Cerf, 1990).
9 Parts of the following study draw on my following articles: 'Ὁλισμός, δυναμισμὸς καὶ σύνθεση: Ἡ ἀνθρωπολογικὴ σκέψη τοῦ Παναγιώτη Νέλλα' [Holism, dynamism, and synthesis: The anthropological thinking of Panayiotis Nellas], *Synaxi* 140 (2016): pp. 30–40; 'Antropocentrismul modern şi oferta antropologiei eclesiale' [Modern anthropocentrism and ecclesial anthropology], *Analele Universităţii din Craiova* [Annals of the University of Craiova], series *Teologie* [Theology] 7 (Craiova: Universitaria, 2002), pp. 216–56, esp. pp. 239–41.
10 See Pierre Teilhard de Chardin: *Christianity and Evolution*, trans. René Hague (Wilmington, MA: Mariner Books, 2002) and *The Phenomenon of Man* (New York: Harper Perennial Modern Classics, 2008).

dental lens. His approach was liturgically and scripturally grounded,[11] informed by the patristic tradition,[12] and attentive to the cultural trends of his own time. I discuss the latter aspect in the final section of this study. What resulted from this blending of perspectives is an anthropology that displays traditional and modern features. At its centre resides the human being configured in the image of Christ as an 'image of the Image' — Christ being God's authentic Image — and therefore as a theological mystery that resists immanentist assessments.[13] This anthropological vision draws upon an 'iconic ontology' (εἰκονικὴ ὀντολογία)[14] which takes the Archetype, that is, Christ, as the supreme criterion for human existence. Ultimately, 'iconic ontology' amounts to a broader 'theocentric and christocentric (θεοκεντρικὸ καὶ χριστοκεντρικό) anthropology.[15] To the implications of this perspective I must now turn.

'Iconic', theocentric, and christocentric anthropology represents a transcendent and comprehensive frame of reference whose implementation demands the wholesale reappraisal of the human being in nonreductionist terms. Against the Cartesian rift separating *res cogitans* and *res extensa*, subject and object, person and nature, mind and body, Nellas's human being is personalised nature and mindful body. It consists of person and nature or rather is a 'person that pertains to nature and that reveals it' (πρόσωπο ποὺ κάνει συγκεκριμένη καὶ ἀποκαλύπτει τὴ φύση).[16] Our being is not a voiceless nature deprived of subjective dimensions; in its case, *res extensa* and *res cogitans* overlap and intersect. Furthermore, ours is not a static being, a given, hopelessly conditioned by inflexible rules. Our being is a work in progress, at once dynamic and purposeful, theologically conditioned and existentially flexible. As a person, the human being has a crucial task to perform in regard to its own nature,

---

11 See the parts on Nicholas Cabasilas and Andrew of Crete. *Ζῶον θεούμενον*, pp. 115–224. *Deification in Christ*, pp. 109–96.
12 Louth, *Modern Orthodox Thinkers*, p. 192. Nichols, *Light from the East*, pp. 171–72.
13 *Ζῶον θεούμενον*, pp. 29–30, 33–34. *Deification in Christ*, pp. 30, 33. See on this Nichols, *Light from the East*, pp. 172–74. For a similar position see Christos Yannaras, *Elements of Faith: An Introduction to Orthodox Theology*, trans. Keith Schram (Edinburgh: T&T Clark, 1991), pp. 62–65. For a recent synthesis of 'iconic' anthropology reminiscent of Nellas's thinking, see Louth, *Introducing Eastern Orthodox Theology*, pp. 82–89.
14 *Ζῶον θεούμενον*, pp. 34, 197. *Deification in Christ*, pp. 34, 173.
15 *Ζῶον θεούμενον*, pp. 165. *Deification in Christ*, pp. 146. See also Louth, *Modern Orthodox Thinkers*, p. 193.
16 *Ζῶον θεούμενον*, p. 25. *Deification in Christ*, p. 27. Nellas advocated a balanced stance on the human constitution as person and nature. See Ioan I. Ică Jr., 'Persoană şi/sau Ontologie în gândirea ortodoxă contemporană' [Person and/or Ontology in contemporary Orthodox thinking], in *Persoană şi comuniune: Prinos de cinstire Părintelui Profesor Academician Dumitru Stăniloae* [Person and communion: Honoring Father Dumitru Stăniloae, Professor and Academician], ed. by Ioan I. Ică jr. (Sibiu: Arhiepiscopia Ortodoxă a Sibiului, 1993), pp. 359–85, esp. pp. 379–80. Nellas's articulation of the person satisfies the criteria of Orthodox anthropology outlined in Ambrose Mong, *Purification of Memory: A Study of Modern Orthodox Theologians from a Catholic Perspective* (Cambridge: James Clarke & Co, 2015), pp. 156–57. However, Mong did not refer to Nellas. For a slightly different articulation of the person-centred perspective, see the classic work of John Zizioulas, *Being as Communion: Studies in Personhood and the Church*, Contemporary Greek Theologians 4 (Crestwood, NY: St Vladimir's Seminary Press, 1997), pp. 27–66.

that is, to make it be and to make it its own, to bring it from potentiality to actuality as it were. However, in order to achieve this, it must listen to the transcendent voice encoded within its genes under the guise of the 'iconic' dimension. This voice calls it to push forward, to undergo gradual changes that culminate in our being's divine transformation. So understood, our existence is from beginning to end an ongoing metamorphosis in the parameters of 'iconic ontology'.

Human transformation began with our creation out of the earthly stuff, which God reconfigured theologically or iconically. Nellas addresses this aspect by way of an interpretive paraphrase of the divine breath in Genesis 2.7. In his words,

> Ἡ κτιστὴ ὕλη, ὁ «χοῦς ἀπὸ τῆς γῆς», ὠργανώθηκε ἔτσι γιὰ πρώτη φορὰ θεολογικά, ἡ ὑλικὴ κτίση ἀπέκτησε μορφὴ καὶ δομὴ κατ᾽ εἰκόνα τοῦ Θεοῦ, ἡ ζωὴ ἔγινε πάνω στὴ γῆ ἐνσυνείδητη, ἐλεύθερη καὶ προσωπική.[17] (Thus, [through the divine breath,] created matter or the [scriptural] 'dust of the earth' was for the first time theologically organised. The material creation gained form and structure in the image of God. Life on earth became conscious, free, and personal.)

The human being cannot be thought of outside the earth's biosphere and the cosmic milieu of its birth. The nature of the cosmos is its own nature. Nor can it be considered apart from the divine agency which makes it someone out of something, so to speak, a reality of a different order, 'conscious, free, and personal'. Against the modern habit of separating humankind from the natural world, the above passage does not emphasise the discontinuity between the human, the biological, and the cosmic levels of the creation. Instead, it brings to the fore their continuity. Long before humankind's arrival, created matter was organised into the cosmos, including 'life on earth' or the earth's biosphere. But its becoming did not stop there.

Divinely conditioned, for the universe's own nature is 'iconic',[18] created matter advanced towards humanisation and, remoulded by divine energy, when it finally engendered humankind, it experienced another reorganisation. Engendering humankind was matter's way of becoming human. It is true that the arrival of humankind was a theological event — under the divine breath, created matter was now 'conscious, free, and personal' — but this event was not unrelated to the transformative processes already at work in the universe. And these processes did not stop there either. Elsewhere we read that the 'iconically' or theologically remade dust, namely, the human being, furthers the reorganisation of created matter as the universe's anthropic transformation.[19] Human creativity is part and parcel of this process.[20]

---

17 Ζῶον θεούμενον, pp. 31–32. *Deification in Christ*, p. 32.
18 Ζῶον θεούμενον, p. 67. *Deification in Christ*, p. 61. The cosmic dimension is central to Nellas's anthropological thinking. Ζῶον θεούμενον, pp. 36, 57–58, 101–14, 158–64, 178–80, 183–96. *Deification in Christ*, pp. 35, 54, 93–104, 141–45, 157–59, 163–72. While his approach fits even on this count the bill of Mong's (*Purification of Memory*, 52–53) outline of contemporary Orthodox theology, Nellas's contribution goes again unnoticed.
19 Ζῶον θεούμενον, pp. 28, 60–61, 171–73. *Deification in Christ*, pp. 29, 56–57, 150–52.
20 Ζῶον θεούμενον, pp. 27–28, 105–14. *Deification in Christ*, pp. 28–29, 97–104.

The solidarity with created matter and the cosmos's anthropic transformation notwithstanding, humankind's 'iconic' condition points to a destination which transcends the parameters of nature. Specifically, as it is potentially godlike, the human being must live accordingly. It must actualise its 'iconic' potential[21] into an existential status without equivalent within the created universe. It must progress towards replicating 'its archetype's wonderful way of life' (στὸ θαυμαστὸ τρόπο ζωῆς τοῦ ... ἀρχετύπου της).[22] In the author's daring words, 'having been created "in the image" of the infinite God, the human being ... is called to transcend the finite boundaries of the creation and to become infinite' (ὁ ἄνθρωπος ἔχοντας πλασθῆ «κατ' εἰκόνα» τοῦ ἀπείρου Θεοῦ, καλεῖται ... νὰ ὑπερβῆ τὰ πεπερασμένα ὅρια τῆς κτίσεως καὶ νὰ ἀπειροποιηθῆ).[23] Nellas shared this conviction with other modern Orthodox theologians, such as Dumitru Stăniloae and John Zizioulas.[24]

This culminating experience cannot be rendered without the aid of paradoxical formulations. Once again turning to Gregory the Theologian's insights,[25] Nellas shows that when the human person reaches this blessed goal, it experiences temporality as well as timelessness[26]—boundaries, insofar as it remains human and created, and limitlessness, insofar as it participates in the divine life and appropriates divine features. The human being therefore attains a 'new mode' (τρόπο νέο) of life, a 'theanthropic' (θεανθρώπινο) or divinehuman condition[27] which qualifies Christian anthropology as 'theanthropology' (θεανθρωπολογία).[28] The 'new mode' amounts to the person's 'real christification' (πραγματικὴ χριστοποίηση)[29] or the attainment of likeness to Christ, the archetype of perfect humankind.[30] Foreshadowed by the virtuous life,[31] 'christified' existence ultimately refers to the human person's life *in* Christ and *with*

---

21 See on this Scott Prather, 'The Body and Human Identity in Postmodernism and Orthodoxy', *American Theological Inquiry* 1:2 (2008): pp. 123–33, esp. p. 129.
22 *Ζῶον θεούμενον*, p. 28 (see also pp. 38, 43–44). *Deification in Christ*, p. 29 (see also pp. 37, 41).
23 *Ζῶον θεούμενον*, p. 27. At p. 28, ἀπεριόριστος καὶ ἀθάνατος ('unlimited and immortal'; see also pp. 131–32). *Deification in Christ*, pp. 28, 29, 119. See the comments of Prather, 'The Body and Human Identity', p. 127.
24 Dumitru Stăniloae, *Studii de teologie dogmatică ortodoxă* [Studies in Orthodox dogmatic theology] (Craiova: Editura Mitropoliei Olteniei, 1990), pp. 157–200. John Zizioulas: *Being as Communion*, pp. 49–65 and his *Communion and Otherness: Further Studies in Personhood and the Church* (London: T&T Clark, 2006), pp. 13–112, 206–48.
25 Gregory the Theologian, *Oration* 38.11.13–19. Building on Gregory's insights, the topic of humankind's call to an unbounded or unlimited existence returned in Saint Maximus the Confessor, quoted in *Deification in Christ*, pp. 36, 37. On the latter's input see the authoritative article of Panayotis Christou, 'Maximos Confessor on the Infinity of Man', in *Maximus Confessor: Actes du Symposium sur Maxime le Confesseur, Fribourg (2–5 septembre 1980)*, ed. by Felix Heinzer et Christoph Schönborn (Éditions Universitaires Fribourg, Suisse, 1982), pp. 261–71.
26 *Ζῶον θεούμενον*, pp. 44–45. *Deification in Christ*, p. 42.
27 *Ζῶον θεούμενον*, pp. 163–64. *Deification in Christ*, p. 145.
28 *Ζῶον θεούμενον*, p. 133. *Deification in Christ*, p. 120.
29 *Ζῶον θεούμενον*, pp. 40–41. *Deification in Christ*, p. 39.
30 *Ζῶον θεούμενον*, pp. 24–25, 35–36, 40–41, 42, 133–58. *Deification in Christ*, pp. 24, 27, 35, 39, 40, 120, 121–39. See also Collins, *Partaking in Divine Nature*, pp. 82, 87.
31 *Ζῶον θεούμενον*, pp. 57–60. *Deification in Christ*, pp. 54–56.

Christ.[32] While it constitutes God's original intention for humankind, the theanthropic mode or our christification becomes a reality within the circumstances of salvation.

But christification is not the only existential road the human person can take. Being 'conscious and free', it can also choose the opposite of God's plan, changing direction and objectives.[33] This it does almost continuously until it stabilises itself on a certain path. Nellas describes the dramatic ambivalence of the human being in great detail, revealing its repeated oscillations between good and evil,[34] holiness and the passionate life,[35] natural and unnatural,[36] theonomy and autonomy,[37] the 'divine image' and the 'garments of skin',[38] rationality and irrationality,[39] theomorphism and zoomorphism.[40] These oscillations depend entirely on our free choices. Nevertheless, they are not without an impact upon the human condition, sometimes resulting in traumatic events and other times in qualitative leaps towards holiness and the theanthropic state. What makes such oscillations register in the physical plane is the dynamic metamorphism of nature. Here, metamorphism does not entail any negative connotations. The same aptitude which makes possible the person's spiritual disfigurement through unnatural choices plays a crucial role in the redress of fallen humankind. Specifically, nature responds to Christ's salvific grace by healing itself from the traumas of sin, becoming whole and wholesome.[41] On this note, I must briefly return to the soteriological aspect.

Nellas believed that there is no way of articulating a complete Christian anthropology without the Savior's restorative activity, thus without soteriology. It is Christ's agency that restores our normal self, profoundly affected by sin, and by which the 'iconic' potential of human existence regains its theocentric orientation.[42] For that reason, to decipher the mystery of human existence one must consider, beyond its condition before and after the fall, the 'new mode' that Christ, our Archetype, inaugurated for us.[43] This existential status is readily available through sacramental participation

---

32   Ζῶον θεούμενον, pp. 21–23. *Deification in Christ*, pp. 23–25.
33   Ζῶον θεούμενον, pp. 198–99. *Deification in Christ*, p. 175.
34   Ζῶον θεούμενον, p. 43. *Deification in Christ*, p. 41.
35   Ζῶον θεούμενον, pp. 206–07. *Deification in Christ*, p. 180.
36   Ζῶον θεούμενον, pp. 46–47, 204–05. *Deification in Christ*, pp. 43–44, 179.
37   Ζῶον θεούμενον, pp. 120, 212 (on p. 31, theonomy is called theocentricity). *Deification in Christ*, pp. 185, 32.
38   Ζῶον θεούμενον, pp. 49, 57–64, 120–21. *Deification in Christ*, pp. 46, 53–60, 110–11. According to the author of the 'Foreword' to the English version, Bishop Kallistos of Diokleia, the sections on the 'garments of skin' are the most original part of the book. See *Deification in Christ*, pp. 9–14, esp. p. 13. In turn, Verna Harrison showed that the 'garments of skin' inspired Nellas to think of a theological perspective on the human activity in the world. See Nonna Verna Harrison, 'The human person as image and likeness of God,' in *The Cambridge Companion to Orthodox Christian Theology*, ed. by Mary B. Cunningham and Elizabeth Theokritoff (Cambridge University Press, 2009), pp. 78–92, esp. p. 88.
39   Ζῶον θεούμενον, pp. 52–53. *Deification in Christ*, pp. 48–49.
40   Ζῶον θεούμενον, pp. 55, 198. *Deification in Christ*, pp. 51–52, 175.
41   Ζῶον θεούμενον, pp. 68–69. *Deification in Christ*, p. 63.
42   Ζῶον θεούμενον, pp. 122–24. *Deification in Christ*, pp. 111–13.
43   Ζῶον θεούμενον, pp. 127–29. *Deification in Christ*, pp. 116–17.

in him.[44] That said, Christ's soteriological and sacramental input does not work by itself. Human beings are not passive recipients of gifts. While christification without Christ is impossible, it still requires human input — the actualisation of our 'iconic' potential by adopting a corresponding cast of mind, thus through conversion, and by exercising one's will through the practice of virtue and prayer.[45] Ultimately, Christian 'theanthropology' views human existence and salvation as synergetic or interactive events.

To summarise, Nellas's representation of the human being is complex, multilayered, and paradoxical. It refers at once to humankind's Archetype, Christ, the Logos incarnate, and the natural origin of our species in the created matter of this world; the 'iconic' condition and metamorphic dynamism of human nature; a range of existential possibilities that depend on free choice; humankind's restored wholeness through Christ's salvific economy and sacramental regeneration; the task to push the entire cosmos to a rich state of complex unity, through virtuous living, in tune with God's intention; and finally the participation of renewed humankind in the boundlessness of the divine life through attaining 'christification' or the 'theanthropic' condition. By consistently referring to the theological dimension of existence, Nellas's is an anthropology which transcends immanentist assessments, but also — due to this fact — one that is overwhelmingly rich and diverse. The resulting human portrait is far from simplistic; it is a polychrome, nuanced representation which accommodates more perspectives than one.

I must now turn to the holistic dimension of Nellas's anthropology, which wraps up together all of the above, paving the way for the last part of my analysis, regarding the integration of theology and science.

Holism

In his own words, Nellas was interested in the 'complementary dimensions of an orthodox, that is, healthy structure of the human being' (ἀλληλοσυμπληρούμενος διαστάσεις μιᾶς ὀρθοδόξις, δηλαδὴ ὑγιοῦς δομῆς τοῦ ἀνθρώπου).[46] The adjectives 'complementary' (ἀλληλοσυμπληρούμενος), 'orthodox' (ὀρθόδοξη), and 'healthy' (ὑγιής) designate the human being restored in its complex entirety, free of the confusion and sickness pertaining to its fallen state. These adjectives also denote a comprehensive anthropology that accounts for human wholeness and wholesomeness. In what follows I focus on the complementary dimension, which is the distinctive feature of an integrative, holistic framework.

The human phenomenon presents traits which the disciplinary perspectives within contemporary anthropology — from biology to genetics and neuroscience and from cultural studies to psychology and sociology — consider in separation

---

44 Ζῶον θεούμενον, pp. 133–45, 161–62. *Deification in Christ*, pp. 122–30, 143–44.
45 Ζῶον θεούμενον, pp. 145–58, 215–18. *Deification in Christ*, pp. 130–39, 187–90.
46 Ζῶον θεούμενον, p. 24. *Deification in Christ*, p. 25.

from one another and partially. Biology does not pay attention to the human being as a personal centre of thoughts, feelings, and choices, while cultural anthropology has no interest in genetics. What conditions their foci are overspecialisation as well as various assumptions. But the same happens at intuitive levels. By calling the human being by a certain word, each language manifests a particular perception of it, in order to ascertain its relation with the earth, its bipedal posture, or its reflective aptitude etc. Against this backdrop, Nellas searched for a holistic framework where the human being can be seen in its layered complexity. For him, this framework was patristic anthropology.

Drawing upon their experience with God and the theological vantage point to which they adhered,[47] patristic authors explored the human phenomenon in all its breadth, length, and depth, connecting its many dimensions. They mapped human nature in the abstract as well as a wide range of concrete existential states, from holiness to sinfulness. Above all, they discerned 'how the human being's nature is when it holds a connection of sorts with God and what happens when it breaks this link' (πῶς εἶναι ἡ φύση τοῦ ἀνθρώπου ὅταν κρατάη τὸ σύνδεσμό της μὲ τὸ Θεό, καὶ πῶς γίνεται ὅταν σπάση τὸ σύνδεσμο αὐτό).[48] Human nature is not invariable. Alongside internal conditions and external factors such as culture and society, what determines its shape and state is the person's own life choices. In processing the various data, from theoretical to observational and practical, patristic authors developed a comprehensive and detailed chart of the human phenomenon. What facilitated their achievements was the incorporation of theological insights, philosophical reflection, and the available scientific information. Nellas replicated this very interdisciplinary approach.

Perceived from a range of perspectives, Nellas's human being is an animal that becomes whatever it eats and does; a person as well as nature; a being that leads a social, political, and rational life; and an animal called upon to become god or, as we have seen above, to experience a theanthropic life. In short, and reiterating the paradoxical articulations discussed in the previous section, the human being is 'at the same time earthly and heavenly, temporal and eternal, visible and noetically apprehended, truly and really a "deified animal"' (ταυτόχρονα ἐπίγειος καὶ οὐράνιος, πρόσκαιρος καὶ αἰώνιος, ὁρατὸς καὶ νοούμενος, ἀληθηνὰ καὶ πραγματικὰ «ζῶο θεούμενο»).[49] Thus, no single definition or disciplinary approach could capture what he construed as the human mystery.

Looking closer at how Nellas approached the human phenomenon, one discerns a cross-section representation and a dynamic, teleological overview. Here is the first representation.

Πρόσωπο συνάμα καὶ φύση ὁ ἄνθρωπος, ποὺ χαρακτηρίζεται θεμελιακὰ ἀπὸ τὸ μυστήριο τῆς ἀγάπης, ποὺ ὠθεῖ ἐσωτερικὰ τὰ πρόσωπα στὴ φυσικὴ κοινωνία· ἐνσυνείδητη προσωπικὴ ὕπαρξη μέσα στὸ χρόνο· ἑνότητα ψυχοσωματικὴ ἀδιάσπαστη, μὲ ἀπροσμέτρητο ψυχικὸ βάθος· ἐλεύθερος· κυρίαρχος· δημιουργός· λογικός,

---

47 Ζῶον θεούμενον, pp. 7–8. Deification in Christ, p. 15.
48 Ζῶον θεούμενον, p. 8. Deification in Christ, p. 16.
49 Ζῶον θεούμενον, p. 7. Deification in Christ, p. 15.

ἐπιστήμων κ.λ.π.⁵⁰ (The human being is both person and nature. The mystery of love which fundamentally characterises the [human] persons pushes them outwards, towards physical fellowship. Experiencing time as a conscious personal existence, it [sc. the human being] is an indivisible psychosomatic unity of immeasurable psychological depth, free, sovereign, creative, rational, endowed with scientific aptitude etc.)

The human being is multifaceted and multilayered. It evolves in the course of time on the existential plans of personhood and nature as a complex psychosomatic being. Self-aware and social, it pursues fulfilment in the company of other persons. It is equipped for enquiry, knowledge, and innovation. One could recognise here descriptors pertaining to a number of fields and approaches, from cultural anthropology to psychology to sociology. As the reference to nature might be an allusion to genetics and biology, the reference to the human being as person could very well denote the frameworks of existentialism and personalism. Moreover, the matter of consciously experiencing time suggests a phenomenological take on the human experience. It appears that Nellas could not part ways with any of the available representations of the human phenomenon, accommodating as many of them as possible. As such, the passage under consideration faithfully mirrors the 'catholic ecclesiological perspective … simultaneously christological, pneumatological, and cosmological' (καθολικὴ ἐκκλησιολογικὴ προοπτική … ταυτόχρονα χριστολογική, πνευματολογικὴ καὶ κοσμολογική).⁵¹ This comparison is illuminating: as the church could not be reduced to any sides of its complex structure, neither could the human experience. It is relevant that Nellas's 'catholic' — comprehensive or holistic — description of the human phenomenon calls on theological anthropology to broaden its scope by integrating data from various contemporary disciplines and viewpoints. Only through a new cultural contextualisation would theological anthropology be genuinely consistent with the patristic tradition which once appraised the human mystery in the parameters of ancient culture.

The second representation, partially encountered earlier, goes as follows:

> … ὁ ἄνθρωπος ἔχοντας πλασθῆ «κατ' εἰκόνα» τοῦ ἀπείρου Θεοῦ, καλεῖται ἀπὸ τὴν ἴδια του τὴ φύση — καὶ αὐτὸ ἀκριβῶς εἶναι ἀπὸ τὴν ἄποψη αὐτὴ τό «κατ' εἰκόνα» — νὰ ὑπερβῆ τὰ πεπερασμένα ὅρια τῆς κτίσεως καὶ νὰ ἀπειροποιηθῆ.⁵² (… having been created 'in the image' of the infinite God, the human being is called by its very nature to transcend the finite boundaries of the creation and to become infinite. From this viewpoint, this, precisely, is what the 'in the image' means.)

Drawing upon the central theme of humankind's 'iconic' configuration, the passage reveals that the structure of the human being, person and nature, is neither a given nor a static reality. Human nature — 'iconically' configured or bearing Christ's archetypal signature — points to a destination above the ontological gap, to the divine life and

---

50 *Ζῶον θεούμενον*, p. 26. *Deification in Christ*, p. 27.
51 *Ζῶον θεούμενον*, p. 177. *Deification in Christ*, p. 154.
52 *Ζῶον θεούμενον*, p. 27. *Deification in Christ*, p. 28.

the uncreated mode of existence pertaining to the theanthropic mode. In the previous section I addressed this matter in detail. My reason for returning to it here is in order to show that this experience entails a dynamic dimension which, implicitly, means that any exhaustive descriptions of the human being are of necessity impossible in its current transitional state. Summarised within the 'in the image' as a promise of things to come, the full description of the human being demands a teleological and/or an eschatological vantage point — one that takes in consideration the ultimate form of our experience, christomorphic and theanthropic.[53] The signs of this experience are currently discernible only on the radiant faces of the saints.[54] Nellas's dynamic anthropology is christologically and hagiologically conditioned.

In short, against reductionist thinking, Nellas' holistic anthropology represents the human mystery as complex and as fulfilled by way of dynamic processes whose aim is participation in the divine life. An important aspect of this anthropological outlook is that it incorporates diverse information from a range of disciplines and viewpoints, in light of which the human phenomenon does not constitute the province of any one-sided perceptions. Basically, an interdisciplinary appraisal of the human phenomenon is in order. To this aspect I must now turn.

The integration of Theology and Science

To articulate the holistic perspective earlier discussed, Nellas, as I have suggested several times already, endeavoured to bridge scientific and theological anthropologies.

Often, he illustrates this commitment in an indirect fashion. For example, he posits that humankind was brought into existence 'out of preexisting biological life' (ἀπὸ τὴν προϋπάρχουσα βιολογικὴ ζωή) and that Christ restored the human being as 'new creation' (καινουργία δημιουργία) 'out of the preexisting human biology' (ἀπὸ τὸ προϋπάρχον βιολογικό ἀνθρώπινο).[55] This statement echoes the dynamic outlook discussed above, while transparently alluding to the modern theory of evolution. What must have facilitated his use of evolutionary anthropology is Gregory the Theologian's insight, already mentioned a couple of times. Gregory talks about the making of humankind out of preexisting structured matter,[56] a stance which Nellas's own echoes. It is noteworthy that Stăniloae proposed a similar theological integration of evolutionary biology by taking as a starting point Maximus the Confessor's views.[57] What matters is that, here, Nellas returns to the topic of created matter's gradual

---

53 Ζῶον θεούμενον, p. 44. *Deification in Christ*, p. 41.
54 Ζῶον θεούμενον, p. 128. *Deification in Christ*, p. 117.
55 Ζῶον θεούμενον, p. 134. *Deification in Christ*, p. 121.
56 See παρὰ μὲν τῆς ὕλης λαβὼν τὸ σῶμα ἤδη προϋποστάσης (God 'took the body from the already structured matter'). Gregory the Theologian, *Oration* 38.11.10–11.
57 See Doru Costache, 'A Theology of the World: Dumitru Stăniloae, the Traditional Worldview, and Contemporary Cosmology', in *Orthodox Christianity and Modern Science: Tensions, Ambiguities, Potential*, ed. by Vasilios N. Makrides and Gayle Woloschak, Science and Orthodox Christianity 1 (Turnhout: Brepols Publishers, 2019), pp. 205–22, esp. pp. 209–12.

metamorphosis into the cosmos, then into life, then into human life — itself a topic not deprived of patristic antecedents.[58]

Against this backdrop, he saw no difficulty in acknowledging the fact that human nature originated in the evolutionary processes of life. He adds however an important detail, which corresponds to his eschatological appraisal of the human phenomenon: evolution means progressing from generic biology to human biology to a spiritually regenerated, transfigured human existence. As humankind emerged from preexisting life, glorified humankind emerges out of human biology. We note that humankind's creation 'out of preexisting biological life' indicates his integration of scientific data into the framework of traditional anthropology.

Earlier in the book, Nellas outlined his position in a straightforward manner. Central is the tenet that the theory of evolution cannot harm 'iconic' anthropology. Christos Yannaras defended a similar position closer to us.[59] Theological anthropology upholds that Christ is the origin, the truth, and the fulfilment of humankind, which conviction science can neither prove nor disprove. The evolutionary processes studied by scientific anthropology represent the external side of humankind's inner movement from being 'in the image' to the theanthropic form. This inner metamorphosis transcends biology and for this reason falls outside the purview of science. Scientific analysis cannot obscure humankind's theological core — its reference to the Archetype who transcends nature — the way to analyse the materials of which a holy icon is made has no impact upon the icon's reference to its original.[60] Here, Nellas adapts Vladimir Lossky's cosmological insights to the area of anthropology. In short, Lossky posited that the theological truth of the Christian worldview remains unaffected by the successive recontextualisation of this truth in various cultural contexts.[61]

Nellas returns to this understanding several pages later. In his words,

> ... ἡ ἀνάπτυξη ἡ ἐξέλιξη τῆς ἀνθρωπότητας καὶ γενικὰ τῆς κτίσεως φωτίζεται ἐσωτερικά, ἡ κατανόησή της δὲν περιορίζεται μόνο στὶς διαδικασίες ἀλλαγῆς ποὺ παρατηροῦνται στὸ ὑλικὸ τῆς εἰκόνας, ἀλλά, χωρὶς ἡ πρώτη αὐτὴ διάσταση νὰ παραθεωρῆται, ἐπεκτείνεται καὶ κατανοεῖται κυρίως ὡς ἀνέλιξη ἡ ὕψωση τῆς εἰκόνας ὡς τὸ ἀρχέτυπο. Ἡ ἀνέλιξη τῆς εἰκόνας ξεπερνάει ἔτσι τὰ ὅρια τῆς κτίσεως ... καὶ φθάνει μέχρι τὸ ἄπειρο. Ἡ ἐξέλιξη μὲ τὸν τρόπο αὐτὸ κατανοεῖται σ' ὅλες της τὶς διαστάσεις — ὄχι μόνο σ' ἐκεῖνες ποὺ προσδιορίζει ἡ ἐπιστημονικὴ παρατήρηση — καὶ καταξιώνεται.[62] (Our understanding of humankind and of creation more generally does not refer only to the process of change observed in the matter of the

---

58 See the patristic sources reviewed in Doru Costache, *Humankind and the Cosmos: Early Christian Representations*, Supplements to Vigiliae Christianae 170 (Leiden and Boston: Brill, 2021), pp. 335–37, 339–41. Doru Costache, 'The King, the Palace, and the Kingdom: Anthropic Thinking in Gregory of Nyssa, John Chrysostom, and Other Witnesses', in *John Chrysostom: Past, Present, Future*, ed. by Doru Costache and Mario Baghos (Sydney: AIOCS Press, 2017), pp. 235–65, esp. pp. 239–43.
59 Yannaras, *Elements of Faith*, pp. 58–62.
60 *Ζῶον θεούμενον*, p. 33. *Deification in Christ*, p. 33. See on this Nichols, *Light from the East*, pp. 175–77.
61 Vladimir Lossky, *The Mystical Theology of the Eastern Church* (Crestwood, NY: St Vladimir's Seminary Press, 2002), pp. 104–06.
62 *Ζῶον θεούμενον*, p. 44. *Deification in Christ*, pp. 41–42.

image. Without ignoring this first aspect, our viewpoint fundamentally extends to and captures the image's evolution towards or ascent to the Archetype. The evolution of the image thus exceeds the bounds of creation ... and arrives at the infinite one. In this manner, development is perceived in all its dimensions and significance, not only those established through scientific observation.)

The passage reaffirms that 'iconic' anthropology goes unaffected by the scientific study of human nature, but without overlooking this study. This is to say that the two perspectives have different competencies and that they complement each other. This understanding anticipates what recent transdisciplinary thinking calls the relationship between various levels of perception. Scientific anthropology explores human nature as such, whereas theological anthropology focuses on personal becoming and fulfilment. Neither of them gives the full picture of the human phenomenon, yet both perspectives contribute towards obtaining a comprehensive picture of the human phenomenon.[63]

Nellas's take on this matter is far from original; he actually believed that his position was profoundly traditional. At the end of his book's first part, he wrote a beautiful tribute to the early Christian theologians — above all John Chrysostom, from whom he quoted at this juncture — who were not afraid of either scientific progress or humankind's technological prowess.[64] In this light, the passage under consideration seems to convey an exhortatory message. Specifically, in the same way patristic authors contemplated human morphology through the available sciences of late Antiquity, out of missional concerns, a theologian of today should rephrase 'iconic' anthropology by any contemporary cultural idioms, evolutionary theory included. The only condition for such an undertaking is that it renders accurately and efficiently the message of 'iconic' anthropology.

The above passage explains, in indirect fashion, what makes possible such an achievement. It is not difficult to piece together the relevant details. Given that 'iconic' anthropology does not ignore the 'process of change' or evolution, the theological

---

63 See Doru Costache, 'Logos, Evolution and Finality in the Anthropological Research: Towards a Transdisciplinary Solution', in *Science and Religion: Antagonism or Complementarity?*, ed. by Basarab Nicolescu and Magda Stavinschi (Bucuresti: XXI Eonul dogmatic, 2003), pp. 241–60.
64 *Ζῷον θεούμενον*, p. 107. *Deification in Christ*, p. 98. Nellas gave also a list of early Christian and Byzantine theologians who, according to him, showed appreciation for research and technological development. *Ζῷον θεούμενον*, p. 110. *Deification in Christ*, p. 100. Contemporary research confirms Nellas's views of the patristic open attitude towards science and technology. Doru Costache, 'The Orthodox Doctrine of Creation', pp. 49–54. Doru Costache, 'The Transdisciplinary Carats of Patristic Byzantine Tradition', *Transdisciplinary Journal of Engineering & Science* 4 (2013): pp. 94–104, esp. 99–102. Doru Costache, 'Making Sense of the World: Theology and Science in St Gregory of Nyssa's *An Apology for the Hexaemeron*', *Phronema* 28/1 (2013): pp. 1–28. Doru Costache, 'Christian Worldview: Understandings from St Basil the Great', in *Cappadocian Legacy: A Critical Appraisal*, ed. by Doru Costache and Philip Kariatlis (Sydney, NSW: St Andrew's Orthodox Press, 2013), pp. 97–126. Knight, 'Natural Theology', p. 216. Andrew Louth, 'The Six Days of Creation According to the Greek Fathers,' in *Reading Genesis after Darwin*, pp. 39–55. Efthymios Nicolaidis, *Science and Eastern Orthodoxy: From the Greek Fathers to the Age of Globalization*, trans. Susan Emanuel (Baltimore: The Johns Hopkins University Press, 2011), pp. 8–12.

discourse cannot only assert its independence from the scientific perspective. The internal and the external dimensions of human existence hold together, and so do, too, theological anthropology and scientific anthropology. Elsewhere Nellas affirms that there is an obvious correspondence between the traditional representation of the human being and 'the most serious conclusions of contemporary anthropological researches' (τὰ σοβαρώτερα συμπεράσματα τῶν συγχρόνων ἀνθρωπολογικῶν ἐρευνῶν).[65] This position is consistent with his conviction on the need to integrate information from various disciplines in order to reach a deeper understanding of 'iconic' anthropology. This conviction, furthermore, relates to his point that one of the tasks appointed to the divinely marked human being is to grow in scientific knowledge.[66]

Verna Harrison observed that for Nellas, as for Stăniloae, scientific advancement is inherent to humankind's growth in God's image, constituting a positive dimension of the 'garments of skin' or our present condition.[67] It is clear that, far from entertaining the fear of certain Christians against shifting scientific paradigms and worldview changes,[68] Nellas emulated the saints' open attitude towards both scientific progress and technological developments.[69] Indeed, it is not progress and change that should worry us; it is the misuse of modern technology[70]—a position recently reiterated by the Holy and Great Council of the Orthodox Church (Crete, 18–26 June 2016).[71] Free of fear, the genuine Christian attitude is to engage, integrate, and transform human creativity, including science and technology.[72]

Nellas showed that the integration of various disciplinary perspectives alongside the theological one is not only possible, but necessary. His approach makes no allowance for the dramatic antagonism between creationists and evolutionists that obstructs current debates. But the final message of the above excerpt — and of the book in its entirety — is that human evolution entails experiences that elude material perceptions and quantitative measurements. Thus understood, in Nellas's case, as for Teilhard de Chardin, the theological take on contemporary scientific anthropology makes room for ethical values as much as it does for research. And although Nellas did not quote de Chardin here, what he proposed is a closely related view, rendered in a language that makes the message digestible for patristically oriented readers.

---

65 Ζῶον θεούμενον, p. 26. *Deification in Christ*, p. 27.
66 Ζῶον θεούμενον, p. 27. *Deification in Christ*, p. 28. Later, Nellas speaks of theology's positive attitude towards the world and of the 'garments' as in a sense God's gift, denoting human creativity. In turn, creativity is indication of a positive evolutionary process. Ζῶον θεούμενον, pp. 105–06. *Deification in Christ*, pp. 97–98.
67 Harrison, 'The human person,' pp. 88–89.
68 See on this, recently, Brown, *The Days of Creation*, pp. 290–97.
69 Ζῶον θεούμενον, p. 107. *Deification in Christ*, p. 98.
70 Ζῶον θεούμενον, pp. 108–09. *Deification in Christ*, pp. 99–100.
71 See *The Mission of the Orthodox Church in Today's World*, F11–F12. <https://www.holycouncil.org/-/mission-orthodox-church-todays-world> [accessed 25 March 2019]. Cf. Doru Costache, 'Orthodoxy and Science: Insights from the Holy and Great Council', *The Ecumenical Review* 72:3 (2020): pp. 396–408, esp. 401–02.
72 Ζῶον θεούμενον, pp. 110–14. *Deification in Christ*, pp. 100–04.

Nellas displayed a profound familiarity with the patristic authors who, aware of the need to communicate the Christian message in adequate ways, borrowed appropriate tools from various cultural frameworks and the available sciences. He replicated their achievements within the contemporary context by articulating Orthodox anthropology in the language of evolution, but avoiding the pitfalls of reductionism. He transfigured scientific anthropology by reinterpreting the available data within a holistic theological framework grounded in the spiritual experience. The title of his work, Ζῶον θεούμενον, 'the deified animal,' captures this accomplishment perfectly. By reinterpreting evolutionary science theologically, he proved that Orthodox anthropology cannot be reduced to a retrospective of mediaeval representations. For him, to look into the past was in order to learn how to proceed within the current circumstances.

HARALAMBOS VENTIS

The Enduring Temptation of Scientistic Reductionism as the Secular Equivalent to Ontotheology and Religious Literalism.

▼ ABSTRACT The present paper intends to address critically the natural human inclination towards reductionism as a perennial temptation scourging both scientific and religious narratives. In the former case, reductionism assumes the form of a strict and unmitigated 'scientism,' a forced narrowing of ontology to what is humanly conceivable, inimical to alternative modes of addressing ultimate questions. With regard to religion, on the other hand, the said tendency translates to an equally presumptuous glorification of human reason premised on its analogical similarity to the mind of God. The common denominator underlying both instances of reductionism is a covert, but hubristic, assumption that reality (physical as well as divine) can and must be cognitively domesticated by being framed in humanly recognizable coordinates, to the detriment of its inscrutable ontological integrity . It is the purpose of this paper to challenge this conceited assumption.

In my paper, I shall endeavor to formulate a critical assessment of scientism as a crude and unexpected instance of philosophical idealism parasitic to real science. My thesis more likely appears to be self-contradictory and will thus require extensive qualification, given the obvious metaphysical basis and implications of idealism, on one hand, and the notoriously anti-metaphysical purposes of scientism, on the other, routinely identified with observable truth and objectivity — virtues considered alien to classical idealism. A significant aspect of my aim here will be to argue that scientism and ontotheology are, appearances to the contrary, two sides of the same ideological coin known as 'reductionism,' and so must be equally rejected as feeble ways of making sense of reality, including the ultimate reality referred to as God.

Reductionism is a richly layered term with several distinct connotations (ontological as well as methodological), sharing a common denominator: the idea that complex systems can always be better understood by being reduced to their individual parts. Though quite useful for making sense of physical reality, reductionism can also become deeply problematic if pushed to extremes serving ideological or idiosyncratic agendas foreign to science proper. Reductionism is frequently identified with materialism, in part thanks to some superficial similarities that the two share, most notably a commitment to Occam's Razor, and Nominalism's overall ontological predilection for physical particulars inhabiting space-time. As denoted here, however, reductionism (αναγωγισμός, in Greek) is not synonymous with materialism *per se*, for materialism need not be ideologically-laden. Science is after all justifiably bent on examining the fundamental building blocks of matter, and the case could be argued that Christianity is likewise thoroughly materialist in its respective ontological commitments — as a faith both premised on God's enfleshment and bodily resurrection, and adamantly insisting on the physical reality of creation (in contrast, say, to eastern forms of spirituality picturing the world and selfhood as illusions, and against certain postmodern misgivings about normative representations of reality, including those of science, as disguised social constructs).

In its scientistic version, reductionism corresponds to an intentional dogmatic shortcut: meaning, an impulsive tendency to explain away qualitatively complex layers of reality in advance, usually in a rush to offer the simplest possible explanation of how the world is constituted and operates. The latter goal, while not necessarily erroneous, does I submit become problematic when existence in its unfathomable totality gets 'cut down to size,' in Thomas Nagel's famous phrase, as soon as it is reduced, that is, to the size of human conceptuality — an arbitrary leap that simply and no less arrogantly assumes with no supporting evidence that reality at large is correlative with our cognitive apparatus, i.e., with what is humanly graspable and testable. Such is the case, for example, with the highly popular eliminativist tendency in the philosophy of mind to explain away all mental activity (and the entire notion of 'mind' as such) not simply in purely physical terms, but as a beguiling fantasy, encompassing the reality of *qualia* as well, — precisely what marks us, that is, as unique persons savoring life in distinctive ways . One major problem with scientistic reductionism is that its metaphysical core goes easily unnoticed because of the covert form of its underlying assumptions, such as the perception that what is unseen or appears to be empirically superfluous must be unreal. Arbitrary leaps like these are habitually assumed as 'self-evident' in our empiricist (or even post-empiricist) culture, in effect granting eliminativism a misleading plausibility. It is these unacknowledged metaphysical premises and their detrimental consequences for real science that I wish to bring to the fore in my paper, with a view to suggesting that contrary to its realist aims, scientistic reductionism amounts actually to a very peculiar, veiled form of *idealism*, injurious to real science.

I. Human beings have rightly been called 'theopoetic' creatures, for they do appear to possess an obvious propensity to create gods after their own image, regardless of whether God, as understood in any of the three monotheistic faiths, in fact exists (a practicing Christian may actually agree with this statement, adding however that once created by God, humankind has been ceaselessly reciprocating the favor by constantly fabricating idols). Interestingly, some of these concocted metaphysical worldviews may even be devoid of theistic content but still be applauded regardless, as long as they purport to make full sense of the world. To comprise an alluring picture, powerful enough to hold us captive, a worldview need not invoke a divine agency at all; all it need do, actually, is to offer an all-encompassing, comprehensive view of reality with ironed-out corners and fully palatable to the human mind. Once the desired goal of furnishing a nuanced (better yet, a *reassuring*) account of reality is met, the ideological undercurrent of such worldviews usually passes unnoticed, and they are embraced for the comfort that they provide against our complex, frighteningly unfathomable cosmos. For that is precisely the purpose of these alluring constructs: they aim at softening the roughness of human encounter with a universe that is so overwhelmingly immeasurable, unpredictable, and hostile in its magnitude as to mandate some measure of its domestication, at least on the psychological level.

Those sufficiently versed in Christian theology may easily recall matching religious instances of this tendency. Biblical literalism, a routine source of fundamentalism, is the most flagrant example of a reductionist scriptural exegesis informing the vision of numerous sects and cults. This cluster of simplified religious narratives serves a satisfactory purpose: it reassures believers of God's steadfast providence and perennial morals in the face of new knowledge that appears to undermine heartfelt revealed truths, albeit of course at the terrible cost of severing all ties with reality. A less known theological counterpart to Biblicism serving the same purpose of reassurance (by resorting to a thinly veiled anthropomorphism), is the concept of 'ontotheology:' this is a controversial theological trend tracing its roots in a branch of medieval Scholasticism that in one way or another fashions God as a being, though to be sure as the greatest and sublimest of all beings.[1] When thusly conceived, God is more easily domesticated, i.e. shrunk to a humanly recognisable proportion than Søren Kierkegaard's and Karl Barth's 'infinite qualitative distance' between God and creation would allow. An alternative, but related, version of ontotheology (which for Heidegger was synonymous with the reification and banalification of being), is the tendency to link God so inextricably to the cosmos as to visualise Him as distinct yet inseparable from it. Platonism is a good example of an ontotheological metaphysics of that sort; for as canvassed in the *Timaeus*, Plato's Demiurge has shared all eternity with a pre-existing lump of unformed matter that He could only give meaningful shape to as opposed to creating it *ex nihilo*. On top of that major limitation, however, the Demiurge's 'divine' freedom and strength are further curtailed as this pre-existing matter imposes its own pattern on what the cosmos ought to look like — in effect, rendering Plato's 'God' more of a cosmic decorator than a creator of the universe in the Judaeo-Christian sense of the term. Critics of ontotheology include Immanuel Kant, Martin Heidegger, and Jacques Derrida as well as preeminent theist philosophers like Jean-Luc Marion, who has integrated antecedent criticisms of ontotheology to his phenomenological pursuits, with a particular eye to offering a robust theological alternative to the much-maligned (on charges of idolatry) concept of ontotheology.

---

1 Thomas Aquinas, *Summa Theologiae*, 1, Question 13 a 11c.

The Christian version of ontotheology is, as already mentioned, a mental image of God as a supreme being, which can be noetically ascended to with the aid of reason and revelation. The well-intended aims behind this notion are clear: 'God as the highest Being' was conceived, among other reasons, as a means of somehow bridging the frightening gap between God and humankind, and was premised on the Aristotelian notion of *analogia entis*, which was to become one of the most distinctive hallmarks of natural theology. The analogical similarity between divine and human personhood forms an integral part of St Thomas Aquinas's teaching,[2] and is also encountered in the writings of other Scholastic theologians, such as Suarez, Cajetan, and John of St Thomas. It is also known as the object of legendary, vehement rejection by the Swiss Protestant theologian Karl Barth, who assailed it as the contrivance of the antichrist, because the concept blurred the vital distinction between God and created beings. As such, *analogia entis* was condemned as an idol generator, in the sense that if the constituents of the created order alone can be assigned the attribute of 'being,' then any reference to God as Being, capitals or not, must denote a glorified creature, not the Creator of all that is.

It is a matter of intense dispute whether Aquinas did in fact mean the analogical similarity between God and humans the way Barth (and, long before him, Luther and Kierkegaard) believed that he did; for a careful reading of Aquinas indicates that the Angelic Doctor only intended to argue that humans bear at best a very deficient similarity to their Maker, and by participation in His divine glory at that, not by nature. Such qualifications, nevertheless, have not by and large managed to spare the notion of *analogia entis* from relentless criticism, hurled by theist and atheist quarters alike. Notwithstanding their disparate purposes, both camps have been elaborately vocal in unveiling the fundamental error bedeviling *analogia entis* and the ensuing falsity of God's ontotheological reification with devastating subtlety: for those theologians countering it, the concept constitutes an outright form of blasphemous idolatry; iconoclasts of an atheist bent, on the other hand, have seen in it a lamentable case of anthropomorphism, the projection to eternity and the divine sphere of a magnified version of human subjectivity, as Ludwig Feuerbach (and, to some extent, Friedrich Nietzsche as well as Karl Marx) so poignantly observed. If, therefore, the critique against the presumed analogy between God and humankind holds, theology is but a fiction amounting to a concealed anthropology, and humans end up worshipping an imaginary entity fashioned after themselves — thereby unsuspectingly succumbing to a mental bondage cashed in by the priesthood — as Cornelius Castoriades would ruefully maintain in his defense of abrogating religion as a prerequisite for the flourishing of democracy.

As already stated, the notion *of analogia entis* constitutes a neat example of an understandable human effort to domesticate ultimate reality (in this case, God) out of a heartfelt need to render it friendlier, more congenial, better understood, and so more palatable to the human mind. Intentions aside, though, this move is reductively enacted; and the reductionism involved in this presumed analogy between God

---

2   Thomas Aquinas, *Summa Theologiae*, 1, 4, 3 ad 3.

and humankind is easily lost on the rushed scoffers of faith, who are by and large content to simply dismiss theology altogether along with its errors with one stroke, in complete disregard of theology's own self-correcting efforts. But such rashness leaves us open to future repetitions of the selfsame error; for human ways of the mind tend to persist and to cut across eras and disciplines clad in misleadingly different garbs, if anything because they are a constitutive aspect of human nature, much like instincts.

It is my contention that in its own, distinctive mode of reductionism, scientism[3] constitutes a covert form of theology; a bad theology, at that, like the one surrounding *analogia entis*.[4] If my thesis is right, it suggests that metaphysics is inevitably lurking even in the most disinterested versions of naturalism. I am well aware of the outrageous resonance of this allegation, inasmuch as scientism purports to be metaphysics-free, objective, and non-ideological, precisely at the opposite end of mythology-laden worldviews, like those of religion. Scientism prides itself as a tested, time-honored form of presuppositionless enquiry into the world, in sharp contrast to theological pursuits, which are habitually chided and dismissed as deplorably non-falsifiable exercises in futility. Such, at any rate, is the critique leveled against free-floating metaphysics (whether based on revelation or not) voiced by such rigorous modern iconoclasts as Immanuel Kant, the logical positivists, and Karl Popper, among others. How would it be possible, then, to even remotely assert a link between scientism and metaphysics, especially when the metaphysics involved is of the pre-Kantian, maximalist sort decried by the partisans of materialism?

A considered attempt to answer this question should first draw a sharp distinction between scientism and real science — a vital demarcation that still gets blurred by the hastiness of scientism's adherents to sell their trade as uniquely dispassionate and objective. In actual fact, scientism is a worldview with its own background presuppositions and commitments, whereas science proper is an ongoing, open-ended, inconclusive enterprise, unconcerned with final ends amounting to comprehensive worldviews, particularly regarding ultimate questions. Admittedly, scientists do not entirely work in an ideological vacuum, if only because, like everybody else, they are

---

3   For a thorough, authoritative review of scientism by leading experts in the philosophy of science and religion, see *Scientism: The New Orthodoxy*, Richard N. Williams & Daniel N. Robinson, eds (London: Bloomsbury Publishing, 2015). For an apologia of scientism, see Alexander Rosenberg, *The Atheist's Guide to Reality: Enjoying Life without Illusions* (W. W. Norton & Company, 2011).

4   For a perceptive, if also unduly confessional, critical look on the Scholastic exploits of Aristotle's concept of *analogia*, see Christos Yannaras, *Heidegger and the Areopagite: On the Absence and Unknowability of God*, Andrew Louth, ed., Haralambos Ventis, trans. (London & New York: T & T Clark International, 2005), esp. pp. 43–47, 59–62, 74–75. To suggest a rendering of God 'beyond being', Yannaras utilises F. Nietzsche's as well as Martin Heidegger's critiques of the idolatrous onto-theological tendency to fashion God as the highest and sublimest of all beings. Contemporary Roman Catholic theology has taken note, and has thus impressively assimilated the critique of ontotheology to its body of thought, as in the pioneering phenomenological work of Jean-Luc Marion: see his emblematic monograph, *God without Being*, Thomas A. Carlson, trans. (Chicago & London: The University of Chicago Press, 1991, 2012), as well as his *In Excess: Studies of Saturated Phenomena*, Robyn Horner and Vincent Berraud, trans. (New York: Fordham University Press, 2002).

very human and thus inevitably influenced by a host of religious and political ideas. They can be skeptics, flat-out atheists, moderately or deeply religious, and prone to espousing either side of the left versus right political spectrum or anything in between. Not infrequently, their research is guided by intuition and gut feeling, or propelled by inherited beliefs. Selfishness, ambition, and vanity are also known to motivate them. At bottom, science is not the emotionally detached, sterilised activity envisioned by superficial idealisers of it.

Nonetheless, despite being humanly susceptible to their own dogmatic axes, conscientious scientists remain alert to the possibility of error and are generally willing to correct themselves in light of documented falsification of their work. If not, academic peers shall unfailingly give them flak, sternly and promptly. In this line of work, it is conclusions that matter, not whatever idiosyncratic beliefs prompted research in the first place. Isaac Newton was, among other things, a learned theologian and a skilled biblical exegete, and some key aspects of his mechanics had been at least partially influenced by his religious beliefs. The same is true of renowned chemist Joseph Priestley. But both made history for their pioneer discoveries in physics and chemistry respectively, not because of their forays in matters of faith. By the same token, Albert Einstein is not known and remembered today as a Spinozist, but as the founder of the Special and General Theories of Relativity. Private philosophical views, as well as faith (or lack thereof) are inconsequential for science and even become bad baggage when allowed to mire research. Hence, a so-called 'Christian science,' like its reverse counterpart (a pronouncedly atheist one), is a contradiction in terms and a betrayal of science's spirit of open-ended query.

The metaphysics tainting scientism concerns the latter's patronizing assumption (tacit or explicit alike) that scientific reasoning can ontologically only endorse and accept what is humanly conceivable . This may sound reasonable but is actually based on a subtle misconception. It is one thing to argue that science must focus on what is observationally and experimentally accessible to the human mind. It is quite another to stretch this tenet to determine what exists solely on the basis of what is constitutively compatible with human modes of apperception. In other words, it is a flagrant error to *reduce ontology to epistemology* and from there to deduce that anything resisting conceptualisation must be deemed irrelevant, nonsensical and ultimately fictitious.

Scientism is routinely guilty of succumbing to this temptation, as is easily observed in the manifestos of the self-styled 'new atheists,' such as Richard Dawkins, Christopher Hitchens et al. The major flaw in the writings of these authors isn't atheism, which is a perfectly reasonable, legitimate, and perceptive (even valuable) standpoint, aptly voiced by towering philosophical figures in the past. The black spot consists rather in the axiomatic dismissal of a transcendent, broader-than-human horizon that could accommodate deep questions resisting quantification. That doesn't mean science's scope should be curtailed to the empirical realm. Science is most certainly entitled to be vocal as regards perennial ontological issues traditionally addressed by religion and pre-Kantian metaphysics: for one thing, because no one must be allowed to monopolise public discourse in the blessed context of constitutional, pluralistic democracy; furthermore because science, with its unique investment in facts and falsification, can more effectively curb ignorance and fundamentalist nonsense than anyone else involved in the exchange of ideas. Scientific forays in cosmology, biology, geology, and particle physics are apt to correct prolonged myths concerning humankind and the cosmos, and can thus render metaphysics more accountable to reality than free-floating, dogmatic intuitions would ever be capable or willing of doing. In view, then, of its purgative performance in opposing falsehoods venerated as sacred truths, scientific scepticism is a valued ally to healthy, accountable, and in essence self-correcting modes of doing theology, certainly not inimical or threatening to the latter, as is often assumed.

Be that as it may, an *in toto* ban on faith, while respectable as a private viewpoint, would be arbitrary and counterproductive if argued in the name of reason and science. How so? Religions have justifiably caught heavy flack for promulgating hopelessly anthropocentric creeds. By the same token, however, science should also guard against the reverse and more insidious kind of anthropocentrism assumed by the current generation of hard-line atheists, as reflected in their stern insistence that in its totality, reality amounts to what is noetically palatable. Far from capitulating to such provincial restrictions, science leaves sufficient room for inscrutable ontological possibilities intrinsically capable of escaping our detection —constitutively and *in principle*. Had it been otherwise, the paradoxical, antinomy-laden field of quantum mechanics wouldn't have gotten off the ground at all.[5] As the fascinating history of twentieth-century physics demonstrates, scientists, without abrogating scepticism and common sense, eventually become accustomed to thinking counter-intuitively in their line of work; meaning they are forced to defy conventional concepts and expectations, the more they ascend or descend to the extreme scales of physical reality (this insight actually forms the main line of Karl Popper's reproach of Francis Bacon's naïve and shallow empiricism, whose inductivist method does not allow us to challenge the obvious, the way Galileo managed to do, because of his counter-intuitive reasoning). To be sure, science does indeed function with an immanentist logic, out of respect for the empirical limits of human cognition. Immanentism, however, need not be reductionist at all, provided it acknowledges that the edges of our cognitive faculties do not necessarily match those of external reality. As long as it maintains this vital ontological asymmetry, scientific immanentism could be designated as *apophatic* in orientation, in the sense of subscribing to a 'top-down'

---

5 A defender of scientism might counter-argue here that for all its paradoxes, Quantum Mechanics does enjoy an unquestionable scientific status because, apart from the accumulated observational data confirming its reality, it has been successfully utilised by modern technology in numerous ways, and so is not in doubt. This much, of course, is true. The impressive record of Quantum Mechanics' technological applications, however, doesn't change the fact that the deterministic mindset, which accords so perfectly with ordinary human experience and ways of thought as these take shape in the macrocosm, still challenges and resists the logic of Quantum Physics; so much so, in fact, that the unresolved incompatibility between the two is often seen as an unbearable scandal sometimes causing experts to try and mitigate or even thoroughly write off (rather unsuccessfully) the more unpalatable principles governing the realm of sub-atomic particles. In that regard, Albert Einstein's discomfort with quantum non-locality and the overall probabilistic character of Quantum theory, masterfully demonstrated in his debate with Niels Bohr, is very instructive.

realism prioritising (at least in principle, as a merest possibility) ontological realms, entities and entire states of affairs more complex and alien than the procrustean, deflated frameworks of post-Enlightenment rationalism and empiricism would ever allow for. In view of all this, reductionism would actually be detrimental to the open-ended spirit of science, appearances — and intentions — of its upholders to the contrary.

II. In its more sophisticated instances, scientistic reductionism is often propounded with the help of a pragmatist philosophy of meaning and language that similarly conflates what is *real* with what can be *known*, except in a more nuanced mode of argumentation. An idiosyncratic version of American Pragmatism has played a key role here, meaning not the early version of the movement, as established by William James, John Dewey, and Charles Sanders Peirce,[6] but the immensely popular late twentieth-century kind championed by Willard Van Orman Quine and Richard Rorty. Despite Rorty's persistent efforts to appropriate Quine as an ally to a common pragmatist cause, the two actually have very little in common, in terms of both strategy and aims: for all his emphasis on 'ontological relativity' and 'indeterminacy of translation,' Quine was no relativist and always maintained that science gives us the best; in that sense, he belonged to the epistemologically rigorous, 'right-wing' camp of Pragmatism. Rorty, by contrast, was so eager to establish the fluidity of the notion of truth, stripped of any inkling of 'objectivity' as part of his agenda to support social mobility, change, and progress, that he would not scruple at conflating scientific claims with the subjectivism of literary insights — fearful as he was that as an objective and normative pursuit, science could be nearly as oppressive as religion. Crucial to his purposes was the doctrine of 'linguistic non-representationalism,' a notion amply shared by Quine and Ludwig Wittgenstein. This concept maintains that reality, as accessed by humans, is always linguistically mediated instead of being directly available to us in its 'raw' form. As such, reality is inescapably subject to a limitless assortment of interpretations (or 'vocabularies,' in Rorty's own terminology), open to change and even total abandonment, should they prove hopelessly anachronistic and useless.

More crucially for the purposes of the present paper, 'linguistic non-representationalism' delimited all meaningful discourse to empirical statements about the world, indispensably relayed in a publicly accepted idiom (Wittgenstein was adamant that there can be no such thing as an intelligible 'private language'). Whilst the latter stipulation is reasonable enough, the underlying idea of this linguistic empiricism is that *sense* as well as *existence* (i.e. ontology) are correlative with what

---

6 In *Recovery of the Measure* (Albany, New York: State University of New York Press, 1989), Robert Cummings Neville defends the ordinary realism of this early generation of American Pragmatists from their stretched appropriation by Richard Rorty and his totalising categories of limitless 'interpretation' and 'conversation': see Ch, 2, esp. pp. 47–52. As Neville indicates, 'unlike both the hermeneutic and structuralist traditions … pragmatism is thoroughly naturalistic' (p. 49). In the process, Neville seizes the opportunity to stave off widespread but shallow and unfair dismissals of pragmatism, often from European quarters, as a 'crass, materialistic, and egoistic' movement (pp. 49–52).

is humanly perceivable and makes sense for *us*. So devised, this new source of immanentism comprises a *linguistic, de-*transcendentalised version of Kant's original non-representationalism: for just as Immanuel Kant had restricted our contact with the external world to the realm of the transcendentally constituted phenomena only, so is our awareness of reality hereby made dependent upon language. Such an intra-linguistic immanentism is prohibitive of the possibility to do philosophical work in the large-scale systematic fashion of, say, Plato and Descartes, or at least as pre-critical (i.e. pre-Kantian) metaphysicians, including Christian theologians, would have it — the reason being that for metaphysical claims to carry any weight, their makers should be able to see the world in its nakedness ('in itself,' as Kant said), unfiltered by language; this possibility may be afforded God, if He exists, but is constitutively denied to human beings, according to these linguacentrist theorists. Quine would be much more in agreement here with Rorty: as he bluntly declared, summarising the epistemological upshot of Wittgensteinian semantics[7] (and his own): *'Truth is immanent and there is no higher. We must speak from within a theory, albeit any of various.'*[8] Or, in Alexander George's condensed form of Quine's dictum, 'nonsense awaits if one fails to recognize that one must work from within, that one cannot leap outside language and all systems of belief [more so in Quine's case] to evaluate these from a distance.'[9]

---

7   Wittgenstein was no Pragmatist, and from all we know about him he'd more likely be appalled to find his insights mobilised in Rorty's cause. Nevertheless, his famous claim in the *Tractatus Logico-Philosophicus* (5.6) that the limits of language, thought, and the world coincide (fully retained in his later, revisionist phase of the *Philosophical Investigations*, e.g. 329, 337, 338, 339, 342, and esp. 344), places him firmly in the tradition of 'linguacentrism.'
8   Willard Quine, 'Things and their Place in Theories,' in *Theories and Things* (Cambridge, MA: Harvard University Press, 1981), pp. 23. Quine's thought revolves around a cluster of highly popularised philosophical catchwords such as 'indeterminacy of translation,' 'ontological relativity,' 'naturalised epistemology,' 'holism,' etc., all of which add up to his eliminative program rendering the concept of truth solely internal to languages and theories. His program of shifting conceptual legitimacy 'from talk of objects to talk of words' is thoroughly laid out in his *Word and Object* (Cambridge, MA: The MIT Press, 1960), wherein Quine declares that '[w]hat comes of the association of sentences with sentences is a vast verbal structure which, primarily as a whole, is multifariously linked to non-verbal simulation [this last reference is indicative of his empiricism]. These links attach to separate sentences (for each person), but the same sentences are so bound up in turn with one another and with further sentences that the non-verbal attachments themselves may stretch or give way under strain. In an obvious way this structure of interconnected sentences is a single connected fabric including all sciences, and indeed everything we can say about the world (p. 12). Thus Quine seems to have championed (along with Wittgenstein and his heir apparent Donald Davidson) the key presupposition of much of the twentieth century, i.e. "linguacentrism", earlier encountered in Willfrid Sellars' influential repudiation of the 'Myth of the [unconceptualised] Given' in 'Empiricism and the Philosophy of Mind,' Science, Perception and Reality (Atascadero, CA: Ridgeview, 1991 and more recently published in monograph form from Harvard University Press, 1997), where Sellars critiques and, to a certain extent revolutionises, classical empiricism by thoroughly conceptualising the most rudimentary bits of sense-data, building his case on arguments reminiscent of the work of Wittgenstein and Quine.
9   Alexander George, 'On Washing the Fur without Wetting It: Quine, Carnap and Analycity,' *Mind*, Vol. 109, No. 433 (January, 2000): 1–24.

Admittedly, this anti-realist approach, a transition from foundationalism[10] and realism to non-representationalist holism[11] has its merits, the most important of those being an emphatic re-affirmation of humanism in epistemology.[12] As Nicholas Wolterstorff explains in his neat summary of the 'realism versus anti-realism'

---

[10] Foundationalism may perhaps best be accounted for by the distinction its adherents have drawn between basic and non-basic beliefs, where the former of these are regarded as infallible and non-inferentially justified, comprising thereby a cognitive bottom-line or foundation upon which the entire epistemic edifice is erected. Such 'basic beliefs' may include faith in the existence of the self [cogito, ergo sum] and God for Descartes, or, alternatively, sense-data for the empiricists. Foundationalists see a real progress in knowledge, which they believe is attained cumulatively. The regress argument is the strongest one employed by the foundationalists, saying that we need basic beliefs so as to terminate what would else be an infinite epistemic regress. This argument originates in Aristotle's *Posterior Analytics*. Justification becomes impossible, so the argument goes, if a statement must be justified ad infinitum by something else. The Cartesian passage habitually cited as the inaugural statement of modern foundationalism is drawn from the set of four cognitive rules listed by Descartes in his Discourse on Method: 'The first rule was to accept nothing as true which I did not evidently know to be such, that is to say, scrupulously to avoid precipitance and prejudice, and in the judgments I passed to include nothing additional to what had presented itself to my mind so clearly and distinctly that I could have no occasion for doubting it. The second, to divide each of the difficulties I examined into as many parts as may be required for its adequate solution. The third, to arrange my thought in order, beginning with things the simplest and easiest to know, so that I may then ascend little by little, as it were step by step, to the knowledge of the more complex, and, in doing so, to assign an order of thought even to those objects which are not of themselves in any such order of precedence. And the last, in all cases to make enumerations so complete, and reviews so general, that I should be assured of omitting nothing.' Descartes: Philosophical Writings, selected & translated by Norman Kemp Smith (New York: The Modern Library, 1958), pp. 106–07.

[11] Best understood in its juxtaposition to foundationalism as a rival epistemological theory, holism (also known as 'coherentism') may be designated as the epistemological attitude that in one way or another undercuts the thick, foundationalist connection between theory and reality by denying their alleged one-to-one correspondence, granting them only a wholesale correspondence at best. Holism should be basically understood as a web of epistemic beliefs, neatly captured in Otto Neurath's famous metaphor of the 'conceptual boat', whose point is to illustrate the sheer impossibility of establishing direct and unmediated Jinks between our linguistic paradigms and extralinguistic reality. This is because we are visualised as being constantly adrift a vessel amidst a boundless linguistic ocean and so forced to reconstruct the boat of cognition plank by plank while afloat, forever denied the chance to build it anew from the privileged point of an extralinguistic 'shore'. Theologian Nancey Murphy draws out a helpful comparison/contrast between the two epistemological models. Holist theories of knowledge, she says, 'differ in several important respects from foundationalism. First, there are no indubitable (unrevisable) beliefs; nor are there any sharp distinctions among types of belief, only degrees of differences in how far a belief is from the experiential boundary. Second, for foundationalists, reasoning (construction) goes in only one direction — up from the foundation. For holists there is no preferred direction, and the kinds of connections among beliefs in the web are many ... In general, what "holism" means is that each belief is supported by its ties to its neighboring beliefs, and ultimately, to the whole; the criterion of truth is coherence'. From her introduction to Theology Without Foundations: Religious Practice and the Future of Theological Truth, edited by Stanley Hauerwas, Nancey Murphy, and Mark Nation, (Nashville, TN: Abingdon Press, 1994), p. 13.

[12] For a rigorous defense of realism in science countering all forms of subjectivism and relativism, see Michael Redhead's 1993 Tarner Lectures delivered at Cambridge University and published under the title *From Physics to Metaphysics* (Cambridge: Cambridge University Press, 1995).

debate: 'At issue is whether or not we are at home in the world. The anti-realist sees metaphysical realism as an alienating perspective; it regards the world and even ourselves as something out there, *over against us* and *alien to us* with which we have to cope [my italics]. The goal of the anti-realist is to show us that this is mistaken; we are not thus alienated. His path toward that goal is making us see that we are the *makers* of our world [italics in the original]. We are no more alien in the world than the artist is alien to his work which mirrors him back to himself as its maker ... But to regard ourselves as world-makers is to regard the world as an expression of ourselves.'[13]

As recapped by Wolterstorff, the project of humanising epistemology relies on an ideological contraction of the world enacted through an isomorphism between mind, language and reality, by which the impenetrable limits of linguistic non-representationalism are supposedly established. This new, updated 'critique of pure reason,' has been sold throughout the twentieth-century as an effective philosophical trick for demarcating sense from nonsense. For all its successful record of helping to keep flamboyant metaphysical claims at bay, however, it cannot be assumed as a truism, given the still moot relation between thought, words, and things. Much less should it be postulated as a foundational pillar for the pursuance of science: above all because science, while stringent in its demands for compelling evidence, cannot exclude the possible existence of inherently unfathomable entities and states of affairs, vastly alien from anything remotely perceptible or imaginable by creatures such as us. This anti-humanist alternative to reductionism reinstates a precious dose of humility in epistemology and must thus be preserved as a matter of principle, regardless of the practical uselessness of maintaining it, and irrespective of the healthy dose of scepticism that must always accompany metaphysical or ultimate concerns. From a philosophical angle, the arbitrariness tainting the above-mentioned contraction should be even more vehemently protested and challenged than blindly endorsed, following the perceptive insights of Thomas Nagel, Michel Marsonet and others. These theorists, falling as they do on the 'realist' camp of modern philosophy, have convincingly chided Wittgenstein's immanentist semantics for being a 'linguistic idealism' of sorts: meaning that his neo-nominalism, along with Quine's,[14] essentially

---

13 Nicholas Wolterstorff, 'Realism Versus Anti-Realism: How to Feel at Home in the World', in Realism: Proceedings of the American Catholic Philosophical Association, Vol. 59, Daniel o. Dahlstrom, ed. (Washington, DC.: American Catholic Philosophical Association, 1984), p. 184.
14 In his essay 'A Comparison of Something with Something Else,' included in his *Words & Life* (Cambridge, MA: Harvard University Press, 1996), pp. 330–50, Hillary Putnam contests the robustness of Quine's realism, setting for himself the bold and unthinkable indeed task (for most people versed in post-positivist philosophy of language) of blurring the lines between Quine's relative ontological commitments and Richard Rorty's historicism. In the process of a careful reconstruction of Quine's arguments, Putnam appears anxious to distance his own 'internal realism' from Quine's doctrine of 'immanent truth.' Quine's replies to critics notwithstanding, that neither the authority of ontology nor the authority of epistemology are in any way impaired by being seen as 'immanent' (ibid. P. 348), a claim he tries to further substantiate by recourse to the materiality of neurology and nerve endings stimulations as the empiricist basis of his system, Putnam still faults his internalism as hopelessly Pythegorean, a sort of 'transcendental Skinnerianism' (p. 349) not

'cuts reality down to size,'[15] to use Nagel's phrase. More elaborately, Wittgenstein's Quine's and Rorty's perception of language, despite their subtle differences, are chided as downsizing meaningful ontology to the capacity and limits of human conceptualisation, thereby rendering the notion of the real commensurate with the possibility of its epistemic justification. As Nagel explains in his groundbreaking *The View from Nowhere*, linguistic, post-positivist idealism, far from making its predecessor's claim that 'to exist is to be perceived' (*esse est percipi*), holds rather that 'what there is, is what we can think about or conceive of, or what we or our descendants could come to be able to think about — and that this is necessarily true because the idea of something that we could not think about or conceive makes no sense.'[16] It stipulates, in other words, that what exists or what is the case, at any rate, *coincides necessarily* with what is a possible object of thought *for us*, in effect subjecting all significant (i.e. meaningful) ontological discourse to the qualifications of the human mind: what there *is* and what we can *think* and therefore *talk* about, are all made co-extensive in a reductive move rendering human understanding the measure of all things. Michel Marsonet draws a similar parallelism between classical and linguistic idealism along the following lines: 'We might say, thus, that for classical idealism whatever is foreign to thought is unknowable, while for the analytic tradition whatever is foreign to language

---

qualitatively different from Rortyan intersubjectivity and culturalism. Putnam reaches his verdict by way of carrying Quine's idea of relative reference through to its ultimate consequences, as he sees them.

In *Ontological Relativity and Other Essays* (New York: Columbia University Press, 1969, p. 49), Quine had already tried to forestall an immediate objection to his theory of reference: If reference is granted sense only relative to a background language, what of the infinite regress into further and further background languages, relative to which each of these would in turn only make sense? Quine's reply invokes the relational doctrine of space, with its lack of an absolute position or velocity, as an analogue to the intra-linguistic relationality and relativity of reference (ibid). But Putnam thinks the analogy is flawed, since even relative position (in pre-relativistic physics) enjoys an absolute or invariant status that should be acceptable to any number of impartial observers at a time, regardless of which coordinate systems they individually use. This isn't the case with relative reference as Quine intends it, because as Putnam shows Quine interjects *interpretation* down to the point of specifying the background language itself without which (i.e. unless one acquiesces to it) there is no fact of the matter as to the truth value of any sentence. The arguments and counter-arguments are long to be recorded here with any justice done to their subtlety. Suffice it simply to state (and thereby conclude) Putnam's worry that 'once truth goes "immanent", there is no reason [as Rorty holds] to privilege science over literature, or over ethics, aesthetics, and so forth' (*Words & Life*, p. 343).

On the flip side to Putnam's portrayal, Jonathan Dancy sketches a more 'conservative' picture of Quine's philosophy, whose holism and internalism are significantly tempered by the suggestion that Quine may also be classified as a foundationalist, on account of the distinction that he draws between observation and non-observation sentences. Quine's coherentism is spared the excesses attributed to it by Putnam as a result of its empiricism, which ensures that for Quine 'there are data and there is theory;' a good reminder, Dancy concludes, that 'one cannot be an empiricist without being a foundationalist. Dancy, Introduction to Contemporary Epistemology (Oxford: Blackwell, 1985), pp. 100–01.

15 Thomas Nagel, *The View from Nowhere* (Oxford & New York: Oxford University Press, 1989), p. 109.
16 Nagel, p. 90.

is unknowable as well.'[17] Quinean scholar George Romanos appears to concur with Marsonet's assessment, albeit more as regards the semantics of logical positivists:

There was more than a slight Kantian flavor, then, to the positivist program ... The cutting edge of Kant's approach was the observation that there could be no pure perception of reality unmediated by human conceptualization ... Thus any knowledge of the world is necessarily relative to such a conceptual scheme, and the idea of any absolute or direct apprehension of reality is rejected as an impossibility. This is essentially the same outlook positivists came to adopt, except that, whereas Kant had located the organizing conceptual manifold through which all experience is filtered on the structure of the human mind, the positivists saw it now embodied in the very language of science ... Kant's strictures against projecting the features of our conceptualizations *onto reality itself* were paralleled by similar positivistic strictures against projecting the features of linguistic systems onto their subject matter ... Shifting the conceptualizing burden from human nature [where Kant had placed it] to language was also important in establishing the logical independence of the new epistemology from the rest of science. It represented a move away from psychological introspection to *purer logical analysis*» (italics provided).[18]

For his part, Nagel protests the Kantian as well as the neo-pragmatist/Wittgensteinian tendency to exhaust ontology in terms of what is conceivable to the mind (a contraction championed on the pretext of humbly 'acknowledging the limits of human cognition,' though in truth by clandestinely doing the reverse, i.e. by making those limits coextensive with the real): 'Any conception of the world must include some acknowledgment of its own incompleteness ... the world,' Nagel counter-argues, 'may contain not only what we don't know and can't *yet* conceive, but also what we could possibly never conceive.'[19] This realist view espoused by Nagel, 'amounts to a strong form of antihumanism: the world is not our world, even potentially,' since 'it may be partly or largely incomprehensible to us not just because we lack the time or technical capacity to acquire a full understanding of it, but because of our natures.'[20] Nagel, himself an agnostic intellectual bordering on atheism, is actually reminiscent here of St. Paul in his sober reminder of the cognitive unevenness between God and humankind: 'But now that you have come to know God, or rather *to be known* by God ...' (Galatians 4.9).

It goes without saying that not all scientifically inclined thinkers subscribe explicitly to this pragmatist epistemology (though often only because of a serious deficit in philosophical training). Nonetheless, and although they would stridently deny it, most appear to work with a tacit, secularized version of idealism's underlying tenet, that the human mind in one way or another determines ontology. From there, it's only a small step to the projection of human subjectivity to a level of ultimacy, either

---

17 Michel Marsonet, 'Linguistic Idealism in Analytic Philosophy of the Twentieth Century,' in *Current Issues in Idealism*, Paul Coates & Daniel D. Hutto, eds (Bristol: Thoemmes Press, 1996), pp. 114–15.
18 George Romanos, *Quine and Analytic Philosophy: The Language of Language* (Cambridge, MA: M. I. T. Press, 1983), pp. 23–24.
19 Nagel, p. 108.
20 Ibid.

in the form of an imaginary, comforting 'God as a Being' (as regards theologians) or in the sense of a minimised ontological horizon that mustn't exceed what is humanly perceivable and thus palatable to our finite sensibilities. In both cases, this idealist tendency constitutes a feeble way to domesticate what so frighteningly exceeds our human frontier.

Like science at its very best, cutting-edge theology likes to think big, outside the tiny box of conventional human modes of perception and imagination. To be sure, science's extraordinary claims are backed by matching extraordinary evidence, apart from which its discourse becomes one more narrative among others, not any closer to reality than fiction and/or coherently sounding conspiracy theories. Theological claims, on the other hand, albeit occasionally purporting to be based at least partially on experience, are of a different nature: they can neither be quantified, nor objectively proven or falsified, yet they are not inescapably irrational and arbitrary on account of being dependent on faith. Christian doctrines, to some extent like scientific theories *mutatis mutandis*, must pass through a series of rigorous tests before being gradually endorsed and validated as normative, despite having been initially premised on revealed grounds: they have a long history of intellectual development and consolidation, in the sense that their truth has been demonstrated by sophisticated arguments over long periods of time, in the context of subtle disputes and counter-arguments. Their truth is also gauged by the degree and manner to which doctrines fit into the overall Christological and Trinitarian architecture, as well as by their capacity to shed light on the human condition, by providing meaningful responses to humankind's deep existential concerns, past as well as present.

Admittedly, such criteria for assessing the stamina of Christianity's doctrinal apparatus are *internal* to faith, and as a result are dissimilar to the evidentialism followed by science. Still, that is but a half-truth applying to doctrines concerning God. Christianity's cosmological and anthropological claims, on the other hand, have an empirical component to them, which surely can and must be tested against the backdrop of modern science. Constructive criticism of that sort should be welcome by theologians, especially in view of the unfinished, on-going character of the Christian Tradition and its progressive, evolving cognitive take on creation — after all, the Christian faith is largely forward-looking by nature thanks to its eschatological orientation, which leaves us enough room for fresh insights, even for reconsideration of past errors leading to unwarranted social prejudices and discrimination. The present lines are written in the belief that science and theology can both serve the human cause in distinct but equally responsible ways: they can do so by being trailblazers, in the sense of stretching the mind to unprecedented lengths, by discovering new terrains, new and expanded modes of thinking, broader and more perceptive ways of looking at the universe, the one inside us and the one at large. For theology in particular, such an expectation translates to a deliberate abrogation of cheap, self-laudatory and backward-looking apologetics coupled by a relentless deconstruction of popular myths and idols, particularly of the *religious* kind still holding Christians hostages to a pharisaic caricature of their faith.

In more concrete terms, to be true to reality and honour it as befits reality's true magnitude, science and Christian theology must break away from the spell of *reductionism*, which as we saw entails a religious counterpart as well. To do so, they must allow, *at least in principle*, for the possibilities of cosmological and theistic forms of radical otherness. Such a bold stance entails the determination to repudiate the placating myth that what is in existence coincides with what can be an object of observation and study *for us*, as in scientism; or (where faith is concerned) by vehemently denying that Scripture and Tradition have infallibly and exhaustively pontificated about creation and humankind forever thereafter. This last precept must be combined with the renunciation of the appeasing but naïve and idolatrous conception of God as a 'Being;' for the latter is but an ideological construct, whose spurious ways, emulate the shallow bigotry of fundamentalists and are disastrously codified in a static, black-and-white 'tradition' by those who adhere to the 'letter' than to the 'spirit' of the Gospel. Only thus can science and Christian theology become truly emancipating activities, and open up our eyes to the limitless wonder of life (John 9.6–7).

BRUCE FOLTZ

Orthodox Christianity and the Archaic Experience Of Nature

▼ ABSTRACT Like science itself, our understanding of nature in modernity has undergone what philosopher of science Thomas Kuhn has called a 'paradigm shift.' This changed understanding of nature is especially notable in environmental thought, which was born not from the science of ecology, but rather began within the lived experience of the natural world, and was typically framed in experiential and often poetic and religious language. Early percursors and founders of environmental thought such as Rousseau and Blake and Hölderlin, Emerson and Thoreau, Muir and Leopold all proceeded from what Leopold, himself first of all a scientist, called 'an intense consciousness of land,' a beginning that this essay will argue is itself rooted in what may be called an 'archaic experience' of nature that ultimately has religious roots. Yet as Leopold also noted, our civilization is headed not toward this intense awareness of the natural world, but rather away from it, for our interaction with the natural environment is mediated not just by concepts, but by innumerable machines and gadgets. Looking deeper, however, we also find that our secularised world is deeply suspicious of the normative implications of such an 'archaic' experience of nature, and ultimately hostile to it, along with its religious moorings. The hesychast or mystical tradition of Orthodox Christianity, then, can perform a critical role in legitimizing this realm of experience, giving ontological and cosmological expression to what Western Christianity has too often come to see as a merely emotive realm. Refusing to separate the realms of nature and grace, this tradition sees 'empirical' nature as in fact an abstraction from our archaic experience of nature as always already spiritually and aesthetically charged. It exhorts us, then, to move not away from our experience of nature, but more deeply into it through what the Hesychast Fathers called *theōria physikē*, seeing 'into' nature to grasp its

Bruce Foltz • Eskerd College

foundations in the divine *logoi* or 'words' through which God articulates the *kosmos* into being and which secure the fundamental meaning of the phrase 'book of nature.' Thus, such 'archaic' experience retrieves and incorporates not only the *archē* or 'ruling beginning' of our own experience, but the *archē* of nature itself. Moreover, the *askēsis* or purification of the soul from worldly attachments that engenders this realm of archaic experience is itself prescriptive for our relation to the natural environment and the mode of economy that — together with sound scientific research — will be able to preserve it.

Science and the Foundation of Ecology

It is a curious feature of intellectual history that schools of thought may undergo dramatic, even seismic changes that may nevertheless go largely unnoticed at the time. We owe to Thomas Kuhn the insight that individual sciences may experience what he called paradigm shifts, involving not just conceptual innovation, but radically new understandings of what is to count as science at all.[1] But although this has taken place with regard to particular sciences, such as physics, the enterprise of science as a whole has also undergone perhaps the most radical shift of all. Beginning in antiquity as an essentially contemplative activity, oriented toward meaning or purpose (*telos*), it has been transformed in modernity into a mode of calculative rationality that seeks only efficient causes, abstracted from those questions of final causality or meaning that inevitably arise when we encounter nature pre-scientifically, i.e. when we experience the natural world not as an object of science, but within what Husserl called the *Lebenswelt* or life-world. In short, science has now come to inhabit a conceptual universe that is to varying degrees, depending upon the individual science, alien to the world as we experience it pre-scientifically.

Parallel to this general shift in the interpretation of science that took place at the threshold of modernity, we may discern a major metamorphosis in our understanding of the natural environment during the last two centuries, one that remains largely unnoticed. Although environmental thought originated in the lived experience of poets and naturalists, it has moved toward a strongly quantitative orientation, defining both problems and solutions in narrowly scientific terms. But there is reason to think that at least some paradigm shifts may be neither inexorable nor irreversible. This essay will argue that the Orthodox understanding of the natural environment should resist this movement away from the primacy of experience into conceptual abstraction, building instead upon the contemplative experience (*theōria physikē*) that is indigenous to it. It is by remaining true to its essentially noetic worldview, and using scientific findings as secondary to its traditional experiential orientation, that it can best contribute to environmental thinking in general.

---

1   Thomas S Kuhn, *The Structure of Scientific Revolutions* (Chicago: University of Chicago Press) 1996.

The Archaic Experience of Nature in Western Environmental Thought

Contrary to popular assumptions, environmental thought originated not in the science of ecology, which developed only later, but in an immediate and often poetic experience of nature, i.e. within what I shall call an archaic mode of experience. Just as modern natural science reached its triumphal zenith, there arose a counter-movement that included Romanticism (in Europe) and Transcendentalism (in America), and it is here that we find the beginnings of environmental thought. In eighteenth-century France, Rousseau contrasted an integral and harmonious sense of 'the natural' with the analytic and mechanistic views of nature in Enlightenment figures such as Newton and Hobbes. A few decades later in England, William Blake maintained that the scientific view of nature represented not an enlightenment or awakening, but a kind of slumber. Blake implored God Himself to save us from 'Newton's sleep,' depicting the great physicist in a remarkable monotype. Here, sitting naked on a large rock within a cave that suggests Plato's allegory in the *Republic*, Newton stares hypnotically at geometric abstractions upon a long scroll, oblivious to the striking environment surrounding him. Meanwhile in Germany, the poet Hölderlin evoked a natural world that still retained traces of its sacramental character, even as he mourned the progressive withdrawal from it of what he called the Holy. Simultaneously in America, Emerson called for the revival of an original, archaic experience of nature: 'The foregoing generations *beheld God and nature face to face; we through their eyes*. Why,' he asks 'should not we also enjoy an *original relation* to the universe?' 'Original,' and this means unmediated by concepts (either scientific or philosophical) that do not originate within our active relation to nature — i.e. he prescribes a mode of experience that is loyal to the origins of nature as it presents itself to us in our naïve, pre-conceptual, pre-reflective experience. His younger friend Thoreau, a hero of modern environmentalism, sometimes even found such an archaic experience of nature almost too powerful to endure. He recalls having stood on the windswept summit of Mt Ktaaden, like Moses on the holy ground of Mt Sinai: 'Nature here was something savage and awful, though beautiful. I looked with awe at the ground I trod on, to see what the Powers had made there, the form and fashion and material of their work. This was that earth of which we have heard, made out of Chaos and Old Night.'[2] Woven throughout the writings of these proto-environmentalists we find an elemental and often numinous encounter with creation.

With John Muir and Aldo Leopold, we arrive at easily the two most admired and influential founders of environmental thought. The son of a Scottish immigrant farmer and itinerant preacher, Muir sees wilderness as the enduring presence of Eden, where it is still possible to walk with God in the cool of the day — where we can encounter 'creation just beginning, the "morning stars still

---

2   Henry David Thoreau, *The Maine Woods*, in *The Library of America: Henry David Thoreau*, ed. Robert F. Sayre (New York: Library of America, 1985) p. 644 f.

singing together."[3] Parallel to the Desert Fathers, Muir sees wild nature as a sanctuary from the fallenness of the city, as that singular realm where "God's love is manifest in the landscape as in a face."[4] His ascetic sojourns in the mountains of North America, often alone and with few provisions, freed and purified him to experience the divine beauty of creation. He was a wilderness activist as well as a writer of poetic prose that enchanted his contemporaries just as it does for us today, and much of the wilderness that is now preserved in North America is indebted to John Muir.

Aldo Leopold, in contrast, was a professional conservationist, trained in the famous Yale University Forestry program. Yet he too wrote poetic, lyrical accounts of nature, which he experienced as inclining toward harmony and order and above all *beauty*. 'Poets sing and hunters scale the mountains,' he wrote, 'primarily for one and the same reason — the thrill to beauty.'[5] Leopold was the first to argue that we should approach the environment ethically, as citizens of a greater community that includes the land itself. But he believed this 'land ethic' must proceed not from something abstract and conceptual, but rather something experiential — not primarily from moral precept or hortatory persuasion, but rather from 'love, respect, and admiration for the land.' And this, in turn, entails something even more fundamental, something he called '*an intense consciousness of land.*'[6] It is something inclusive of this intense consciousness that I want to call 'archaic experience,' and which this essay itself will attempt to circumscribe, if not altogether define. And it is of great interest that Aldo Leopold, this very practical man who died helping to put out a wildfire, this very rigourous man whose training was scientific, sees the enterprise of environmental conservation as resting not primarily upon sound scientific findings, but upon a very personal mode of experience. 'Conservation' itself, he writes, is 'a state of harmony between men and land,' as opposed to a state of 'violence.'[7] These words convey moral and aesthetic intuitions, not scientific concepts — akin to the 'fierce green fire' he sees lingering in the eyes of a dying wolf — akin to the 'hidden meaning' of being in wolf country, that 'tingles in the spine of all who hear wolves by night,' — akin to what he calls 'thinking like a mountain' — indeed, akin to key terms such as order, harmony, and even beauty which still remain current in environmental theory, but with little awareness that their basis is ultimately aesthetic and theological rather than scientific.'[8]

---

3 John Muir, *My First Summer in the Sierra* (Boston: Houghton Mifflin, 1944) p. 213.
4 John Muir, *The Cruise of the Corwin*, in *John Muir: His Life and Letters and Other Writings*, ed. Terry Gifford, (London: Baton Wicks, 1996) p. 746.
5 Also Leopold, 'Goose Music,' in Aldo Leopold, *A Sand County Almanac and Other Writings on Ecology and Conservation*, ed. Curt Meine (New York: Library of America, 2013) p. 221.
6 Aldo Leopold, 'The Land Ethic,' in *A Sand County Almanac*, p. 187; italics added.
7 Leopold, pp. 175, 184 f.
8 Leopold, pp. 114 f.

The Decline of Archaic Experience in the West

But there is an elegiac note in his essays as well. For Leopold emphasised that 'our educational and economic system' is headed in the wrong direction, 'away from and not toward' this intense, poetic, archaic awareness of nature. We are, he laments, 'separated from the land by many middlemen, and by innumerable physical gadgets.'[9] Bored with the land, unless it is a golf course, we are unconcerned whether the food we eat or the clothes we wear come from the land itself or from chemical factories. In the sardonic words of C. S Lewis: '[We] are almost free of Nature, attached to her only by the thinnest, finest cord.'[10]

What has caused this decline of the 'intense consciousness of nature'? Why the eclipse of this archaic or poetic experience of nature, luring our children away from playing freely outdoors, and imprisoning them instead in solipsistic cyberspaces. Why is nature losing its tang, its zest and savour, at best holding interest for us only as we see it through the viewfinder of our camera phones, readying our next post for social media. Why have environmental concerns themselves shifted away from local matters such as preserving wild areas, fixating instead on increasingly intractable and often nebulous global issues that are typically buried within mountains of scientific data and computer modelling — with the sole panacea of ubiquitous governmental control relieving us of the need for a personal relation to living nature? Finally, why are environmental concerns now defined purely scientifically, as involving a larger domain of objects (the "natural environment") whose otherwise stable homeostasis is being upset by a smaller field of component parts (i.e. human beings)—a trope which is in fact more myth than science, as is shown by chaos theory and disturbance ecology?

One explanation is that proponents of this archaic experience of nature were fighting a losing battle all along, swimming from the beginning against a very strong current. Writing in 1917, the German sociologist Max Weber ironically refers to science using the Calvinist understanding of *Beruf* or 'calling,' ironic because he argues that a scientific calling must be premised upon the belief that our lives 'are not ruled by mysterious, unpredictable forces, but that, on the contrary, we can in principle *control everything by means of calculation.*'[11] For Weber, this means that nature is now 'disenchanted,' no longer holding either mystery or meaning for anyone other than those he dismisses as 'overgrown children' whose religious beliefs show they lack intellectual integrity. And he is even more dismissive of those who look to science as a 'path to God,' asserting 'today no one can really doubt in his heart of hearts that *science is alien to God.*'[12] From Weber's perspective, then, the figures just discussed are intellectual smugglers, trying to sneak past the customs inspectors (such as Weber himself) religious goods under the guise of philosophy and science, while

---

9 Leopold, p. 187.
10 C. S. Lewis, *That Hideous Strength* (New York: Macmillan, 1968) p. 178.
11 Max Weber, 'Science as a Vocation,' in *The Vocation Lectures* (Indianapolis: Hackett, 2004) p. 13; italics in original.
12 Weber, 'Science as a Vocation,' p. 1; italics added.

still relying, often unawares, upon an essentially Christian view of nature as creation, manifesting a divinely instituted harmony and order.

It is noteworthy that each of these six figures in fact drew, often tacitly, upon a childhood Christianity that shaped their early experiences of nature, but that they could no longer either practice or believe in any traditional form. Each lived during a time when the secularisation of Christianity in Western Europe and America was at a mid-point, a time when its first or second half-life had been reached — in which Christian valuations and sensibilities still remained engaging, and capable of sustaining a rich experience of nature as divine creation, even as they were becoming detached from the beliefs and practices that had originally animated and supported them.

Orthodox Views of Creation, Nature, and Environment

Looking toward the Orthodox East, however, matters are quite different. For while the Protestant Christianity that each of the previously mentioned figures had inherited was rapidly losing its few remaining sacramental moorings in physical reality, Orthodoxy retained its deep and essential roots in its experience of nature as divine creation.

A. Orthodox Christianity characteristically defines environmental issues from within its own experience of nature, drawing upon the findings of science not for its underlying principles, but only secondarily, to inform practical judgments about courses of action. As Metropolitan Kallistos Ware has put it, 'The [environmental] crisis is not really outside us ... It lies not in the ecosystem, but in the human heart.'[13] Or as stated even more strongly by Ecumenical Patriarch Bartholomew: 'The crisis that we face is ... not primarily ecological but religious; it has less to do with the environment and more to do with spiritual consciousness.'[14]

B. Nature is not seen as a self-enclosed, self-sufficient sphere that can be fully grasped through empirical science. The realms of nature and grace are not separated, as has been the case in the West since the Late Middle Ages. Vladimir Lossky states this succinctly: "he Eastern tradition knows nothing of 'pure nature' to which grace is added as a supernatural gift. For it, there is no natural or 'normal' state, since grace is implied in the act of creation itself ... Nature and grace do not exist side by side, rather there is a mutual interpenetration of one another, the one exists in the other ..."[15]

C. At the heart of the Orthodox approach to the environment is what since the fourth century has been called *theōria physikē*, the contemplative 'seeing' of nature, spiritual apprehension of the meaning of creation in relation to God and to ourselves. This is not a specialised pursuit for some few, but the second stage of spiritual

---

13 Kallistos Ware, *Ecological Crisis, Ecological Hope: Our Orthodox Vision of Creation*, cited in Andrew Louth, *Modern Orthodox Thinkers: From the Philokalia to the Present* (Downers Grove, IL: Inter Varsity Press, 2015) p. 346.
14 Ecumenical Patriarch Bartholomew, Foreword, in Margaret Barker, *Creation: A Biblical Vision for the Environment* (London: T & T Clark, 2010) p. IX.
15 Vladimir Lossky, *The Mystical Theology of the Eastern Church* (Crestwood, NY: St Vladimir's Seminary Press, 1976) pp. 101, 126, 131.

development in general, following the initial stage of *askēsis*, i.e. purification of the soul from the distorting effects of the passions. *Theōria physikē* sees the heavenly within the earthly, the eternal within the temporal, the energies of the Creator at work within creation. It is the culmination and perfection of what we have called the archaic experience of nature, for it is 'archaic' not only by encountering creation in a primordial manner — preceding both the abstractions of science and the conventions and distractions of society or 'the world' — but archaic in the truest sense that because it is ascetically purified, it experiences creation as it emerges from the hand of the Creator, removing its sandals to approach the *archē* proclaimed in the first verse of Genesis: 'In the *archē* or beginning, God created Heaven and Earth' (Gen. 1:1)

Archē is appropriately the first noun in the Bible, for the word signifies a beginning that is not left behind, but rather rules throughout the life of what it has inaugurated, prescribing not only its inception but its end (*telos*) as well. Just as appropriately, we find in the last chapter of the Bible that Christ, through Whom all things are created, names Himself 'the Alpha and the Omega, the Beginning (*Archē*) and the End.' (Rev. 22:13) To undergo some degree of *askēsis* — even if it is at Walden Pond just outside of Boston, rather than in the Egyptian Thebaid, and however incomplete or corrupted that experience may be—and through this purification to experience nature archaically, is to experience it in greater proximity to the Creator than everyday living often allows us.

D. With reference to us, *theōria physikē* experiences the *logoi* of created things, i.e. the inner essences (Bradshaw), the depth of meaning (Louth), the creative and singular 'thought-wills' of God (Lossky) that inhere uniquely in each creature. These *logoi* or 'sayings' are what God has to 'say' to us — not just to humanity in general, but even more importantly to each of us individually, as He addresses us within creation. They are inimitable, unrepeatable, unique reflections of the Logos Himself, encounters with Christ in this original or archaic mode of revelation that precedes Holy Scripture. Thus, we find St Isaac the Syrian insisting: 'The first book given by God to rational beings was the nature of created things. But the instruction set down in writing [i.e., scripture] was given after the transgression.'[16] So too St Ephraim the Syrian: 'in his book [of *Genesis*] Moses described the creation of the natural world, so that both Nature and Scripture might bear witness to the Creator.'[17]

And here we may note the absurdity, and perhaps even blasphemy, of certain founders of modern science who presumed to be the first to understand the language of God as He revealed Himself in His creation. Is it not both comic and hubristic to believe that God sought to speak to us through creation, but only in the hope that someday telescopes and microscopes, the infinitesimal calculus and differential equations would be invented so that we human beings

---

16 St Isaac the Syrian, *The Ascetical Homilies of St Isaac the Syrian*, trans. Holy Transfiguration Monastery (Boston: Holy Transfiguration Monastery, 1984) p. 41.
17 St Ephraim the Syrian, *Hymns on Paradise*, trans. Sebastian Brock (Crestwood, NY: St Vladimir's Seminary Press, 1998) p. 102.

could finally decipher what He had been trying to say all these many years? This is not, of course, to suggest that the Creator cannot be revealed to us through scientific results, for everything about creation is revelatory — its grandeur, its symmetries and regularities, and sometimes its disorder or fallenness, for nature is not always 'natural' in the archaic manner of its creation.[18] But the *primary* and *enduring medium* for God's self-revelation through creation, to which the Fathers consistently attest, must be understood as prescientific experience, and not any set of concepts, whether scientific or philosophical. Is this not why the Psalms and the other Wisdom Books of Holy Scripture — not to mention the preaching of Jesus, which often draws upon images of nature — present this divine revelation in nature symbolically, allegorically, poetically, not through the scientific concepts or mathematical theorems? Within Holy Scripture, God is revealed to us in nature primarily as a poet, and only secondarily as an engineer.

E. With reference to God, *theōria physikē* encounters the divine energies. And in contrast to the Western insistence on a divine simplicity that places God beyond earthly experience, the Orthodox East has maintained since the fourth century that while the divine essence or *ousia* is indeed forever shrouded in mystery, the *energeiai*, the energies or activities of the Creator can be, and should be, experienced everywhere within His creation. This powerful insight affirms that God is truly present in nature, without recourse to the pantheistic premises employed by certain environmentalists seeking to 're-enchant' nature through neo-pagan motifs.

F. Finally, Orthodoxy acknowledges the cosmic dimensions of Fall and Redemption that Western Christianity has largely dismissed as mythological. Orthodox Christianity still affirms that nature has been corrupted, distorted, and fallen due to human transgression. And this, in turn, rests upon the Orthodox belief that the highest calling of humanity is not to scientific activity, as Weber believed, but to draw together the great divisions of creation across which we are uniquely situated; St Maximus the Confessor delineates these polarities as uncreated and created, noetic and sensible, heavenly and earthly, paradise and inhabited world, and finally male and female. It is indeed because of this high calling to serve as cosmic mediator, that human disorder could generate such essential devastation in the world. Humanity, then, is not primarily a part of the environment, as deep ecology asserts, nor even merely its microcosm as is sometimes claimed, but as St Maximus affirms, we are ourselves the macrocosm, singularly called to celebrate and consecrate all creation and offer it up in praise and thanksgiving to its Creator. It is for this same reason that Christ became incarnate as a human being, the New Adam redeeming the cosmic chaos introduced by the first Adam, and calling us to work towards not just a restoration of the original paradise, but its higher transfiguration. And here

---

18 In a fallen world, much that is found in empirical nature, such as cancer, is quite unnatural, i.e. contrary to the order of creation that its Creator has bestowed. As the Fathers often remind us, disease and corruption are symptoms of the Fall, which nevertheless do not vitiate the inherent goodness and beauty of creation.

lies the deepest meaning of archaic experience, for we are called to help prepare for a New Beginning, a New *Archē*. Citing St Maximus, Florensky formulates this great calling lucidly: 'Through Christ man is deified; through man all creation will be deified.'[19]

The Environmental Challenge for Orthodox Christianity

Leopold was right, and to a certain extent strikingly consonant with Orthodox figures such as Metropolitan Kallistos and Patriarch Bartholomew: what we call 'environmental crisis' will not be resolved without an intensified experience of creation — although he is less clear that this will require some major manner of asceticism and some measure of spiritual transformation. And indeed, an Orthodox orientation must surely incorporate the best science, but it cannot base itself upon a scientific worldview. On the contrary, scientific implementations must themselves be directed not by further scientific analysis, but by the archaic experience of nature that is, in fact, the foundation upon which we always already stand, albeit often like Blake's Newton, we are oblivious to it, enchanted by theories, concepts, and abstractions. Not surprisingly, we find a parallel conclusion in secular thinkers such as Edmund Husserl, founder of phenomenology, whose last writings focused upon the problematic relation of science to society, a problem that he argued derives from science as an abstract and derivative mode of consciousness that must be re-connected with its roots in living, archaic experience for which, for example, the earth must always be not one planet among others; it is and must be the very 'ark' upon which we necessarily depend not just for our sustenance, but also the 'referential foundation for our spatial orientation as such.'[20] And it is a great challenge for Orthodox Christianity to show how its theology and practice can most truly evoke, shape, and elevate this archaic, pre-scientific, living experience of nature.

Parallel to the succession of environmental founders in the West discussed earlier, we could easily assemble a splendid Eastern lineage whose encounter with creation goes much deeper, and carries the exposition of archaic nature much farther. In Dostoevsky, for example, we find in the speeches of Elder Zosima a vision of nature

---

19 Pavel Florensky, *The Pillar and Ground of the Truth: An Essay in Orthodox Theodicy in Twelve Letters*, tr. Boris Jakim, (Princeton: Princeton University Press, 1997), p. 525, n. 479.
20 'The earth is the ark which makes possible in the first place the sense of all movement and all rest as a mode of movements. But its rest is not a mode of movement.' Edmund Husserl, *Foundational Investigations*, Marvin Farber trans., cited in Maurice Merleau-Ponty, *Husserl at the Limits of Phenomenology, Including Texts by Edmund Husserl*, ed. Leonard Lawlor and Bettina Bergo (Evanston: Northwestern University Press) 2002, p. 89 'We have a surrounding space as a system of locations — i.e., as a system of possible terminations of motions of bodies. In that system all earthly bodies certainly have their particular "place", but not the earth itself.' Edmund Husserl, *Foundational Investigations of the Phenomenological Origin of the Spatiality of Nature: The Originary Ark, the Earth, Does Not Move*, cited in Merleau-Ponty, p. 122.

as infused with divine energies, saturated with divine grace.[21] In the early work of Bulgakov, we find a philosophy of economy based upon an experience of the Edenic foundations that endure in creation, and upon our human calling to actualise them within human community.[22] In Florensky, himself a scientist and mathematician of international distinction, we find a phenomenology of creation, along with a powerful critique of how the Enlightenment worldview distorts our ability to experience God in creation.[23] In Yannaras, created nature is comprehended not through the Western language of *substance* but through the living language of *relation*, with nature seen as everywhere issuing an invitation or *klesē* to hear God speaking to each of us individually, through this particular flower, that very cloud overhead. Nor should we ignore the great monastics of recent time such as St Paisios and St Porphyrios, who eloquently articulate the glory of natural creation as speaking the language of its loving Creator.

Beyond Muir, Leopold, and the others, whose theological foundations are often inchoate and improvised, these writers, thinkers, and monastics of the Orthodox East (and there are a host of others) are rooted in two millennia of Orthodox tradition. They recall environmental thought not just to its own *archē*, but call it forward to the promise of a deeper and more enduring beginning. It is up to Orthodox Christians themselves to facilitate their reception not just in the secular West, but throughout those Eastern lands that are not yet deeply secularised, and where only an ecology that is soundly based upon a religious foundation will ever be taken seriously.

Modern natural science has been of incalculable benefit to the world, not only through practical applications such as modern medicine, but through uncovering formerly hidden aspects of God's revelation in creation. But when science overflows its boundaries and becomes the basis for a worldview, it gets distorted and hybridised into that modern sphinx called scientism, a profoundly unscientific conflation of science and metaphysics. As Heidegger put it, science then becomes 'the theory of reality.' For traditional Christianity, however, there is only one theory of reality, itself rooted in a radical empiricism exceeding that of modern science — the empiricism of *theōria physikē*, which has taught with unfailing inter-subjective verification throughout two millennia that reality is itself Christological. If our understanding of the natural environment is to comport with a Christian worldview — rather than subvert and disenchant it, as Max Weber foresaw a century ago — it must proceed from the Cosmic Logos through Whom the divine energies invite us to communion with God Himself.

---

21 See, for example, Bruce V. Foltz, 'The Glory of God Hidden in Creation: Eastern Views of Nature in Fyodor Dostoevsky and St Isaac the Syrian' in *The Noetics of Nature: Environmental Philosophy and the Holy Beauty of the Visible*, (New York: Fordham University Press, 2014), pp. 187–202.
22 See Foltz, *Noetics*, chapter 'The Resurrection of Nature: Environmental Metaphysics in Sergei Bulgakov's *Philosophy of Economy*,' pp. 88–112.
23 See Bruce V. Foltz, *Byzantine Incursions on the Borders of Philosophy: Contesting the Boundaries of Nature, Art, and Religion* (Cham, Switzerland: Springer, 1991).

GEORGIOS MESKOS

Science at the edge of Eternity

▼ ABSTRACT Many physicists and other scientist researchers, in order to overcome the deadlocks of Quantum Theory and the General Theory of Relativity, or the issues related to the mind-brain problem and the nature of consciousness, end up adopting an extended physical reality. A line of thought represented among others by Julian Barbour, Roger Penrose and Lee Smolin seeks to construct the extended physical reality with the tools of physics and mathematics alone. Wolfram Schommers believes that basic physical reality goes beyond the image of reality that our brain forms and on this premise develops its own mode about reality. Large number of researchers, of all specializations, extends and deepens the study of the relationship between mind and physical reality by formulating a variety of scientific views, some of which are indeed impressive. All these researchers introduce, in one way or another, an extended physical reality that has as a common denominator some kind of eternity from which temporality emerges by physical processes. In this sense, many religious experiences are the result of the structure of the physical world. Iain McGilchrist in *The Master and His Emission, The Divided Brain* and *The Making of the Western World*, gives us all the means to explain and interpret why the human brain, although it comes in contact with and knows this eternal reality, had to rediscover it through the language of mathematics and physics.

Introduction

Modern science describes the natural world with the help of two great theories, Quantum Theory (QT) and General Theory of Relativity (GTR). So, she develops her ontology, that is, attempts to describe everything that exists, the universe and what this includes, life, humans, consciousness and cognition with the help of these two theories, or possibly with another that will unify and replace them.

Georgios Meskos • Independent Scholar

The QT and GTR are extremely successful theories and they make predictions that have been verified with great accuracy. Yet from the very beginning they have been accompanied by what we call paradoxes. That is, they predict and describe situations that are fundamentally opposed to what we call daily experience. At the same time, they are fundamentally incompatible with each other. These issues have been studied and described in many ways by many experts.

Quantum paradoxes are the most well-known and somehow easiest to perceive. Indeed, it is easy to conceptualise a paradox as some physical entity being simultaneously at many locations, or as many physical entities communicating in zero time to each other. We cannot understand how this is done, but we understand, more or less, what we are talking about. On the contrary, the paradoxes of the GTR are extremely tricky and unclear. It is not easy to feel what contraction of time or space expansion is, much less so to understand how this can happen.

Both the QT and the GTR have significant philosophical consequences, primarily because they affect our image of what we call ultimate physical reality. The QT, because it is obvious that we do not yet have a sufficient understanding of what is really happening in the quantum world. And this is true, in spite of the fact that for more than one hundred years, the best physicists and mathematicians tried to resolve her paradoxes albeit unsuccessfully, and the reality of her many practical applications. So, there is a big hole in the ontology of physics that is not foreseed to close. The existential consequences of this hole in QT are not so great because in our lives we do not happen to encounter quantum phenomena.

The Theory of Relativity

On the contrary, philosophical questions posed by GTR are much more difficult, but also immediate. Indeed, they relate directly to what we are and what we are going to be, both us and the world we live in. This theory leads to two major conclusions and acceptance of them entails significant contradictions and difficulties. The first is the idea of the Big Bang, i.e. the idea that whole Universe started from an anomaly. Initially this was a theoretical conclusion, but over the decades and with the development of technology, it is now supported by a variety of empirical observations. Cosmology is now an empirical science.

The Big Bang is associated with many unanswered questions of a technical nature, but also two issues of particular existential interest. The first is the question about what existed before the Big Bang. A theological type of answer[1] is not satisfactory for many and various reasons, which I will not discuss here. There are several scientific answers which are also problematic, especially in the light of the second question.

The second question is related to the fact that the universe we observe has proved to be extremely, extremely, exceptional. It is the famous problem of the natural

---

1 Paul Davies Niels and Henrik Gregersen, *Information and the Nature of Reality, From Physics to Metaphysics* (Cambridge: University Press, 2010).

constants, where a multitude of them is incredibly accurately regulated. That is, if it were infinitesimally different, this universe, and we, could not have existed. It is now commonly accepted that the universe is not what it is, randomly. The important question that remains unanswered by current cosmology is why the universe exists and why it is what it is.

In this discussion the QT is also involved because the moment of the Big Bang is in its own field. So, the GTR leads us to the Big Bang where the QT is dominant, and at the same time we know that QT and GTR are fundamentally incompatible with each other. At this point the concerns, though delicate and often obscure, do not raise strong controversy. This is not the case with the other major issue raised by the GT — the problem of time.

The ontological connection between space and time leads to the well-known concept of space-time and its paradox, i.e. the dependency of time flow rate on the velocity and the change in length as a function also of the velocity. All of this is well known. What is not particularly well-known is the fact that when space is connected with time, then the concept of time as we know it and believe it disappears. This is the idea of Block Universe.

Block Universe

At the heart of this idea, which if it is to be fully understood requires a familiarity with mathematics and physics, is the ontological equivalence of the past, present and future. In other words, there is no difference between the past, the present and the future. If the present is real and exists, the past is also real, that is, it has not ceased to exist, and the future is as real as if it is already present. So, Parmenides defeats Heraclitus: There is nothing new under the sun.

The argument that leads to this conclusion is extremely solid, but the conclusion is completely inconceivable.[2] How is it possible for the past to exist equally alongside the present and the future? In such a universe what can be the idea of freedom? For these reasons and for others that can be added, many of those who come to deal with these issues reject strongly and emphatically the GTR, which is subject to intense controversy in all possible ways. However, it is consistently outperforming any experimental or observational test. The dilation-contraction of space and time has been experimentally verified many times, even in the dimensions of everyday life, cosmological observations confirm it, and the discovery of gravitational waves has come to further enhance her credibility.

So, at this moment, when we are discussing the ultimate physical reality, we have the following situation. As far as the microcosm is concerned, QT is extremely successful, but strongly resists every attempt to interpret it. Many possible interpretations have been proposed, but none have been generally accepted. As far as the macrocosm is

---

2   See for example Vesselin Petkov, 'Is There an Alternative to the Block Universe View?' in by Dennis Dieks, ed, *The Ontology of Spacetime vol. 1* (London: Elsevier, 2006), p. 207.

concerned, GRT is similarly successful, but leads to conclusions that are considered unacceptable. Both theories are incompatible with each other.

This incompatibility is illustrated in the way they treat time. For the QT, time is real, and it is an independent variable, for GRT time is a dependent variable and therefore not autonomous and practically non-existent. These issues are known from the early twentieth century, during which all the great physicists struggled to deal with them, but in the twenty-first century it is now becoming a common belief that it cannot be done. On the contrary an increasing number of scientists are looking for different ways to resolve these issues. Among them we find top names of modern physicists and cosmologists.

Brain, Mind and Physical Reality

Before we discuss these new directions, we should mention another area of scientific research which is directly involved in the debate on the nature of the ultimate physical reality. This area is the relationship of mind and brain. Although knowledge about brain function has greatly increased, it is unclear how thoughts, feelings, memories and, in general, mental functions are connected with the brain. Nevertheless, what we think of as the universe — a natural realm along with whatever is in it — is nothing more than decoded information that enters our brain through our sensory system, followed by an optical representation of this information, constructed by our brain.

Our attempt to understand the relationship between physical reality, brain, and mind, that is, mental representations of physical reality and physical reality itself, is undermined by the fact that the brain understands the world through the brain, and it is self-referential. Finally, there are two major issues. First, whether the ultimate physical reality has a one-to-one correspondence with the mental representation of the ultimate physical reality that our brain creates. In other words, whether there are physical realities out there that our brain, due to its structure, cannot perceive.

The second issue is the question of whether our brain is the physical space where our mental representations are stored or whether they are 'located' somewhere else. Although the idea that our brain works as computer is losing ground as time passes, I will use the computer image to define the above question which may take the following form: Is the brain the entire computer, or is it just the keyboard and the processor, whilst information is stored at means that are located elsewhere?

Before we move forward, we need to make a clarification that is often ignored by those dealing with these issues. The distinction between ontology and epistemology. The distinction between what is real by itself and what we as a human species can know as real. There is a fundamental discrimination between ontological reality and epistemic reality, something that is typically reflected in quantum indeterminacy, which is supposed to be ontological, and uncertainty due to chaotic phenomena which are by their nature epistemic.

Classical and Extended Ultimate Physical Reality

Thus, in the search for the ultimate physical reality, we can distinguish two lines of scientific thought. According to the first, there exists only what we can 'see' either directly or indirectly, with our sensory faculties and our scientific instruments. The ultimate physical reality that is accepted as real by this line of thinking I call classical ultimate physical reality, whose ontology is the ontology of modern physics or a smooth extension of this ontology. In this sense, dark matter and strange energy, the multiverse, or a universe of many spatial dimensions that predict various theories are classical ultimate physical realities

The second scientific line of thought extends the ultimate physical reality beyond what we can 'see' with our corporeal senses and our scientific instruments, into realities of different ontological status, so we can call the ultimate physical reality that accepts this scientific line of thought, as extended ultimate physical reality.

For more than a century, scientists have tried to solve the issues of QT and GTR within the context of classical ultimate physical reality. But early on, the other line of thought appeared within an interpretation of the QT, the interpretation of David Bohm, that of the hidden variables, which naturally encountered a fierce reaction.[3] But over the decades and after the disappointment experienced trying to solve the problems within the context of classical ultimate reality, more and more scientific papers have been published, exploring the possibilities of an extended ultimate physical reality.

Next, we will present a brief summary of the core ideas and suggestions of well-known scientists to unfold these fascinating puzzles and to intergrate the image of the universe and ourselves within it. Needless to say, the reference to these theories is short and quite basic so it must be noted that these are scientific proposals, highly worked out and developed, which utilise the ability of modern mathematics to describe and handle abstract or generalised concepts.

Julian Barbour

We start with Julian Barbour a physicist who is perhaps one of the first who wanted to address the issue of the compatibility of the QT and the conceptualisation of time according to GTR. In his book, *The End of Time: The Next Revolution in Our Understanding the Universe*[4] he introduced the concept of successive moments, he called them Nows[5] in which we live our everyday life. Barbour's work is extensive; he and his collaborators continue to work on his ideas and develop and update

---

3 Sheldon, Goldstein, "Bohmian Mechanics", in Edward N. Zalta, ed, *The Stanford Encyclopedia of Philosophy* (Summer 2017 Edition), (https://plato.stanford.edu/archives/sum2017/entries/qm-bohm /).
4 Julian Barbour, *The End of Time: The Next Revolution in Our Understanding the Universe*, (Oxford University Press, 1999).
5 Julian Barbour, The End of Time, p. 16.

them. We are interested in how he extends physical reality to form a suitable, for him, model of the universe.

Initially, he did something quite expectable in attributing a status of ontological substance to the phase space, which is usually considered to be a mathematical entity use by scientists to describe the evolution of natural systems. The phase space is by definition timeless, so in this case eternal. Everything that exists in the universe we see corresponds to a curve, a geometrical path in the phase space. The ontological background of beings lies in this, and as it resembles the world of Plato's ideas, he calls this phase space, Platonia[6].

Interestingly, the study of Platonia's evolution leads him to the conclusion that in Platonia, all that is true are shapes that are scale invariant, therefore the proportions are kept unchanged, which reminds us of the concept of logos-logoi (reasons-ratio) of ancient philosophy[7]. These shapes in combination with numbers, are expressed in the beings we observe in the universe[8]. We should point out that these are not the result of conceptual thinking and reasoning, but of extensive processing of physics and mathematics, which has not been completed yet, but has inspired other scientists, such as Lee Smolin who will be mentioned later. It is worth observing that he accepts without questioning that there is an external objective physical reality and that there is a one-to-one match between it and our daily experience.[9]

Summarizing, Barbour's extended ultimate physical reality includes a natural background which is eternal and unchanged, there is no change in it depending on the time, and it comprises nothing else but sizes (numbers) and shapes in a phase space.

Roger Penrose

Another well-known physicist, with strong philosophical concerns, is Roger Penrose, known for his extensive writings and scientific work. One of his latest research projects is described in his book, *The Cycles of Time, an Extraordinary New View of the Universe*,[10] where he investigates the issues we examine here and formulates the conclusions of his life's work. The fundamental issue that concerns him is to answer the question of how the universe has emerged and why it has the characteristics it does. As he is a leading scientist who has been occupied for decades by these issues, his work is thorough and at the same time modest. He investigates this question

---

6 Julian Barbour, The End of Time, p. 44.
7 Georgios Meskos, "The notion of Logos from Heraclitus to modern physics" (https://www.academia.edu/12881725/THE_NOTION_OF_LOGOS_FROM_HERACLITUS_TO_MODERN_PHYSICS).
8 Julian Barbour, Tim Koslowski, and Flavio Mercati, "A Gravitational Origin of the Arrows of Time", Physical Review Letters 113, 181101 (2014).
9 Barbour et al, A Gravitational Origin of the Arrows of Time, p. 50.
10 Roger Penrose, *The Cycles of Time, an Extraordinary New View of the universe* (The Bodley Head, London, 2010).

based on the concept of entropy. The main question takes the form: how entropy reached a terrifyingly negligible value for the universe that we see to emerge under the impact of the second thermodynamic axiom[11]. If you take seriously the notion of entropy, and Penrose and others do, then every idea of a circular history of the universe is impossible. The idea of a big crunch cannot lead to a big explosion because it is accompanied by a maximisation of entropy[12].

The solution therefore is that the ultimate physical reality consists of a sequence of universes that follow each other. Each universe inherits some of the characteristics of the previous one and develops some news ones, through an evolutionary process, so that at some 'moment', our own universe emerges. He calls every such universe Aeon from the corresponding Greek word. So, there *is* a succession of Aeons.[13]

Every Aeon, that is, every universe is the manifestation of a massless reality[14] defined by natural laws that are conformal, i.e. they maintain proportions regardless of the scale of magnitude, from the infinitely small that correspond to the moment of the Big Bang, to the infinitely large, the time of the thermal death of the universe. At this time of infinite expansion there is a smooth transition to a period of infinite contraction and a new universe appears with slightly different characteristics. The period of an Aeon is estimated at 10^{100} years![15]

Penrose's model is very similar to that of Barbour, since at the core of both are homeomorphisms of the shapes in the space of phases, which is nothing other than the homeomorphism of natural laws. The novelty of Penrose's ideas lies in the fact that he speaks neither of a pulsating universe nor of parallel universes but of successive universes. In this way he answers the question of why our universe has the characteristics it has, something that probably does not concern Barbour.

Lee Smolin

The well-known physicist Lee Smolin in his book, *Time Reborn*[16] develops his positions thoroughly. He first explains with great success why the classic approach to modern physics leads to the annihilation of time. This is particularly disturbing to him because if there is no time then there is no change and if there is no change then things simply 'are' and therefore cannot be explained. His ultimate goal is to answer the question of why this universe exists though it might well not exist[17].

The model it develops has the following characteristics. He initially distinguishes two types of time, although he does not state it clearly, probably because he has no way of doing it philosophically. He distinguishes the time that 'exists' inside

---

11 Roger Penrose, The Cycles of Time, p. 122.
12 Roger Penrose, The Cycles of Time, p. 124.
13 Roger Penrose, The Cycles of Time, pp. 146–47.
14 Roger Penrose, The Cycles of Time, p. 147.
15 Roger Penrose, The Cycles of Time, p. 145.
16 Lee Smolin, *Time Reborn* (Houghton Mifflin Harcourt, Boston, New York, 2013).
17 Lee Smolin, Time Reborn, p. 97.

the universe from the 'time' that exists outside the universe. His central choice is the rejection of the idea of multiverse and the development of the concept of the evolution of natural laws[18]. This choice fundamentally differentiates his perception of the ontological background of the universe from other ontological models developed by other scientists and gives the notion of time a dominant position without introducing some kind of teleology, as does e.g. Amoroso whom we will discuss next.

The theory of the multiverse claims that there are infinite universes, one of which happens to have the characteristics of our own universe. Smolin rejects this idea and explains why, but he does not adopt Penrose's idea for a sequence of universes with different inherited attributes that arise from the differentiation of the original conditions and chooses the idea of evolution of natural laws themselves. So, at some stage of their evolution the universes will acquire the features we see now[19].

So natural laws acquire an ontological priority over the universe and to simplify things, the question arises as to where 'laws' lie. To answer this question, he manipulates the QT according to the interpretation of a special kind of hidden variables[20]. He adopts the idea of shape dynamics, developed by Julian Barbour[21], but instead interprets the GTR in a very specific way. He reforms GTR so that its basic substance is not space but time[22]. For these ideas to work, we again reach the conclusion that there is a deeper natural background from which all beings emerge[23].

This background has no spatial dimensions, everything 'is' together![24] Within this non-local background there exist the laws that defined all the beings that we find in our universe, so time is 'measured' by the rate of change of these laws. He describes the way by which, the space and time we live in is emerging. He hasn't been able to fully explain this natural process up to now but gives enough details about.[25] It is obvious that from an ontological point of view, time is different in the non-local background from time in the world we live in. As far I have noticed by now, he has not at all processed this substantial distinction.

Throughout this extensive and complex development of physics and new ideas, he takes no account of the question of the relationship between the reality we see with that which really exists.[26] The relationship between the physical world and the brain is an issue that concerns other researchers and creates other problems and opens up new horizons.

---

18 Lee Smolin, Time Reborn, pp. 123, 132.
19 Lee Smolin, Time Reborn, p. 124.
20 Lee Smolin, Time Reborn, pp. 155, 162.
21 Lee Smolin, Time Reborn, p. 168.
22 Lee Smolin, Time Reborn, p. 170.
23 Lee Smolin, Time Reborn, p. 172.
24 Lee Smolin, Time Reborn, p. 191.
25 Lee Smolin, Time Reborn, p. 188.
26 Lee Smolin, Time Reborn, p. 112.

Wolfram Schommers

Wolfram Schommers in his book, *Mind and Reality, The Space-Time Window*[27] deals exactly with this issue. We do not have direct access to what actually exists, which he calls external or basic reality. Information coming from this reality enters through different paths in our brain and our brain automatically reproduces the image of the world we 'see'. The major question is whether there is a one-to-one match between the basic reality and the image that our brain constructs.[28]

While the aforementioned physicists give, without discussion and reflection, an affirmative answer to this question and work with the tools of physics and mathematics to describe this basic reality, Schommers with strong arguments gives a negative answer.[29] The immediate consequence is that the external reality is purely metaphysical, while the inner one, which we perceive as external, is the product of the biological evolution of the living organisms on our planet and obeys its rules.[30] Something very plausible since the process of biological evolution determines the amount and the type of information that the biological brain must 'process', from the outside reality and which is necessary for the survival and growth of biological organisms.

Within this context, space and time do not exist in the external reality but are categories of the inner reality created by the brain. But the brain, that is, the image we have of the brain, is an element of the inner reality, that is, a mental construction. In this sense, there is no distinction between mind and brain; there is only mind and what is 'out there' about which we have no direct knowledge.[31]

The inner world, which is all 'intellectual', is organised at various levels. At the first level there is what we consider 'matter' and 'material', on another level there are concepts or natural laws.[32] On the other hand, the external reality must not be discriminatory, it must be all present at the same time, a unified reality, a single entity in which there is neither space nor time.[33] With all this equipment Schommers examines the role of evolution, the role of observer and of course gives his own answers to the big questions of modern physics.

The Universe from Inside

From the moment the quest for the ultimate reality entered the field of the relationship between mind, brain and the natural world, scientists from many other disciplines

---

27 Wolfram Schommers, *Mind and Reality, The Space-Time Window*, (World Scientific Publishing Co. 2015).
28 Wolfram Schommers, p. 5.
29 Wolfram Schommers, p. 189.
30 Wolfram Schommers, p. 114.
31 Wolfram Schommers, p. 125.
32 Wolfram Schommers, p. 89.
33 Wolfram Schommers, p. 92.

have been involved in the debate and this field of research has expanded considerably. At the centre of their interest is the question whether the study and description of the natural world is objective or not. This question arises from the realisation that we observe the natural world from within it and not from outside, so by definition we cannot have a complete picture of the natural world but only a partial one. We are also in constant interaction with it and therefore the image that we have, has subjective elements. This raises the need for an endo-physics, a physics that will take this into account. A series of texts on this subject can be found in *Endophysics, Time, Quantum and the Subjective*.[34]

When subjectivity comes to the forefront, then the question about consciousness and its nature becomes essential, and a variety of human experiences, such as psychological, religious, artistic, and extrasensory, are at the heart of the interests of the researchers. The reasoning is simple: a complete understanding of the ultimate physical reality cannot leave out of its quest this entire range of human experiences.

In this perspective, over the past 20 years, dozens of papers have been published on the theme of the combination of mental and physical realities. However, unlike the majority of similar work in the past that did not follow the scientific methodology and denigrated the research in this area, the most recent papers aspire to have an acutely technical scientific character. Among them we decide here to illustrate the ideas of Richard L. Amoroso,[35] not because they are the most convincing but due to their originality and his effort to include the fullness of human experience, both sensory and spiritual, within a scientific physical theory. His ambitious programme aims at the synthesis of at least six scientific fields, psychology, philosophy, biology, physics, cosmology and computer science![36]

Although, as far as it has come to our attention, he does not declare it clearly, Amoroso must be a follower of the connection of theology and science[37] within a frame of a version of the Intelligent Design[38]. He extends the fundamental background of physical reality with a single cognitive field[39] which coexists with other known fields of traditional physics. The peculiarity of this field is that it has a teleological character, that is, it causes and leads the evolution of beings in one direction, leading to self-organisation, and to the emergence of ever more complex forms and is correlated with consciousness. This cognitive field has nothing to do with intelligent beings or intellect, but it is part of an integrated cosmology.

---

34 Rosolino Buccheri, Avshalom C. Elitzur, Metod Saniga, editors, *"Endophysics, Time, Quantum and the Subjective"*, (World Scientific Publishing 2005).
35 Based on his extensive text, Richard Amoroso, "Through the Looking Glass: Discovering the Cosmology of Mind with Implications for Medicine, Psychology and Spirituality", in the *"Aspects of Consciousness Essays on Physics, Death and the Mind"*, edited by Ingrid Redriksson, (McFarland & Company, Inc., Publishers 2012), p. 147.
36 Amoroso, Through the Looking Glass, p. 148.
37 Amoroso, Through the Looking Glass, p. 175 and p. 149.
38 Amoroso, Through the Looking Glass, p. 151.
39 Amoroso, Through the Looking Glass, p. 164.

The work of Amoroso and his associates is interesting because it relates the human spiritual experience with 'hard' science. He does not hesitate to use all the tools offered by physics and mathematics to give a technical and scientific character to his view.[40] He makes predictions that if disproven will betray his error.[41] Some of these predictions were unfortunate because the discovery of the gravitational waves and the Higgs particle did not match his expectations. In any case, his attempt should be considered as exploratory and not definitive.

The Common Denominator

Most physicists and cosmologists would wish to explain the existence and structure of the universe without the introduction of entities which we cannot observe directly or indirectly. If the universe was static and the QT had not developed this would be easily feasible. But the universe is not static, it is not true that it just 'is'. It evolves, therefore it is in a continuous becoming, without ceasing to be. On the other hand, the QT is prooved to be not local. In some incomprehensible way, the entities that form the universe at the same time are 'being' and 'becoming' and at a fundamental level are in instantaneous and constant correlation with each other. And all of them are wonderfully coordinated by laws, natural laws.

For over a century, attempts to include all the above in a narrative that would not extend the ontology of natural sciences with new elements, failed, so we arrive to the quite safe conclusion that this enrichment of physics' ontology is inevitable. And already many scholars of all disciplines are working in this direction by developing a wide range of such model-narratives.

For those who care about philosophical and existential enquires, it is obvious that the world we see emerges from another deeper reality which, in all its candidate versions, involves the characteristics of non-locality and timelessness. We have seen that even Smolin who wants to revive time, speaks about the time, which is not the time we are living, but a time that measures another reality, that measures another kind of change, the change of natural laws.

Every element of our world is in direct connection with this deeper reality. Hence, human existence is by definition part of both physical realities, and the brain may be proved to be the link between the experience of everyday life and non-local and timeless physical reality. It does not matter what type of mathematics a scientist uses to describe all of this, and it does not matter what at any given time is the prevailing natural theory that will describe this deeper physical reality. It is important that human existence is involved both in everyday life reality, and in such a deep natural eternity.

---

40 Richard L. Amoroso, "The Physical Origin of Subtle Energies: The Principle of Self-Organization Driving Living Systems" in Richard L. Amoroso, ed, *Complementarity of Mind and Body: Realizing the Dream of Descartes, Einstein and Eccles*, (Nova Science Publications, 2010), pg 240–75.
41 Richard L. Amoroso, *The Holographic Anthropic Multiverse, Formalizing the Complex Geometry of Reality*, (World Scientific Publishing, 2009).

Iain Mcgilchrist

At this point, the baton must be passed to the book of Iain McGilcrist, *The Master and his Emissary, The Divided Brain and the Making of the Western World*.[42] This is an extensive work with an enormous amount of information coming from clinical observations and other scientific research into the functioning of our brain. Some time ago, he published a summary of this book in which he sets out the most important conclusions of his study entitled '*Ways of Attending, How Our Divided Brain Constructs the World*'[43] in which we will make references.

Should any of the previously mentioned, or especially the unmentioned theories, finally proved to be true, whatever that means, the tool with which we come into interaction with the outside reality is our brain and therefore in this sense the brain is what creates the reality we see. McGilchrist then examines the effect of the biological structure of our brain on the image of the world it constructs.

His interest is focused on the fact that our brain, as in all mammals, consists of two hemispheres. So why do the two hemispheres exist? McGilchrist systematically explains the reasons, but here we are interested in the view he has also developed analytically, that the two hemispheres have different and conflicting 'personalities', two different wishes, actions and plans for the future and approaches about the world.[44] The composition of these two different realms is us.

Simplifying McGilcrist's extensive analysis, we can say that the right hemisphere has a holistic, intuitive and systemic understanding of the world, in constructing the image of the world we see, while the left hemisphere approaches the world analytically, inductively by observing details.[45] While at the beginning of human history and the origin of civilisation the right hemisphere is the dominant one, the left is dominant as we approach the modern age in the Western world. In other words, it is a fact that in antiquity, and I would say in pagan cultures more generally, the metaphysical, theological and intuitive philosophical thinking is the result of the dominance of the right hemisphere. The prevalence of science, of rationality and scepticism is the result of the left hemisphere's dominance.

Without being an expert, I think it is a matter of cultivation and training in the context of our specific culture so that our conscious mind can more or less utilise one or the other hemisphere of our brain or, to be precise, the information they provide each of them. Eventually I think that 'we' at all times are involved in the battle of the hemispheres as they strive to gain our attention.[46]

The path that McGilchrist opens up with extensive arguments, is indeed unique because it enables us to understand that the intuitions of ancient religious and philosophical traditions are no different from the intuitions of modern scholars. In

---

42 Iain McGilcrist, *The Master and his Emissary, The Divided Brain and the Making of the Western World* (Yale University Press, 2009).
43 Iain McGilcrist, *Ways of Attending, How Our Divided Brain Constructs the World*, (Routledge, 2019).
44 Iain McGilcrist, Ways of Attending, p. 20.
45 Iain McGilcrist, Ways of Attending, pp. 19 and 22.
46 Iain McGilcrist, Ways of Attending, p. 20. and 25.

antiquity, the human brain stands against the outside world and understands and describes it based on the data of the right hemisphere and later with utilisation of the left hemisphere's capabilities, one studies, analyses and finally describes the outside world based on information provided by the left hemisphere.

However, as this analysis and knowledge advance, the formation of an image very similar to that of the right hemisphere is inevitable. We are not schizophrenic. Whether we like it or not, so long as the left hemisphere gradually broadens and deepens knowledge of the world, it will gradually approach the understanding of the right hemisphere. And of course, the understandings of the right hemisphere will lose their magical or supernatural character and will become elements of the natural world. We are on the threshold of natural eternity.

The Reality of the Religious Experience

The religious experience, as all religious people live it, has some common characteristics. These include the feeling of communicating with something or someone beyond the perceivable world, the experience of forecasting the future, or distant events, or even the feeling of temporarily leaving the body, believing in eternal life, or believing in reincarnation. The faithful believers of religions interpret all these experience in the context of the supernatural and they often use them as evidence of the truth of their faith. On the other hand, sceptics place them in the realm of imagination, or psychological delusions, denying any reality of religious experiences.

However, developments in scientific thinking and the new knowledge that we gain, as we have described above, open up new ways of understanding the religious experience. It is the structure of physical reality that allows us to have these experiences. We are by definition involved in the timeless natural reality, but in some, yet inconceivable way, we are experiencing the life of temporality. This is an experience of real dichotomy, but in the context we have described here it has a different explanation, as it could be a characteristic of a unitary ultimate physical reality.

Someone could ask, therefore, do religious beliefs and rituals play any role in the religious experience? Why is the miracle happening preferentially in the religious world? These questions find reasonable responses when one acknowledges attention as an important factor of our mental functioning. By controlling attention, the complex mind-brain, is capable of experiencing the ultimate reality without the constraints of space and time because physical brain is immersed in the timeless reality. Each religious tradition develops its own techniques, methods and ways that some of its believers can experience the supernatural, that is, the ultimate physical reality.

The path of scientific research and thought that we have described is an authentication of religious experience and emotion, but also a great challenge for theologies of religions, and especially for Christian theology. To connect or even identify the ultimate reality with the notion of deity, is something perhaps feasible. The great challenge for Christian theology is to connect this reality with the concept of a personal God.

CHRISTOPHER C. KNIGHT

Incarnational Naturalism: A Solution to the Problem of Miracles?

▼ ABSTRACT The concept of "miracle" is often understood in terms of some kind of understanding of the "supernatural." However, because the Orthodox tradition has a different understanding of the term "natural" than is to be found in Western Christianity, those events which are spoken of as miraculous may be affirmed in terms of a kind of "enhanced" naturalism that is based on the doctrine of the incarnation. This "incarnational naturalism" conforms to St. Maximos the Confessor's understanding of the presence in all created things of the divine Logos spoken of in the fourth gospel. Augustine of Hippo's conception of "higher laws of nature" reflects this understanding, which is reinforced when the Orthodox understanding of the sacramental mysteries is expanded so as to be applicable to all divine action. In particular, the patristic understanding of the empirical world as in some sense "sub-natural" can be used to see the miraculous, not in terms of God "interfering" with autonomous natural processes, but as a return to the truly natural world intended by God in his creation of it. This understanding of divine action has been seen as a component of the "theological turn" that has recently begun in discussions of divine action in both East and West. The advantages of this model are, it is argued, both theological and apologetic.

Miracles and the Laws of Nature

One of the results of the scientific revolution in the early modern era was an increasing stress on the functioning of the world according to 'laws of nature.' Because of the new science, phenomena that had previously been attributed to God's direct action increasingly became understandable in terms of these laws, and some began to wonder whether eventually all events would come to be understood in this way.

Christopher C. Knight • Institute for Orthodox Christian Studies, Cambridge

Eighteenth-century philosophers sometimes went further and argued that, to all intents and purposes, this understanding was in fact already substantiated, so that the notion of miracles — with the possible exception of the act of creation itself — had become redundant. (Among those who accepted this view were the deists, who accepted the validity of arguments from design and so did not become atheists. The God that they believed in was not, however, the God of classical Christian belief, but simply a creator of the cosmos who, after the moment of creation, had become nothing more than what has been called an 'absentee landlord.')

At the heart of this Enlightenment period discussion was a set of assumptions that had at least some of their origins in mediaeval Western thinking. Already, before the rise of scholasticism, there had been a tendency to think about nature as something to which divine grace was added as a supernatural gift. This tendency continued in scholasticism, in which, although God was still seen as the 'primary' cause of all events, normal events were seen as also having a 'secondary', natural cause. In the case of miracles, it was believed that there was no secondary cause, so that such events were seen as entirely supernatural.

This scholastic picture did have a certain subtlety, not only because God — as 'primary' cause — was still seen as active in natural processes, but also because grace was always seen as 'completing' nature. In the Enlightenment period, however, there was a tendency for this subtlety to be lost. The natural world was increasingly seen as a kind of clockwork mechanism understandable through science, and those who still believed in miracles tended to see God's continuing action in the world as limited to those events for which no scientific explanation could be found. There was thus a new emphasis on 'gaps' in scientific explanation, and a view of God developed that is sometimes now referred to as the 'God of the gaps.'

In recent Western Christian discussion — especially within Protestantism, though also with effects in the Roman Catholic world — there has been a reaction against this model. This has led to a new stress on the way in which God should be seen as working *in, with and under* the laws of nature. However, because Western Christian thinking has tended to assume a separation between God and the world, this stress inevitably poses the question of how 'special' divine action can occur. If God is assumed to be 'outside of' the world, then the question of how He can 'get in' remains. This understanding of separation, with its emphasis on the autonomy of the cosmos's normal functioning, tends to see special divine action as requiring what is sometimes called a *causal joint* between God and the world, through which God can manipulate the outcome of those laws. Much effort has been expended in attempting to identify this causal joint in a way that is scientifically literate. Typically, the non-determinism of the quantum mechanical picture of the world has provided the conceptual foundation for this effort. However, in an important study by Nicholas Saunders, the success of this model has been questioned.[1]

---

[1] Nicholas Saunders, *Divine Action and Modern Science* (Cambridge, Cambridge University Press, 2002) This model, which has set the terms of the debate about divine action within the so-called science-theology dialogue of the last half century, has been seen by Wesley Wildman as based on

Naturalism

As an alternative to this approach I have — in my book, *The God of Nature*[2] and in my recent book, *Science and the Christian Faith*[3] — advocated an approach that is based both on philosophical arguments about the concept of naturalism and on important aspects of Orthodox theology. In the philosophical component of this argument, I have argued that we need to take into account, not only miracles with a religious meaning, but all reported events of a paranormal kind. I have urged that — despite the difficulties of dealing with anecdotal evidence — we need not only to recognise the possibility of such events, but also to see them in a naturalistic way. This is possible, I have argued, by defining naturalism more broadly than it sometimes is: not in terms of what can in principle be uncovered by the scientific methodology, but in terms of the more general belief that the world always functions consistently — that is, in a way that we can describe in terms of obedience to 'fixed instructions.' These instructions, in their simpler manifestations, I see as susceptible to investigation through the scientific methodology, and thus nothing that represents robust scientific theory need, in my view, be challenged. However, I argue that not all such instructions are necessarily susceptible to investigation through the scientific methodology, since at levels of high complexity — such as that of the *personal* — these fixed instructions will simply not be susceptible to the *repeatability* criterion that is so important for scientific methodology. (We cannot, for example, put two people in a laboratory and tell them to fall in love so that we can observe the process.) This is not to deny that such processes follow what we might call law-like patterns, with identical outcomes arising from identical situations. Rather, it means that there is an *epistemological* barrier to our exploration, in that the criteria for identifying identical situations are simply not available to us.

In terms of this understanding, I have suggested that naturalism need not, *a priori*, preclude events that are seen as paranormal or miraculous, since neither of these terms has any necessary connotations of the supernatural. (The root meaning of the term *miracle*, for example, is simply 'that which excites wonder.') Such events, I have suggested, may be seen as coming within the bounds of naturalism because they may be seen as analogous to what in physics are known as changes of regime, such as the onset of superconductivity in certain materials when they are cooled to below a particular temperature. In such changes, once a certain threshold is crossed, discontinuities in properties occur. The difference between this kind of regime change, which may be explored scientifically, and what is considered paranormal, lies only,

---

a "personalistic theism" that represents "a distinctively Protestant deviation from the mainstream Christian view." See Wesley Wildman, "Robert John Russell's Theology of God's Action", in Ted Peters and Nathan Hallanger, eds *God's Action in the World: Essays in Honour of Robert John Russell* (Aldershot, Ashgate, 2006) 166.

2 Christopher C. Knight, *The God of Nature: Incarnation and Contemporary Science* (Minneapolis, Fortress Press, 2007).

3 Christopher C. Knight, *Science and the Christian Faith: A Guide for the Perplexed* (Yonkers NY, St. Vladimir's Seminary Press, 2020).

I have suggested, in the way in which, in the latter, the repeatability criterion is not straightforwardly applicable at a practical level, so that investigation through the scientific methodology becomes difficult or impossible.

Theological Considerations

It is at this point that patristic theological considerations come into play. The first of these considerations relates to an aspect of Western theological thinking in the period before that thinking became dominated by scholastic understandings. This is the way in which the philosophical distinction that I have made — between natural processes that are straightforwardly susceptible to scientific investigation and those that are not — may be understood in terms of the way in which St Augustine of Hippo, in the late fourth century, wrote about miracles. The point here is that we might now interpret his view as suggesting a distinction between 'lower' and 'higher' laws of nature. Miracles are not, in this approach 'supernatural' events but instead are to be seen — in much the way that I have suggested — as outcomes of 'higher' laws of nature that are not susceptible to our investigation.[4]

This understanding is, I believe, also supported by aspects of the Eastern patristic tradition. At the heart of my interpretation of this tradition is my observation that it rejects the separation between grace and nature that has influenced most Western theological systems (and has its origins in other aspects of the thinking of Augustine than that to which I have already alluded.) For Orthodoxy, there is — as Vladimir Lossky has noted — no concept 'of "pure nature" to which grace is added as a supernatural gift. For it, there is no natural or "normal" state, since grace is implied by the act of creation itself'.[5] This is linked to the way in which the notion of the *supernatural* is not used in Orthodoxy in the same way as it is in the West.[6]

The Orthodox view of the cosmos is one that is based on what is sometimes called panentheism: the notion that the world is not separated from God but is, in some sense, 'in God.' This panentheistic dimension of Orthodox understanding is perhaps manifested most clearly in the notion of divine energies in the work of St

---

4 See St. Augustine, *Of the Advantages of Believing* 34, cf. *City of God* 21:6–8; see also the comments in Wolfhart Pannenberg "The Concept of Miracle", *Zygon: Journal of Religion and Science* 37 (2002) 759–62.
5 Vladimir Lossky, *The Mystical Theology of the Eastern Church* (Cambridge, James Clarke, 1957), 101.
6 The term *supernatural* is, in the East, sometimes used of events in a way that points to their paranormal character rather than to anything that can be related to the Western use of the term *supernatural*. Indeed, the use of the distinction between the natural and the supernatural is far less common in Orthodox writing than is the distinction between the created and the uncreated. The latter distinction is interesting in that created entities include things like angels, which traditional Western systems regard as supernatural. For Orthodoxy, atoms and angels belong to the same category, not to different ones as in the West. This is in part because of what Elizabeth Theokritoff has called the Orthodox stress on "solidarity in createdness". See Elizabeth Theokritoff, "Creator and creation", in Mary B. Cunningham and Elizabeth Theokritoff, eds, *The Cambridge Companion to Orthodox Christian Theology* (Cambridge, Cambridge University Press, 2008) 65.

Gregory Palamas.[7] Certain aspects of Orthodox panentheism are, however, made clearer in the work of St Maximos the Confessor, who — in a way that reflects the range of meanings of the Greek term *logos* — speaks, not only about the divine *Logos* incarnate in Christ (John 1.1–14) but also about the *logos* of each created thing, which he sees as being, in some sense, a manifestation of the divine *Logos*. As Metropolitan Kallistos of Diokleia has put it, in Maximos's understanding, 'Christ the creator Logos has implanted in every created thing a characteristic logos, a "thought" or "word", which is God's intention for that thing, its inner essence which makes it distinctively itself and at the same time draws it towards the divine realm.'[8]

An important point to note here is that Maximos's understanding of the *logoi* of created things includes — as Metropolitan Kallistos has noted — a sense of the way in which those things are, by their very nature, drawn towards their eschatological fulfilment. This insight, as I have observed in the books I have cited, seems to anticipate the kinds of teleological possibilities that in recent years have crept back into interpretations of scientific thinking, both through the notion of convergent evolution developed by Simon Conway Morris[9] and through some understandings of the astrophysicist's perception of the 'fine tuning' of the universe.[10] Here, I have argued, we find a convergence between insights based on a naturalistic understanding and what I have called the *teleological-christological* insights of St Maximos, for whom — as Vladimir Lossky has put it — the world, 'created in order that it might be deified' is by its very nature 'dynamic, tending always towards its final end.'[11]

Incarnational Naturalism

An understanding based on this convergence between naturalistic and theological perspectives may, I have suggested, be spoken of in terms of what I have called *incarnational naturalism*. This use of the term *naturalism* is reinforced for me by the way in which another aspect of the Orthodox Tradition — its understanding of both sacraments and miracles — may also be interpreted in terms of a kind of naturalism. This is related to the Orthodox belief that the world has suffered a transformation in 'the Fall,'[12] and will undergo another transformation when its eschatological fulfilment

---

7   Kallistos Ware, "God Immanent yet transcendent: The Divine Energies according to St. Gregory Palamas", in Philip Clayton and Arthur Peacocke, eds, *In Whom We Live and Move and Have Our Being: Panentheistic Reflections on God's Presence in a Scientific World* (Grand Rapids, Eerdmans, 2004), 157–68.
8   Kallistos Ware, "God Immanent yet transcendent ", p. 160.
9   Simon Conway Morris, *Life's Solution: Inevitable Humans in a Lonely Universe* (Cambridge, Cambridge University Press, 2003).
10 John D. Barrow and Frank J. Tipler, *The Anthropic Cosmological Principle* (Oxford, Clarendon, 1986) is now slightly outdated but still provides perhaps the best comprehensive review of the issues.
11 Lossky, *The Mystical Theology of the Eastern Church*, 101.
12 The Fall is not always seen in Orthodox thinking as a historical event. In the Origenist tradition — which has had a significant effect on Eastern Christian thinking despite aspects of it being considered heretical — there is a strong sense that the Fall represents a descent *into* our present

is accomplished. In this sense, as Panayiotis Nellas has pointed out, the world as we now experience it is seen in Orthodox theology as being far from what God originally intended and ultimately wills, so that in a sense it should be seen as 'unnatural'[13] or — perhaps better — sub-natural. The traditional Orthodox interpretation of the 'garments of skin' given by God to humans after their rebellion against God (Genesis 3.21) is that they represent our present, sub-natural, psychosomatic make-up, and that this make-up is reflected in the entire sub-natural world in which we find ourselves.[14] Miracles, for this understanding, are often at least implicitly seen in the same way as the sacraments explicitly are:[15] not as 'supernatural' events in the Western sense of that term, but as a restoration of the world's 'natural' state i.e. as an anticipation of its eschatological transformation, brought about through the faithful response of creatures to their Creator.[16]

In this perspective, when the universe 'changes' so as to bring about miraculous events, it is a sign and a foretaste of what is to be when all the purposes of God have been fulfilled. In such an event, created things are, in the deepest sense, simply becoming themselves as they are in the intention of God. As the grime of fallen human nature gets wiped away in any person through response to God in faith, not only is the fullness of human potential that is revealed to us in the person of Jesus Christ actualised in that person to some degree, but in addition, the world around that person may also be cleansed and become 'natural' once more. In this perspective, miracles and human sanctity are inextricably linked, so that it is, for example, no accident that anticipatory experiences of 'the wolf laying down with the lamb' (Isaiah 11. 6) are linked, in the memory of the Christian community, to the 'miraculous' response of wild animals to people like St Cuthbert of Lindisfarne and St Seraphim of Sarov.

The central argument of my books, *The God of Nature* and *Science and the Christian Faith*, is that the philosophical arguments that I have outlined may be combined

---

space-time world, not an event within it. In this sense it is seen, not as a historical event but as something meta-historical.

13 See the comments in Panayiotis Nellas, *Deification in Christ: Orthodox Perspectives on the Human Person* (Crestwood, St.Vladimir's Seminary Press, 1997).
14 An aspect of this sub-natural character of the world is that there exists within it what Western Christian analysis would call "natural evil."
15 . Alexander Schmemann calls the sacrament "a revelation of the genuine *nature* of creation." See Alexander Schmemann, *The Eucharist: Sacrament of the Kingdom* (Crestwood, St.Vladimir's Seminary Press, 1987) 33 f. In a comparable way, Philip Sherrard has also stressed this aspect of the Eastern patristic understanding, noting that a sacrament is not "something set over against, or existing outside, the rest of life ... something extrinsic, and fixed in its extrinsicality, as if by some sort of magical operation or *Deus ex machina* the sacramental object is suddenly turned into something other than itself." On the contrary, he goes on, "what is indicated or revealed in the sacrament is something universal, the intrinsic sanctity and spirituality of all things, what one might call their real nature." See Philip Sherrard, "The Sacrament"; in A. J. Philippou, ed., *The Orthodox Ethos: Essays in Honour of the Centenary of the Greek Orthodox Archdiocese of North and South America* vol. 1 (Oxford, Holywell Press, 1964) 134–35.
16 See Knight, *The God of Nature*, 86–95; cf. Christopher C. Knight, "The Fallen Cosmos: An Aspect of Eastern Christian Thought and its Relevance to the Dialogue Between Science and Theology", *Theology and Science* 6 (2008) 305–15.

with these essentially theological insights in a new synthesis. In this synthesis, the classic Western distinctions between special and general modes of divine action and between the natural and the supernatural are made redundant.

Orthodox Input to Divine Action Discussions

This argument has been seen by Sarah Lane Ritchie as an important component of what she calls a 'theological turn'[17] in twenty-first century discussion of divine action. In this theological turn, my own arguments, based on Orthodox insights, may be seen as anticipating aspects of more recent Western developments within that discussion. Ritchie has explored the way in which I — together with the Western proponents of this theological turn — reject the assumption on which most recent Western debate about divine action has been based: that of an essentially autonomous universe, which God must influence from the 'outside'. Those of us who challenge this kind of naturalism instead posit, in our various ways,[18] a different kind of naturalism, based on a universe that is to be understood ultimately only in terms of God's presence within it. As Ritchie observes, we argue that standard Western understandings of divine action "are dependent upon question-begging metaphysical commitments, which in turn inadequately frame the entire divine action conversation. These presuppositions involve basic ontological questions about the God–nature relationship, and especially the question of what, exactly, it means to be properly 'natural.'"[19]

In relation to the concept of miracles, this 'theological turn' manifests important parallels between my own approach, based on Orthodox insights, and that of a few Western Christian scholars, especially those who emphasize the work of the Holy Spirit and have developed what Ritchie calls a 'pneumatological naturalism.' As we have seen, in my own way of expressing the Orthodox understanding, miraculous events are an aspect of the 'natural' functioning of the world that requires human response to God to be activated. In a comparable way, the pneumatological approach is, as Ritchie puts it, one in which the way that 'some events seem more supernatural than others … is due the varying levels of creaturely response and openness to the Spirit.'[20] Here she quotes James Smith as saying that such events are 'sped-up modes

---

17 Sarah Lane Ritchie, "Dancing Around the Causal Joint: Challenging The Theological Turn in Divine Action Theories", *Zygon: Journal of Religion and Science* 37 (2017) 362–79. This This paper has been expanded in a recent book Sarah Lane Richie, *Divine Action and the Human Mind* (Cambridge, Cambridge University Press, 2019).
18 Ritchie sees two main components of the Western dimension of the "theological turn": the revision of scholastic assumptions in Michael Dodds, *Unlocking Divine Action: Contemporary Science and Thomas Aquinas* (Washington DC. Catholic University of America Press, 2012), and the "pneumatological" versions to be found in Amos Yong, *The Spirit of Creation: Modern Science and Divine Action in the Pentecostal-charismatic Imagination* (Grand Rapids, Michigan: Eerdmans, 2011) and James A. K. Smith, *Thinking in Tongues: Pentecostal Contributions to Christian Philosophy* (Grand Rapids, Michigan, Eerdmans, 2010).
19 Ritchie, "Dancing Around the Causal Joint", 362.
20 Ritchie, "Dancing Around the Causal Joint", 375.

of the Spirit's more regular presences',[21] and this clearly parallels my own view of the way that such events may be seen as the outcome of the presence of the *Logos* in both 'lower' and 'higher' laws of nature. (Indeed, since Orthodox perspectives are always Trinitarian, the views of the Protestant pneumatologists are already implicitly present in Orthodox thinking about the presence of this *Logos*.)

My argument has been, then, that the occurrence of miraculous events is not to be denied, but that equally they are not to be understood in terms of the kind of naturalism that sees their occurrence as requiring that God either sets aside the laws of nature or else manipulates those laws through some kind of causal joint. I have posited, as an alternative, a different kind of naturalism — an *incarnational naturalism* — based on the way in which St Maximos the Confessor interprets the incarnation of the divine *Logos* in terms of the presence of that *Logos* in all created things. Here, I have argued, the Augustinian notion of higher laws of nature provides a useful way of thinking about miraculous events, but it is supplemented in an important way when Orthodox insights are taken into account. For if the Augustinian notion is interpreted in terms of a picture of God and the creation as separated, then it is in danger of falling into a deistic, 'absentee landlord' understanding that is different from classical deism only insofar as it manages to avoid the deistic belief that miracles cannot occur. If, however, the notion of 'higher laws of nature' is interpreted in terms of St Maximos's panentheistic picture, then any hint of the 'absentee landlord' God of deism is removed because those events that we describe as miraculous — together with those that we can understand through science — are ones from which God is not absent. Rather, in all events He can be seen as active and present.

The advantages of this model are, I would argue, both theological and apologetic. At the theological level, the Orthodox doctrines of creation and incarnation are fully acknowledged by the model, while the notion of supernatural intervention — which is based on an understanding of the cosmos that has non-Orthodox roots — is replaced by a more subtle understanding. In this understanding, divine action through the *logoi* of created things and the 'laws of nature' — some but not all of which may be explored through the scientific methodology — are identified with each other.

At the apologetic level, the widespread suspicion of the notion of 'supernatural events' in our scientific age is acknowledged as at least partially justified. In this sense, the model promises to do what was made possible in the early centuries by apologists such as St Justin Martyr and St Clement of Alexandria, who set out to convince their contemporaries that the Christian faith was compatible with important elements of the philosophy of their time. We do not — as some seem to think — have to challenge the naturalism that is almost instinctive among our contemporaries. Rather, we must interpret it theologically, expanding it in such a way that we can acknowledge both the validity of the scientific enterprise and the occurrence of those events that we call miraculous. The model that I have presented is able, I believe, to allow this interpretation to be made.

---

21 James A. K. Smith, "Is the Universe Open for Surprise? Pentecostal Ontology and the Spirit of Naturalism." *Zygon: Journal of Religion and Science* 43 (2008) 892.